Mediatized Worlds

Mediatized Worlds

Culture and Society in a Media Age

Edited by

Andreas Hepp and Friedrich Krotz
University of Bremen, Germany

First published 2014 by
PALGRAVE MACMILLAN

Palgrave Macmillan in the UK is an imprint of Macmillan Publishers Limited,
registered in England, company number 785998, of Houndmills, Basingstoke,
Hampshire RG21 6XS.

Palgrave Macmillan in the US is a division of St Martin's Press LLC,
175 Fifth Avenue, New York, NY 10010.

Palgrave Macmillan is the global academic imprint of the above companies
and has companies and representatives throughout the world.

Palgrave® and Macmillan® are registered trademarks in the United States,
the United Kingdom, Europe and other countries.

ISBN 978–1–137–30034–8

This book is printed on paper suitable for recycling and made from fully
managed and sustained forest sources. Logging, pulping and manufacturing
processes are expected to conform to the environmental regulations of the
country of origin.

A catalogue record for this book is available from the British Library.

A catalog record for this book is available from the Library of Congress.

Contents

Figures and Tables

Figures

Tables

Contributors

Matthias Berg is a research associate at the Centre for Communications, Media and Information Research (ZeMKI), University of Bremen, Germany. He is a member of the German Research Foundation (DFG) priority programme 'Mediatized Worlds' and works within the project 'Mediatized Everyday Worlds of Translocal Communitization'. His research interests are communication and media studies, with a focus on the interrelations of communication and mobility as well as media and popular culture. His publications include *Mediatisierte Welten der Vergemeinschaftung: Kommunikative Vernetzung und das Gemeinschaftsleben junger Menschen* (with A. Hepp and C. Roitsch, 2014).

Andreas Breiter is Professor for Information Management and Applied Informatics in the Department for Mathematics and Computer Science at the University of Bremen, Germany. He is also Scientific Director of the Institute for Information Management Bremen GmbH, a not-for-profit research centre at the University of Bremen, and Co-chair of the Centre for Communications, Media and Information Research (ZeMKI), University of Bremen. He was member of the German Research Foundation (DFG) priority programme 'Mediatized Worlds' and headed the project 'Schools as Mediatized Social Organizations'. His research interests are media integration in educational systems, IT governance and information systems for data-driven decision-making. His publications include *Medienintegration in der Grundschule* (2013), *Medienkompetenz in der Schule* (2011) and *School Information Systems and Data-Based Decision-Making* (2008).

Miyase Christensen is Professor of Media and Communication Studies at Stockholm University and a guest professor in the Department of Philosophy and History of Technology at the Royal Institute of Technology (KTH), Sweden. She is an editor of *Popular Communication: International Journal of Media and Culture* and Chair of the Ethnicity and Race in Communication Division of International Communication Association (ICA). Christensen's research focuses, from a social theory perspective, on globalization processes and social change; technology, culture and identity; and politics of popular communication. Recent co-edited books include *Understanding Media and Culture in Turkey: Structures, Spaces, Voices* (in press), *Media and the Politics of Arctic Climate Change: When the Ice Breaks* (2013) and *Online Territories: Globalization, Mediated Practice and Social Space* (2011).

Lynn Schofield Clark is Professor of Media, Film and Journalism Studies and Director of the Estlow International Center for Journalism and New Media at the University of Denver, USA. She is an ethnographic researcher who focuses on the role of media in social change, particularly as related to families, young people and world religions. She is author of *The Parent App: Understanding Families in a Digital Age* (2013) and *From Angels to Aliens: Teenagers, the Media, and the Supernatural* (2005), and co-author of *Media, Home, and Family* (2004).

Nick Couldry is Professor of Media, Communications and Social Theory in the Department of Media and Communications at London School of Economics and Political Science, UK. His research and teaching interests are very wide and include media rituals and anthropological approaches to media, reality TV, media and democracy, alternative and community media, media ethics, and social and cultural theory. He is the author or editor of ten books, including most recently *Media, Society, World: Social Theory and Digital Media Practice* (2012) and *Why Voice Matters: Culture and Politics after Neoliberalism* (2010).

Mark Dang-Anh is a research assistant in the postgraduate programme 'Locating Media' at the University of Siegen, Germany. He was a member of the German Research Foundation (DFG) priority programme 'Mediatized Worlds' and worked within the project 'Political Deliberation on the Internet'. His research interests are media linguistics, political communication, social movements and social media. His publications include 'Computer-Assisted Content Analysis of Twitter Data' (with J. Einspänner and C.Thimm in K. Weller et al., *Twitter and Society*, 2014), 'Mediatisierung und Medialität in Social Media: Das Diskurssystem Twitter' (with J. Einspänner and C. Thimm in K. Marx and M. Schwarz-Friesel, *Sprache und Kommunikation im technischen Zeitalter. Wieviel Technik (v)erträgt unsere Gesellschaft?*, 2013) and 'Twitter als Wahlkampfmedium' (with C. Thimm and J. Einspänner; *Publizistik*, 2012).

Mark Deuze is Professor of Journalism and Media in the Department of Media Studies of the University of Amsterdam, the Netherlands. His research interests include the cultural and technological convergence of media culture in general and the creative industries in particular. He is the author of seven books, including *Media Work* (2007) and *Media Life* (2012).

Jessica Einspänner is a research assistant in the Department of Media Studies, University of Bonn, Germany. She is a member of the German Research Foundation (DFG) priority programme 'Mediatized Worlds' and works within the project 'Political Deliberation on the Internet'. Her research interests are social media and political communication, online privacy and online journalism. Her publications include 'Computer-Assisted Content Analysis of Twitter Data' (with M. Dang-Anh and C. Thimm, in Weller et al., *Twitter and Society, 2014*), 'Wahlkampf im Web 2.0.: Blogs im US-Wahlkampf' (in M. Anastasiadis and C. Thimm, *Social Media – Theorie und Praxis digitaler Sozialität*, 2011), and 'Digital Public Affairs – Lobbyismus im Social Web' (in G. Bender and T. Werner, *Digital Public Affairs. Social Media für Unternehmen, Verbände und Politik*, 2010).

Johan Fornäs is Professor of Media and Communication Studies at Södertörn University, Sweden, and Editor-in-Chief of *Culture Unbound: Journal of Current Cultural Research*. Having initiated the Bank of Sweden Tercentenary Foundation's (Riksbankens Jubileumsfond) Sector Committee for the Mediatization of Culture and Everyday Life, his research interests concern media culture, intermediality, popular music and intersectional identity issues, with publications including *Cultural Theory and Late Modernity* (1995), *Digital Borderlands: Cultural studies of Identity and Interactivity on the Internet* (2002), *Consuming Media: Communication, Shopping and Everyday Life* (2007), *Signifying Europe* (2012) and *Capitalism: A Companion to Marx's Economy Critique* (2013).

Andreas Hepp is Professor of Media and Communication Studies at the Centre for Communications, Media and Information Research (ZeMKI), University of Bremen, Germany. He is co-initiator of the German Research Foundation (DFG) priority programme 'Mediatized Worlds' and leads the projects 'Mediatized Everyday Worlds of Translocal Communitization' and 'A Qualitative Longitudinal Study about the Mediatization of Social Relationships' (with Friedrich Krotz). His main research areas are media and communication theory, media sociology, mediatization research, transnational and transcultural communication, cultural studies, media change, and methods of media culture research. Publications include *Media Events in a Global Age* (ed. with N. Couldry and F. Krotz, 2010), *Cultures of Mediatization* (2013) and *Mediatisierte Welten der Vergemeinschaftung: Kommunikative Vernetzung und das Gemeinschaftsleben junger Menschen* (with M. Berg and C. Roitsch, 2014).

Stig Hjarvard is Professor of Media Studies in the Department of Media, Cognition and Communication at the University of Copenhagen, Denmark. He is Vice-Chair of the department, chief editor of the journal *Northern Lights* and head of the collaborative research project 'Mediatization of Culture: The Challenge of New Media'. Among his research interests are journalism, media and globalization, media history, media and religion, and mediatization theory. His publications include *The Mediatization of Culture and Society* (2013), *Mediatization and Religion: Nordic Perspectives* (ed. with M. Lövheim, 2012) and *News in a Globalized Society* (2001).

Hubert Knoblauch is Professor of General Sociology at the Technical University of Berlin. He is working in areas such as the sociology of knowledge, sociology of religion, communication, death and qualitative methods, particularly videography. He is a member of several scientific societies, editor and board member of various scientific journals and currently Speaker of the Research Network 7 (Sociology of Culture) of the European Sociological Association. Publications in English include *Powerpoint, Communication, and the Knowledge Society* (2013), 'Visual Analysis: New Developments in the Interpretative Analysis of Video and Photography' (ed. with A. Baer, E. Laurier, S. Petschke and B. Schnettler; Special issue of *Forum: Qualitative Social Research*, 2008) and 'Communicative Constructivism and Mediatization' (in *Communication Theory* 23 (2013), 297–315).

Friedrich Krotz is Professor of Media and Communication Studies at the Centre for Communications, Media and Information Research (ZeMKI), University of Bremen, Germany. He is initiator and coordinator of the DFG priority programme 'Mediatized Worlds' and leads the project 'A Qualitative Longitudinal Study about the Mediatization of Social Relationships' (with Andreas Hepp). His research interests are media change and mediatization, social communication theory, cultural studies and methodology. His publications include *Mediatisierte Welten: Forschungsfelder und Beschreibungsansätze* (ed. with A. Hepp, 2012), 'Mediatization: A Concept to Grasp Media and Societal Change' (in Lundby, *Mediatization: Concept, Changes, Consequences*, 2009) and *Mediatisierung: Fallstudien zum Wandel von Kommunikation* (2007).

Knut Lundby is Professor of Media Studies in the Department of Media and Communication, University of Oslo, Norway. His research interests are in mediatization theory, digital storytelling and the relation between media and religion. Publications include *Digital Storytelling, Mediatized Stories: Self-Representations in New Media* (ed., 2008), and *Mediatization: Concept, Changes, Consequences* (ed., 2009).

Katy McDonald is Senior Lecturer in Journalism and Radio at the University of Sunderland, UK. Her research interests are in radio journalism and in the mediatization of everyday life, specifically the uses of media technology when in romantic relationships. Recent work has been on the influence of citizen journalism on commercial radio news, and the changing landscape of the newsroom.

James Miller is Professor of Communications in the School of Cognitive Science at Hampshire College, USA. His primary teaching and research interests are political culture, especially the increasingly cultural experience of citizenship, and public diplomacy; issues of design and architecture as they pertain to media; and the phenomenology of emerging new media. His international work includes appointments as a Fulbright researcher attached to the Center for the Study of French Political Life in Paris, as a short-term East European studies scholar at the Woodrow Wilson International Center for Scholars and as visiting professor at Goldsmiths, University of London. Recent publications include 'NGOs and the "Modernization" and "Democratization" of Media' (*Global Media and Communication*, 2009) and 'Mainstream Journalism as Anti-vernacular Modernism' (*Journalism Studies*, 2012).

Jan-Hendrik Passoth is a postdoctoral researcher in the Department of Sociology, Technische Universität Berlin (Berlin Institute of Technology), Germany. He was a member of the German Research Foundation (DFG) priority programme 'Mediatized Worlds' and co-headed the project 'Calculating Inclusion' (with Tilmann Sutter and Josef Wehner). His research interests are socio-technical infrastructures and the material circumstances of social practice. He is the author of *Technik und Gesellschaft* (2007) and 'Actor-Network State: Integrating Actor-Network Theory and State Theory' (with N. J. Rowland; *International Sociology*, 2010) as well as co-editor of *Agency without Actors: New Approaches to Collective Action* (ed. with B. Peuker and M. Schillmeier, 2012), and *Quoten, Kurven und Profile. Zur Vermessung der sozialen Welt* (with J. Wehner, 2013).

Corinna Peil is a postdoctoral researcher in communications at the University of Salzburg's Center for Advanced Studies and Research in ICTs and Society (ICT&S Center), Austria, where she is part of the Innovation in Cultural and Creative Institutions unit. Until 2012, she was a member of the DFG priority programme 'Mediatized Worlds' and worked within the project 'The Mediatized Home'. She specializes in mobile communications, media innovations in everyday life, convergence culture, the changing ecology of news and the history and future of television. Her latest publications include 'Using the Domestication Approach for the Analysis of Diffusion and Participation Processes of New Media' (in Bilandzic et al. eds, *The Social Use of Media. Cultural and Social Scientific Perspectives on Audience Research*, with J. Röser, 2012), and *Mobilkommunikation in Japan. Zur kulturellen Infrastruktur der Handy-Aneignung* (2011).

Cindy Roitsch is research associate at the Centre for Communications, Media and Information Research (ZeMKI), University of Bremen, Germany. She is a member of the German Research Foundation (DFG) priority programme 'Mediatized Worlds' and works within the project 'Mediatized Everyday Worlds of Translocal Communitization'. Her research interests are communication and media studies, with a focus on media culture and communication theory. Publications include *Mediatisierte Welten der Vergemeinschaftung: Kommunikative Vernetzung und das Gemeinschaftsleben junger Menschen* (with A. Hepp and M. Berg, 2014).

Jutta Röser is Professor of Communications at the University of Münster, Germany. She is a member of the German Research Foundation (DFG) priority programme 'Mediatized Worlds' and leads the project 'The Mediatized Home'. Her research interests include media and communication technologies in everyday life, the domestication of the internet, audience and reception research, media sociology, cultural studies and gender media studies. Röser's publications include 'Using the Domestication Approach for the Analysis of Diffusion and Participation Processes of New Media' (in Bilandzic et al. eds, *The Social Use of Media. Cultural and Social Scientific Perspectives on Audience Research*, with C. Peil, 2012) and *MedienAlltag: Domestizierungsprozesse alter und neuer Medien* (ed., 2007).

Thomas Steinmaurer is Professor of Communication Studies in the Department of Communication Science, University of Salzburg, Austria. His research interests are theory and history of mediatization, media and cultural change, media systems and regulation. Publications include *Tele-Visionen: Zur Theorie und Geschichte des Fernsehempfangs* (1999).

John Storey is Professor of Cultural Studies and Director of the Centre for Research in Media and Cultural Studies at the University of Sunderland, UK. He has published extensively in cultural studies, including ten books. The most recent book is *From Popular Culture to Everyday Life* (2014). His work has been translated into 16 languages. He is also on the editorial and advisory boards of journals in Australia, Canada, China, Germany, Spain, the UK and the USA, and has been a visiting professor at the University of Vienna, the University of Henan and the University of Wuhan.

Tilmann Sutter is Professor of Sociology at the Faculty of Sociology, Bielefeld University, Germany. His research interests are media sociology, socialization and qualitative social research. He was a member of the DFG priority programme 'Mediatized Worlds' and co-headed the project 'Calculating Inclusion' (with Jan-Hendrik Passoth and Josef Wehner). Publications include *Medienanalyse und Medienkritik. Forschungsfelder einer konstruktivistischen Soziologie der Medien* (2010), *Medienwandel als Wandel von Interaktionsformen* (ed. with A. Mehler, 2010) and *Interaktionistischer Konstruktivismus. Zur Systemtheorie der Sozialisation* (2009).

Caja Thimm is Professor of Media Studies and Intermediality at the University of Bonn, Germany. She is a member of the German Research Foundation (DFG) priority programme 'Mediatized Worlds' and leads the project 'Political Deliberation on the Internet'. Her main research interests are online communication theory, social media, and organizational and political communication online. Her publications include *Social Media: Theorie und Praxis digitaler Sozialität* (ed. with M. Anastasiadis, 2011), 'Virtual Worlds: Game or Virtual Society?' (in J. Fromme and A. Unger eds, *Computer Games and New Media Cultures: A Handbook of Digital Games Studies*, 2012) and 'The Visuals of Online Politics: Barack Obama's Web Campaign' (in V. Depkat and M. Zwingenberg eds, *Publications of the Bavarian American Academy*, 2012).

Josef Wehner is a lecturer at the Faculty of Sociology, University of Bielefeld, Germany. He was a member of the German Research Foundation (DFG) priority programme 'Mediatized Worlds' and co-headed the project 'Calculating Inclusion' (with Jan-Hendrik Passoth and Tilmann Sutter). His research interests are media sociology and sociology of technology and communication. He is the author of 'Numerische Inklusion – Medien, Messungen und Modernisierung' (in T. Sutter and A. Mehle eds, *Medienwandel als Wandel von Interaktionsformen*, 2010) and ' "Social Web" – Rezeptions- und Produktionsstrukturen im Internet' (in M. Jäckel and M. Mai eds, *Medien und Macht*, 2008), and co-editor of *Quoten, Kurven und Profile. Zur Vermessung der sozialen Welt* (with J.-H. Passoth, 2013).

1
Mediatized Worlds – Understanding Everyday Mediatization

Andreas Hepp and Friedrich Krotz

1. Mediatization: A concept emerges

While mediatization as a concept is nothing new in media and communication research, it has recently emerged as an international term: in 2008, Sonia Livingstone referred to 'mediatization' in her address as president of the International Communications Association (ICA) when she reflected the increasing 'mediation of everything' and its relation to changing approaches of media and communication research (Livingstone, 2009). Various panels and papers at the recent ICA conferences referred to 'mediatization' as a research-guiding concept. And, in 2011/12, the European Communication Research and Education Association (ECREA) set up a working group on mediatization. In addition to this, various special issues relating to the concept have been published over the past few years. For example, a special issue of *Communications: European Journal for Communication Research* (2010, 35(3)) focused on empirical perspectives on mediatization, an issue of *Culture and Religion* (2011, 12(2)) on the mediatization of religion debate, an issue of *Empedocles: European Journal for the Philosophy of Communication* (2013, 3(2)) on mediatization as part of more general 'media processes', a thematic issue of *MedieKultur* on mediatization and cultural change (2013, 29 (54)), and, most recently, an issue of *Communication Theory* (2013, 23(3)) on conceptualizing mediatization. In addition, Knut Lundby (2009c) edited the book *Mediatization: Concepts, Changes, Consequences* to present international reflections on mediatization across various research fields. And a comprehensive handbook on mediatization is in preparation, again edited by Lundby. Various other books and journal articles have been published with 'mediatization' in the title.

So how can we explain this intensifying discussion about mediatization? Fundamentally speaking, Sonia Livingstone is right in relating the growing attention to the concept to the increasing everyday relevance of

1

communication mediated by the media. As she writes about the recent development within media and communication research:

> It seems that we have moved from a social analysis in which the mass media comprise one among many influential but independent institutions whose relations with the media can be usefully analyzed to a social analysis in which everything is mediated, the consequence being that all influential institutions in society have themselves been transformed, reconstituted, by contemporary processes of mediation.
>
> (Livingstone, 2009, p. 2)

This said, the concept of mediatization represents such a move. However, while this empirical appraisal explains many aspects of the increasing interest in mediatization research, it is important to bear in mind that the concept itself has a far longer history within social sciences.

'Mediatization' as a term can be traced back to the early 20th century, and therefore to the beginning of so-called 'mass communication research' (Averbeck-Lietz, 2014). One example is Ernest Manheim (1933) in his post-doctoral thesis *The Bearers of Public Opinion* (German: 'Die Träger der öffentlichen Meinung'), which he had to withdraw because of the pressures in Nazi Germany. In this book he writes about the 'mediatization of direct human relationships' (German: 'Mediatisierung menschlicher Unmittelbarbeziehung', p. 11). He uses this term in order to describe changes of social relations within modernity, changes that are marked by the so-called mass media. Jean Baudrillard (1995, p. 175), in *Simulacra and Simulations*, described information as mediatized because there is no measure of reality behind its mediation. Within his 'theory of communicative action' (German: 'Theorie des kommunikativen Handelns'), Jürgen Habermas (1988a; 1988b) uses the term 'mediatization' to describe a sub-process of the colonialization of the lifeworld. However, he does not refer to communication media but to generalized symbolic media like power and money. In his edited volume *Medier och kulturer*, Ulf Hannerz (1990) characterized the cultural influence of media as such (that is, beyond their contents) on culture as mediatization. John B. Thompson (1995) writes in his book *Media and Modernity* about the 'mediazation of culture', meaning the increasingly irreversible mediation of culture by institutionalized mass media. These examples demonstrate that the term 'mediatization' in its different variants is deeply related to social and cultural research as a whole. However, a more detailed substantiation of the concept took place in media and communication studies. This, for example, started as early as 1995 in Germany, where related concepts like 'mediatized communication' were used (Krotz, 1995).

Within this discipline, two traditions of mediatization research emerged: an 'institutionalist tradition' and a 'social-constructivist tradition'. While it is not possible here to discuss the traditions in detail (see for this Couldry and Hepp, 2013; Hepp, 2013b), at least a fundamental understanding of them is necessary to grasp the further development of the concept.

In the 'institutionalist tradition', media are understood more or less as independent social institutions with their own sets of rules. Mediatization, then, refers to the adaptation of different social fields or systems like politics or religion, for example, to these institutionalized rules. The latter are described as a 'media logic' (Altheide and Snow, 1979; Asp, 1990); that is, in the widest sense of the word, institutionalized formats and forms of staging. This 'media logic', on the one hand, takes up non-mediatized forms of representation. On the other hand, non-media actors have to accommodate to this 'media logic' if they want to be represented in the (mass) media or if they want to act successfully in a media culture and media society. Starting with such a preliminary understanding of 'media logic', the concept became differentiated within that tradition, while the link to these original ideas remains (Hjarvard, 2013, pp. 8–40).

The understanding of mediatization from a 'social-constructivist' point of view moves the role of various media into the foreground as part of the process of the construction of social and cultural reality. Mediatization, then, refers to the process of a construction of socio-cultural reality by communication (Berger and Luckmann, 1967; Knoblauch, 2013; Krotz, 2001) and the status of various media within this process is analyzed (Hepp, 2013a, pp. 54–68). Mediatization describes how certain processes of the construction of reality by communication become manifested in certain media and how, in turn, existing specifics of certain media have a contextualized 'influence' on the process of the communicative construction of socio-cultural reality.

Having these different traditions of mediatization research in mind, a shared fundamental understanding of mediatization has developed across them in recent years. Basically, the term 'mediatization' does not refer to a single theory but to a more general approach of media and communication research. In this sense, *mediatization is a concept used in order to carry out a critical analysis of the interrelation between the change of media and communication, on the one hand, and the change of culture and society on the other.* Based on such a fundamental understanding, mediatization refers to something other than mediation (cf. Couldry, 2012, pp. 134–7; Hepp, 2013a, pp. 31–8; Hjarvard, 2013, pp. 19–20): mediation is a concept to describe the process of communication in general, that is, how communication has to be grasped as a process of mediating meaning construction. Mediatization is a category to describe a process of change. In a certain sense we can link both concepts as follows: mediatization reflects how the process of mediation has changed with the emergence of different kinds of media. This said, the concept of mediation describes a very fundamental moment of communication as symbolic interaction. In contrast to this, mediatization is much more specific in analyzing the role of various media in the further process of socio-cultural change. However, it has to be linked to an analysis of communication as symbolic interaction (c.f. Krotz, 2001, pp. 51–2).

At this point, we can see significant similarities to – but also differences from – the *medium theory* as it was originally introduced by Harold Innis (1950) and Marshall McLuhan (1994) and brought forward by others (cf. for an overview Meyrowitz, 1995). Two similarities are striking. First, both mediatization research and medium theory focus not (only) on media content but also on the role media as such play in altering communication. Joshua Meyrowitz – one of the most prominent present scholars of medium theory – put this as follows: 'To observe [...] potential media effects – whether in the past, present or future – one needs to shift from the content of media to the nature and capacities of each medium itself' (Meyrowitz, 2009, p. 518). Mediatization research does not argue along the lines of the effect paradigm (not even in an alternative manner, as medium theory does), but it emphasizes in addition the necessity to focus on 'capabilities' (Lundby, 2009b, p. 115), 'moulding forces' (Hepp, 2013a, pp. 54–5), 'affordances' (Hjarvard, 2013, p. 18) and the 'dissolution of media boundaries' (Krotz, 2001, pp. 188–9). Second, both medium theory and mediatization research understand their respective approaches as being inclusive across the micro, meso and macro levels. For medium theory, this is explicitly expressed by Meyrowitz (1995; 2009) in his distinction between 'microlevel' and 'macrolevel medium theory': while the 'macrolevel medium theory' is focused on long-term and comprehensive changes across centuries, for example, from 'modern print culture' to 'global electronic culture', the 'microlevel medium theory' is interested in a detailed analysis of the altering of interaction orders by such comprehensive changes. Moreover, mediatization research at the level of certain interactions and/or institutions is interested in more general statements on the change of culture and society. This becomes thickened in the idea of understanding mediatization as a 'meta-process' (Krotz, 2009, p. 22). Bearing these two similarities in mind, it is no wonder that both paradigms are in dialogue with each other (cf., for example, Hug and Friesen, 2009 and Schofield Clark in this volume).

This said, a number of differences between medium theory and mediatization research are striking – differences which substantiate the uniqueness of the mediatization approach. In this introduction we can name only the four most important points, while a more comprehensive discussion can be found in other publications (cf. Hepp, 2013a, pp. 11–17; Hjarvard, 2013, p. 12; Krotz, 2014). First, mediatization research is sceptical about the narration of change as introduced by 'macrolevel medium theory'. This narration of change is based on the idea that each culture and society is dominated by a single medium, which is more or less stable over time. Within mediatization research many examples can be found that demonstrate the shortcomings and under-complexity of this idea. This already refers to the second point, namely the transmedial perspective of mediatization research. Increasingly, the scholars of mediatization research emphasize the necessity to focus (also historically) on the interrelation of various media and not solely on a single medium. This is because the media-related transformation we are confronted with is 'driven' by the interaction of these various media in certain contexts. It's not just the mobile phone that makes the difference for our present everyday lives, but how the mobile phone interacts with social media, e-mail, digital television and so on. Third, within mediatization research the specificity of media is also core, albeit understood as one moment of the 'double articulation' (Silverstone and Haddon, 1996) of the media as objects and bearers of meaning. Mediatization research considers both. Fourth, mediatization research is in the trajectory of a 'non-media-centric' (Morley, 2009) media and communication research. The idea is not to take media without question as the source of change – there are many contexts in which 'new' media come up but are not the sources of change. Mediatization research wants to consider the *interrelation* between the change of media and communication, on the one hand, and culture and society, on the other. This also implies that the driving forces of change might not be the media at all. In sum, it becomes obvious that mediatization research is something different from medium theory.

In such a general orientation, the term 'mediatization' implies quantitative as well as qualitative aspects. With regard to quantitative aspects, mediatization refers to the increasing temporal, spatial and social spread of media communication. That means that over time we have become more and more used to communicating via media in various contexts. With regard to qualitative aspects, mediatization refers to the role of the specificity of certain media within the process of socio-cultural change. This means that it does 'matter' which kind of media is used for which kind of communication. Some researchers understand this process of mediatization as a long-term process that has more or less accompanied the whole history of humankind (Hepp, 2013a, pp. 46–54; Krotz, 2009). Seen from such a perspective, human history is, besides other things, a process of intensifying and radicalizing mediatization. In contrast to this, other researchers use the term 'mediatization' to describe the process of an increasing social and cultural relevance of the media since the emergence of so-called independent 'mass media' (print, cinema, radio, television) (Hjarvard, 2013, pp. 21–3; Strömbäck, 2011).

It is in this general discussion that we also have to locate the volume at hand. It includes articles from authors of both traditions of mediatization research as well as articles that discuss across the lines of these different traditions. As such, it can be understood as an attempt to bring these different traditions of mediatization research closer together. However, this attempt is related to a certain idea – and that is the importance of linking mediatization more closely to an analysis of changing everyday lifeworlds and social worlds. This is the point at which the term 'mediatized worlds' comes in, which frames the different chapters of this volume.

2. Mediatized worlds: Everyday mediatization

Within media and communication research, the concept of 'media worlds' has a certain tradition. David L. Altheide and Robert P. Snow (1991), for example, relate their understanding of 'media logic' to 'media worlds' when they use the latter term to describe social worlds marked by a 'media logic'. Elizabeth Bird (2003) describes the everyday use of (mass) media from an ethnographic perspective as 'living in a media world', as she writes in the subtitle of her book. Faye D. Ginsburg, Lila Abu-Lughod and Brian Larkin (2002) characterize the cultural anthropology of the media as analyses of different 'media worlds'. Leah A. Lievrouw (2001) sees a relation between the establishment of 'new' digital media and the pluralization of lifeworlds. David Morley (2001, p. 443) reflects on questions of belonging in the 'present mediated world'.

However, in a general sense, 'media worlds' is no more than a metaphor for the fact that various contexts of present everyday life are marked by media communication. That said, we use the concept of 'mediatized worlds' in a much more concrete sense when referring to (1) social phenomenology and (2) symbolic interactionism (see, for the following, Hepp, 2013a, pp. 75–83; Krotz, 2009; Krotz and Hepp, 2013).

1. Within *social phenomenology*, Alfred Schütz and Thomas Luckmann have described the everyday world as a very special part of the lifeworld of a human being: 'The everyday life-world is [...] that province of reality which the wide-awake and normal adult simply takes for granted' (Schütz and Luckmann, 1973, vol. 1, p. 3). The everyday lifeworld is accepted without question, not the 'private world' of individual(s), but intersubjectively: '[T]he fundamental structure of its reality is shared by us' (p. 4). As such, the everyday world does not only include nature but also the social and cultural world in which a person exists.

Very early on, Benita Luckmann (1970) emphasized the fragmentation of everyday lifeworlds into various 'small life-worlds'. For her, these are the 'segments' (Luckmann, 1970, p. 81) of everyday life that exist as specificity within organizational as well as private contexts: 'The life round of modern man is not one piece. It does not unfold within one but within a variety of small "worlds" which are often unconnected with one another' (Luckmann, 1970, p. 587). Empirically, Benita Luckmann refers to 'worlds' of different jobs, of social clubs, of political parties, religious communities, subcultures and so on. Therefore, in present (post-)modern societies, we are confronted with a variety of 'socially constructed part-time-realities' (Hitzler and Honer, 1984, p. 67) which impact more and more on the experience of men and women.

2. Within *symbolic interactionism*, the concept of 'social worlds' is well established and can be linked to our outlined understanding of mediatized worlds. Here, three points are especially striking:

The first point is that *mediatized worlds have a 'communication network' beyond the territorial.* It was Tamotsu Shibutani (1955) who in the 1950s reflected on the characteristics of what he called 'social worlds'. One of his key arguments was that, already at that time, media played an important role in the construction of social worlds. However, as these mediated 'communication networks are no longer coterminous with territorial boundaries, cultural areas overlap and have lost their territorial bases' (Shibutani, 1955, p. 566). Quoting Shibutani, our argument is not that questions of (re)territorialization will not matter for the analysis of mediatized worlds. More specifically, the argument is that mediatized worlds are at least partly articulated by mediated communication networks, and that these communication networks transgress various territories with increasing mediatization. To take one of our above-mentioned examples: the mediatized world of stock exchange dealing is something that takes place not only in the stock exchange building itself but at nearly every place where bankers as well as private persons can deal their stocks via desktops and laptop computers or smartphones. It is the mediatized communication network by which this mediatized world gets constructed, not a territoriality.

A second important point is that *mediatized worlds exist on 'various scales'.* Some years later than the publication by Tamotsu Shibutani, it was Anselm Strauss (1978) who reflected Shibutani's arguments somewhat further. In so doing, he perceives one important indication of why the concept of social worlds (and, therefore, also our conceptualization of mediatized worlds) presents a highly promising starting point for empirical research. Strauss argues that they 'can be studied at any scale, from the smallest (say, a local world, a local space) to the very largest (in size or geographic spread)' (Strauss, 1978, p. 126). Therefore, the concept of mediatized worlds offers an approach for investigating mediatization empirically by defining an investigation perspective, meaning the perspective of the thematic core of a mediatized world. At the same time, the concept is not so narrow that it is reduced to a micro-concept of interaction at a certain place. We can use it on various levels or scales, across which we can conduct mediatization research.

The third point is that *mediatized worlds are 'nested/interlaced' with each other.* Again, we can refer here to the arguments by Anselm Strauss. Discussing Shibutani's ideas, he remarks that 'social worlds *intersect*, and do so under a variety of conditions' (Strauss, 1978, p. 122). We are also confronted with the '*segmenting* of social worlds' (Strauss, 1978, p. 123), not only in the sense that they segment the totality of lifeworlds but also in the sense that they segment internally, producing 'specifiable subworlds'. We can take as examples here the mediatized worlds of popular cultural scenes like hip hop, black metal or techno: the ongoing articulation of their mediatized worlds is likewise an ongoing segmentation and (re)invention process. That said, researching mediatized worlds also entails investigating the transgression from one mediatized world to another as well as the processes of demarcation.

It is within these two frames of discussion that we want to use the concept of 'mediatized worlds'. Mediatized worlds are still lifeworlds in the phenomenological sense and social worlds in the perspective of symbolic interactionism, and at the same time new versions of these already existing concepts, as they are mediatized worlds and should be studied in this sense. They are *structured fragments of social lifeworlds with a certain binding intersubjective knowledge inventory, with specific social practices and cultural thickenings*. Mediatized worlds are the everyday concretization of media cultures and media societies. They are the level where mediatization becomes concrete, where people use media in specific contexts and with specific interests and intentions, and by virtue of this can be analyzed empirically. To give some examples: while it is impossible to research the mediatization of a culture or society as a whole, we can investigate the mediatized world of stock exchange dealing, of schooling, of the private home and so on. Analyzing these 'socially constructed part-time realities' as mediatized worlds means researching empirically in what way their communicative construction is shaped by various media, as well as how this communicative construction changes in the sense outlined above. If we raise the question of how this can be done in practice, a look at the already existing studies of Anselm Strauss, for example, and at other work in the frame of symbolic interactionism may be helpful, as well as the existing studies in phenomenological sociology and sociology of knowledge. This is done in practice, for example, in the priority programme *Mediatized Worlds* (see below).

The analysis of various mediatized worlds and their change by virtue of becoming mediatized can, of course, be only one starting point for undertaking empirical mediatization research. However, the idea is to start at this concrete level to get different 'grounded theories' of how media communicative change and socio-cultural change are interlaced with each other, and how this interplay can be theorized in an appropriate way as part of the meta-process of mediatization. The deployment of a good number of such grounded theories of mediatized worlds makes it possible to develop a more general theory of the present mediatization.

If we link mediatization in such a way with a social (life)world perspective, the concept of mediatization begins to speak in a new way: if we follow the above-mentioned argument that one main moment of present mediatization is the situation of an increasing 'media saturation' (Lundby,

2009a, p. 2), the 'media manifold' (Couldry, 2012, p. 16) and 'polymedia' (Madianou and Miller, 2013, p. 172), mediatization research is not so much concerned with investigating the 'influence' of one single medium, but more with the changing role of a variety of media in our lives. While such an argument is theoretically striking, the main problem is how to turn it into empirical research. One possibility for this is not to start the research with one medium but to take one kind of social world or (small) lifeworld as a unit of research. Then it becomes possible to investigate how this social world or (small) lifeworld changes with mediatization – or, in other words, how it changes as a mediatized world.

Such a move, however, also emphasizes that mediatization does not offer a closed theory, as, for example, the system theory within sociology does. This is not the idea of mediatization research. Recently, Sonia Livingstone and Peter Lunt (2014) compared mediatization research with a Twitter 'hashtag'. By this they want to emphasize that mediatization is a 'meta-project' of integrating various detailed studies into and overall analysis of transformation and change. This metaphor points to one very important aspect of current mediatization research, because of the complexity of its undertaking – to research the interrelation between the change of media and communication, on the one hand, and culture and society on the other – various detailed and competing analytical concepts are necessary, as well as various methods. However, a group of scholars who have gathered around the term 'mediatization' are engaged in bringing this form of analysis forward. With this volume, we hope to bring the discussion one step forward by introducing the concept of 'mediatized world' to ground mediatization research better in an everyday perspective.

3. About this volume: Background, structure and arguments

The aforementioned shift of mediatization is the reorientation we adopted with the priority programme *Mediatized Worlds*. Since 2010, funded by the German Research Foundation (DFG), 12 research projects have investigated the mediatization of various social worlds or (small) lifeworlds. Topics are the everyday world of community building, the world of sport betting, 'scopic media' in various social worlds, mediatized business models in social worlds, the mediatized home, and the mediatized world of political deliberation and of members of the parliament, of security policy and of music – and how to investigate the changing social relations of present mediatized worlds in a long-term perspective (for detailed information about the projects, see http://www.mediatizedworlds.net).

While these projects operationalize the idea of mediatized worlds in very concrete ways, it is nevertheless linked with an argument that goes beyond this specific research. This is the argument for bringing mediatization research closer to the everyday world. As such an argument is much more general, in 2011 the priority programme hosted a conference at the University of Bremen with the title 'Mediatized Worlds: Culture and Society in a Media Age'. The idea of this conference was to discuss internationally such a shift in mediatization research. In all, 54 presentations were given by scholars from 14 different countries. The present volume consists of revised versions of the best of these papers. In addition, a number of authors were invited who have been more recently engaged in the discussion about linking mediatization research with a social and lifeworld perspective.

The volume comprises six parts. Part I, 'Rethinking Mediatization', opens with a chapter from Knut Lundby, 'Mediatized Stories in Mediatized Worlds'. In this chapter, Lundby, on the one hand, introduces the mediatized story project which played an important role in the present international push of mediatization research. On the other hand, he reflects on how far the phenomenon of mediatized storytelling is related to the idea of living in mediatized worlds. The core argument of this chapter is that a mediatized story is, for sure, not a mediatized world. However, living in mediatized worlds means that mediatized stories gain relevance in a number of these social worlds.

In the following chapter, Johan Fornäs argues for a culturalizing of mediatization. With the move to a more concrete investigation of mediatized worlds, he links the argument that more culturally oriented approaches to mediatization should be revitalized. Such a cultural orientation means looking more carefully into the different levels and kinds of mediatization and relating mediatization more deeply to process concepts such as modernization, lifeworld colonization and reflexivity. For this, a reconnection of mediatization to anthropologically and hermeneutically inspired theorizations of the early 1990s is a help.

Nick Couldry, too, links the idea of mediatized worlds to a new 'grounding' of mediatization research. However, this 'grounding' needs an appropriate foundation in social theory, for which especially the field theory in the tradition of Pierre Bourdieu is helpful. This theory is, on the one hand, linkable to the idea of mediatized worlds – different fields consist of various, though characteristic, mediatized worlds. On the other hand, linking the mediatization approach with field theory makes it possible to explain that mediatization results in different phenomena depending on which part of culture and society one investigates.

Friedrich Krotz in his article 'Media, Mediatization and Mediatized Worlds' rethinks what mediatization means in the frame of a social (life)world perspective. His core argument is that, if we take this perspective seriously, the idea of a 'media logic' is less helpful. Therefore, we must clarify what a medium is. This makes it possible to conceptualize mediatization as a process related to the social construction of the word. This process is always related to changing demands, expectations and interests of the people. Therefore, mediatization reminds us that there is a social entity that becomes mediatized – and, in this sense, the concept does not simply describe media change, but also its consequences.

Part II of the volume deals with mediatization and new media. However, we cannot fully grasp the relation of mediatization to *current* new media without contextualizing it historically. This contextualization is given by Thomas Steinmaurer in his chapter on the historical traits of telephony and theoretical considerations about a new dispositive of communication. A look back to the origins of telecommunications makes it possible to detect 'techno-cultural traces' of interactive communication throughout the history of telephony. In addition, it becomes evident that the development of interactive technologies of communication is shaped by certain social structures whenever the technological system as such is characterized by a certain openness of use. In such a view, the present 'newness' of digital media loses its singularity.

In his chapter, James Miller posits that present mediatized worlds are marked by the omnipresence of media in all situations. Linking this with media technologies related to mobile communication, he speaks about 'everyware media' and, based on that, reformulates the idea of a 'media logic' within the institutionalist tradition of mediatization research. His argument is that, originally, the dimension of technology was not integrated as inclusively as it should have been. In short, the fear of technological determinism ought not to constrain the consideration of technology in mediatization.

The final chapter of the second part is by Stig Hjarvard, who discusses the institutionalization of new media. The aim of this chapter is to take more recent points of critique against an institutionalist view on mediatization as a starting point to reflect forms of mediatization related to digital media. Hjarvard argues for linking mediatization research more closely to the theoretical framework of institutional logics, also when it comes to digital media: 'new' digital media, too, have institutional properties, however different they may be compared with the 'old' mass media. Such a move also opens the original idea of media logic when analyzing present mediatized worlds.

In Part III, mediatized communities are the focus of analysis. In the first chapter, Hubert Knoblauch develops an approach on the mediatization of religion that makes it possible to understand the change of present religious communities. Taking the example of the visit of Benedict XVI to Germany, he demonstrates a substantial change in the role of the media in religion and in the structure of communicative action which may be called religious. His research makes accessible the transformation of religious communication and religion by interactive and digital technology towards a new kind of 'popular religion' with its own mediatized worlds.

Miyase Christensen examines the relation of technology, place and mediatized cosmopolitanism in present lifeworlds. Based on empirical research in Sweden and drawing on Bourdieu's field theory and social phenomenology, she analyzes the role of place and technology in shaping current modes of 'mediation' and 'communicative practice' in everyday lifeworlds that make new forms of 'mediatized cosmopolitanism' possible.

Andreas Hepp, Matthias Berg and Cindy Roitsch discuss the 'mediatized worlds of communitization' of young people. Based on ethnographic and qualitative network research and referring back to Max Weber's idea of understanding communities more as a process of 'communitization', they argue that present mediatization results in 'mediatized horizons'. This means that each individual positions him- or herself in a variety of communities which are increasingly articulated by media practice. This kind of research makes it possible to distinguish between young people as 'localists', 'centrists', 'multi-localists' and 'pluralists'.

The fourth part of this book moves private life into the foreground of analyzing mediatized worlds. Mark Deuze begins this move by reflecting on the relation between his understanding of 'media life' and processes of the mediatization of the lifeworld. His argument is that we need to analyze the 'invisibility of media' – their disappearance into 'natural user interfaces' – if we want to understand present-day mediatized worlds. Therefore, his aim is to develop a conceptual approach for making the 'unseen disappearance of media into the lifeworld' accessible.

This is followed by John Storey's and Katy McDonald's chapter on 'Media Love'. Via a detailed analysis of qualitative interviews, it becomes evident that 'love' in present mediatized worlds means something different than it used to: their research demonstrates that contemporary romantic practices have become 'entangled in, and almost unthinkable without, media'. This does not mean that all moments of love are related to media. However, with mediatization it has become a matter of fact that people increasingly appropriate media as 'part of the architecture and choreography of a romantic relationship'.

The third chapter of Part IV discusses the meaning of 'home' in the context of digitization, mobilization and mediatization. Based on empirical data drawn from an ethnographically oriented panel study of 25 households, Corinna Peil and Jutta Röser argue that, also in times of increasing mediatization, the 'home' remains the main location of media appropriation. However, it becomes a 'mediatized home' when new media technologies are integrated into everyday domestic life, and the coexistence of old and new media is managed at home.

Part V moves the analysis from private life to organizational contexts. The first organizational context under consideration is politics – or, more concretely, mediatized politics. Based on detailed quantitative and qualitative research, Caja Thimm, Mark Dang-Anh and Jessica Einspänner explore the structures and strategies of discursive participation and online deliberation on Twitter. While their point of departure is related to a single medium – the 'functional operator model of Twitter' – their analysis ends with a reflection of the overall change within the mediatized worlds of politics.

Jan-H. Passoth, Tilmann Sutter and Josef Wehner investigate another organizational context: the context of media distribution. Informed by ethnographic studies and theoretical reflection, they demonstrate how far new, technology-based 'audience measurement techniques' play a role in these mediatized worlds. Their argument is that the internet opens 'new opportunities for measurement' that take individual media behaviour more strongly into consideration. However, this 'measurement' is not just a basis for decision-making but enters directly and automatically, as well as indirectly and mediated, into the creation of content.

The third organizational context discussed in this part of the volume is schools as mediatized network organizations. Andreas Breiter's argument is that educational reform in the process of mediatization can be framed by looking at schools as mediatized worlds. Based on empirical research in various projects, Breiter develops a three-level model of educational governance with reference to the micro level (media and the classroom), the meso level (media and school organization) and the macro level (media, school governance and educational policy).

The final Part VI of this volume consists of the concluding chapter 'Mediatization: Concluding Thoughts and Challenges for the Future' by Lynn Schofield Clark. The focus of this chapter is to discuss – based on the analysis of various mediatized worlds in this volume – future possibilities for mediatization research. In so doing, the main argument is that 'abductive reasoning' should gain more space in mediatization research. Referring back to the medium theory of Marshall McLuhan as well as linking forward to the idea of a better involvement in critical media-related movements, Schofield Clark argues that thought experiments rooted in visionary pragmatism develop mediatization theory even further than the present reflection of mediatized worlds.

In sum, our hope is that this volume will stimulate media and communication research in general, and mediatization research in particular, by linking the concept of mediatization more strongly than before to the everyday lives of people. The argument is that mediatization is nothing abstract, taking place in spheres of life socially far away. Rather, mediatization is about changes in our personal lives, our experiences and our belongings that are deeply related to media and communication change. The idea of this volume is, through the selection of its chapters, to invite such an analysis by presenting related theoretical reflections as well as empirical research.

References

Altheide, D. L. and Snow, R. P. (1979) *Media logic* (Beverly Hills: Sage).
Altheide, D. L. and Snow, R. P. (1991) *Media worlds in the postjournalism era* (New York: Aldine).
Asp, K. (1990) 'Medialization, media logic and mediarchy'. In: *Nordicom Review*, 11(2), pp. 47–50.

Averbeck-Lietz, S. (2014) *Soziologie der Kommunikation: Die Mediatisierung der Gesellschaft und die Theoriebildung der Klassiker* (München: Oldenbourg Wissenschaftsverlag).

Baudrillard, J. (1995) *Simulacra and Simulations* (Ann Arbor, MI: University of Michigan Press).

Berger, P. L. and Luckmann, T. (1967) *The social construction of reality: A treatise in the sociology of knowledge* (London: Penguin).

Bird, S. E. (2003) *The audience in everyday life. Living in a media world* (New York, London: Routledge).

Couldry, N. (2012) *Media, society, world: Social theory and digital media practice* (Cambridge, Oxford: Polity Press).

Couldry, N. and Hepp, A. (2013) 'Conceptualising mediatization: Contexts, traditions, arguments'. In: *Communication Theory*, 23(3), pp. 191–202.

Ginsburg, F. D., Abu-Lughod, L. and Larkin, B. (2002) 'Introduction'. In: Ginsburg, F. D., Abu-Lughod, L. and Larkin, B. (eds.) *Media worlds. Anthropology on new terrain* (Berkeley: California UP), pp. 1–36.

Habermas, J. (1988a) *Theorie des kommunikativen Handelns. Bd. I. Handlungsrationalität und gesellschaftliche Rationalisierung* (Frankfurt am Main: Suhrkamp Verlag).

Habermas, J. (1988b) *Theorie des kommunikativen Handelns. Bd. II. Zur Kritik der funktionalistischen Vernunft* (Frankfurt am Main: Suhrkamp Verlag).

Hannerz, U. (ed.) (1990) *Medier och kulturer* (Stockholm: Carlsson).

Hepp, A. (2013a) *Cultures of mediatization* (Cambridge: Polity Press).

Hepp, A. (2013b) 'The communicative figurations of mediatized worlds: Mediatization research in times of the "mediation of everything"'. In: *European Journal of Communication*, 28(6), pp. 615–629.

Hitzler, R. and Honer, A. (1984) 'Lebenswelt – Milieu – Situation. Terminologische Vorschläge zur theoretischen Verständigung'. In: *Kölner Zeitschrift für Soziologie und Sozialpsychologie*, 36(1), pp. 56–74.

Hjarvard, S. (2013) *The mediatization of culture and society* (London: Routledge).

Hug, T. and Friesen, N (2009) 'The mediatic turn: Exploring concepts for media pedagogy'. In: Lundby, K. (ed.) *Mediatization: Concept, changes, consequences* (New York: Peter Lang), S. 63–83.

Innis, Harold A. (1950) *Empire and communications* (Oxford: Clarendon Press).

Knoblauch, H. (2013) 'Communicative constructivism and mediatization'. In: *Communication Theory*, 23(3), pp. 297–315.

Krotz, F. (1995) 'Elektronisch mediatisierte Kommunikation – Überlegungen zu einer Konzeption einiger zukünftiger Forschungsfelder der Kommunikationswissenschaft'. In: *Rundfunk und Fernsehen*, 43(4), pp. 445–62.

Krotz, F. (2001) *Die Mediatisierung kommunikativen Handelns. Der Wandel von Alltag und sozialen Beziehungen, Kultur und Gesellschaft durch die Medien* (Opladen: Westdeutscher Verlag).

Krotz, F. (2009) 'Mediatization: A concept with which to grasp media and societal change'. In: Lundby, K. (ed.) *Mediatization: Concept, changes, consequences* (New York: Peter Lang), pp. 19–38.

Krotz, F. (2014) 'Mediatization as a mover in modernity: Social and cultural change in the context of media change'. In: Lundby, K. (ed.) *Handbook mediatization* (Berlin: de Gruyter), in print.

Krotz, F. and Hepp, A. (2013) 'A concretization of mediatization: How mediatization works and why "mediatized worlds" are a helpful concept for empirical mediatization research'. In: *Empedocles. European Journal for the Philosophy of Communication*, 3(2), pp. 119–34.

Lievrouw, L. A. (2001) 'New media and the "pluralization of life-worlds". A role for information in social differentiation'. In: *New Media & Society*, 3(1), pp. 7–18.

Livingstone, S. M. (2009) 'On the mediation of everything'. In: *Journal of Communication*, 59(1), pp. 1–18.

Livingstone, S. and Lunt, P. (2014) 'Mediatization: An emerging paradigm for media and communication research?' In: Lundby, K. (ed.) *Handbook mediatization*. Berlin, New York: de Gruyter, in print.

Luckmann, B. (1970) 'The small life-worlds of modern man'. In: *Social Research*, 37(4), pp. 580–96.

Lundby, K. (2009a) 'Introduction: "Mediatization" as a key'. In: Lundby, K. (ed.) *Mediatization: Concept, changes, consequences* (New York: Peter Lang), pp. 1–18.

Lundby, K. (2009b) 'Media logic: Looking for social interaction'. In: Lundby, K. (ed.) *Mediatization: Concept, changes, consequences* (New York: Peter Lang), pp. 101–19.

Lundby, K. (ed.) (2009c) *Mediatization: Concept, changes, consequences* (New York: Peter Lang).

Madianou, M. and Miller, D. (2013) 'Polymedia: Towards a new theory of digital media in interpersonal communication'. In: *International Journal of Cultural Studies*, 16, pp. 169–87.

Manheim, E. (1933) *Die Träger der öffentlichen Meinung. Studien zur Soziologie der Öffentlichkeit* (Brünn, Prag, Leipzig, Wien: Verlag Rudolf M. Rohrer).

McLuhan, M. (1994) *Understanding media: The extensions of man* (Cambridge, London: MIT).

Meyrowitz, J. (1995) 'Medium theory'. In: Crowley, D. J. and Mitchell, D. (eds.) *Communication theory today* (Cambridge: Polity Press), pp. 50–77.

Meyrowitz, J. (2009) 'Medium theory: An alternative to the dominant paradigm of media effects'. In: Nabi, R. L. and Oliver, M. B. (eds.) *The Sage handbook of media processes and effects* (Thousand Oaks, CA: Sage), pp. 517–30.

Morley, D. (2001) 'Belongings: Place, space and identity as mediated world'. In: *European Journal of Cultural Studies*, 4(4), pp. 425–48.

Morley, D. (2009) 'For a materialist, non-media-centric media studies'. In: *Television & New Media*, 10(1), pp. 114–16.

Schütz, A. and Luckmann, T. (1973) *The structures of the life-world*, 2 volumes (Evanston: Northwestern UP).

Shibutani, T. (1955) 'Reference groups as perspectives'. In: *American Journal of Sociology*, 60, pp. 562–9.

Silverstone, R. and Haddon, L. (1996) 'Design and the domestication of information and communication technologies: Technical change and everyday life'. In: Silverstone, R. and Mansell, R. (eds.) *Communication by design. The politics of information and communication technologies* (Oxford: Oxford University Press), pp. 44–74.

Strauss, A. (1978) 'A social world perspective'. In: *Studies in Symbolic Interactionism*, 1(1), pp. 119–28.

Strömbäck, J. (2011) 'Mediatization of politics'. In: Bucy, E. P. and Holbert, R. L. (eds.) *Sourcebook for political communication research* (London, New York: Routledge), pp. 367–82.

Thompson, J. B. (1995) *The media and modernity. A social theory of the media* (Cambridge: Cambridge University Press).

Part I
Rethinking Mediatization

2
Mediatized Stories in Mediatized Worlds
Knut Lundby

1. Introduction

Youth use digital media for self-representations in different life settings, and young people practise 'digital storytelling' in particular 'mediatized worlds'. This book aims to explore the extent to which contemporary social worlds and lifeworlds are mediatized. The international *Mediatized stories* project may throw light on digital storytelling in mediatized worlds, and the dimensions of mediatized worlds – as laid out in the introduction to this volume – may help analyze findings from the *Mediatized stories* research. This is the double ambition of this chapter: to locate digital storytelling in mediatized worlds and to reinterpret those mediatized stories with the analytical categories of mediatized worlds.

The project *Mediatized Stories. Mediation Perspectives on Digital Storytelling among Youth*[1] linked up scholars from media and communication studies, informatics and education sciences across seven countries, among them David Brake, Tone Bratteteig, Nick Couldry, Kirsten Drotner, Ola Erstad, Larry Friedlander, David Gauntlett, Stig Hjarvard, Birgit Hertzberg Kaare, Glynda Hull, Sonia Livingstone, Mia Lövheim, Mark Evan Nelson, Lotte Nyboe, Elisabeth Staksrud, Nancy Thumim and James V. Wertsch. Some of them brought their larger projects into this frame of cooperative research.

This chapter, first, gives an overview of findings in the *Mediatized stories* project, highlighting how it has influenced contemporary mediatization research and explored digital storytelling among young people and the informal learning processes involved. Second, cases of digital storytelling from the *Mediatized stories* research are analyzed with the categories of mediatized worlds. Finally, a conclusion is drawn on the relation between digital storytelling practices and mediatized worlds.

2. Mediatized stories

Exploring how people – youth in particular – use self-representation in digital storytelling, the *Mediatized stories* project had three research objectives: first, to clarify theoretically the contrast between the concepts of mediation and mediatization; second, to analyze the socio-cultural dynamics of mediatization in digital storytelling when people shape and share their lives; and, third, to investigate how self-representation in digital storytelling may build competence and media literacy through informal learning.

Understanding 'mediatization': The role of the *Mediatized stories* project

To understand how stories can be 'mediatized', we had to dive into the emerging discourse on mediatization. The project actually came to contribute some significant pieces of work in this field of media and communication research.

The British participants initially avoided 'mediatization' because it is 'a clumsy neologism' in English (Livingstone, 2009b, p. 6). Inspired by Raymond Williams (1988, pp. 204–7) and in particular by Roger Silverstone (2002; 2005; 2007), they were sticking to the technological and social 'mediation' to denote transformations following the 'dialectical process in which institutionalized media of communication are involved in the general circulation of symbols in social life' (Silverstone, 2007, p. 109). These processes of communication 'change the social and cultural environments that support them as well as the relationships that participants, both individual and institutional, have to that environment and to each other' (Silverstone, 2005, p. 189).

Silverstone acknowledges the 'telling of stories about ourselves and others' to be at the heart of mediation processes in public space (2007, pp. 52–3). Nancy Thumim applied mediation in this sense to understand self-representation and digital culture (Thumim, 2008; 2009; 2012). Sonia Livingstone prepared a draft of her address 'On the Mediation of Everything' as part of the *Mediatized stories* project (Livingstone, 2009b, p. 13).

In another much-cited piece, Nick Couldry discussed the concepts of mediatization versus mediation in understanding 'the emergent space of digital storytelling' (Couldry, 2008). At that time he argued for mediation, in line with Silverstone, and found 'mediatization' too linear and one-sided to capture 'the broader social consequences of media' (p. 389). He later changed his mind (cf. his chapter in this volume). ' "Mediatization" has emerged as that term', Couldry admits, which covers 'media's general effects on social organization' (Couldry, 2012, p. 134). This is the most suitable concept to grasp the particular transformations in media-saturated societies. Couldry, however, does not apply a narrow media-centric approach. He has a perspective on social processes in general and asks how mediatization may be identified as operating in different types of social processes. In a 'media age', mediatization is the concept that would 'acknowledge media as an *irreducible* dimension of all social processes' (Couldry, 2012, p. 137, emphasis in original). This, further, refers to communication as part of all social processes, to how media shape communication processes (p. 136). Friedrich Krotz (2009) introduced this perspective on mediatization as

> grounded in the modification of *communication as the basic practice* of how people construct the social and cultural world. They do so by changing communication practices that use media and refer to media. Hence, mediatization is *not* a technologically driven concept, since it is not the media as a technology that are causal, but the changes in how people communicate when constructing their inner and exterior realities by referring to the media.
>
> (p. 25, emphases in original)

When Krotz terms mediatization a 'meta-process' alongside globalization, individualization and commercialization (Krotz, 2007; 2008a), this perspective on how communication becomes mediated is at the heart of it. 'The concept of mediatization opens up a particular panorama of the world', as Andreas Hepp (2013, p. 50) writes with reference to Bruno Latour's concept of 'panoramas' (Latour, 2005, pp. 183–90). The mediatization of communication, then, creates a *life horizon* for those immersed in a media-saturated environment or in the more specific media worlds.

Stig Hjarvard, in contrast, views this environment from the *institutions* that initiate mediated communication as part of the social interaction. Institutions, like politics, education or religion, increasingly take on a 'media logic' in the way they operate. The institutions in society adapt to the requirements of the media. Social interaction and communication with the institutions, as well as within and between the institutions, take place to a greater degree via the media (Hjarvard, 2008). The media themselves, then, strengthen their position and take on a semi-institutional character (Hjarvard, in this volume).

Initially, Hjarvard identified mediatization with social or cultural activities and not with institutions. While digital storytelling is not an institution as such, it is a social and cultural activity. Hjarvard's working definition was that mediatization 'implies a process through which core elements of a social or cultural activity (like work, leisure, play etc.) assume media form' (Hjarvard, 2004, p. 48). Hence, when it becomes common to turn the old human practice of storytelling into digital forms, it becomes 'mediatized'. However, the same could have been said when storytelling was done with books, or with film, radio and television.

Institutions or fields of 'activity', as Hjarvard observes, are not 'worlds' in the sense in which they will be discussed here. Still, there may be insights to take from his institutional perspective on mediatization to the encounter with 'mediatized worlds'.

Hjarvard became the main guide on the Scandinavian route to mediatization, developed as a theory of the media as agents of social and cultural change (Hjarvard, 2008; 2013). Mediatization, for Hjarvard, is quite close to Silverstone's concept of mediation. They both take care of the long-term social and cultural transformations in which media play an inherent, crucial role (Lundby, 2008b, p. 12). For Hjarvard, 'mediation' is simply the communication that takes place through a technical medium (Hjarvard, 2008, p. 114, and chapter in this volume). Couldry is right that the real debate is, rather, about the type of explanation we aim at and not about terminology. He observes a general scholarly agreement on a pervasive media influence in all spheres of social and cultural life and that new causal complexities emerge in media-saturated societies, which we now try to understand and specify (Couldry, 2012, p. 134).

I support Hepp (2013, pp. 37–8) in saying that 'mediation' and 'mediatization' are complementary rather than opposing concepts. Mediation is the basic process of communication that may or may not lead to the forms of social and cultural transformations denoted by 'mediatization'.[2]

The *Mediatized stories* project led into a general outline of mediatization, as can be seen in the volume *Mediatization: Concept, Changes, Consequences* (Lundby, 2009c), in which German-speaking scholars contributed from their long record of research in this conceptual terrain (Friesen and Hug, 2009; Hartmann, 2009; Hepp, 2009; Krotz, 2009; Schrott, 2009; Strömbäck and Esser, 2009; Thomas, 2009). American scholars added to this mostly European debate (Clark, 2009; Hoover, 2010; Rothenbuhler, 2009).

'Mediatization' denotes processes of change 'moulded' by the media, as Andreas Hepp (2009; 2012) has aptly termed the work of media in society and culture. The changes 'may have the character of *transformations*, as the changes incurred by the media may change the direction, the form or character of the actual social or cultural activities' (Lundby, 2009a, p. 11). Mediatization implies long-term *structural* transformations of the relation between media and modern society at large (Hjarvard in this volume, my emphasis). However, this is 'a matter not merely of the transformation of media, but also of the transformation of *symbolic forms*, and so of *communication* bound up with the media' (Hepp, 2013, p. 31, my emphases). I take this into 'the emergent space of digital storytelling' (Couldry, 2008). From the socio-cultural approach to mediation[3] I take that both narratives and digital media work as cultural tools (Erstad and Wertsch, 2008). There is a cultural dynamic to digital storytelling.

Dynamics of digital storytelling: Researching communication in 'mediatized worlds'

New forms of digital storytelling emerge to enhance communication within mediatized worlds. These are usually small-scale and 'self-made' media

(Hartley, 2008). The second aim of the *Mediatized stories* project was to analyze the socio-cultural dynamics inherent in mediation and mediatization when people shape and share their lives through self-representation in small-scale digital storytelling. This takes us into cultural and social transformations with digital stories.

What is to be regarded as 'mediatized' with digital storytelling was initially presented in the volume *Digital Storytelling, Mediatized Stories. Self-representations in New Media* (Lundby, 2008a). Considering digital storytelling, I introduced mediatization on three levels of transformation: narrative or semiotic transformations, institutional transformations and cultural transformations (Lundby, 2008b). This distinction corresponds with, and is partly inspired by, Nancy Thumim's work on digital storytelling and other kinds of mediated self-representation, among them projects at the Museum of London and in BBC's *Capture Wales*. Her research is summarized in her book on *Self-representation and Digital Culture* (Thumim, 2012). In good British tradition, she applies 'mediation' as the concept with which to grasp the transforming processes. She finds that we can now speak of a genre of self-representation across diverse settings and contexts.

Thumim observes three dimensions of transforming mediation, in textual, institutional and cultural processes, respectively. The concept of 'text' is used in a broad, multimodal sense. A digital story is a 'text' in its combination of digital modes: images, words, graphics, music. 'Textual mediation' is the multimodal composition of a mediated self-representation with digital tools and the reception of it. Thumim argues that analysis of texts is crucial to understanding how self-representations are mediated in digital culture but has to be explored in relation to the institutional and cultural context in which it is produced. The 'institutional mediation' points to the context within which the digital stories are produced. 'Cultural mediation' refers to the points of view – the abilities, expectations and understandings – that 'ordinary people' bring with them when they act to create digital stories. Tensions occur in all three forms of mediation and between them (Thumim, 2012, pp. 58–62). Such tensions contribute to the cultural and social transformations that digital storytelling may be part of and help to 'mould'.

Where Thumim observes 'tensions', I look for 'transformations'. Basically, we refer to the same kind of processes and contexts for self-representation in digital storytelling. She captures them with the concept of mediation while I stress the potential changes to the 'text' and to the institutional and cultural context by applying the term 'mediatization'.

The *Mediatized stories* project initially concentrated on small-scale personal storytelling, short multimedia tales as performed according to the global outreach of the Center for Digital Storytelling in California (www.storycenter. org) (Lambert, 2009b). 'Digital storytelling', in this sense, is 'a workshop-based practice in which people are taught to use digital media to create short audio-video stories, usually about their own lives' (Hartley and McWilliam, 2009a, p. 3). The idea for the digital production is developed with fellow storytellers and an instructor sitting in a ring, a 'story circle' (Hartley and McWilliam, 2009b), later shaped in pre-defined steps into a story to share (Lambert, 2013).

This form of digital storytelling had its particular place in time and space: it was no coincidence that it started in California, close to Silicon Valley, where computers with easily accessible multimedia software were developed (Lundby, 2009b). This form of digital storytelling soon inspired the BBC *Capture Wales* project (Meadows and Kidd, 2009), one of the cases Nancy Thumim studied, and later expanded throughout the world (Hartley and McWilliam, 2009b). This form of digital storytelling also went 'beyond individual expression' (Watkins and Russo, 2009) into various institutions that found it useful (McWilliam, 2009). However, the institutional purposes may create tensions and transform the genre, in particular because the personal, emotional aspect may be lost (Kaare, 2012). Schools or other institutions that would like to tell 'the whole story' of their activity within a short digital story may not be able to keep the personal, poetic aspect which gives these stories their strength (Jamissen and Skou, 2010).

However, there are other forms of small-scale digital storytelling with capacity for self-representation. Such cases will be explored throughout this chapter. Digital narration with a personal twist may be done in animation (Nyboe and Drotner, 2008), blogging (Mortensen and Walker, 2002; Rettberg, 2008) and on SNSs, social network(ing) sites (Beer, 2008; boyd and Ellison, 2008). SNSs were only in their embryonic stages when the *Mediatized Stories* project was planned in 2005. As it progressed, the project had to turn its interest towards self-representation in social media as well: David Brake studied 'Shaping the "me" in MySpace: The framing of profiles on a social network site' (Brake, 2008) and Sonia Livingstone (2008) sat with teenagers to learn how they represent themselves online.

Informal learning: Building competence for 'mediatized worlds'

Practices of personal digital storytelling, in 'classical' short-story form, in blogging or on social network sites, build competence for participation in mediatized worlds.

Sonia Livingstone, in her *Mediatized stories* project, was keen to find out how young people learn informally through their self-representational practices in social networking, how they 'uncover the subtle connections between online opportunity and risk' (Livingstone, 2008, p. 393). This tension between children's handling of online risk and opportunity has been further explored within *Mediatized stories* by Elisabeth Staksrud (2013).

Self-representation in various forms of digital storytelling may build competence and media literacy through the informal learning that takes place during this narrative activity with computers. This learning perspective, inspired by the New Literacy movement (e.g., Knobel and Lankshear, 2007), was central when Glynda Hull and her colleagues did their research with children in after-school activities in the DUSTY project – *Digital Underground Storytelling for Youth* (Hull, 2003; Hull and James, 2007; Hull and Katz, 2006; Hull and Zacher, 2004). DUSTY actually became the inspiration that sparked off *Mediatized stories*. 'The paradox of digital competence formation' (Drotner, 2008, p. 65) is that so much knowledge building takes place outside formal learning sites in play and social engagement with information and communication technologies. 'Unwittingly, many youngsters are busy rehearsing for their adult existence through digital storytelling in gaming, blogging, and through multimodal editing of visuals, graphics and sound' (Drotner, 2008, pp. 67–8). The ability to express oneself through digital storytelling also challenges the formal educational context in schools. There is agency in digital storytelling (Erstad and Silseth, 2008). 'When young people are given the opportunity to blend the informal "cultural codes" with the more formal ones in their own learning processes, agency might be fostered in a new way, with implications for democratic participation' (Erstad and Silseth, 2008, p. 214).

Digital media and mediatization: Does it matter that it is digital?

In digital storytelling, 'computational power meets human contact' (Hartley and McWilliam, 2009a). The *Mediatized stories* project aimed to understand transformations in the age-old practices of storytelling that have become possible with new, digital media (Lundby, 2008b, p. 1). Does it matter that it is digital? Yes, definitely. Tone Bratteteig (2008) answers the question in the affirmative from her viewpoint in participatory computer studies. 'The mediatized story is characterized by the digital: It makes use of many data types presented digitally using the computer's ability to present digitized data of all types in a sequence of programmed operations "playing" the digital story' (Bratteteig, 2008, p. 281). Mastering the digital equipment, the digital storyteller is able to 'play' as well as to produce stories. As Erstad and Wertsch (2008, p. 36) note, the digital tools 'create new performance spaces where young people in particular take advantage of these new meditational means to engage themselves in digital storytelling'.

It is the multimodal capability of digital media that first and foremost makes digital storytelling 'mediatized'. Multimodality is nothing new in storytelling. Telling stories face to face, one may play with the mode of orality as well as with the mode of facial expression. Digitalization, however, expands the multimodal space through combinations of text, music, visuals and graphics via the same binary codes. Glynda Hull and Mark Nelson (2005) explored the 'semiotic power of multimodality' in a detailed study of a particular digital story. They concluded that it could not have been told in the way it was if it had not been for the applied digital tools. The story was shaped – mediatized – with these tools.

'Digital narratives aspire to the variety and plenitude of a "world" rather than to the fixed structure of a text', Larry Friedlander (2008, p. 185) argues.

Although this primarily refers to larger, three-dimensional configurations in interactive game-narratives, small-scale digital storytelling offers some of this multimodal capability. As small-scale narratives, they open small-scale worlds. To what extent could these worlds in the cases of *Mediatized stories* be studied with the analytical dimensions of mediatized worlds?

3. Digital storytelling in mediatized worlds

Various forms of digital storytelling take place within different mediatized worlds. How far could a mediatized-world perspective be helpful in understanding digital storytelling – and how may the mediatized-world perspective be extended, based on the mediatized storytelling research?

I select four cases from the *Mediatized stories* project to explore this. They represent different forms of digital storytelling among youth: first, the 'classical' personal digital story; second, a digital animation; third, self-representation on social network sites; and, finally, successful personal blogs. Before embarking on these cases, it is necessary to recapitulate the analytical dimensions of the mediatized-worlds perspective (cf. the introduction to this book).

The mediatized-worlds perspective: Actions, networks, contexts, lifeworlds

How could forms of digital storytelling be understood within the dimensions of mediatized worlds? Initially, 'mediatized worlds' were identified through social relations on three levels: (1) actions and forms of interaction, (2) networks and (3) contexts (Krotz, 2008b).[4]

Mediatized worlds take shape with 'changing forms of communication and accordingly, related forms of *action and interaction*' (Krotz, 2008b, p. 8, my emphasis). People still interact face to face, but new forms of interaction with digital media 'directly affect the forms of social coexistence and collaborations' (Krotz, 2008b, p. 8). A mediatized world 'is based on the participation of people in specific configurations and therefore it requires specific media-related interaction and communication practices' (Krotz, 2008b, p. 9).

'Today's mediatized worlds are expressed in a change of professional as well as private *networks* and forms of relationships [...] increasingly maintained via digital media' (Krotz, 2008b, p. 9). Such networks depend on connectivity and act in flows (Hepp, Krotz, Moores and Winter, 2008).

Current mediatized worlds 'must not be considered on an isolated level since they are located in diverse social *contexts*. These contexts are to be understood as highly socially mediated. That means: embedded in certain "institutions" [...] which are again part of "social fields"' (Krotz, 2008b, p. 10, my emphasis).

The concept of mediatized worlds is theoretically refined in a three-step move: first, as 'social worlds', then into the more specific 'media worlds', and finally to 'mediatized worlds', as explained in the introduction to this book. W. Barnett Pearce's explication of 'social worlds' applies to the first step, although not referred to by Krotz and Hepp (2013). With them, Pearce shares a communication perspective on social worlds. We create social worlds that are 'complete' within their own horizons; there are many social worlds, each of them is shaped through interaction and communication, and everyone is an agent in the making of social worlds (Pearce, 2007, pp. 40–53). Where Pearce sticks to interpersonal communication, Krotz and Hepp look for mediated communication. They share a phenomenological perspective on the multiple realities of our everyday lifeworld. Krotz and Hepp make a particular reference to Benita Luckmann's observation of 'the small life-worlds of modern man' (1978):

> Mediatized worlds are, in our understanding, mediatized small life-worlds. As such, they are *structured fragments of life-worlds with a certain binding intersubjective knowledge inventory, specific social practices, and cultural thickening.*
>
> (Krotz and Hepp, 2013, p. 128)

Mediatization plays out in different ways in different 'worlds'; it is through these 'worlds' that mediatization can be grasped empirically (Hepp, 2013, pp. 75–83). Beside the social, relational aspects of interaction, networks and contexts, we may look for the phenomenological characteristics of a particular 'world' as a lifeworld.

What could cases from the *Mediatized stories* gain from a reinterpretation with these analytical dimensions in the mediatized worlds' perspective? David Gauntlett, in a project linked to *Mediatized stories*, asked for 'Young people's creative understanding of their mediaworlds'.[5] Young people are the agents. In addition to actions, networks, contexts and the lifeworld characteristics, it is necessary to specify who are the agents or storytellers. Let us re-examine the four cases from the *Mediatized stories* project. To what extent and in which ways could they be regarded as practices in mediatized worlds?

The classical form of digital storytelling: Digital faith stories

The first case is my own study, with Birgit Hertzberg Kaare, on digital faith stories (Kaare, 2008; Kaare and Lundby, 2008a; 2008b; Lundby, 2011; Lundby and Kaare, 2007). They were modelled on the 'classical' form of digital storytelling developed at the Center for Digital Storytelling in California (Lambert, 2009; 2013). The storytellers were 16–18-year-old post-confirmands.

The immediate *context* was an experimental faith education programme in their local parish in the Church of Norway, located just outside the capital city Oslo. The complexity and multilayered character of the context soon become visible. The community is located in a rich municipality with a high educational level. The local church is a medieval building. A great majority of the population are members of the national, Lutheran church, although most people rarely go to regular services and religion is not usually talked about. In 2003, the Norwegian parliament decided to fund a reform of religious education, to take place within the religious communities and not in the schools. The aim of the reform within the Church of Norway was to socialize children and youth within a religious tradition and help them to master life rather than to convey a package of theological knowledge. From 2005, this particular congregation was hosting a project to try out digital storytelling as a method in such identity formation among young church members (Lundby, 2006).

The participants in the digital faith stories project were part of several *networks*. Being young people, they had network relations with peers in school and leisure time. Most of them had cell phones and were used to digital tools, which they could apply for networking purposes alongside face-to-face contacts. However, this was in the early stage of social network media and before smartphones were on the market. The storytellers had some network relations to the local church through youth club activities and the confirmation programme, in particular through the youth minister, who was also the leader of the digital faith stories project. However, usually, they did not have a very extensive and long-lasting network activity with their church. This project established a temporary network in itself among the group of seven participants who took part in the first round of storytelling production. Similar numbers came with the following 'generations' of storytellers. The project lasted for a few years.

What did they actually do? What kind of *action and forms of interaction*? They first met in a 'story circle' with instructors experienced in this 'classical' form of digital storytelling and further developed their ideas in a workshop with the youth minister and other leaders. Each participant produced a digital story on a chosen topic related to his or her own life. They told how they had confidence or 'faith' in themselves rather than being specific about God or Jesus. However, they gave several more or less subtle cues to the religious tradition, thus confirming a belonging to the national and local church. Just making the digital stories in a church setting was a marker of interaction with this tradition, an expression of their point of view back to the church. However, when the digital story was done, they left. The church did not manage to keep them, as planned, as instructors for the next group of storytellers.

The participants in the digital faith stories project shared a *lifeworld* in terms of the joint school experience in their suburban, affluent, late-teenage life. In this lifeworld, the old church building occupies a significant space in consciousness and cultural landscape. The participants confirm their belonging to the dominant cultural–religious tradition by joining the storytelling project. However, they only committed themselves to a limited extent, withdrawing when their story was produced. This project never became a fully mediatized world. The particular interaction and network did not last. However, through their digital faith stories, the young participants confirmed and renewed their relation to the context in which the national church and its religious and cultural tradition (still) have a role.

Animation as digital storytelling: Digital narration and multimodal learning

Lotte Nyboe and Kirsten Drotner (2008) researched digital storytelling with computer animation. Their case study was with pupils from the sixth and tenth grades: children who were 12–13 and 15–16 years old, respectively, when the fieldwork was done in 2005.

The *context* was a provincial town in Denmark, where the two school classes were introduced to digital animation by professional animators and storytellers. This took place over three weeks at workshops in the Media School, the Computer Clubhouse and the Animation School, all connected to a Danish experimental culture centre for young people. The children already had some experience and competence in digital narration, like other children of their age in this period of digital developments. This exercise took it further: 'The digital animation project formed part of a larger cultural venture, incorporating also professional drama, oral storytelling and museology – a venture with the ambition to empower the young culturally' by teaching them about these aesthetic and artistic expressions and invite them to make their own stories with these skills (Nyboe and Drotner, 2008, p. 162).

This introduced the children to new *networks*. They did the digital animation as part of their known setting at school, but they also spent time at the workshop sites and got some impression of the professional networks based there. This work was mostly offline, although they used various digital tools on the computers. The pupils worked in groups with different animation technology.

The *action and forms of interaction* centred on the instruction and production of their animations. One workshop facilitated the use of Photoshop, the second, the use of computer animation, and the third, stop-motion animation. During the four phases of the aesthetic work process – introduction, storyboarding, production and screening – the pupils developed their multimodal competencies and their ability in digital narration. They found the sources for their narrative representations in their own everyday experiences as well as in the media culture they knew. Although the aim was a digital product, the pupils were surprised how much physical non-digital work they had to perform in preparation for the digital part.

This case unfolded in a constructed *lifeworld*: a cultural production experiment in which professional media facilities and facilitators coached school children in their animation work. The project created an intense mediatized world, but just for the few weeks it lasted. These experimental media productions encouraged a controlled mediatization. Although the participating children may have acquired competencies and experience that helped express and shape their identities, they did not share a lasting mediatized world.

Digital storytelling on social network sites: Telling stories online

During the summer of 2007, Sonia Livingstone sat down with 16 teenagers, 13–16 years old, half and half boys and girls. She wanted to observe and ask them about their use of social network sites, still in a fairly early stage of expansion at that time but already a significant part of life for these youngsters. The research is reported separately (Livingstone, 2008) as well as in the larger work on *Children and the Internet* (Livingstone, 2009a, ch. 4).

The wider *context* is teen culture in the UK with the available SNSs and their various affordances at the time of the field study. The particular ethnographic contexts are the bedrooms of those 16 teenagers where Livingstone was allowed in to follow the online connections from their PCs. Again, this was before the mobility of the smartphone made SNS use available on any corner.

SNSs are in themselves *networks* for social communication. The 16 participants did not know each other in a face-to-face social network. However, they all created and confirmed individual networks of friends through their SNS use. Livingstone found that the young internet users went beyond the simple distinction of 'friend' versus 'not-friend' on SNSs at that time. The teenagers operated a graded conception of 'friends', she observed.

The *action and forms of interaction* in the SNS use of these teenagers aim at staying in touch and managing the various levels of friendship. The self-representation given on the profile page of the SNS becomes crucial, a way of telling a story of oneself online. This is expression of identity. Livingstone found that the younger teenagers preferred to use the multimodal digital tools to 'recreate continuously a highly-decorated, stylistically-elaborate identity', while the older teenagers 'favour a plain aesthetic that foregrounds their links to others, thus expressing a notion of identity lived through authentic relationships' (Livingstone, 2008, p. 393).

The teenagers in Sonia Livingstone's study were recruited by a market research agency from the greater London area to represent a mix of socio-economic status categories and living locations (Livingstone, 2008, p. 397). They did not share a *lifeworld* beyond their overall media-connected teenage experience in the UK capital. However, to some extent they created a range of small lifeworlds in their internet exchange on Bebo, MySpace or Facebook. These British teenagers live in a kind of mediatized world as long as they stay in the virtual space of their own SNS activity. However, they also meet many of their online friends face to face. Online as well as offline, this is an individual world, as each young person has his or her own defined, layered network of friends. As such, it does not achieve the definition of a mediatized world.

Blogging as digital storytelling: Top-bloggers in ethical spaces

Mia Lövheim studied Swedish female top-bloggers, how they tried to be popular and personal at the same time (Lövheim, 2011a), how they carved out their blogs as 'ethical spaces' (Lövheim, 2011b), and the relation between these bloggers and their readers (Lövheim, 2012). The analysis is based on the content, characteristics and structure of 20 top-ranked blogs written by young women in 2009. The authors were between 18 and 28 years old.

The overall *context* is given with the Swedish blogosphere. The sample is taken from two top-ranked blog lists. These blogs are written in Swedish and thus only accessible within the country and for Swedish-reading internet users abroad.

The technological and discursive infrastructures make *networks* on several levels: the internet provides the overall network structure; the blogging lists are more limited networks, while each individual blog with its readers and commentators also makes up a separate network. We do not know to what extent these female bloggers and their followers also create face-to-face social networks, but we may assume that this is basically a virtual activity. However, the bloggers are usually involved in commercial structures outside the blog-world, as they attract marketing attention from various companies.

The *action and forms of interaction* in the top-blogs, first, relate to the content these bloggers put on the web. They concentrate on everyday life, fashion and beauty. These top-blogs got many comments – a great majority of them more than 50 written responses a day, mostly from women. Ethical considerations and negotiations on how to behave in life and in the commercial environment make up much of the discourse. Many take part as listeners or lurkers: 17 of the 20 sites had more than 28,000 visits every week, some considerably more (Lövheim, 2011a, pp. 5–6). Hence, these blogs are large communicative or 'ethical' spaces, particularly for young women, in contemporary society.

The top-bloggers operate on an individual basis in a large internet space. Their many followers may not interact at all, but share an interest in how to perform and represent oneself and how to handle life in late-modern society. In this sense, they share a generalized *lifeworld* as a backdrop for the communication in and beyond the particular blogs.

Each of these blogs or ethical spaces may be said to make a mediatized world. They have references to life offline, but the actual mediatized world takes place online. But how stable or persistent are these mediatized worlds as social worlds? To borrow book titles by Zygmunt Bauman (2000; 2007), they are part of the *Liquid modernity*, of *Living in an age of uncertainty*.

4. Conclusion

Starting from different forms of personal digital storytelling, it is not easy to identify lasting mediatized worlds with clear boundaries. Digital storytelling as such does not make a mediatized world of its own. Mediatized worlds are typically articulated across various media practices, of which digital storytelling may be just one. In this chapter, I discuss cases where new forms of digital storytelling have been introduced in emerging or project-based settings, and where these environments may be considered to take on some of the characteristics of mediatized worlds through the storytelling practices.

In the case of the digital faith stories, the group of young storytellers came together for the task of producing the stories. They never did create a lasting mediatized world. In the production of digital animations, the storytellers came closer to establishing a mediatized world through tighter interaction with the digital tools, each other and professional instructors. However, it did not last for more than three weeks. Interestingly, all interaction and media use was offline. In the third case, of teenagers expressing themselves on social network sites, they are in a mediatized setting as long as they operate in the virtual space of the SNSs. However, this is just a fluid part of their interaction, network and context and, thus, makes no lasting mediatized world. In the final case, top-bloggers and their community of followers make online mediatized worlds. However, these worlds are in flux and may not last.

The concept of mediatized worlds does not fully capture contemporary forms of digital storytelling. However, on the contrary, digital storytelling – in its various forms – has become a practice that articulates participation, self-representation and interaction in various mediatized worlds. Here this chapter meets the one on mediatized worlds of communitization by Andreas Hepp, Matthias Berg and Cindy Roitsch. Both chapters study communication practices among young people.

Beside the social relationships of mediatized worlds – interactions, networks and contexts – they make particular lifeworlds. Digital storytelling is not a practice to 'produce' a certain mediatized world, but, rather, a practice that nurtures and contributes to (segments of) 'mediatized lifeworlds'.[6] Storytelling is the practice that mediates the tension between the 'stories lived' and the 'stories told' (Pearce, 2007, p. 211). Stories are part of the communication in all social worlds. *Digital* storytelling enhances communication in *mediatized* lifeworlds.

Notes

1. http://www.uv.uio.no/iped/english/research/projects/mediatized-stories/index. html. The author of this chapter was director of the project (2006–11), which was funded by the Research Council of Norway.
2. I have another take on 'mediation' in the book on *Religion across media. From early antiquity to late modernity* (Lundby, 2013a; 2013b) in relation to Birgit Meyer's work (2013).
3. Vygotsky and others (cf. Drotner, 2008).
4. 'Mediatized Worlds' is a research programme under the German Research Foundation (DFG Priority Program 1505).
5. http://www.uv.uio.no/iped/english/research/projects/mediatized-stories/studies/ young-people.html
6. I am grateful to Andreas Hepp for suggesting this line of thought on my material.

References

Bauman, Z. (2000) *Liquid modernity* (Cambridge: Polity).
Bauman, Z. (2007) *Liquid times. Living in an age of uncertainty* (Cambridge: Polity).
Beer, D. (2008) 'Social network(ing) sites . . . revisiting the story so far: A response to danah boyd and Nicole Ellison'. In: *Journal of Computer-Mediated Communication*, 13, pp. 516–29.
boyd, d. m. and Ellison, N. B. (2008) 'Social network sites: Definition, history and scholarship'. In: *Journal of Computer-Mediated Communication*, 13, pp. 210–30.
Brake, D. (2008) 'Shaping the "me" in MySpace: The framing of profiles on a social network site'. In: Lundby, K. (ed.) *Digital storytelling, mediatized stories: Self-representations in new media* (New York: Peter Lang).
Bratteteig, T. (2008) 'Does it matter that it is digital?' In: Lundby, K. (ed.) *Digital storytelling, mediatized stories: Self-representations in new media* (New York: Peter Lang).
Clark, L. S. (2009) 'Theories: Mediatization and media ecology'. In: Lundby, K. (ed.) *Mediatization: Concept, changes, consequences* (New York: Peter Lang).
Couldry, N. (2008) 'Mediatization or mediation? Alternative understandings of the emergent space of digital storytelling'. In: *New Media & Society*, 10, pp. 373–91.
Couldry, N. (2012) *Media, society, world. Social theory and digital media practice* (Cambridge: Polity).
Drotner, K. (2008) 'Boundaries and bridges: Digital storytelling in education studies and media studies'. In: Lundby, K. (ed.) *Digital storytelling, mediatized stories: Self-representations in new media* (New York: Peter Lang).
Erstad, O. and Silseth, K. (2008) 'Agency in digital storytelling: Challenging the educational context'. In: Lundby, K. (ed.) *Digital storytelling, mediatized stories: Self-representations in new media* (New York: Peter Lang).
Erstad, O. and Wertsch, J. V. (2008) 'Tales of mediation: Narrative and digital media as cultural tools'. In: Lundby, K. (ed.) *Digital storytelling, mediatized stories: Self-representations in new media* (New York: Peter Lang).
Friedlander, L. (2008) 'Narrative strategies in a digital age: Authorship and authority'. In: Lundby, K. (ed.) *Digital storytelling, mediatized stories: Self-representations in new media* (New York: Peter Lang).

Friesen, N. and Hug, T. (2009) 'The mediatic turn: Exploring concepts for media pedagogy'. In: Lundby, K. (ed.) *Mediatization: Concept, changes, consequences* (New York: Peter Lang).

Hartley, J. (2008) 'Problems of expertise and scalability in self-made media'. In: Lundby, K. (ed.) *Digital storytelling, mediatized stories: Self-representations in new media* (New York: Peter Lang).

Hartley, J. and McWilliam, K. (2009a) 'Computational power meets human contact'. In: Hartley, J. and McWilliam, K. (eds.) *Story circle. Digital storytelling around the world* (Malden, MA: Wiley-Blackwell).

Hartley, J. and McWilliam, K. (eds.) (2009b) *Story circle. Digital storytelling around the world* (Malden, MA: Wiley-Blackwell).

Hartmann, M. (2009) 'Everyday: Domestication of mediatization or mediatized domestication?' In: Lundby, K. (ed.) *Mediatization: Concept, changes, consequences* (New York: Peter Lang).

Hepp, A. (2009) 'Differentiation: Mediatization and cultural change'. In: Lundby, K. (ed.) *Mediatization: Concept, changes, consequences* (New York: Peter Lang).

Hepp, A. (2012) 'Mediatization and the "molding force" of the media'. In: *Communications: The European Journal of Communication Research*, 37, pp. 1–28.

Hepp, A. (2013 [2011]) *Cultures of mediatization* (Cambridge: Polity).

Hepp, A., Krotz, F., Moores, S. and Winter, C. (eds.) (2008) *Connectivity, networks and flows. Conceptualizing contemporary communications* (Cresskill, NJ: Hampton Press).

Hjarvard, S. (2004) 'From bricks to bytes: The mediatization of a global toy industry'. In: Bondebjerg, I. and Golding, P. (eds.) *European culture and the media* (Bristol: Intellect).

Hjarvard, S. (2008) 'The mediatization of society. A theory of the media as agents of social and cultural change'. In: *Nordicom Review*, 29, pp. 105–34.

Hjarvard, S. (2013) *The mediatization of culture and society* (London: Routledge).

Hoover, S. M. (2010) 'Complexities: The case of religious cultures'. In: Lundby, K. (ed.) *Mediatization: Concept, changes, consequences* (New York: Peter Lang).

Hull, G. A. (2003) 'Youth culture and digital media: New literacies for new times'. In: *Research in the Teaching of English*, 38, pp. 229–33.

Hull, G. A. and James, M. A. (2007) 'Geographies of hope: A study of urban landscapes, digital media, and children's representations of place'. In: O'Neill, P. (ed.) *Blurring boundaries: Developing writers, researchers and teachers. A tribute to William L. Smith* (Cresskill, NJ: Hampton Press).

Hull, G. A. and Katz, M.-L. (2006) 'Crafting an agentive self: Case studies of digital storytelling'. In: *Research in the Teaching of English*, 41, pp. 43–81.

Hull, G. A. and Nelson, M. E. (2005) 'Locating the semiotic power of multimodality'. In: *Written Communication*, 22, pp. 224–61.

Hull, G. A. and Zacher, J. (2004) 'What is after-school worth? Developing literacies and identities out-of-school'. In: *Voices in Urban Education*, 3, pp. 36–44.

Jamissen, G. and Skou, G. (2010) 'Poetic reflection through digital storytelling – a methodology to foster professional health worker identity in students'. In: *Seminar.net. International Journal of Media, Technology & Lifelong Learning* [online], 6.

Kaare, B. H. (2008) 'Youth as producers: Digital stories of faith and life'. In: *Nordicom Review*, 29, pp. 189–201.

Kaare, B. H. (2012) 'The self and the institution. The transformation of a narrative genre'. In: *Nordicom Review*, 33, pp. 17–26.

Kaare, B. H. and Lundby, K. (2008a) 'Mediated lives: Autobiography and assumed authenticity in digital storytelling'. In: Lundby, K. (ed.) *Digital storytelling, mediatized stories: Self-representations in new media* (New York: Peter Lang).

Kaare, B. H. and Lundby, K. (2008b) 'The "Power of configuration" in digital storytelling'. In: Gächter, Y., Ortner, H., Schwarz, C. and Wiesinger, A. (eds.) *Erzählen – Reflexionen im Zeitalter der Digitalisierung/Storytelling – Reflections in the age of digitalization* (Innsbruck: Innsbruck University Press).

Knobel, M. and Lankshear, C. (eds.) (2007) *A new literacies sampler* (New York: Peter Lang).

Krotz, F. (2007) *Mediatisierung: Fallstudien zum Wandel von Kommunikation* (Wiesbaden: VS).

Krotz, F. (2008a) 'Media connectivity. Concept, conditions and consequences'. In: Hepp, A., Krotz, F., Moores, S. and Winter, C. (eds.) *Connectivity, networks and flows. Conceptualizing contemporary communications* (Cresskill, NJ: Hampton Press).

Krotz, F. (2008b) 'Mediatized worlds: Communication in the medial and social change'. Application to the DFG for implementation of a priority programme. Deutsche Forschungsgemeinschaft.

Krotz, F. (2009) 'Mediatization: A concept with which to grasp media and societal change'. In Lundby, K. (ed.) *Mediatization: Concept, changes, consequences* (New York: Peter Lang).

Krotz, F. and Hepp, A. (2013) 'A concretization of mediatization: How mediatization works and why "mediatized worlds" are a helpful concept for empirical mediatization research'. In: *Empedocles – European Journal for the Philosophy of Communication*, 3 (2), pp. 119–134.

Lambert, J. (2009) 'Where it all started. The center for digital storytelling in California'. In: Hartley, J. and McWilliam, K. (eds.) *Story circle. Digital storytelling around the world* (Malden, MA: Wiley-Blackwell).

Lambert, J. (2013) *Digital storytelling. Capturing lives, creating community*, 4th edition (New York, London: Routledge).

Latour, B. (2005) *Reassembling the social. An introduction to actor-network theory* (Oxford: Oxford University Press).

Livingstone, S. (2008) 'Taking risky opportunities in youthful content creation: Teenagers' use of social networking sites for intimacy, privacy and self-expression'. In: *New Media & Society*, 10, pp. 393–411.

Livingstone, S. (2009a) *Children and the internet. Great expectations, challenging realities* (Cambridge: Polity).

Livingstone, S. (2009b) 'On the mediation of everything'. In: *Journal of Communication*, 59, pp. 1–18.

Lövheim, M. (2011a) 'Personal and popular. The case of young Swedish female top-bloggers'. In: *Nordicom Review*, 32, pp. 3–16.

Lövheim, M. (2011b) 'Young women's blogs as ethical spaces'. In: *Information, Communication & Society*, 14, pp. 338–54.

Lövheim, M. (2012) 'Negotiating emphatic communication'. In: *Feminist Media Studies*, iFirst, pp. 1–16.

Luckmann, B. (1978 [1970]) 'The small life-worlds of modern man'. In: Luckmann, T. (ed.) *Phenomenology and sociology* (Harmondsworth: Penguin Books).

Lundby, K. (2006) 'Transforming faith-based education in the church of Norway: Mediation of religious traditions and practices in digital environments'. In: *Studies in World Christianity*, 12, pp. 5–22.

Lundby, K. (ed.) (2008a) *Digital storytelling, mediatized stories: Self-representations in new media* (New York: Peter Lang).

Lundby, K. (2008b) 'Introduction: Digital storytelling, mediatized stories'. In: Lundby, K. (ed.) *Digital storytelling, mediatized stories: Self-representations in new media* (New York: Peter Lang).

Lundby, K. (2009a) 'Introduction: "Mediatization" as key'. In: Lundby, K. (ed.) *Mediatization: Concept, changes, consequences* (New York: Peter Lang).

Lundby, K. (2009b) 'The matrices of digital storytelling: Examples from Scandinavia'. In: Hartley, J. and McWilliam, K. (eds.) *Story circle. Digital storytelling around the world* (Malden, MA: Wiley-Blackwell).

Lundby, K. (2009c) *Mediatization: Concept, changes, consequences* (New York: Peter Lang).

Lundby, K. (2011) 'Mediatizing faith: Digital storytelling of the unspoken'. In: Bailey, M. and Redden, G. (eds.) *Mediating faiths. Religion and socio-cultural change in the twenty-first century* (Farnham: Ashgate).

Lundby, K. (2013a) 'Introduction: Religion across media'. In: Lundby, K. (ed.) *Religion across media. From early antiquity to late modernity* (New York: Peter Lang).

Lundby, K. (2013b) 'Media and the transformations of religion'. In: Lundby, K. (ed.) *Religion across media. From early antiquity to late modernity* (New York: Peter Lang).

Lundby, K. and Kaare, B. H. (2007) 'The sacred as meaning and belonging in digital storytelling'. In: Furseth, I. and Leer-Salvesen, P. (eds.) *Religion in late modernity. Essays in honor of Pål Repstad* (Trondheim: Tapir Academic Press).

McWilliam, K. (2009) 'The global diffusion of a community media practice: Digital storytelling online'. In: Hartley, J. and McWilliam, K. (eds.) *Story circle. Digital storytelling around the world* (Malden, MA: Wiley-Blackwell).

Meadows, D. and Kidd, J. (2009) ' "Capture Wales". The BBC digital storytelling project'. In: Hartley, J. and McWilliam, K. (eds.) *Story circle. Digital storytelling around the world* (Malden, MA: Wiley-Blackwell).

Meyer, B. (2013) 'Material mediations and religious practices of world-making'. In: Lundby, K. (ed.) *Religion across media. From early antiquity to late modernity* (New York: Peter Lang).

Mortensen, T. and Walker, J. (2002) 'Blogging thoughts: Personal publication as an online research tool'. In: Morrison, A. (ed.) *Researching ICTs in context* (Oslo: Unipub forlag).

Nyboe, L. and Drotner, K. (2008) 'Identity, aesthetics and digital narrative'. In: Lundby, K. (ed.) *Digital storytelling, mediatized stories: Self-representations in new media* (New York: Peter Lang).

Pearce, W. B. (2007) *Making social worlds. A communication perspective* (Malden, MA: Blackwell).

Rettberg, J. W. (2008) *Blogging* (Cambridge: Polity).

Rothenbuhler, E. W. (2009) 'Continuities: Communicative form and institutionalization'. In: Lundby, K. (ed.) *Mediatization: Concept, changes, consequences* (New York: Peter Lang).

Schrott, A. (2009) 'Dimensions: Catch-all label or technical term'. In: Lundby, K. (ed.) *Mediatization: Concept, changes, consequences* (New York: Peter Lang).

Silverstone, R. (2002) 'Complicity and collusion in the mediation of everyday life'. In: *New Literary History*, 33, pp. 745–64.

Silverstone, R. (2005) 'The sociology of mediation and communication'. In: Calhoun, C., Rojek, C. and Turner, B. (eds.) *The Sage handbook of sociology* (London: Sage).

Silverstone, R. (2007) *Media and morality. On the rise of the mediapolis* (Cambridge: Polity Press).

Staksrud, E. (2013) *Children and the online world: Risk, regulation, rights* (Farnham: Ashgate).

Strömbäck, J. and Esser, F. (2009) 'Shaping politics: Mediatization and media interventionism'. In: Lundby, K. (ed.) *Mediatization: Concept, changes, consequences* (New York: Peter Lang).

Thomas, T. (2009) 'Social inequalities: (Re)production through mediatized individualism'. In: Lundby, K. (ed.) *Mediatization: Concept, changes, consequences* (New York: Peter Lang).

Thumim, N. (2008) ' "It's good for them to know my story": Cultural mediation as tensions'. In: Lundby, K. (ed.) *Digital storytelling, mediatized stories: Self-representations in new media* (New York: Peter Lang).

Thumim, N. (2009) 'Exploring self-representations in Wales and London. Tension in the text'. In: Hartley, J. and McWilliam, K. (eds.) *Story circle. Digital storytelling around the world* (Malden, MA: Wiley-Blackwell).

Thumim, N. (2012) *Self-representation and digital culture* (Basingstoke: Palgrave Macmillan).

Watkins, J. and Russo, A. (2009) 'Beyond individual expression. Working with cultural institutions'. In: Hartley, J. and McWilliam, K. (eds.) *Story circle. Digital storytelling around the world* (Malden, MA: Wiley-Blackwell).

Williams, R. (1988) *Keywords* (London: Fontana Press).

3
Culturalizing Mediatization

Johan Fornäs

1. Introduction

The term 'mediation' denotes that something functions as a linking device between different entities. Media are socially organized technologies made for being used in the practices of communication that are prime examples of such mediating processes. 'Mediatization' refers to some kind of historical process whereby such media 'increasingly come to saturate society, culture, identities and everyday life' (Fornäs, 1995, p. 1).[1] However, there are many difficulties hidden in this concept of mediatization. Some of these issues will be identified and discussed here, in an effort to help clarify how the idea of mediatization can be made useful for transdisciplinary studies of contemporary media processes, with a focus on the value of revitalizing culturally oriented approaches.

First, some definitional problems are analyzed, hinting at how a cultural perspective on signifying practices of meaning-making helps in identifying 'if', 'when', 'where', 'what' and 'how' issues of interpreting mediatization. The idea of 'a media age' is scrutinized, based on a tension between conceiving mediatization as a long-term process and as a dateable historical event. This leads to proposing a model of different levels and kinds of mediatization, making use of cultural theory.

In a second main section, mediatization is related to modernization, lifeworld colonization, reflexivity and culturalization. The meaning of culture in relation to society is discussed, based on a combination of cultural studies and Paul Ricoeur's critical hermeneutics.

Third, the contested genealogy of the concept of mediatization is discussed, emphasizing repressed routes through cultural research of anthropological and hermeneutic inspiration. Mediatization discourse has developed in the interface between media studies and other branches of the humanities and social sciences, with a particular affinity to cultural theory. Strategic considerations end in a plea for continued transdisciplinary dialogue as the best means for understanding mediatization today.

2. Conceptual difficulties

In the late 1980s, Swedish social anthropologist Ulf Hannerz attracted me to the concept of mediatization, inspiring theoretical development of its main dimensions. Since then, the discourse on this historical process has gone through several phases, involving complex dialogues between different regional research traditions in Germany (where it seems to have its oldest roots), the Nordic countries, Britain and Latin America. Its genealogies remain to be traced.

> There is in world history, in the modern era, and most particularly in its current late-modern phase, an accelerating growth, spread, diversification and interlacing of communications media across the globe. Media use constitutes increasingly greater parts of everyday life for a growing number of people around the world. This historical process of mediatization draws a widening range of activities into the sphere of media, making mediation an increasingly key feature of society and everyday life. All contemporary major social and cultural issues directly implicate uses of media. Debates on war, science, ethics, ecology, gender identities, ethnic communities, generation gaps and socialization – all immediately raise questions of media power. Media no longer form a distinct sector, but are fully integrated in human life. This paradoxically means that their enormous influence can never be adequately 'measured', since there is no media-free zone with which to compare their effects.
>
> (Fornäs, Becker, Bjurström and Ganetz, 2007, p. 1)

This passage expresses some common assumptions. Inferences are often made between, on the one hand, the growing number of media technologies, of mediated text genres and of practices of media use, and, on the other, an assumedly increasing importance of these technologies, texts and practices for society, culture and identity. It is often thought that these trends result in specific changes in social, cultural and personal life, induced by the effects of the irresistible imposition of a kind of 'media logic'. This is sometimes seen as a long-term historical process, but often certain decisive steps or turning points are identified in recent decades, to support the talk of a late-modern 'media age'.

Such discourses and ideas are not only upheld by media scholars but are rather widespread in the humanities and social sciences, as well as in society at large, not least in the political field, but also in social movements, in science and in the aesthetic fields. Everywhere people seem to agree that media have never been so important to so many aspects of social and cultural reality.

This discourse seems to have had new impetus during the last years. For instance, without using the term itself, Roger Silverstone (2005, p. 202) talks of mediation in general, but also hints at the 'increasing centrality of media for the exercise of power as well as for the conduct of everyday life in modern society', which is precisely the historical process that the related concept mediatization stands for. In Norway, Knut Lundby (2009, p. 4) has defined mediatization as 'the transformations in society and everyday life that are shaped by the modern media and the processes of mediation'. In a more developed analysis, Danish media scholar Stig Hjarvard (2008, p. 113) has defined mediatization of society as

> the process whereby society to an increasing degree is submitted to, or becomes dependent on, the media and their logic. This process is characterized by a duality in that the media have become *integrated* into the operations of other social institutions, while they also have acquired the status of social institutions *in their own right*.

Thus, there seems to be an almost universal consensus that our age is primarily characterized by the accelerating presence and importance of communication media. But there are several tricky problems of definition, extension and application involved here. A first – and very reasonable – question is whether there is any process of mediatization at all, and, if so, when does it arise or peak, along which historical contour does it develop, is it equally insistent globally, which are its causes and effects, and which areas, aspects or levels does it mainly affect?

1. *If?* – Is there currently a general process of mediatization? This depends on what is meant. There are more and more media available, their use tends to fill larger portions of most people's everyday life, and at least some kinds of activities are increasingly dependent on texts and technologies of communication media. There are, thus, many good reasons to argue that this accelerating and increasingly complex mediation of widening circuits of human life and society surely must have certain existential and societal effects that might be described by the term 'mediatization'.

However, one should perhaps be at least a bit careful here, and not draw conclusions too quickly. It has, for instance, been argued that Scandinavians' knowledge of the USA is today totally media-dependent (Hjarvard, 2008, p. 115). But was that not equally true in the 19th century, when an even smaller proportion of Scandinavians had ever visited America themselves, and all one knew about it was mediated through letters, books or the press? Another example: in medieval Europe, so many of people's worldviews and understandings were dependent on one particular mediated text – the Bible – that it is difficult to judge whether media influence us more or perhaps less today. A third historical comparison between the French and American revolutions in the late 18th century and the 2011 Arab revolutions at first seems obvious, as the internet and mobile phones were so central in the latter, but, after all, pamphlets and posters also played a decisive role in Paris in 1789, and today many participants in the Tunisian and Egyptian events testify that the role of instant messaging and Facebook for what happened in early 2011 may have been slightly exaggerated by western media, as the most decisive steps were still taken at face-to-face meetings in activists' homes and mass manifestations in the streets.

This is not to deny the huge impact of new media on political and social life of today, but only a reminder that there were also old media that were crucial for many processes ages ago. Actually, in some cases the presence of scarce and singular media forms may in certain respects have been of even greater relative importance than the whole spectrum of contemporary communication tools. Abundance does not automatically imply importance. Scarcity (of media texts or technologies) can in some conditions produce an aura that makes the rare media form more central to people than when media are routinized and endlessly present everywhere. Compare, for instance, how vinyl records were sometimes enormously important to teenagers in the 1950s – not *in spite of* but rather *because of* their scarcity, whereas today, when almost all music can easily be downloaded, this does not *automatically* imply that it has a more central role for identity formation in everyday life.

There are doubtlessly lots of more media in place today, and their specific use fills a much bigger proportion of everyday lifetime, but there is no direct line between such hard facts and the actual significance of media texts or technologies in various levels of social, cultural or personal life. This cannot be taken for granted, but has to be empirically verified by cultural research asking how people made various aspects of life meaningful in shifting modes of communication. There is a need for more precise historical analysis, and, in particular, for interpretive studies that strive to understand what various media have meant to those people and contexts using them. I do not wish to refute the mediatization thesis, but only argue that it may be useful to qualify the concept both empirically and theoretically.

2. *When?* – In which phases has mediatization developed historically? Mediatization is conceivable as a long-term process, parallel to modernization, urbanization, secularization or individualization and other similar tendencies that pass through shifting phases in different world regions. But some researchers have been tempted to regard it as particularly bound to a relatively recent phase of history, resulting in a current 'media age' that has qualitatively shifted basic conditions of life and society. One example is Stig Hjarvard (2008, p. 113 and several other places), who has argued that, while mediatizing processes have been in play for a long time, there has been a qualitative leap in that media have now become leading societal institutions of key importance to all sectors, rather than serving as just one sphere among others. There may well have been a decisive shift in institutional balances some time during the last half-century, but the technological, social and textual levels of mediatization do not seem so easily dateable to any specific decade. I remain unconvinced that mediatization should be confined to its recent period, as mediatizing processes can be discerned for a much longer historical period – yes, they may actually be interpreted as one of the basic dimensions not only of modernization but of the civilizing process as a whole, as Friedrich Krotz (2009) has argued.

Learning from the 1980s' postmodernity debate, it is wise not to subscribe too quickly to any belief in a sudden and unique historical break, but rather to see history as a dialectical process of complexly interacting transitions which are rarely coordinated into singular nodes in time, but stretch out across wide spans. It is often tempting to exaggerate changes in the short term, as the modern era is characterized by a constant focus on the passing moment, on newness. In the words of Walter Benjamin (1999 [1982], p. 545):

> There has never been an epoch that did not feel itself to be 'modern' in the sense of eccentric, and did not believe itself to be standing directly before an abyss. The desperately clear consciousness of being in the middle of a crisis is something chronic in humanity. Every age unavoidably seems to itself a new age. The 'modern', however, is as varied in its meaning as the different aspects of one and the same kaleidoscope.

There are surely some periods that are more densely filled with key changes than others, but a certain delay of time may be needed to correctly identify such historical shifts, and, in any case, mediatization cannot be reduced to one specific point of transition from a pre- to a post-mediatized world. Mediatization is more of a long-term process than a dateable historic event.

3. *Where?* – Is mediatization a global or a geographically situated phenomenon? I have no clear and definite answers to this question, which again needs to be investigated through careful interpretive and comparative empirical research. Mediatization processes may well appear all over the world, but it is safe to presume that they look different in different regions. Hjarvard (2008, p. 113) confines mediatization to 'a development that has accelerated particularly in the *last years of the twentieth century* in *modern, highly industrialized, and chiefly western societies*'. I have already discussed the first part of this argument, and its last few words present a cautionary position that humbly strives to avoid accusations of ethnocentrism. This can be linked to corresponding arguments that globalization, modernization and other similar processes with which mediatization has so many affinities are mainly western phenomena. I am not convinced that this is the best way to recognize global diversity. One may, instead, actually argue that some aspects and

elements of all these processes are particularly intense and visible, not in Western Europe and North America, but in Africa or other developing world regions. The impact of mobile phone technology on everyday life in Africa, for instance, seems even more decisive than in more industrialized countries, where it is embedded in a much richer wealth of other communication tools. Different dimensions of modernization, globalization and mediatization take different forms and shifting intensities during different historical phases, and it would be wrong to believe that the strong and affluent centres always take 'the lead': some steps are more important in various 'peripheries', which may actually, in some respects and periods, serve as vanguards. Historical and geographical specificity is needed to map the routes through mediatization that coexist in the world.

4. What? – Which processes or areas are the main targets affected by mediatization? The questions raised so far point at a need to differentiate between phases and regions in these processes. It should, further, also be discussed which aspects and practices mediatization affects. Empirical and historical investigations are needed to specify which societal processes are mainly affected by mediatization: the political or the cultural public sphere, collective or individual identities, cognitive or emotive faculties and so on. In the first instance, mediatization influences communication practices, since media are in themselves technologies of communication. But it may then be asked which genres and kinds of communication are pulled into the flows of mediatization in each case: whether it is mainly mass or personal communication modes, which symbolic modes (writing, speech, images, music) are primarily targeted and so on. And, as communication practices are modes of mediation rather than self-sufficient goals in themselves, their changes in turn always also have effects on other spheres of practice, where one may discern distinct transformations in politics, economy, education, work, leisure, the arts, intimate relations or identification in terms of class, gender, ethnicity, age and so on.

In order to avoid sweeping generalizations, it might be useful to discern some key aspects and dimensions. Certain practices have for ages been dependent on mediation. For instance, knowledge of the past or the distant – of old times or foreign places – has always been based on tales, travel reports and other forms of mediated communication. While new channels are available today for such purposes, one cannot here talk of any move from a non-mediatized to a mediatized phase. Other social practices have 'before' been less media-dependent, and one may find key phases when institutionalized technologies became more involved in them. It is, for instance, probably hard to deny that interaction among peers has become much more media-dependent, or that media use for most people fills more daily time than before. For social practices like making love, war, music or sports, it is fairly easy to see how new media have in certain historical periods been introduced and deeply affected their dynamics. But then again, for some categories media have 'always' been central: not least for cultural producers active in aesthetic fields and public spheres. Since books are media themselves, authors in the literary field have always focused on mediation processes, and even their supplementary interaction with readers was as media-dependent 100 or 200 years ago, when a famous author could perhaps receive and respond to tens of thousands of letters, as it is today, when this interaction is mainly based on blogs, chats and e-mails.

5. *How?* – What main effects and forms of mediatization are there? It finally remains unclear precisely how mediatization actually works. When Hjarvard and others, following Altheide and Snow (1979), talk of a 'media logic' spreading like a virus across society, this can invite an essentialist reification of the multifarious processes engendered by mediated communications. Others have also, with good reasons, opposed any such talk of a given and unitary 'media logic', arguing that the media are both highly diversified and deeply embedded in social relations, and therefore do not follow or prescribe any specific 'logic' which is identifiable as such and distinguishable from other mechanisms of interaction. One example is Knut Lundby (2009, p. 117), who has concluded that 'it is not viable to speak of an overall media logic; it is necessary to specify how various media capabilities are applied in various patterns of social interactions' and that 'a focus on a general media logic hides these patterns of interaction'.

What are the main motors of mediatization? Is it mainly a matter of expanding and diversifying media technologies that interfere in an increasing proportion of human affairs, and/or an increasing number of mediated texts, symbols and narratives that underpin our ideas and understandings? One may distinguish between technological, institutional, social, textual and discursive mediatization. *Technological* mediatization is when tools of communication accumulate in everyday life; *institutional* mediatization concerns the growing size and influence of media enterprises; *social* mediatization is when everyday practices make increasing use of these technologies; *textual* mediatization is when mediated texts dominate the intersubjective circulation of ideas; and *discursive* mediatization is when dominant discourses explicitly give this media world a central position. They are clearly mutually interrelated, but may not always run in total parallel.

Distinctions such as these would help dissolve some aporias in mediatization theory. For instance, while media institutions of journalism and cultural industries are increasingly independently organized into a relatively autonomous field, media technologies and texts are dispersed into all corners of everyday life and thus remain integrated into all other social and cultural spheres (Hjarvard, 2008, pp. 115ff.). There is no paradoxical duality or contradiction in such a diagnosis – no more than, for instance, in seeing how banks or churches strengthened their institutional autonomy at the same time as money or religiosity intervened in all societal sectors. This indicates the importance of transcending an institutional perspective, combining it with an awareness of social, cultural and subjective facets.

I do not wish to abandon but, rather, to qualify my initially cited typical formulations on the increased scope and weight of media in contemporary societies, and the growing inseparability of media from other aspects of society and everyday life. The mediatization diagnosis is useful – it may just be crucial to decide on what level to place it, and to make detailed historical interpretations.

3. Interlocking social and cultural transformations

Mediatization has links to several other concepts that describe recent epochal trends in culture and society (Fornäs, 1995, pp. 45, 90–3, 210–21). It may, for instance, be seen as a constituent of *modernization*, in particular its late-modern period. In Habermas' interpretation, it was also connected to a *colonization of the lifeworld(s)*, whereby bureaucratization and commercialization let power and money take over from symbolic communication in areas where this is dysfunctional for the development of knowledge, norms and identities. However, if media of symbolic communication (rather than of money and power) are in focus, they have an ambiguous position and cannot be reduced to institutionalized instrumental rationality, as Habermas himself concluded (1987 [1981], pp. 390–391) in *The Theory of Communicative Action*, against his own earlier (1989 [1962]) diagnosis in *The Structural Transformation of the Public Sphere*. In late modernity there is, further, an increasing level of *reflexivity* in individuals, society and culture, whereby institutions, patterns of social interaction and the media demand continuous self-definitions and offer increasingly more resources for such self-referentiality. Mediatization can be a tool for reflexivity, adding elements of de-/recontextualization and self-distanciation by expanding the intermediary zone of signifying texts between selves and others (Ricoeur, 1981 [1975], pp. 131ff.). Being exposed to media may increase reflexivity, but growing reflexive needs in everyday life may also induce the spread of media. Colonization is only the negative side of reflexivity and mediatization – their positive side is a growing communicative competence and rationality that strengthens the capacity of the lifeworld(s) to resist systemic colonization. From several angles, mediatization is therefore a core concept to approach ongoing transformations in the conditions for communication, community and identity-production.

It is common to talk of 'mediatization of culture and society'. This standard formula of 'culture and society' deserves some focused reflection. Social science approaches are defined by a primacy of social institutions and interactions between people and groups, and from such an angle mediatization of politics and societal institutions tends to be in focus. Others, with a more humanities-oriented profile, have added that there is also a mediatization of culture, whatever that may mean. Mixed terms such as 'socio-cultural' hint at the difficulty in distinguishing the social from the cultural.

With its hundreds of different definitions, culture has been described by Raymond Williams (1988 [1976], p. 87) as 'one of the two or three most complicated words in the English language', with a wealth of distinct or partially overlapping meanings (Fornäs, 1995; 2012; Fornäs, Aronsson, Becker, Beckman, Bjurström, Friberg, Kylhammar and Qvarsell, 2007; Fornäs, Becker, Bjurström and Ganetz, 2007). One may differentiate between four main spheres of meaning. First, in an *ontological* sense, culture is the opposite of nature and thus denotes everything made by human beings that is more than natural functions shared with things, plants and animals. This definition is the oldest, as the term 'culture' goes back to words for cultivation, gradually transferred from gardening to self-cultivation of the human mind and of social communities. Second, German Romanticism developed another, 'sociological' or *anthropological* concept of culture as lifeform or as a 'whole way of life', in Williams' (1968 [1958], p. 18) widespread formulation. This made it possible to differentiate between many different cultures and also polarized culture and civilization instead of identifying them with each other. This potentially relativist pluralization of the concept was later in the 19th century contrasted with a third, *aesthetic* interpretation, according to which culture is constituted by the various arts (and, later again, possibly also including popular culture and everyday aesthetics). This is the version that underpins the 'institutional' concept of culture defining cultural politics and the cultural sector. This version is, in a way, again universal (as the faculties of arts are regarded as belonging to all of humanity), but, while the anthropological concept encompassed virtually everything in a particular community, culture in the aesthetic sense constitutes a distinct and rather exceptional sphere of activities and institutions within any society.

During the last half-century or so, a fourth definition has proven increasingly useful. A 'semiotic' or, rather, *hermeneutic* concept of culture as 'signifying practices' of meaning-production is the currently most promising definition. In a late text, Williams (1981, pp. 12–13) himself abandoned his older 'whole way of life' concept as misguiding for complex, modern societies, and instead subscribed to the hermeneutic one, which had already been championed by cultural studies colleagues such as Stuart Hall. Ulf Hannerz (1990, p. 7) has in a similar spirit described cultures as social phenomena of 'consciousness and communication' or 'socially organized meaning'. This line of thought goes back to social anthropologist Clifford Geertz (1973), who was in turn explicitly inspired by the hermeneutic philosopher Paul Ricoeur (1970 [1965]).

Depending on which concept of culture one refers to, 'mediatization of culture' may mean 'mediatization of everything human', 'mediatization of specific ways of life' or 'mediatization of the arts'. As there are strong reasons to favour the latter definition, since it can be shown to unite and underpin the others as well, the main interpretation refers to an increasing media-saturation of meaning-making practices. As I will soon try to show, this has intriguing consequences.

'Society' is, in turn, the 'most general term for the body of institutions and relationships within which a relatively large group of people live' but also the 'most abstract term for the condition in which such institutions and relationships are formed' (Williams, 1988 [1976], p. 291). Geertz (1973, pp. 4–5, 144, 169) has distinguished analytically between 'the cultural and social aspects of human life', defining culture as 'webs of significance' or 'an ordered system of meaning and of symbols, in terms of which social inter-action takes place', while social system is 'the pattern of social interaction itself'. The two are, therefore, 'not mere reflexes of one another but indepen-dent, yet interdependent, variables'. The cultural is defined as related to how signifying practices link meanings to phenomena that are perceived as texts, whereas the social concerns norms and community formations through interpersonal interaction. Ricoeur (1984 [1983], pp. 195–6) likewise distin-guishes between society and culture: the former consisting of individuals living in an organized community with territorial, institutional and norma-tive dimensions, whereas the latter 'covers all of the achievements stemming from social creations and implicated in individual use that are transmitted by a tradition: language, techniques, arts, philosophical or religious attitudes and beliefs'. He adds that the difference is 'difficult to maintain in all cases', yet there is a possible difference in focus, even though the two are always intertwined and coexisting.

Mediatization of society and of culture may thus be seen as complemen-tary processes. The former would, then, imply that social institutions and relationships are becoming increasingly dependent on processes of (textual and technological) mediation. However, there is a particular complication involved in the latter. Mediatization of culture appears to be a more tricky concept than that of society, since culture is *always* mediated: it is the process of mediation of intersubjective relations through constructing and interpreting textualized meanings.

Inspired by Marshall McLuhan, among others, Hannerz (1990, p. 7) has defined media as the 'specific technology of culture', that is, of commu-nicating meaning. As 'machineries of meaning', media relate to three core levels of culture: to textually based *meaning contents*, to *technological modes* of externalization, and to the *interactional relations* in which they circulate (Hannerz, 1992, pp. 26ff.). As technologies for communication, media are tools for producing and sharing meaning across distances in time and space. This is the defining characteristic of culture as signifying practice. Therefore, mediatization is closely related to what might be described as a process of *culturalization*. This concept deserves critical scrutiny at least as intense as that of mediatization, since one may well problematize in which senses culture (meaning-making and the work of interpretation) is more central or important today than earlier (Fornäs, Aronsson, Becker, Beckman, Bjurström, Friberg, Kylhammar and Qvarsell, 2007). Still, in at least some senses this may well be defended, and then this process is closely linked to that of mediatization. The question is how the two processes may be interrelated.

Culturalization is a process of expansion of the universe of meanings: an overflow that multiplies the inherent surplus of meaning in all textual practice, from everyday life and popular culture to the cultural turn in many fields of research. 'Late modernity is saturated by communication media, which increasingly put culture in focus', resulting in 'a double process' of mediatization of culture and culturalization of the media (Fornäs, 1995, p. 1). Mediatization and culturalization are in some respects two facets of the same composite historical process. Given that media are the specific technologies for culture, and culture is the meaning-making or signifying practice of communication, there is a close link between mediatization and culturalization, since a growing scope and centrality of media imply a combined expansion of meaning-making and of its technologies. Mediatization and culturalization are linked to each other, but not quite identical, which points to a need for conceptual clarification and for mediatization studies in the cultural field.

Mediatization and culturalization have 'enabled new ways of theorizing the modern processes, social spheres and subjective identities which are both their conditions and their results' (Fornäs, 1995, pp. 1–2). Further work is required to fully grasp the complex dialectics between these interrelated concepts, which in turn demands revitalized dialogues between scholars in the mutually overlapping fields of social, cultural and media studies.

4. Discourse routes

The term 'mediatization' has old roots, in particular in Germany, where Ferdinand Tönnies' pupil, sociologist Ernest Manheim (1979 [1933]), already in the early 1930s talked of a mediatization of human relations. By this he meant a more general tendency for societal institutions, not least the printed press, to organize social interaction. In volume 2 of *Theory of Communicative Action* (1987 [1981], pp. 186, 196, 305), Jürgen Habermas used the same term in a very wide and general sense. He differentiated between two main kinds of media: steering media (money and administrative power) as tools of the market and state systems, and generalized forms of communication based in the lifeworld(s). However, when Habermas discussed mediatization, it was only applied to the former, as a kind of systemic colonization of the lifeworld. His discussion of the ambivalent developments of the mass media never really made much further use of that mediatization concept, leaving it open to others to consider mediatization not only as a social-systemic steering mechanism through money and administrative power but also (and not least) as a cultural phenomenon related to signifying practices of meaning-making through the use of media technologies. It remains an important task for the current mediatization discourse to draw full conclusions from a decidedly cultural perspective on this concept and phenomenon. This entails focusing not only on technical and institutional changes but also, and not least, on how late modernity has enabled and required media and communication processes to reach more deeply into the signifying processes which shape the identities and social relations of everyday life. In this sense, one might talk of mediatized (life)worlds when people's lifeworlds are becoming mediated not only by the societal institutions of the market and the state but also by the growing mass of texts and technologies that underpin communicative practice itself.

Roger Silverstone (1999, p. 13) has narrowed down the concept of mediation to the 'circulation of meaning': a process involving contacts between media texts and their users, 'the movement of meaning from one text to another, from one discourse to another, from one event to another', in a 'constant transformation of meanings'. Then, he argued that 'action itself is a kind of mediation' (Silverstone 1999, p. 71), since all experience is already mediated by symbolic modes, in a similar way as Ricoeur (1981 [1971]; see also Fornäs, 2000) had argued.

In Sweden, Kent Asp (1986; 1990) used the term in a narrow sense to describe an increasing role of mass media in politics. A more culturally reflected interpretation was offered by Ulf Hannerz (1990, p. 8; see also Fornäs, 1995; Hannerz, 1996), who in turn influenced culturally oriented media scholars such as myself to develop it further in this direction. Hannerz talked of a historic tendency, particularly in the 20th century, for people's lives to be increasingly mediatized, 'impregnated by media': 'We have contact with big parts of the world and of humanity through the media; what we believe, know or think is to a great part derived from them, and the very forms which our consciousness works with may be influenced by them.' In Britain, media sociologist John B. Thompson (1990, pp. 4–5; see also 1995; the term he used was actually 'mediazation') – sharing with me a hermeneutic perspective partly inspired by Ricoeur – simultaneously also found it useful to talk of a mediatization 'of modern culture', implying 'the general process by which the transmission of symbolic forms becomes increasingly mediated by the technical and institutional apparatuses of the media industries'.

In recent years, Maren Hartmann and Andreas Hepp (2010), Stig Hjarvard (2008), Friedrich Krotz (2001; 2007; 2009), Knut Lundby (2009), Winfried Schulz (2004) and others have again thematized the concept, now more firmly situating themselves within a media studies agenda. This is to be warmly welcomed, but in this situation it is crucial not to lose touch with the more cultural or humanities-oriented approaches, or with ideas from disciplinary fields other than dedicated media studies. Reconnecting to ideas of mediatization in more culturally oriented scholars like Hannerz and Thompson helps not only to restore the full genealogy of the concept but also to regain key insights and perspectives from the cultural theories to the ongoing media studies debate.

There is here a great need – and a welcome opportunity – for interdisciplinary cooperation between media and communication studies and surrounding research fields in the humanities and social sciences, for two reasons. First, the interfaces between mediatization and culturalization need to be further theoretically worked through, which demands a transdisciplinary effort of critical dialogue between media scholars and cultural researchers from many other fields.

A second reason is the character of mediatization itself. If it implies that the reach and weight of media are expanding, then this expansion can only partly be analyzed 'from the inside', that is, from a media-centric perspective. As Nick Couldry (2006) and David Morley (2009) have argued, applying a 'non-media-centric' perspective will help to better understand whether or how media saturate a wide range of political and social fields and practices. Media-centric media studies may well analyze the mechanisms of mediated communications as such, but sociological, anthropological, ethnological, historical and aesthetic perspectives are needed to study how these mechanisms interact with other aspects and domains in society and individuals' lives, since these interactions may be easier to discern from a kind of side angle and placed within a larger socio-cultural context (Fornäs, 1994, p. 63). Mediatization can then be seen not only as a technical or institutional mechanism of relevance to the media industries, but, more importantly, as a social and cultural process that transforms the lifeworlds in which people experience the world. A non-media-centric perspective helps to discern mediatizing processes of lifeworlds, not just of political or economic systems.

A media-centric focus on (a set of) media such as film, TV, telephones, computers and so on will predictably always lead to the conclusion that these media are expanding. Starting with a focus on a medium, it will be hard to ever reach the conclusion that its role in society is diminishing. If one really wants to study the fluctuating degrees and modes in which media function in social and cultural contexts, it is more productive to focus instead on something else – institutions, genres, ideas, practices or aspects of life – and see whether and how (or how much) mediatization is discernible in those contexts. This invites collaboration with scholars from disciplines other than media studies.

To be a little bit more specific in terms of offering examples, one might conclude that, with a focus on new digital network media, it will almost always seem as if their importance is growing at a fast and accelerating rate.

However, if one were instead to make comparative interpretive studies of, say, revolutionary events during the last 500 years, one would be able to get a much more nuanced and complex picture of what media texts and technologies played what roles for whom at what points, and thus to discern both qualitative facets of the workings of mediatization (or sometimes, perhaps, also de-mediatization) and long-term estimations of the total level of mediatization in a specific (spatial or social) context.

In the current period, when media scholars are again turning to the mediatization concept, partly as an instrument of legitimizing their own research agenda and arguing for their own importance as a particular discipline within the academy, it is crucial not to lose sight of the approaches to mediatization proposed by others. Mediatization will then not only be used as an argument for the centrality and importance of media studies, but equally as an argument for an increased trans- and interdisciplinary exchange between media studies and a wide range of other fields. This concept has the potential to become a new driving force for intensified cross-disciplinary debate that might revitalize cultural research in general. It is striking how certain concepts and phenomena can, in specific periods, take on the function of crystallizing communication across disciplinary boundaries in order to deal with urgent contemporary issues for the humanities and social sciences. This was once true for concepts like structure, subject, postmodernity and discourse. Irrespective of their ultimate sustainability (and I am, for my part, sceptical about several of them), they did manage to trigger creative dialogues across disciplinary boundaries. Might 'mediatization' perhaps today have such a potential as well?

While the world might become increasingly media-centric, media studies may well gain in strength by becoming *less* media-centric, or at least by conceiving of media in less essentialist and more complexly differentiated ways, not just focusing on media technologies or media institutions, mass media, news contents or journalistic practices, but, rather, acknowledging the full interplay between textual, subjective, social, institutional and technical dimensions and accepting that the phenomenon of mediation is at the basis of human culture as signifying practice and is therefore a legitimate focus of attention, not only to media scholars but to all the humanities and social sciences.

These meditations on mediatization are just preliminary thoughts. Further theoretical work is needed to fully develop this into a comprehensive model. Tracing historical processes whereby media (in several dimensions) become increasingly many, complex and dominant in different societal spheres is a task that demands humble cooperation between media, cultural and social researchers. Against such a genealogical background, mapping and interpreting discourses of mediatization or the contemporary facets of an increasingly mediatized world is another key task for such joint ventures. I therefore suggest that we as media scholars renew our efforts to link our revitalized mediatization topic to relevant agendas in neighbouring disciplines and fields, inviting them not only to passively consume our insights but, rather, to enter an innovative development of new, hybrid knowledge in the borderlands of mediation.

Note

1. This article is partly based on Fornäs (1994; 1995), Andersson and Fornäs (2010) and a paper for the conference 'Mediatized Worlds: Culture and Society in a Media Age' at the University of Bremen on 14–15 April 2011. I am grateful for inspiring comments and discussions at that conference and at the Swedish 'Mediatisation of Culture, Politics, Everyday Life and Research' symposium organized in Stockholm on 18–19 August 2011 by the Bank of Sweden Tercentenary Foundation (Riksbankens Jubileumsfond). Fornäs (2014) deals with the mediatization of popular culture.

References

Altheide, D. L. and Snow, R. P. (1979) *Media logic* (Beverly Hills: Sage).
Andersson, M. and Fornäs, J. (2010) 'Mediekulturperspektivets möjligheter. Ett samtal i kulturaliseringens tecken'. In: *Nordicom-Information*, 32(1), pp. 3–22.
Asp, K. (1986) *Mäktiga massmedier. Studier i politisk opinionsbildning* (Stockholm: Akademilitteratur).
Asp, K. (1990) 'Medialisering, medielogik, mediekrati'. In: *Nordicom-Information*, 4/1990, pp. 7–12.
Benjamin, W. (1999 [1982]) *The Arcades project* (Cambridge MA/London UK: The Belknap Press of Harvard University Press).
Couldry, N. (2006) *Listening beyond the echoes: Media, ethics, and agency in an uncertain world* (Boulder/London: Paradigm Publishers).
Fornäs, J. (1994) 'Medier, kommunikation och kultur'. In: Carlsson, U., von Feilitzen, C., Fornäs, J., Holmqvist, T., Ross, S. and Strand, H. (eds.) *Kommunikationens korsningar. Möten mellan olika traditioner och perspektiv i medieforskningen* (Göteborg: Nordicom-Sverige), pp. 47–67.
Fornäs, J. (1995) *Cultural theory and late modernity* (London: Sage).
Fornäs, J. (2000) 'The crucial in between: The centrality of mediation in cultural studies'. In: *European Journal of Cultural Studies*, 3(1), pp. 45–65.
Fornäs, J. (2012) *Kultur* (Stockholm: Liber Förlag).
Fornäs, J. (2014) 'Mediatization of popular culture'. In: Lundby, K. (ed.) *Handbook of Communication Science (HoCS), Volume 21: Mediatization of communication* (Berlin: Mouton de Gruyter).
Fornäs, J., Aronsson, P., Becker, K., Beckman, S., Bjurström, E., Friberg, T., Kylhammar, M. and Qvarsell, R. (2007) *Culture unbound: Dimensions of culturalisation* (Linköping: Tema Q/Linköping University Electronic Press).
Fornäs, J., Becker, K., Bjurström, E. and Ganetz, H. (2007) *Consuming media: Communication, shopping and everyday life* (Oxford/New York: Berg).
Geertz, C. (1973) *The interpretation of cultures. Selected essays* (New York: BasicBooks).
Habermas, J. (1987 [1981]) *The theory of communicative action. Vol 2: Lifeworld and system: A critique of functionalist reason* (Cambridge: Polity Press).

Habermas, J. (1989 [1962]) *The structural transformation of the public sphere. An inquiry into a category of bourgeois society* (Cambridge: Polity).

Hannerz, U. (ed.) (1990) *Medier och kulturer* (Stockholm: Carlssons).

Hannerz, U. (1992) *Cultural complexity: Studies in the social organization of meaning* (New York: Columbia University Press).

Hannerz, U. (1996) *Transnational connections: Culture, people, places* (London/New York: Routledge).

Hartmann, M. and Hepp, A. (eds) (2010) *Die Mediatisierung der Alltagswelt. Festschrift zu Ehren von Friedrich Krotz* (Wiesbaden: VS Verlag für Sozialwissenschaften).

Hjarvard, S. (2008) 'The mediatization of society: A theory of the media as agents of social and cultural change'. In: *Nordicom Review*, 29(2), pp. 105–34.

Krotz, F. (2001) *Die Mediatisierung kommunikativen Handelns. Wie sich Alltag und soziale Beziehungen, Kultur und Gesellschaft durch die Medien wandeln* (Wiesbaden: Westdeutscher Verlag).

Krotz, F. (2007) *Mediatisierung. Fallstudien zum Wandel von Kommunikation* (Wiesbaden: VS Verlag für Sozialwissenschaften).

Krotz, F. (2009) 'Mediatization: A concept with which to grasp media and societal change'. In: Lundby, K. (ed.) *Mediatization: Concept, changes, consequences* (New York: Peter Lang), pp. 21–40.

Lundby, K. (ed.) (2009) *Mediatization: Concept, changes, consequences* (New York: Peter Lang).

Manheim, E. (1979 [1933]) *Aufklärung und öffentliche Meinung. Studien zur Soziologie der Öffentlichkeit im 18. Jahrhundert* (Stuttgart/Bad Cannstatt: frommann/holzboog).

Morley, D. (2009) 'For a materialist, non-media-centric media studies'. In: *Television & New Media*, 10(1), pp. 114–16.

Ricoeur, P. (1970 [1965]) *Freud and philosophy: An essay on interpretation* (New Haven, CT/London: Yale University Press).

Ricoeur, P. (1981 [1971]) 'The model of the text: Meaningful action considered as a text'. In: Ricoeur, P. (1981) *Hermeneutics and the human sciences: Essays on language, action and interpretation* (Cambridge: Cambridge University Press).

Ricoeur, P. (1981 [1975]) 'The hermeneutical function of distanciation'. In: Ricoeur, P. (1981) *Hermeneutics and the human sciences: Essays on language, action and interpretation* (Cambridge: Cambridge University Press), pp. 131–44.

Ricoeur, P. (1984 [1983]) *Time and narrative. Volume 1* (Chicago/London: University of Chicago Press).

Schulz, W. (2004) 'Reconstructing mediatization as an analytical concept'. In: *European Journal of Communication*, 19(1), pp. 87–101.

Silverstone, R. (1999) *Why study the media?* (London: Sage).

Silverstone, R. (2005) 'The sociology of mediation and communication'. In Calhoun, C., Rojek, C. and Turner, B. S. (eds.) *The Sage handbook of sociology* (London: Sage), pp. 188–207.

Thompson, J. B. (1990) *Ideology and modern culture: Critical social theory in the era of mass communication* (Cambridge: Polity Press).

Thompson, J. B. (1995) *The media and modernity: A social theory of the media* (Cambridge: Polity Press).

Williams, R. (1968 [1958]) *Culture and society 1780–1950* (Harmondsworth: Penguin).

Williams, R. (1988 [1976]) *Keywords: A vocabulary of culture and society* (London: Fontana).

Williams, R. (1981) *Culture* (London: Fontana Press).

4
When Mediatization Hits the Ground

Nick Couldry

1. Introduction

How best can we think about the effects of media institutions' existence on *the space of* the social, that is, on the *underlying possibilities* of social organization? I use the term 'the space of the social' not primarily in a geographical sense, but simply to refer to the whole mass of ways in which the social is organized. That is the question I want to discuss in this chapter. I will stay close to social theory, because there are some issues around mediatization's relationship to social theory that need, I believe, to be sorted out. I will work towards resolving them, in part, by returning to some earlier work of mine on media meta-capital but also through a wider assessment of where mediatization research stands today.[1]

The wider context of this chapter is the way that recent debates on mediatization (and in some countries the related term 'mediation') have served to bring together a range of scholars interested in the social-theoretical implications of the increasing prominence of media contents and media institutions in the social world. While aspects of this debate are already far advanced, I am particularly interested here in considering the wider implications for social theory, and in particular for media research's developing relations with the field theory of Pierre Bourdieu.

2. The problem

If, as Sonia Livingstone (2009a, p. x) argues, we now experience 'the mediation of everything', including 'social institutions – government, commerce, family, church, and so forth', then such a large relationship (media/society) cannot be conceived in a linear way, as the working through of discrete effects of media 'onto' society: for 'society' itself merely refers to a whole mass of interconnecting and overlapping processes, many of which are now, in part sometimes, dependent on, or saturated with, media.

One way of systematizing our understanding of what media do in, and to, the social world has been the idea that media disseminate the *formats* required for everyday performance. The pioneers of this approach were David Altheide and Robert Snow. In their work in the late 1970s and early 1980s, they offered a novel approach to media power: arguing that it derives not simply from institutional resources but from the way everyone in society interrelates with media. Seeing media as the new 'collective consciousness' (Snow, 1983, p. 11), they found the mechanism of this growing influence in the adoption of a 'media logic' across everyday life: 'Media are powerful', they wrote, 'because people have adopted a media logic' (Altheide and Snow, 1979, p. 237).

Altheide and Snow's idea of media logic was based not on any analysis of the systematic patterning of the social, but on their assessment of 'the role and influence of the form and logic of major media in our lives' (Altheide, 1985, p. 9). This emphasis on media formats was offered in contrast both to Goffman's notion of the 'frames' through which we orient ourselves to the world and to Simmel's notion of social forms as the constant patterns that underlie social relationships. What Altheide and Snow had in mind was a rather more arbitrary grafting of media formats *onto* specific contexts and forms of social action.

Altheide and Snow tended to assert that the effect of 'mediation' (as they called it) has *already* taken place and is now pervasive. They risked blurring a number of different 'logics': actual media presentation *formats* which may be adopted in specific circumstances and for specific purposes; the wider *evaluation* of media's authority and importance; people's changing *definition* of what is real, and what is not; and related *desires* for that media reality. As a result, the reference point of the term 'media logic' in Altheide and Snow's work keeps switching from the quite specific to the most general, as here: 'If television reality is more believable and more desirable than everyday life, and if television personalities and characters are more acceptable than people in face-to-face encounters, cultural change is bound to occur' (Snow, 1983, pp. 151–2). This comment says nothing about social ontology, a point to which I will return.

There are other problems if we try to explain media's social effects through a single 'media logic'. First, do all media have a logic? Is it the same logic? If not, what is the common 'logic' that unites their logics into some overall 'media logic' (a problem that becomes more acute with digital media's proliferation of outputs)? Second, when media platforms and outlets change over time, do they acquire a wholly new media logic, or is there something that remains constant? Third, if we limit the notion of media logic to media *formats*, does that capture *enough* of how media influence the social?

These problems, I have argued, persist in some recent work that develops the concept of 'mediatization'. Thus, Stig Hjarvard in some earlier work – his current position is different – defined 'mediatization' as 'the process whereby society to an increasing degree is submitted to, or becomes dependent on, the media and their logic' (Hjarvard, 2009, p. 160), while Andrea

Schrott defines 'mediatization [...] as a social process of media-induced social change that functions by a specific mechanism [...] [that is] the institutionalization of media logic in social spheres' (Schrott, 2009, p. 47). But, as Knut Lundby (2009; compare Couldry, 2008) argues, it is very difficult to see a single logic which would explain the range of general effects to which mediatization claims to point. We already saw the multiple processes gathered under this term by Altheide and Snow; in more recent accounts, media are assumed to be both environment and system, which leaves uncertain, for example, the role of audiences in this media logic – no role if we look for mediatization within production, a major role if we analyze it as an environment for open interpretation. Further uncertainties arise when we look at the types of process that different theorists bring together under the term 'mediatization'. While some see mediatization in the sense primarily of a 'format' (Altheide and Snow's earlier emphasis), Mazzoleni uses 'mediatization' to refer to 'the whole of [the] processes that eventually shape and frame media content' (Mazzoleni, 2008; quoted in Lundby, 2009, p. 8), and Winfried Schulz shifts the emphasis to two new factors: the extension of human capacities and the structural organization of social life (Schulz, 2004, p. 90).

There is a deeper problem here: a lack of *specificity about social ontology* in which some accounts of mediatization theory are involved. We saw earlier that Altheide and Snow were silent about social ontology, except to say that it is transformed by media! But on what basis do we believe that the social world is *liable* to be transformed by media materials so easily, or at least so directly? Are we to imagine the whole of social space as available to be influenced by the same media logic, spreading out without resistance or adaptation? Such claims would be fundamentally at odds with, for example, one important sociological approach – Pierre Bourdieu's field theory – which insists that the space of the social is not unitary but differentiated into multiple fields of competition (such as education, politics, medicine, law), so apparently throwing into doubt the very idea that there *can be* a single media logic that transforms the whole of social space.

Mediatization theory, in its more detailed and specific claims, is also silent about its relationship with theories of value plurality in the social world. Luc Boltanski and Laurent Thévenot (2006) argue – against Bourdieu – that there is no single value framework embedded in social space, which could ground a version of social critique such as Bourdieu's; yet 'justifications' (and arguments about value) go on everywhere in the social world, and their basis, they argue, is in multiple 'regimes of justification', each with *its own* 'proofs' and logics. Interestingly, one of those regimes is 'fame', and so there are potential links from Boltanski and Thévenot's ontology (of social value) to accounts of media logic, but they are very provisional links and rule out, at the start, the idea that values from any one institutional source (such as media) have an *automatic* privileged role in the social world. It may be, of course, that Boltanski and Thévenot's ontology (their work was published in French in 1991) needs to catch up with media's growing influence, but at the very least mediatization theory must engage with their very different starting point.

A similar argument can be made regarding the lack of engagement in earlier mediatization theory with Norbert Elias' (1994) much earlier account of social order built up through emergent solutions to complex problems of interdependency in an increasingly convergent and large-scale social world. Elias' historically based account in *The Civilizing Process* of 'figurations' such as table manners avoids arguing that influences from any one direction can automatically impose their categories or forms on the social world as a whole (compare Hepp, 2013 for a recent discussion). Such an outcome can only emerge in his approach from the detailed interdependencies between social actors and their actions for which a particular set of institutional forms (such as media formats) constitute 'solutions'. That shifts the debate away from 'media logic' towards a consideration of '*social* logics', to which media no doubt contribute, but not exclusively.

I am arguing so far that much debate on mediatization has been too silent (or at least too unspecific) on social ontology. To be sure, it has claimed that media change the nature of the social world, but without producing an explicit account of the understanding of that wider social world on which that claim, even its very possibility, relies. As a result, many accounts of mediatization leave themselves open to flat denial by those who work from social ontologies which do not fit with mediatization's account. As discussed later, this is particularly important if we want to do comparative mediatization research.

3. Ways forward

How to avoid these problems? By far the clearest solution, I believe, is provided by Friedrich Krotz's approach to mediatization. Krotz sees mediatization not as a specific process, but as 'a meta-process that is grounded in the modification of communication as the basic practice of how people construct the social and cultural world' (Krotz, 2009, p. 26). Krotz is not concerned with whether a 'logic' is transferred from media to other social processes, but with the increasing involvement of media in all spheres of life so that 'media in the long run increasingly become *relevant* for the construction of everyday life, society, and culture as a whole' (2009, p. 24). This approach allows 'mediatization' to encompass different types of process across different sites. In an article in *New Media & Society* (Couldry, 2008), and following other English colleagues, I defended the term 'mediation' in preference to 'mediatization', but I must acknowledge that I was not yet taking Krotz's work into account. Now, I too want to align my argument in that earlier piece with Krotz's view of mediatization as an overarching meta-concept, not identifiable with any single logic operating at a specific level.

Another way of putting this is to say that mediatization points to the *changed dimensionality of the social world*. Through the concept of mediatization, we acknowledge media as an irreducible extra dimension of all social processes. This, however, still leaves open *how* exactly we see the media dimension operating in different areas of social life. One way, at the level of individual processes, is to look at how non-media rituals such as weddings are increasingly filled with, and framed through, media content and media scripts, as Elizabeth Bird (2010, p. 88) suggests in a recent paper. Instead, because it will take us further in thinking about the *wider* effects of mediatization on social organization, I want to pursue mediatization within the specific framework of field theory, as developed by Pierre Bourdieu (1993).

Mediatization processes seen from the perspective of field theory

Suppose we repeat our initial question – what are media's general consequences for the space of the social? – but from the starting point of field theory. Bourdieu insists that we cannot analyze sociological processes without first relating them to what goes on in specific 'fields' of practice where particular forms of capital are at stake. We are all familiar with the analyses of the artistic, the literary or the journalistic field from this perspective. Within field theory, prima facie, media's *only* way of influencing the social world is through how journalists or other agents in the media field interact with agents in other fields, for example the medical field, as in Champagne and Marchetti's account (2005) of a medical scandal played out in the French press. But this falls far short of the questions about media influence raised by mediatization theory.

I wrote earlier that some accounts of mediatization are incompatible with the social ontology offered by field theory. But, to be fair, there is a tension between field theory and Bourdieu's *own* attempts to totalize about the social field, whether in his early work on religion and ritual or in his later controversial comments on media's influence on the social field. Indeed, there are similar tensions in the accounts of some followers of field theory, such as Patrick Champagne. Champagne in his 1990 book *Faire L'Opinion* analyzes the media's impacts on contemporary politics: the journalistic field, he says, has a relationship with the political field so close that he is tempted to refer to it as 'a journalistic-political field'. By a 'circular logic' (1990, p. 39), both journalists and politicians 'react' to a version of public opinion which *they* have largely constructed, through the framing of questions for opinion polls, the reported reactions to those polls' results, and the influence of journalists' accounts of politics.

But how exactly – within field theory – *do representations* made by actors in *one* field (media) come to have such influence on the actions and thoughts in *another* field (politics)? Champagne here introduces the notion of 'media capital' (1990, p. 239) to capture people's relative ability to influence journalistic events. Either Champagne is claiming that media capital is a new *basic* form of capital in operation *everywhere* (a claim he never makes as such), or there is a tension with field theory's basic assumptions: *where exactly*, we might ask, is media capital acquired and exercised? In the media field or in the field (political, medical, academic, etc.) where the agent in question primarily acts? Or is it a more general cross-field effect that Champagne is getting at?

Yet Bourdieu's official account is clear, and remains incompatible with *any* idea (including mediatization theory's claims) that media impact on all social space at once. So I want to ask: what bridges can be built between Bourdieu's mature field theory and the intuition of mediatization analysis (with which I agree!) that *some* of media's consequences must be understood in a more generalized way than standard field theory seems to allow?

I want to suggest two such bridges. The first *is* some version of the idea of 'media capital', building on Champagne. Unless we assume that media capital is a new basic *type* of capital, as basic as cultural or economic capital, which is a big claim indeed, problems arise, as I have just noted, in explaining how 'media capital' of a more local sort works: I would prefer to call this 'media-*related* capital' (to avoid, as yet, the suggestion that it is a new *basic* form of capital). Yet *media-related* forms of capital in a field such as politics certainly exist (Davis and Seymour, 2010). The bridge between this phenomenon and field theory involves, however, a further step, which draws on Bourdieu's late work on the state: this is the idea of media meta-capital that I explored in an earlier article. In this way, we can build an account of how, in the future, media capital, as a new basic form of capital, *might* emerge, from the spreading influence of *media meta-capital* across more and more separate fields. Let me explain (for a fuller account, see Couldry, 2003b).

Bourdieu takes over and extends Weber's notion of the state, conceptualizing the state as a monopoly of not just legitimate physical violence but also legitimate *symbolic* violence. What is the resulting power that the state exercises over the rest of social space? Bourdieu, in his book *The State Nobility* (1996), is interested in the state's pre-eminence over social definitions, for example of legal status and educational status: this influence works not in one field only, but across all fields. The state, he writes, is 'the site of struggles, whose stake is the setting of the rules that govern the different social games (fields) and in particular, the rules of reproduction of those games' (Bourdieu in Wacquant, 1993, p. 42). More precisely, the state influences the 'exchange rate' (1996, p. 265) between the fundamental types of capital at stake, in each individual field (for example, economic versus cultural capital).

If we can admit the idea that an institutional bloc like the state has influence over what counts as capital in any particular field, why not allow the same type of influence to another institutional bloc: media institutions? This, too, would be a form of 'meta-capital' through which *media* exercise power over other forms of capital (hence *meta*-capital). In the case of media, this could, I suggest, take the particular form, initially, of influence over what counts as 'symbolic capital' in each particular field.

This broad concept of media meta-capital has important advantages. First, it gives clear theoretical shape to Bourdieu's own interesting insights (in his much-derided book *On Television and Journalism*) about media exposure's consequences for many contemporary fields of competition, such as the academic field. Second, it looks at media's influence on the social world, not only through what goes on in the media field, but through media's influence over the opportunities for competition within multiple fields that derives from media's increasing role in the formation of *symbolic* capital everywhere. And so the notion of media meta-capital introduces a level of analyzing media's effects on social space which is *not* exclusively routed via the operations of the media field itself. For media, like the state, influence the whole of social space through their strategic *representations* of the social world, and through the *categories* for understanding and acting in the world which media circulate.

So if we take, for example, the case of the *Pop Idol/American Idol* format which has spread across the world, it is, certainly, worth asking: what is the influence of such formats? But the answer is likely to be complex, once we introduce the social ontology of field theory. It must be a matter of more than people adopting the *Pop Idol* format (its rhythms and styles) in everyday life. So how would the explanation of *Pop Idol*'s effects go? First, supplementing Altheide and Snow's media logic type account, we need to look at how the authority within the show of Simon Cowell, the judge of *X-Factor*, *American Idol* and so on, one of the best-paid persons in global television, is based in his capital within the broad media and creative industries field. Second, we clearly cannot stop with that first point, but need, supplementing conventional field theory, to acknowledge that the very idea that a television show is a plausible way of judging singing talent is related to media's growing meta-capital, that is, the growing influence of media institutions over what counts as symbolic capital in many specific areas of competition. Third, also supplementing field theory and consistent with the media meta-capital concept, is the idea that media representations and categories, by circulating more generally in social space (that is, within and beyond specific fields of competition), become embedded in social action: such representations and categories become available as reference points in, and frames for, everyday desires, arguments, 'proofs' (in Boltanski and Thévenot's term). This is the second bridge between field theory and mediatization theory, and it relates to the arguments around media-based categories which I have developed in my work on media rituals (Couldry, 2003a).

To summarize, a format such as the global *Idol* format is part of the mediatization story. But it has social effects in particular places, not through imitation of the television format itself but through the forms of authority relied upon, and the forms of success and category membership enacted, *within* the format. This approach to mediatization allows very varied types of 'effect' as we look more closely at the workings of particular fields. In some fields (such as politics – or the popular music industry) the interdependencies with the journalistic field (and, indeed, the whole media production field) are so intense that it perhaps *does* make sense to say that their internal logics have come to incorporate media logic in some way: that may well be why so much of the work on mediatization has focused on politics, but later I want to complicate even this point. But the political (or pop music industry) field represents only one possibility. In other fields the interdependencies with the media field may be less direct, or at least more complex, leading to more subtle forms of mutual influence. Indeed, seeing 'mediatization' as a meta-concept *allows for* varied dynamics at the level of specific sites and fields, and so allows us to differentiate also between the greater or lesser *intensity* of mediatization in different media cultures. I will return to the issue of international comparisons later, but I want to look first at the quite specific version of mediatization as it works through the sample fields of religion, art and politics.

Mediatization and the fields of religion, art and politics

An increasing number of researchers see media as a key dynamic in shaping not merely how religion is represented, but the very *practices* and *beliefs* that today are regarded as religious. There is a deep basis to religion's relations with media, because both religious and media institutions draw on a very general form of *symbolic power to represent the world*: perhaps that is why many scholars claimed, but surely too simply, that in the 20th century media became the 'new religion'. In some countries with very strong, authoritative religious institutions (such as Iran, the Philippines, even parts of the USA), religion's ability to describe the world and consecrate important types of authority *might* constitute a third type of meta-capital to set alongside that of the state and media. But, even in those countries, religious institutions, like the state, are *themselves* increasingly reliant *on media's particular form of symbolic power* – to represent religions' actions and aims – and so they are increasingly vulnerable to media-based scandal, as John Thompson (2001) has analyzed for the political field. That became clear with the Catholic Church's vulnerability to media, in the difficult build-up to and then the actual playing-out of the Pope's visit to Britain in September 2010, when, after the scandals that affected the days before the tour, the Church used media spectacle to its advantage in the Pope's media appearances during the tour.

A great deal of religious practice now involves the use of media, at all levels, and virtually all religious leaders and movements now use media resources to disseminate their arguments and messages. Indeed, building one's own media channel or media distribution facility is in many places a critical tool in *building* alternative religious standing: an example is Ansar Dine, the movement of Sharif Ousmane Haidera in Mali, discussed by Dorothea Schulz (2006). Indeed, there are clear cases of charismatic religious leaders whose symbolic capital encompasses both media prowess and spiritual qualities, from US televangelists (Billy Graham to Benny Himm) to Islamic preachers such as Yusuf Al-Qaradawi. This is not accidental, but derives from religion's basis in the constitution of community, that is, if we maintain Durkheim's understanding of the social bases of religion for an age when a key means of constituting 'community' in general is media.

Another, perhaps even more fundamental, way of understanding the mediatization of religion is via authority. Religious texts and commentary can now be circulated freely, far beyond the limited communities that once controlled access to them. Whereas once religious texts' *interpretation* was controlled by religious elites, theological interpretation and commentary is now open online to a very wide range of contributors. 'Theology becomes a communal activity', as Heidi Campbell puts it (2010, p. 154). Meanwhile, the expanding scale of digital communications enables new religious communities to form, even without face-to-face contact, around very specific religious identities. As a result, many (Hoover and Kaneva, 2009, p. 8; Meyer and Moors, 2006, p. 8; Turner, 2007) now see a change in the nature of religious authority itself. One case, much discussed, is Islam. But in many Islamic countries the above factors coincide with a recent acceleration in mass literacy and wider disputes about the nature and direction of modernity. And these changes are too complex and too important to be reduced to one single media logic; in any case, Islam, as Peter Mandaville (2007) notes, has *always* been relatively decentralized in its authority structure, much more so than, for example, Christianity. So the mediatization of religion takes a complex form, because authority is of particular importance in religion and because the historic nature and significance of authority within the particular frameworks of religious belief vary.

The visual arts offer a different example of how mediatization plays out. The visual arts are a competitive field that is highly specialized in its focus, even if some artists have strayed into claims of general authority that have seemed quasi-religious or quasi-political (Joseph Beuys, Marina Abramovic). Given the lack of agreement about the values, reference points and basic aims of art, there is *no inherent reason* why the art field should have any particular relation to media. While art is, of course, an act of communication, it need not rely on mass or distance communication. Yet under certain circumstances art does get close to media, as with the Young British Artists ('YBA') of the 1990s such as Damien Hirst. Why? The YBA are interesting because, at least for some of them, media exposure and media-related capital (rather than the use of media *formats* in their art production) came to seem of overwhelming importance. Tracey Emin is a painter and sculptor, but in her practice her media appearances seemed to become as important as the art objects themselves.

This process is rather different from a generalized saturation of the art world by media reference points (for example, advertising content). Media's role in the YBA and in parts of today's art world is more plausibly based in the media-related capital on which certain artists increasingly rely as part of their everyday practice of self-promotion and career advancement. But the artistic field is large and plural enough to have sectors where media-related capital is of intense importance, and others where it is not. So, for certain YBA (or, indeed, Andy Warhol and Jeff Koons from different generations of the New York Art scene), artistic logic and a narrowly defined media logic have seemed to overlap. But there is no reason to interpret this as a symptom of a general media logic at work in the artistic field.

What about politics? German political scientist Thomas Meyer (2003) uses the term 'media democracy' to capture the situation where 'the media have acquired a decisive role in the political process, above all in shaping public opinion and decision-making on political issues'. The mediatization of politics has, of course, been intensely researched: it is arguably the clearest example of a sector where *something like* a 'media logic' is at work, in the day-to-day operations of policy generation, policy implementation and public deliberation. Yet any 'media logic' in contemporary politics must involve many things: the time-cycles of politics and news; the influences of media institutions over what counts as political news and policy; and, more broadly, the construction of what politics *is*, the ontology of politics. The term 'media logic' is clearest, I suggest, if we limit it to referring to how media are involved in the logic of action, that is, where media outcomes become *a primary aim* of political action. In this sense, 'media logic' *does* seem to capture the inescapable *force* that media have in contemporary politics, a force from which no political actor is immune at whatever level, from incumbent presidents to local political challengers to non-governmental organizations seeking to influence political agendas from outside the mainstream.

But even in this sense the operation of a 'media logic', if that is what it is best called, is complex and varied. The idea that media outputs become the aim of political action cannot be applied literally. Are media outcomes the *ultimate* end of politicians? Rarely, if we leave aside the former regime of Silvio Berlusconi. Are media outcomes the immediate end at which effort is aimed? Often. Are media outcomes one of the means through which other ends are pursued? Almost always. Politics is concerned with the influencing of collective and institutional action: in large-scale societies, it cannot operate without having media as an instrument. So media skills and media capacity (of some sort) produce 'capital' within the political field: what earlier I preferred to call media-*related* capital, not media capital. But, as Aeron Davis and Emily Seymour (2010) note in their analysis of the rise of the

UK prime minister, David Cameron, there are many types of such capital: it may be more or less institutionalized, more linked to social networks, or, alternatively, to individual performance skills in front of the camera. But then political actors have to deal with feedback loops that result from the fact that almost *every* other political actor is trying to use media as their instrument, too. So large-scale political strategies become unstable, always liable to interruption by other actors. This complicates the application of media-related capital.

The mediatization of politics, I suggest – understood as a meta-process, in Friedrich Krotz's sense – is immensely complex because of the feedback loops that result from the interactions of large numbers of political actors competing for capital in a large field operating across multiple scales. One reaction to this might be to say that, because of these complexities, 'mediatization' as a term can tell us very little about the large field of politics. I do not agree, but, if the term is useful, it must help us identify some *distinctive* types of outcome within this complexity. Let me suggest *three* types of outcome in the field of politics which do not converge on a single media logic, but which do suggest something important about how political ontology is changing through mediatization, that is, through the unavoidable media dimension of politics.

The first is that the space of political values is reshaped – or, we might say, *flattened* – through the value that all political actors share, which is their positive evaluation of actions which result in positive media coverage. As Richard Rogers (2004, p. 173) notes in his study of Dutch NGOs' media practice, however radical their leanings, 'commercial press coverage' remains for them 'demonstrable evidence of worth'. This requires all political actors to shape the 'logic' of their actions, at times at least, towards outcomes that can be 'read' positively somewhere within mainstream media. Actions which under particular historic and cultural conditions are very unlikely to be read positively by mainstream media become difficult to pursue, difficult even to formulate. Neoliberal politics can be seen, I suggest, as linked in part to this flattening of political values. Because media institutions produce their representations for audiences, this flattening in turn cannot be separated from the wider process of media meta-capital that I discussed earlier.

The second distinctive aspect of the mediatization of politics is that the practical energies of political actors converge around the problems of *reacting to*, and attempting to *control*, media inputs and media outcomes. Today in the early 21st century it is the incessant deluge of information and events from all directions with which rulers, governments and politicians must deal, creating challenges for bureaucratic process, political authority and political memory, and for individual politicians' ability to reflect on policy and generally cope with their jobs. Christopher Foster's account of working under the UK prime minister Tony Blair and his predecessor John Major is vivid: 'We no longer had [...] the time or the capability to be thorough enough to explain *to ourselves*, to Parliament and the public just what we were attempting, and therefore to make reasonably sure what was practical and would work' (Foster, 2005, pp. 1–2). This is not so much a matter of value as a practical question of what politicians now do every day: they deal with media.

The *third* distinctive outcome is politics' unavoidable entanglement in what I have called the ongoing contests over the myth of the mediated centre (Couldry, 2012). Large political actors *must* be concerned with maintaining their hold on citizen attention; so, too, are corporate advertisers and media corporations themselves. In one way, this generates possibly more open politics: if national audiences' attention cannot be assumed, then it must be fought for, which means that increasing numbers of actors have a stake in the very framing of politics, and in maintaining key institutional structures ('the media') through which political *attention* is framed.

Media's *saturation* of the field of politics goes, then, much *further* than political actions taking on a 'media format'. Yet the consequences of this saturation are difficult to compress into one *single* media logic. And yet – and this is the force of much of the work done on the mediatization of politics – there is, in a very particular field of intense competition, politics – something logic-like at work, that is, a structuring force far beyond the control of specific actors. Here, as an example, I want to mention Justus Uitermark and Amy-Jane Gielen's (2010) interesting study of a battle in an Amsterdam neighbourhood over attempts to build a major new mosque whose catchment area was inhabited by poor migrants at the bottom of the labour market. The balance of media-related capital between local mosque spokespersons and local government representatives was highly unequal, and the consequence of this imbalance was fundamental. The background was the intense tensions between the majority Dutch population and the Muslim minority following the murder of Theo Van Gogh in November 2005. The chair of the neighbourhood government was well aware of the wider national audience (mainly white Dutch) that mainstream media coverage of this local battle would give him:

> You can think, 'It's just a neighbourhood' [...] [but] there are phenomena on all kinds of levels: the family, the street, education, health, the city, the world – and all that comes together in this one neighbourhood. So if you want to be a player in that [local political] game, you have to use the media [...] The media wants a story and we have a story. We give the story.
>
> (Jaap van Gils, quoted in Uitermark and Gielen, 2010, p. 1331)

The result, this politician suggests, is a *local* 'government [that necessarily] orients itself towards the outside', as some, even all, actors' strategies in the local scene are (Uitemark and Gielen's words, 2010, p. 1340) 'guided or motivated by their actual or anticipated representations in the media'. Anything local with potential relevance to mainstream media narrative reference points becomes a *resource* – or a problem – for local political actors and so gets drawn *by that fact alone* into the potential sphere of politics. Meanwhile, local political actors are differentiated by the level of likely access to positive mainstream media coverage that their relations to potential media narratives give them. The local white politician willing to exploit *national* white anxieties about Islam acquires *local political* capital because he can transmute local actions into events of mainstream and national media significance. This quite particular media-related logic of political competition is, to be clear, not necessarily positive. Indeed, in this sort of case it is probably dangerous, even corrosive.

Media, then, in some societies (in North America and Europe) plausibly have a meta-capital that does not work in the abstract, but through the interrelations between media representations in circulation and the particular dynamics of action in each part of each particular field of competition.

4. Looking ahead

It is clear that, if the nature and intensity of the meta-process we call 'mediatization' depend, among other things, on particular sorts of interfield relations, then its usefulness as a concept – its salience across a whole range of societies – must, in turn, depend on the organization of resources and capital within those societies. If so, the status of the term 'mediatization' must be provisional, always subject to further empirical exploration. Indeed, that consequence follows, even if you do not agree that field theory offers useful ground on which to explore how mediatization works out in detail: it is important here, in passing, to acknowledge the sceptical point of Bernard Lahire that much of social and cultural space is not (yet or ever?) organized into a field (Lahire, 1999).

The undeniable fact that mediatization has emerged as a common analytic frame for understanding a wide diversity of phenomena is surely evidence of two things: the maturing of an international field of media research that puts researchers into regular interface with each other, but quite probably also some common and underlying changes in the organization of communication in many contemporary societies. It was the sense of a shared window on change, and the urgent need to understand that change, that made plausible Sonia Livingstone's argument (Livingstone, 2009) that terminological differences among scholars loyal to the term 'mediatization' or the term 'mediation' should be resolved quickly in favour of whichever single term worked most naturally for the majority of scholars: the result was a decisive shift in favour of the term 'mediatization' rather than the multiply ambiguous term 'mediation'. The shorthand phrase 'media-saturated societies' is normally used as a gesture towards the nature of those underlying changes. I have certainly used that shorthand myself. But it is clear that individuals are 'media-saturated' to different degrees (Bird, 2003), and, more importantly, spaces of action – and whole societies – are 'saturated' with media to different degrees, and quite possibly in very different ways that are yet to be investigated.

If so, this reframes the debate (Hjarvard, 2013; Krotz, 2009) about whether mediatization is a fundamentally new phenomenon or a permanent dimension of the whole long history of communication. Surely both are correct, yet neither quite emphasizes the point that is crucial. To explain: (1) if mediatization is a meta-concept (Krotz's position, that I made the starting point for this chapter), then it can be understood as pointing to a dimension of the organization of communication in *all societies*: there is no society without some technology of communication, and the set of technologies of communication throughout history is certainly much wider and more diverse than acknowledged within contemporary discourses about 'media' (Innis, 1991; Mattelart, 1994). But (2) the emergence in recent decades of a particular intensification of the role in people's lives of technological platforms for communications and their infrastructures is the key reason behind the emergence of mediatization as a frame for mainstream media research. One can see that emergence on more than one time-scale: the emergence of mass broadcasting from the mid-20th century, and so of media institutions that, in principle, had the *capacity to* saturate social space with their contents; but also, decisively, the later emergence of the computer 'screen' and 'computer literacy' that Ivan Illich admits was the pretext for his elegant *retrospective* analysis of how new modes of reading and textuality emerged in the 12th century AD (Illich, 1993, pp. 3, 5). So the point of associating mediatization with key communication developments within modernity remains: to neglect this would be to ignore what holds this emerging field of communication research together.

However, there remains a third and wider point that is implied but not emphasized in (1) and ignored or de-emphasized in (2): that the relevance to mediatization today as a key frame for understanding social space and the dynamics of social change is *dependent* on the *degree* of social space's 'saturation' by media, and, indeed, dependent on assuming as a reference point particular types of technological arrangements (as media) rather than others; for not all media *can* saturate space to the same degree. Most specific mediatization research to date has been formed around the assumption of broadcasting media as a reference point, and, more recently, around the emergence of a common informational infrastructure that makes possible 'mass self-broadcasting' (Castells, 2009). It is an important task of mediatization research in the future to make this assumed reference point explicit, so that it can genuinely work as a meta-concept that facilitates comparative research across contexts in which the degree of their media-saturation, by what media and under what conditions, is precisely what is at stake.

Some of the most influential communication theory of our time (e.g., Castells, 2009) simply fails to make explicit its implication in such assumptions. While authorizing a certain type of international intersocietal comparison (Castells, 2009), this work tends to rely on a notion of 'network society' that works to transform the societies it compares *in advance* into social spaces that make sense as 'network' societies. But, as I have argued elsewhere (Couldry, 2012, Chapter 5), this commits an error common to much commentary on the 'digital age', which is to neglect the question of 'the social' itself, or to substitute for it a thinner discourse about how networks traverse space and 'connect' us to each other in certain ways. As a result, such a frame of comparison – network society analysis – cannot take account of the very different ways in which the social is constituted in different societies, even as (in some of its offshoots) it produces remarkably perceptive comparative work (see Qiu, 2009 on working-class 'network society' in China).

With its local assumptions made explicit, however, the mediatization frame can work as a very powerful tool for focusing comparative research across and between the full range of more *or less* media-saturated societies, and for grasping different modalities in which 'saturation' (if that is how it is best described) does *not only* work within certain societies and worlds of experience that tend to dominate published outputs in the media research field (particularly those from Europe and North America).[2]

5. Conclusion

Certain challenges for mediatization research, as it hits the ground as a widely accepted frame for comparative media and communications research, follow. I will conclude this chapter by summarizing them.

First, mediatization research must affirm its reference to a meta-process (Krotz), not merely to a particular type of local phenomenon involving media technologies. Second, it must acknowledge the precisely *local* (not universal) nature of the transformations, particularly in European and North American societies, on which the mediatization debate has so far been focused, and must make explicit the local (not universal) nature of the empirical reference points that have made such transformations seem of paramount importance for the field of media and communications research, especially since the mid-2000s (the pioneering contribution of Snow and Altheide becomes more, not less, important within this perspective). Third, it must develop mid-range theoretical concepts for better grasping those locally significant phenomena and their relevance for the longer tradition of social theory. Some candidates for such useful mid-range concepts would be: 'categories' (in Durkheim's sense), norms and values (Boltanksi and Thévenot), meta-capital (discussed above) and figurations (Elias). What is crucial is that these mid-range concepts do not directly refer to media.

Fourth, and provisionally, mediatization research must explore the possibility of using the same (or an extended) set of mid-range concepts to grasp the *differences* between societies and contexts which are more *or less* media-saturated, and so where 'mediatization' as a phenomenon is more *or less* salient to understanding social, political and economic transformation.[3] In other words, and finally, mediatization research needs to find and make explicit its limits.

It can only do this by translating its concerns with the underlying dynamics of social order into a language that is not media-centric, a language that ultimately is concerned to grasp *social* form, not media formats, contents or frames. In this sense, a critical version of mediatization research could make a decisive contribution to the transvaluation of media studies, turning it inside out to reveal more clearly than before the always contingent foundations of our contemporary obsessions with those processes that for now we call 'media'.[4]

Notes

1. This chapter began life as a keynote address to the *Mediatized Worlds* conference at the University of Bremen in April 2011. I have since revised it and added two final sections. For a fuller version of my argument, see Chapter 6 of *Media Society World* (Polity, 2012). The consent of Polity Press for this republication is gratefully acknowledged.
2. I thank Don Slater here for the stimulation of conversations about what is at stake in the term 'media' itself: see Slater (2008 and forthcoming).
3. I have approached this same issue from another direction through the notion of 'the myth of the mediated centre', in both its original (Couldry, 2003a) and now more contested (Couldry, 2009; 2012) status.
4. On the need to transvalue media studies from a non-media-centric perspective, see Couldry (2006a, pp. 185–6; 2006b, pp. 13–15).

References

Altheide, D. (1985) *Media power* (Beverly Hills: Sage).
Altheide, D. and Snow, R. (1979) *Media logic* (Beverly Hills: Sage).
Bird, S. E. (2003) *The audience in everyday life* (London: Routledge).
Bird, S. E. (2010) 'From fan practice to mediated moments: The value of practice theory in the understanding of media audiences'. In: Brauchler, B. and Postill, J. (eds) *Theorising media and practice* (Oxford: Berghahn Books), pp. 85–109.
Boltanski, L. and Thevenot, L. (2006) *On justification* (Princeton: Princeton University Press).
Bourdieu, P. (1993) *The field of cultural production* (Cambridge: Polity).
Bourdieu, P. (1996) *The state nobility* (Cambridge: Polity).
Campbell, H. (2010) *When religion meets new media* (London: Routledge).
Castells, M. (2009) *Communication power* (Oxford: Oxford University Press).
Champagne, P. (1990) *Faire l'opinion* (Paris: Editions Minuit).
Champagne, P. and Marchetti, D. (2005) 'The contaminated blood scandal: Reframing medical news'. In: Benson, R. and Neveu, E. (eds) *Bourdieu and the journalistic field* (Cambridge: Polity), pp. 113–34.

Couldry, N. (2003a) *Media rituals: A critical approach* (London: Routledge).
Couldry, N. (2003b) 'Media meta-capital: Extending the range of Bourdieu's field theory'. In: *Theory and Society*, 32(5/6), pp. 653–77.
Couldry, N. (2006a) 'Transvaluing media studies: Or, beyond the myth of the mediated centre'. In: Curran, J. and Morley, D. (eds) *Media and cultural theory* (London: Routledge), pp. 177–94.
Couldry, N. (2006b) *Listening beyond the echoes* (Boulder, CO: Paradigm Books).
Couldry, N. (2008) 'Mediatization or mediation? Alternative understandings of the emergent space of digital storytelling'. In: *New Media & Society*, 10(3), pp. 373–92.
Couldry, N. (2009) 'Does "the media" have a future'. In: *European Journal of Communication*, 24(4), pp. 437–50.
Couldry, N. (2012) *Media society world: Social theory and digital media practice* (Cambridge: Polity).
Davis, A. and Seymour, E. (2010) 'Generating forms of media capital inside and outside a field: The strange case of David Cameron in the UK political field'. In: *Media Culture & Society*, 32(5), pp. 739–59.
Elias, N. (1994 [1939]) *The Civilizing process* (Oxford: Blackwell).
Foster, C. (2005) *British Government in crisis* (Oxford: Hart Publishing).
Hepp, A. (2013) *Cultures of mediatization* (Cambridge: Polity).
Hjarvard, S. (2009) 'Soft individualism: Media and the changing social character'. In: Lundby, K. (ed.) *Mediatization* (New York: Peter Lang), pp. 159–77.
Hjarvard, S. (2013) *The mediatization of culture and society* (London: Routledge).
Hoover, S. and Kaneva, N. (eds) (2009) *Fundamentalisms and the media* (London: Continuum).
Illich, I. (1993) *In the vineyard of the text: A commentary to Hugh's Didaskalion* (Chicago: Chicago University Press).
Innis, H. (1991) *The bias of communication* (Toronto: University of Toronto Press).
Krotz, F. (2009) 'Mediatization: A concept with which to grasp media and societal change'. In: Lundby, K. (ed.) *Mediatization* (New York: Peter Lang), pp. 19–38.
Lahire, B. (1999) 'Champ, hors-champ, contre-champ'. In: Lahire, B. (ed.) *Le travail sociologique de Pierre Bourdieu – dettes et critiques* (Paris: La Découverte/ Poche), pp. 23–58.
Livingstone, S. (2009) 'On the mediation of everything'. In: *Journal of Communication*, 59(1), 1–18.
Lundby, K. (2009) 'Media logic: Looking for social interaction'. In: Lundby, K. (ed.) *Mediatization* (New York: Peter Lang), pp. 101–19.
Mandaville, P. (2007) 'Globalization and the politics of religious knowledge: Pluralizing authority in the Muslim world'. In: *Theory Culture & Society*, 24(2), pp. 101–15.
Mattelart, A. (1994) *The invention of communication* (Minneapolis: Minnesota University Press).
Mazzoleni, G. (2008) 'Media logic'. In: Donsbach, W. (ed.) *The international encyclopedia of communication*, Volume VII (Malden, MA: Blackwell), pp. 2930–2.
Meyer, B. and Moors, A. (2006) 'Introduction'. In: Meyer, B. and Moors, A. (eds) *Religion, media and the public sphere* (Bloomington: Indiana University Press), pp. 1–28.
Meyer, T. (2003) *Media democracy* (Cambridge: Polity).
Qiu, J. (2009) *Working-class network society* (Cambridge, MA: MIT Press).
Rogers, R. (2004) *Information politics on the web* (Cambridge, MA: MIT Press).
Schrott, A. (2009) 'Dimensions: Catch-all label or technical term'. In: Lundby, K. (ed.). *Mediatization* (New York: Peter Lang), pp. 41–62.

Schulz, D. (2006) 'Morality, community, publicness: Shifting terms of public debate in Mali'. In: Meyer, B. and Moors, A. (eds) *Religion, media and the public sphere* (Bloomington: Indiana University Press), pp. 132–51.

Schulz, W. (2004) 'Reconsidering mediatization as an analytical concept'. In: *European Journal of Communication*, 19(1), pp. 87–101.

Slater, D. (2008) 'New media development and globalization', Keynote to EASA Media Anthropology Network 2nd Workshop, *Media practices and cultural producers*. Barcelona, 6–7 November.

Slater, D. (forthcoming) *New media development and globalization* (Cambridge: Polity).

Snow, R. (1983) *Creating media culture* (Beverly Hills: Sage).

Thompson, J. (2001) *Political scandals* (Cambridge: Polity).

Turner, B. (2007) 'Religious authority and the new media'. In: *Theory, Culture & Society*, 24(2), pp. 117–34.

Uitermark, J. and Gielen, A.-J. (2010) 'Islam in the spotlight: The mediatization of the politics in an Amsterdam neighbourhood'. In: *Urban Studies*, 47(6), pp. 1325–42.

Wacquant, L. (2003) 'On the tracks of symbolic power: Prefatory notes to Bourdieu's "state nobility"'. In: *Theory, Culture and Society*, 10(3), pp. 1–17.

5

Media, Mediatization and Mediatized Worlds: A Discussion of the Basic Concepts

Friedrich Krotz

1. Open questions and a conceptual base for answers

The discourse about mediatization (cf. Lundby, 2009) is still an open one. Different labels, different definitions and different ideas are being used. Also, there are a lot of open questions about how to do empirical research on mediatization, what to research exactly, and which methods and procedures to use.

In addition, one of the special qualities of the discussions about mediatization is that most authors do not explain how they use elementary concepts like 'communication' and 'media'. For example, the concept 'media' is frequently understood in the sense of mass media, and also often in a very broad sense as 'extensions of man', referring implicitly or explicitly to McLuhan (1964). However, it is obvious that such different concepts may lead to quite different results. Communication is also often reduced to the reception of mass media content, more or less in the sense of the Lasswell formula. However, this does not take into consideration interactive, interpersonal or group communication, or that the production, including individual production, of media content is, or may be, part of communicative action. And a lot of empirical research about mediatization still takes place in the tradition of the mainstream communication research of the last decades of the 20th century. These are mostly media-centred studies, or they concentrate on individual media. All these implicit habits or explicit assumptions in advance of every theoretical argumentation or empirical work reduce what might be found out about mediatization and also make problematic the discussion about what this concept exactly means.

For example, political communication researchers mostly confine themselves to mass media as social institutions. Those media used to serve democracy by reporting what happens in accordance with journalistic criteria, commented on that and served as an arena for discussion by others

(Newcomb and Hirsch, 1986). From this perspective, mass media today are more and more becoming actors in the political field, and, of course, powerful ones. As a consequence, the traditional political actors must share their power with the media and must accommodate their influence. This, then, is understood as mediatization or the medialization of politics. It is frequently explained as the transfer of a media logic into the political sphere by, for example, Mazzoleni (2008a; 2008b), Mazzoleni and Schulz (1999) and Schulz (2004; 2008), who all refer to Altheide and Snow (1979).

Without doubt some (but not all) mass media today play another role than in the past. But this is not all that has changed in the field of political communication in the last decades: interpersonal and interactive communication has also changed, and offers new ways of communicating in the political sphere, as is shown, for instance, by Wikileaks, flashmobs, blogs or websites that try to critically accompany parliaments, governments and political administrations. Furthermore, I observe, for example, a development of political communication in computer games or services like the 'Wahlomat', a website that helps people to find the political party closest to their opinions – such services also contribute to changes in political communication.

In addition, I doubt that there is such a thing as a media logic (cf. also Hepp, 2013) that is relevant for all different forms of communication, whether mass communication, interpersonal communication or interactive communication. Even if one takes only mass media into consideration, such a media logic would have to be implied by technology, as is assumed by Innis and McLuhan and their followers. But if I compare TV in Iran with that in Los Angeles, or if I take into account the long-term development of the mass medium 'newspaper', then there are no indicators for such a stable media logic. Alternatively, such a media logic has to be provided, in the sense of Altheide and Snow (1979), by the formats and genres of the mass media 'as a way of seeing and interpreting social affairs', as Mazzoleni (2008a, p. 2930) describes this idea. Yet again, such a media-guided representational system must, of course, consist of changing forms over time, and, thus, it is misleading to call it a media logic that holds true over time. Of course, in a capitalist system the media try to adapt to the habits and expectations of the people in order to catch them and sell them to the advertising industry, as Dallas Smythe (2001) puts it: the audience is the commodity. Thus, if there is any logic in the media system of today, it is a capitalist one.

A further problem of the debate on mediatization is that the concept 'mediatization' includes two specific assumptions which are frequently misunderstood. *First of all, 'mediatization' is conceptualized as a process, as is suggested by the word itself, in similar fashion, for example, to individualization and globalization.* It thus assumes that the media's role in society is changing, for instance, as the result of upcoming new media and media change, but also due to changing demands, expectations and interests.

Second, the word 'mediatization' reminds us that there must be something that becomes mediatized – in this sense, the concept does not simply describe media change, but also its consequences. Both assumptions are relevant for any concept of 'mediatization', as I will argue in the following.

Concerning the first assumption, I can say that we know from archaeology and history that media were invented more or less together with human communication and language. For example, at all times pictures or material signs have been created by human beings to control space and time or to remain in contact with a god. As culture and society are processes, and as mediatization takes place in culture and society, mediatization must also be understood to be a complex long-term meta-process; a process of processes. Because of this, it is possible and necessary to study human history to learn about the role of media in their relation to communication, culture and society, from those media in early times until the digital media of today, controlled by 'intelligent' computers. It follows from the above that today no final state of mediatization exists. Instead, mediatization has to be understood to be an ongoing development, similar to modernization, globalization or individualization.

With respect to the second problem, the question arises as to what exactly is meant by mediatization. This will be answered in Section 4. In order to do that, I will develop an understanding of the complexity of mediatization. Based on that, I will describe the difference between mediated, media-related and mediatized. *Mediated* just means that media are used to perform a communicative act – you need, for example, a mobile phone in the case of mediated interpersonal communication, a computer in the case of interactive communication, a mass medium like a newspaper in the case of reading and so on. A communicative act is *media-related* if it refers to questions, emotions, experiences, knowledge and so on which have already been generated or influenced by the use of media. In other words, media-related communication by definition refers to media-related contexts. And I speak of *mediatized* communication if a communicative act not only is media-related but also takes place in the context of a broader media-related field of culture and society and can only be understood in such a context (such a field of culture could be called a mediatized field if core parts and relations were media-related). For example, for centuries the European universities belonged to a book culture, as the learning and the discussions there referred to this book culture, even if the learning and discussing took place as face-to-face communication: universities at that time were mediatized by book culture, whereas today they are being mediatized once again by digital media culture. Similarly, I call an enterprise, an organization or an institution mediatized if this enterprise, organization or institution structurally depends on media in the sense that it is part of a mediatized culture. As a third example, I call a culture, a democracy, the socialization of children, or whatever, mediatized if it is socially constructed with reference to media in a relevant way (about the social construction of reality, cf. Berger and Luckmann, 1980). Being mediatized, thus, not only is a characteristic of a single act but also always includes a reference to the framing culture as being mediatized and as being dependent on media.

In Section 2, I show the complexity of the mediatization meta-process by means of an historical case study about the development of books in the Middle Ages and the ongoing process of raising the levels of literacy among European societies. In Section 3, I then use this to develop a concept of media for a mediatization approach. Finally, in Section 4, I will develop the concept of mediatization and discuss questions of mediatization research, especially of (mediatized) social worlds.

2. From monastery reading to scholastic reading: Conditions for mediatization through written media in the Middle Ages

In this section, I refer to the historian and social philosopher Ivan Illich (2010). Illich analyzed the book *Didascalicon*, written in the 12th century by the monk Hugo of St Victor, in a monastery close to Paris. Hugo's book addresses the question of how we should read. As is well documented, during the post-Roman Empire period, the monasteries in the European Middle Ages were the places where people collected books, wrote, and engaged in reading (cf. Raible 2006; Stein 2010). We know about this time also from Umberto Eco's book *The Name of the Rose* (2005), which later became a movie.

Hugo's account of the way one reads and even should read, however, is quite different from everything we currently understand as 'reading'; Illich explains how this specific type of reading worked. In the 12th century, one could only read books in Latin, Greek or Hebrew, as books did not exist in any other European language, not even in the languages that the people or even the monks used for interpersonal communication in their everyday life. It was unknown that the alphabet used could also be used to write German or French, for example. Thus, the books that could be read were books that did not refer to any actual happenings and were not written for entertainment, practical use or analytical thinking.

At the time when Hugo lived it was unusual for people to read a written text silently; instead, books were usually read aloud, with the reader using his entire body to express what was written. Thus, all the people present could follow him reading and speaking, while the reader himself was listening to his own words with an interest in understanding what he was reading. The comprehension of written text, therefore, did not occur simply by reading the words, but also involved the act of listening – it was reading with eyes and ears. Consequently, if a person was unable to speak, for example, due to illness, she or he was also told not to read.

The reason for this becomes clear if one takes into account how books were written at that time: no page numbers, no chapter headers, no overviews or summaries, no paragraphs, no punctuation marks; even the words were not separated from one another. You can only read such a book letter by letter, and thus construct words and by that reconstruct a sense. In general, one could say that to read a text at those times meant that the reader followed the text sign by sign. No critical reading was known, and this was also not necessary, because you could only read texts of religious or philosophical authorities. Because people read the same book again and again, they often knew many parts of the book by heart. Particularly in the monasteries, a culture of murmuring, as Illich called it, took place: anyone who could read recited the same text over and over again in order to memorize it. People started reading anywhere in the text, followed the text from there, and ended anywhere with an accepting and affirmative meditation about God or the Greek philosophers of former times.

This type of reading, described by Hugo of St Victor, is called by Ivan Illich *monastic reading*. Following Illich, Hugo of St Victor was probably sensitive to questions of reading because it was during his time that it changed. Another type of reading emerged in the 12th century, which Ivan Illich calls *scholastic reading*. This was the onset of a more analytical way of reading – with reference to the logic of Aristotle, people developed an interest not just in following a given text but in analyzing it, understanding and testing the arguments, understanding the logical structure of the book, and thus in being able to reconstruct whether an argumentation in a text was valid and held true or whether it did not. This scholastic type of reading emerged long before the invention of the printing press. It happened at the same period in which the European university was invented – in Italy, France, Germany, England and elsewhere. The scholars of that time were devoted to pragmatic thinking and wanted to find out whether an argument or reference was true. They aimed at reading a book with the intention of learning something they could use, and not just of following the text and of ending in meditation.

All this – according to Illich – took place with further changes in reading and writing, as new forms of trading between faraway places came into existence and other forms of economy and agriculture became predominate. As a result, books started to be written in German and other languages, an increasing number of ordinary people learned how to read, and books began to take on the form that we know today so that they could be read more easily: they acquired a table of contents, summaries, page numbers, indices and punctuation marks, and sequences of letters became separated into words. Scholastic reading, thus, was a new form of reading that could help people analyze texts critically and use them pragmatically. Writers did not intend to refer a reader to God or to the eternal truth of Aristotle or other philosophers, but to describe a piece of the real world, thereby forcing the reader to question whether or not it was true.

Books at that time changed when the interests and needs of the readers changed, and not the other way around. It was some centuries later that Gutenberg invented the printing press, whereby he created an organization for the production of books that included all those technical machines and organizations that already existed before him. While his invention was initially spurred by a medieval motivation to print the best Bible, the printing press ultimately ushered in a new era.

To put it differently, sub-processes of mediatization may also begin by changing the needs and interests of people, as in the case described here. The necessary change of media, then, came later, as more and more people learned to read and to write and the demand for useful books increased. While Gutenberg's invention was helpful in fulfilling all these needs for, and interests in, more affordable and readable books as we know them today, the growing number of people who could read and expected knowledge and information from books initially emerged as the result of other developments, not because of the printing press or the invention of books.

We can draw three conclusions from this historical case study. First of all, it shows that changes of communication, culture and society do not only result from the *rise of new media*, but may also emerge *as the result of changing media* – in this case, the changing book culture. Second, it shows that media changes do not necessarily start with a change in technology, but can also be initiated by demand as people need other media. It is also true that a book before this development was different from a book afterwards, and that reading as a form of media-related communication was different after this development. Third, it shows that media change can be a complex process, which in this case consisted of separate sub-processes. At first, the 'book' as technology changed to accommodate the demands of people who had changed. This led to new forms of intellectual work and socialization, for example, to the foundation of the European universities, and so was a relevant precondition for the invention and success of the printing press by Gutenberg and its use, for instance, in the religious developments and wars of the 16th century and later on.

I would like to unfold a further idea. The development described by Illich was probably a precondition and one step in the slow and long process of the European societies becoming literate. With the emergence of schools and universities, higher education and books grew together: learning to read became the prerequisite for entering the social world of university and thus making a career in the society of those times. The university was created as a mediatized social world; learning and debate took place face to face, but also in letters and books, and learning, thinking and debate mostly referred to other books and papers. It was not only a book-related institution but also a crucial part of the emerging book culture, which was much more than just book-related. While at the beginning the social world of the monks and the social world of the university were mediatized worlds of handwritten books, they later became mediatized worlds of printed media.

However, if we follow the historians, processes in the 19th century in Europe were quite different. At that time, more or less the whole of society became literate – but this happened because of industrial development. People were forced to learn to read and write because industry needed them to be able to read and to write (Osterhammel, 2011; Stein, 2010). Literacy in schools was, thus, not supported as a way for people to learn something that was opening to them a new understanding of the world, nor was it a step towards a broader democracy; it just happened because of the needs of the economy.

3. Defining media as technological and social structure and as a situational space of experiences for content set in scene

In the last section, we learned that media may emerge as a result of people's needs, and that new needs for old media, as well as new media, may be relevant for media and cultural change. We have also seen that media are always in some way related to power: the control of media, as in the monasteries, or the control of media literacy in schools, is still important today.

In this section I will use the case study of Illich, and arguments and ideas presented above, to define a concept of media helpful for studying mediatization. However, as I do this by generalizing, I refer to books as the media of texts and image representations, using a concept of Friedrich Kittler (1985), who called them 'Aufschreibsysteme' (systems of noting), and, in the case of printed books, typographical systems of noting, which is a much more functional label for 'book'. I do so because the concept of 'book' and other printed media, like newspapers, is highly ideologically loaded, as printed media are still seen as the main carrier of human culture. But this view ignores the increase in media, and is frequently related to the idea that books must be printed on paper and that other carriers, such as screens, contribute to the ruin of book culture. Today this is only an assumption.

If I speak about media as visual media of texts and image representations or about digital media, two things can be addressed: a concrete book or any other visual medium of this type, or the whole class of these media, similar to the book as a specific type of a medium. Both cases must be discussed separately.

A single concrete book is a material object which contains symbols and pictures that can be read. Reading means an activity by one or more individuals in a specific situation and includes the interpretation of symbols and pictures found in the book. Similarly, the book must be written before one can read it, and this can be done by a person, for example, manually, or by a group or an organization of people. The book can be printed, or, as is nowadays possible, be 'written' on a screen or elsewhere. If I use the concept of media of text and image representation in this concrete sense, I call this *the situational or pragmatic dimension* of such a visual medium of text and image representation. This dimension thus refers to the fact that the content and form of such a medium are produced by a person or a group of persons who set content in scene, and that it is read by a person or a few people who use this medium as a space of experience.

Against this, all books together are a type of medium and constitute a whole book culture. There is a group of people in society who belong to this culture of books, and whom we call *the readers* and label *literate*. There are other groups, like the authors, the publishers, the book store owners and so on – they all together constitute this book culture. This book culture, of course, consists of much more than the single technology 'book' and groups of people: it consists of social and cultural institutions that organize and care for books, their production, access to them and how to use them, like schools and libraries or book stores. It also consists of institutions that forbid pornography or work as censors, of rules and laws which, for example, deal with property rights or copyrights. Book culture also means that, at least in Germany, by law children can be forced to go to school, and their parents to send them. If we use the concept of media of text and image representation in this general sense as the label for an important cultural influence, we include in our thinking and our social action the technical base and the societal form of these media; we see a book or such visual medium in its *structural dimension*, as a generator of book culture.

A medium, then, should be defined as a single object and a type of object which serves the existence, and the transformation and modification, of communication. It has a situational existence, as it consists of symbolic expressions which are set in scene for this medium, and as it serves as a space of experience for its users. At the same time, a medium has a structural dimension, as it consists of a specific technology and demands specific practices, and is constitutive for a specific media-related culture, consisting of institutions, rules and so on. This is shown in Figure 5.1.[1] Now, let us close this section with some additional remarks.

First, it is important to understand that no technology is a medium 'by nature'. Media are constructed by people in the context of and as a specific part of a culture. It may start with a technology, but this technology only becomes a medium if it is used for communication by people, if it becomes embedded in culture and society and if a media-related culture emerges. The users are then labelled as readers, TV audiences, internet users and so on.

Second, it is evident that the above description of what a medium is holds true not only for books or media of visual presentation but also for other communicative media of similar type. These are media that were formerly known as mass media, but today should be called *media of standardized content which are addressed to everybody*. This includes TV, radio, internet sites, the cinema, all printed media and others. They all present content that

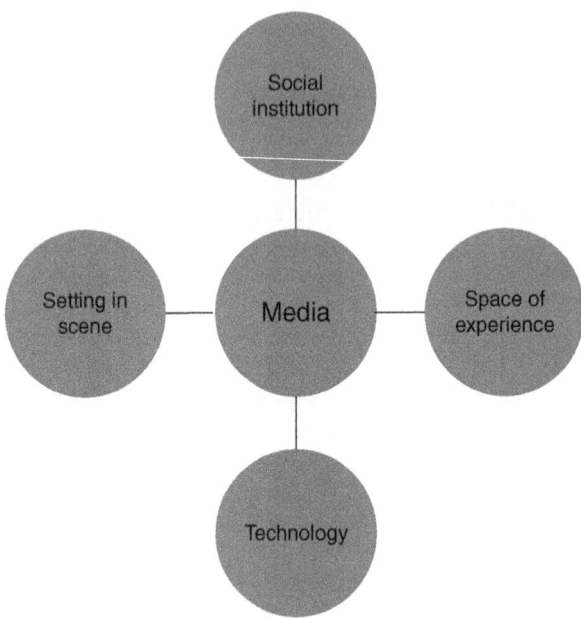

Figure 5.1 Structural and situational dimensions of a book

is always produced by a single person or an organized group of people. Communication here is separated into production and reception.

However, there are also media of *mediated interpersonal communication*, for example, phones, letters or chat. And there exist media of interactive communication, like computer games or GPS systems (cf. also McMillan (2004) for an adequate definition of 'interactive'). Within those types of media, there also exist socially guaranteed structures. They consist of those enterprises and institutions that organize the production, the networks or the transport, people's rights, the rules, how to use them and so on. The above definition of 'media' fits these media, too, as one can easily see.

Third, we have here a *semiotically oriented definition of media*. According to Ferdinand de Saussure, language is, on the one hand, a structure; on the other hand, it is a situational practice. Language vs. parole was Saussure's concept of this duality (Saussure, 1998). With the above definition of media as a structure and a situational practice, I have shown that it makes sense to give media a form analogous to language: they are, in a similar sense, outlasting structure and situational practice at the same time. In this way, media may be seen as a second-order language, a language that consists of other languages or, at the very least, is constructed on the basis of other languages.[2]

4. Researching mediatization by studying media change and mediatized worlds

The above definition of media can now be used for a more diligent explanation of the mediatization meta-process, since with this it is possible to grasp the media change more precisely. On the basis of this we can explicitly define what is meant by 'mediatization' and the attribute 'mediatized'. Further, we can draw some conclusions about mediatization research. This is how I will conclude.

Let us start with a look at the above examples of media change and their consequences for culture and society. When the book culture in the Middle Ages, as described by Ivan Illich, changed, an already existing medium had changed. The demand for that came from culture and society. As a consequence, the book culture adapted to these needs by changing the organization of the technology 'book'. As a further consequence, the mediatized social world of the monasteries changed as far as they were concerned with books. In addition, new book-related social worlds like the universities emerged. What happened in addition was that people communicated with books and printed matter and, on this basis, in different ways than before, and thus, in the long run, also experienced reality, thought and constructed the social world differently.

Another interesting case is the invention and distribution of the mobile phone, as described by Höflich (2010). Here, we find the patterns of domestication approach according to Silverstone and Haddon (1996) (cf. also Hartmann, 2008; Röser, 2005; Silverstone, 2006). Media change in this case was initiated by industry, insofar as the mobile phone was used for speaking with others. It was, thus, a creation of a culture of mediatized interpersonal communication. Besides that, as is well known, young people created an SMS-culture, much to everyone's surprise. They probably did so because it was cheaper, because it allowed more differentiated use and to set themselves apart from the adults. Additionally, the ongoing development of these media may be influenced by culture and society, by industrial interests, by people's practices, by the development of other media like the internet and so on. Here, a lot of empirical studies already exist. It should be mentioned that such studies also exist for historical media: for instance, Degele (2002, pp. 111ff.) cites studies that show that the telephone in the years after 1880 spread in the more open society of the USA much faster than in the UK, which was far less socially mobile.

Mediatization, however, does not always have to be produced primarily as a technology by the industry, as was shown above with the technology 'book'. In addition, the invention of broadcasting in the last century was spurred by governments and was used for the first time during World War I between 1914 and 1918. The idea behind broadcasting was to use this technology to transmit information to soldiers on the front lines. Mediatization can also be prompted by technical changes on the production side if existing media are being used for new functions. One example of this is the cinema of today, which is starting to produce 3D-movies and to transmit opera and sports events. Other examples include the production of new genres with new target groups, for example, Teletubbies for small children.

I thus conclude that *mediatization research must analyze media change as a condition of mediatization*; a theory of media change is necessary as well. This must include the emergence of new forms of media and communication, but also changes to already existing media. In general, it seems necessary to take the whole media system of a culture into consideration in order to understand the development of each individual medium in relation to the others. In addition, it is necessary not to limit research to technological questions – instead, social and cultural developments must also be analyzed. For example, today digital media are the same throughout the world, but it is evident that the social and cultural consequences are rather different in the different nations and cultures.

Related to this question is a further fundamental problem: in what way do changes in media impact on changes in culture and society?

In order to answer this, I will introduce a theoretical idea. If we follow Berger and Luckmann (1980) and also George Herbert Mead (1934), symbolic interactionism and related theoretical positions, we can assume that society and culture and all other social and cultural entities are socially constructed by people. Then, we can conclude *that communication is the relevant connection between media change and changes in culture and society*. This is the case in the above examples: it is the step from communication to mediated or media-related communication which is the direct consequence of media change.

I will explain this in more detail. The direct consequences of the emerging new media or changes to already existing media are (1) new mediated forms of communication, as in the case of interactive media, (2) different forms of already mediated communication, as in the case of changes to the technology 'book', and (3) the substitution of face-to-face communication or of other activities by mediated communication, as resulting from the invention of the mobile phone. This might mean that *mediated communication* becomes more frequent. On the basis of this, it is possible that also *media-related communication* emerges. *Media-related* here means that the contexts in which communication takes place and makes sense, and which are necessary for expressing oneself and for understanding others, refer to media: maybe we communicate in the presence of media, about media or about media content, or are involved in experiences and emotions or on the basis of knowledge we have acquired from media. In other words, more and more 'parts', 'objects', 'relations' and 'fields' of culture and society are then constructed under media-related conditions and contexts. If all this happens, we can speak of the emergence of a media-related culture – and we then call these activities, parts, relations, objects, fields and societies *mediatized*. Thus I can say: *Mediatization should be understood to be a process of mediatization of communication that has consequences for other cultural and social entities. We then have mediated communication, media-related communication, the emergence of a media culture and, thus, mediatized forms of communication. While in the past this may have taken place in specific social worlds like the monasteries or the universities, we live today in a more complex situation in cultures and societies that are mediatized by different media in different ways.*

With this I have also defined a mechanism of *how* the changing or upcoming media contribute to societal and cultural change. It is neither the differentiation of media, nor technology or media logic, that changes conditions of communication. It is simply communication: people use the different changing or upcoming media, and thus communicate differently and construct reality differently, as they think and experience differently, too (for a detailed outline, see also Krotz, 2007).

I can finally use this to discuss empirical approaches employed to analyze mediatization. What I have shown already is that the analysis of media change is important for mediatization research. In addition, we were able to state that it will be a complex task to describe mediatization, as this meta-process is a multi-layered and dialectical process in different directions and different in various cultures, especially if we take into consideration that it takes place on the micro, meso and macro levels. Mediatization may even happen reflexively, in the sense that after a mediatization process another one may follow, maybe resulting from the development of new media or media services, or because of socially and culturally created demands that arise as a consequence of existing media pushes. This, for example, is the case if we look at the university as an institution that was formerly mediatized by books and handwritten culture, then print culture, and which today is obviously mediatized by computer culture, which, nevertheless, has not replaced the old developments at all.

We could, further, say that mediatization must be understood to be a dismantling process, as the growing role of media separates the unity of every instrumental action into a communicative and an instrumental action. Instead of giving a piece of metal a form, you tell this to a machine or a robot. Instead of killing a person in a war, you order a drone to do so – the killing process is separated from the control over killing.

Other developments that we can observe today are changes in old media – for example, newspapers becoming news screens – such as writing acquiring a new material carrier. At the same time, the role of the visual culture is changing, as people, for example, increasingly express and represent themselves through pictures, for instance, on Facebook. Audio culture is also changing, as the use of music is still growing with respect to time and realized opportunities. These are similar sub-processes in all cultures, but there are, of course, also sub-processes in different directions, such as the cinema, radio or newspapers looking for new niches.

Besides these media-centred studies of mediatization sub-processes, an important empirical approach will be provided by the concept of *social worlds*, which are changed by mediatization processes and may become mediatized worlds on different levels (cf. www.mediatizedworlds.net). By 'social world' I mean a specific, thematically defined sphere of activity (or a field in culture and society) that is constructed and structured by specific forms of human communication. This may be the social world of a poker player, of a fitness studio client or, as explained above, the written-media mediatized world of a university student in the Middle Ages. Of course, the world of a university student today is mediatized not only by book culture but also by the technical media culture, and is being mediatized again by digital media. In contrast to earlier times, today all areas of life are mediatized.

The social world idea was developed by Tamotsu Shibutani (1955) and by Anselm Strauss (1978; cf. also Unruh, 1980) more than 50 years ago. In phenomenological sociology, there is the idea of the existence of different areas of human activity, such as everyday life, the dream and so on (cf. Berger and Luckmann, 1980; Schütz, 1971; and especially Benita Luckmann, 1970). It now turns out to be a helpful idea to study the mediatization of social worlds, as it is obvious that the social worlds, which differ in topic and main communicational forms, but also in the specific interests of the inhabitants and relations to other social worlds, are mediatized in specific ways, and thus each one must be studied by itself.

Let us look at the social world of a car driver, sitting in her or his car and driving from A to B. Traditionally, she or he may have been accompanied by a radio and a map. From time to time she or he will have seen advertising texts on walls or bulletin boards outside the car. However, this was yesterday. Today, the radio may also show pictures and the driver may speak to GPS devices and even the car. Also, the mobile phone or even a tablet or a notebook may be used (which, of course, might be forbidden). There is even more mediatization, as the car may be connected with service stations, observed by cameras, photographed by satellites to control whether fees for using a street must be paid, followed by drones and whatever, not to mention those cars that do not need a driver. Thus, driving home is participation in a mediatized world, and one of the next steps here is what is called augmented reality for the car driver.

Augmented reality is the result of the intention of physicists and information science researchers to teach us new ways of viewing. A good example of how this works is the well-known situation of driving a car at night: if, for example, some hundred metres in front of us and thus too far ahead for us to see there are people walking on the street, and sensors have already investigated those pedestrians and projected them onto the windscreen, we can pretend that we see them already. This can be done by using our knowledge about the central perspective (e.g., Schmeiser, 2002): it is well known where the driver is sitting and in which direction he is looking. And the point where the pedestrians appear on the windscreen is thus provided as if he can see them already, and can recognize their size. If the car drives round a bend, the figures will change their position on the windscreen or disappear, just in the same way as if the driver were really seeing them. Similar things are already possible today using a smartphone. If, for example, you were taking a walk in Berlin and looking at the places around you, not only using your eyes but also via the screen of your smartphone, and if you were supported in your observations by specific augmented reality software, then you could see the Berlin Wall in specific streets, as if it still existed.

Of course, the drive to develop such technologies accrued from the commercial use of augmented reality – you can be shown virtual advertising (and you will be), and the names of shops or restaurants will be highlighted. Nevertheless, this is based on old ideas – to take the example of the car, the exact moment when the pedestrians must appear on the windscreen is determined by using human knowledge of the central perspective, and this is explained by the rules of how the central perspective works. These rules describe how a three-dimensional reality must be projected on a two-dimensional screen so that we have the illusion that we see the whole space. The idea of the central perspective was developed in the European Renaissance in the 13th and 14th centuries, and this mode of representing three-dimensional objects on a two-dimensional surface has been used since then by architects, painters and photographers. Today this is still the way we expect to see the space in front of us. But this mode of viewing is learned, as all modes of viewing are learned, and not natural.

Thus, the new forms of media-supported viewing refer to the old knowledge of the central perspective (cf. Krotz, 2012) and are part of an ongoing development that started centuries ago. The development of media in this sense may happen accumulatively, and so our communicational development, a long process, accompanies us over time.

The concept of mediatized worlds may thus be seen as a systematic step to understanding the ongoing mediatization processes. Researchers, of course, must always take into account that there are other long-term meta-processes, like globalization and individualization, which are intertwined with mediatization. In addition, again and again we see that commercial interests and also the interest in gaining power and in the stabilization of power are important movers of media change. Because of this, mediatization research cannot only take place as research about current and historical developments, but must also include *critical research*. This is what we need, because just following the interests of enterprises and political institutions might, in the long run, lead us into situations which are dangerous for democracy and for the development of human beings.

Notes

1. It should be noted that this media concept can also be connected to an understanding of media as found in the apparatus theory that is based on the ideas of Foucault.
2. It should be noted that we here understand a language not as a medium, but as a constitutive human practice.

References

Altheide, D. L. and Snow, P. R. (1979) *Media logic* (Beverly Hills: Sage).
Berger, P. L. and Luckmann, T. (1980) *Die gesellschaftliche Konstruktion der Wirklichkeit* (Frankfurt am Main: Fischer).
Degele, N. (2002) *Einführung in die Techniksoziologie* (München: Wilhelm Fink).
Eco, U. (2005) *In the name of the rose* (Random House: Vintage).
Hartmann, M. (2008) 'Domestizierung 2.0: Grenzen und Chancen eines Medienaneignungskonzeptes'. In: Winter, C., Hepp, A., and Krotz, F. (eds) *Theorien der Kommunikationswissenschaft* (Wiesbaden: VS), pp. 401–16.
Hepp, A. (2013) *Cultures of mediatization* (Cambridge: Polity).
Höflich, J. (2010) 'Mobile communication and the change of everyday life: A short introduction'. In: Höflich, J., Kircher, G. F., Linke, C. and Schloge, I. (eds) *Mobile media and the change of everyday life* (Frankfurt am Main: Lang), pp. 7–15.
Illich, I. (2010) *Im Weinberg des Textes* (München: C. H. Beck).
Kittler, F. (1985) *Aufschreibsysteme 1800/1900* (München: Fink).
Krotz, F. (2007) *Mediatisierung von Kommunikation: Fallstudien zum Wandel von Kommunikation* (Wiesbaden: VS).
Krotz, F. (2012) 'Von der Entdeckung der Zentralperspektive zur Augmented Reality: Wie Mediatisierung funktioniert'. In: Krotz, F. and Hepp, A. (eds) *Mediatisierte Welten* (Wiesbaden: VS), pp. 27–59.
Luckmann, B. (1970) 'The small life-worlds of modern man'. In: *Social Research*, 37(4), pp. 580–96.
Lundby, K. (ed.) (2009) *Mediatization. Concept, changes, consequences* (New York: Peter Lang).
Mazzoleni, G. (2008a) 'Media logic'. In: Donsbach, W. (ed.) *The international encyclopedia of communication*, vol. VII (Malden, MA: Blackwell), pp. 2930–2.
Mazzoleni, G. (2008b) 'Mediatization of politics'. In: Donsbach, W. (ed.) *The international encyclopedia of communication*, vol. VII (Malden, MA: Blackwell), pp. 3047–51.
Mazzoleni, G. and Schulz, W. (1999) ' "Mediatization" of politics: A challenge for democracy?' In: *Political Communication*, 16, pp. 247–61.
McLuhan, M. (1964) *Understanding media* (New York: McGraw/Hill).
McMillan, S. (2004) 'Exploring models of interactivity from multiple research traditions: Users, documents and systems'. In: Lievrouw, L. and Livingstone, S. (eds) *Handbook of new media*, reprint of 2002 (London: Sage), pp. 163–83.
Mead, G. H. (1934) *Mind, self and society. From the standpoint of a social behaviourist* (Chicago: Chicago University Press).
Newcomb, H. M. and Hirsch, P. M. (1986) 'Fernsehen als kulturelles Forum'. In: *Rundfunk und Fernsehen*, 34, pp. 177–91.
Osterhammel, J. (2011) *Die Verwandlung der Welt. Eine Geschichte des 19. Jahrhunderts*, special edition (München: C. H. Beck).

Raible, W. (2006) *Medienkulturgeschichte. Mediatisierung als Grundlage unserer kulturellen Entwicklung* (Heidelberg: Universitätsverlag Winter).

Röser, J. (2005) 'Das Zuhause als Ort der Aneignung digitaler Medien: Domestizierungsprozesse und ihre Folgen'. In: *Merz – Medien & Erziehung. Zeitschrift für Medienpädagogik*, 49(5), pp. 86–96.

Saussure, F. de (1998) 'Grundfragen der allgemeinen Sprachwissenschaft'. In: Mersch, D. (ed.) *Zeichen über Zeichen: Texte zur Semiotik von Peirce bis Eco und Derrida* (München: DTV), pp. 193–215.

Schmeiser, L. (2002) *Die Erfindung der Zentralperspektive und die Entstehung der neuzeitlichen Wissenschaft* (München: Fink).

Schulz, W. (2004) 'Reconstructing mediatization as an analytical concept'. In: *European Journal of Communication*, 19(1), pp. 87–101.

Schulz, W. (2008) *Politische Kommunikation*, 2nd edition (Wiesbaden: Verlag für Sozialwissenschaften).

Schütz, A. (1971) *Gesammelte Aufsätze*, 2nd vol. (Den Haag: Nijhoff).

Shibutani, T. (1955) 'Reference groups as perspectives'. In: *The American Journal of Society*, 60(6), pp. 562–9.

Silverstone, R. (2006) 'Domesticating domestication. Reflections on the life of a concept'. In: Berker, T., Hartmann, M., Punie, Y. and Ward, K. (eds) *Domestication of media and technology* (London: Open University Press), pp. 229–48.

Silverstone, R. and Haddon, L. (1996) 'Design and the domestication of information and communication technologies: Technical change and everyday life'. In: Mansell, R. and Silverstone, R. (eds) *Communication by design. The politics of information and communication technologies* (Oxford: Oxford University Press), pp. 44–74.

Smythe, D. W. (2001 [1981]) 'On the audience commodity and its work'. In: Durham, M. G. and Kellner, D. M. (eds) *Media and cultural studies: Keyworks* (Malden, MA: Blackwell), pp. 253–79.

Stein, P. (2010) *Schriftkultur. Eine Geschichte des Schreibens und Lesens*, 2nd edition (Darmstadt: Wiss. Buchgesellschaft).

Strauss, A. L. (1978) 'A social world perspective'. In: Denzin, N. K. (ed.) *Studies in symbolic interaction* (Greenwich: JAI Press), pp. 119–28.

Unruh, D. R. (1980) 'The nature of social worlds'. In: *The Pacific Sociological Review*, 23(3), pp. 271–96.

Part II
Mediatization and New Media

6
Mediatized Connectivity: Historical Traits of Telephony and Theoretical Considerations about a New Dispositive of Communication

Thomas Steinmaurer

1. Introduction

We are currently witnessing a process of mediatization which is, in turn, establishing a new dispositive of communication. Emerging out of the realm of mobile communication, techno-cultural developments have laid the foundation for a new status of 'perpetual contact' (Katz and Aakhus, 2002, p. 2), which is now on its way to a further extension as processes of convergence between the fields of mobile communication, the global infrastructure of the internet and additional applications of ubiquitous computing are setting new frameworks for communication. Today, we find the individual embedded within a structure of permanent connectivity, which on the one hand offers new chances for participation in media and communication structures, but on the other hand carries implied constraints and risks within a new communication structure that we can identify as a dispositive of 'mediatized connectivity'.

With reference to the approaches of medium theory, my perspective seeks to trace the developments of how technologies of communication evolved to become integrated elements within the structures of everyday life. We can trace the emergence of technical configurations of communication over time, setting pre-configurations to new forms of a 'habitualization of social action' that lead to different types of a 'communicative construction of reality' (Hepp, 2013, pp. 6–7). Along a diachronic development, certain levels of connectivity to communication technology correspond to specific 'mediatization waves' (Hepp, 2013, p. 13) and finally lead to a now-dominant dispositive of perpetual connectivity.

Looking back to the origins of telecommunications, we are first of all able to detect techno-cultural traces of interactive communication throughout the history of telephony. Following those lines, we find that the development of this interactive technology of communication has been shaped by specific social structures whenever the technological system as such was characterized by a certain openness of use. These findings, therefore, offer us indications pertaining to the interdependency of technology and society on the level of a specific communication technology with a high impact on structures of mediatization. The key question in this context is: what kinds of interdependencies are we to assume between technical and social impact forces – between approaches of techno-determinism and the social shaping of technology – that configure a certain techno-cultural development? Furthermore, we also have to observe how this interdependency has developed during the different historical periods of telephony. Conversely, we might address the theoretical considerations of how to conceptualize the current status of a dispositive of 'mediatized connectivity'. Processes characterizing that structure – such as individualization, mobility and domestication – are transformed in certain ways. In addition, notions of space and structures of time have to be taken into consideration when we speak of a new dispositive of communication. The following reflections, therefore, aim to observe the techno-cultural traces of a certain communication technology that, in its current stage of development, can be conceptualized within the new theoretical framework of a dispositive – a theoretical framework that might help us to understand processes of mediatization within society in a specific critical perspective.

2. Techno-cultural traces of telephony

The following arguments might offer insights into the different pathways of the development of a communication technology and its integration into everyday life. In the case of telephony, we can find a specific openness of its technical and cultural form at the beginning, and after that certain techno-social stages of its usage in society, formatted by social patterns within different societies as well as by economic impact forces and peculiarities in different markets. The specific outcome of this interplay between the different forces shapes the integration of a specific communication technology into the social field, and, by that, its potential as a factor for mediatization. It is, therefore, of great interest to consolidate knowledge about the historical traces of techno-social conditions for structures of mediatization within society.

Three steps to interactivity

Perhaps more than any other communication technology, the initial stages of telephony were characterized by a conceptual openness and flexibility concerning its socio-technical system. Arguing in Brian Winston's (1998) terms, the early phase of 'ideation' was mainly based on scientific and technical cognitive experimentations, with no major product-orientated propositions at the outset. Implementations on the level of business or private usage turned out to be merely subordinate at this stage of development. A certain shaping on the technological side was brought in by the system of telegraphy, which 'informed' telephony insofar as it preconfigured the idea of unidirectional flows of information in its early days. It was Alexander Graham Bell himself who was guided by this idea in his initial technical investigations. Following this path, telephony should, therefore, be used as a communication device for unidirectional transmissions of orders and instructions. Similarly, the first 'ideations' for implementations in the business world as well as in the military argued that telephony should be used first and foremost as an instructional tool for command and control. And, in private households, the technology served in its early days as a kind of electric bell or a tool to call for servants. These usage patterns particular to telegraphy shaped early telephony's first implementation as a communication technology for more or less unidirectional transfers of information (see Rammert, 1989).

That particular concept of more or less unidirectional information processing, called the 'transport concept' by Werner Rammert (1989, pp. 80–1), should, in a second step, lead to the 'radio concept', which 'simulated' a broadcasting service within the technological system of telephony. The most famous example of that historical curiosity was the so-called Telefon Hirmondó in Budapest, which, until 1944, reached up to 10,000 subscribers (see Becker, 1989a, p. 21; 1989b, p. 71). In other European cities like Paris, Amsterdam, Berlin or Munich, similar services also functioned for a certain period of time (see Becker, 1989a; Genth and Hoppe, 1986). People could receive music programmes or transmissions from opera houses as well as news programmes at home or in public places via the technological infrastructure of telephony.

But finally it would take a third implementation step for telephony to establish itself as a tool of interactive and dialogically orientated communication. One might conclude that the impact of social patterns and the pre-configuring structures of existing technologies shape the formation of a socio-technical system to a certain extent – an argument with which scholars like Werner Rammert (1989), Brian Winston (1998) or Klaus Beck (1989) might agree. Beck, for example, suggested an understanding of the technological system of telephony as a catalyst that is able to transform social needs and demands within a socio-technical system into certain forms of implementation. He stands for a social-historic and culturalist approach similar to the techno-sociological approach of Rammert. And it was Carolyn Marvin (1988) who argued 'that the early history of electric media is less the evolution of technical efficiencies in communication than a series of arenas for negotiating issues crucial to the conduct of social life' (p. 4). We may additionally stress a valid argument for a strong bias in terms of the social shaping of technology, as it also has to be pointed out that the specific openness of the whole technical system at the very beginning created space for trial and error through several technical implementations until the system of telephony found its specific 'medial and cultural form' (Williams, 1975).

Mutual shaping of telephony within society

Additionally, it is interesting to follow the diffusion of telephony, where we encounter different patterns and rates of adoption in various countries. Once again we find arguments strengthening the idea that powerful social forces and socio-cultural layers, rather than technical pre-configurations, are shaping the diffusion of a certain communication technology. Rammert (1993), in his observations on the diffusion processes of telephony in four different countries (the USA, Germany, Great Britain and France), demonstrates how the different cultural biases and patterns of communication within a certain society can have a major impact on the speed of the diffusion of telephony. The following graph illustrates the varying diffusion patterns of telephony in different countries (Figure 6.1).

The accelerated diffusion rate in the USA can be accounted for in part by the lack of any major 'potentials of radical suppression' (Winston, 1998) on the level of market restrictions or state regulation. Rammert's crucial argument is that we also have to take into account the cultural and social

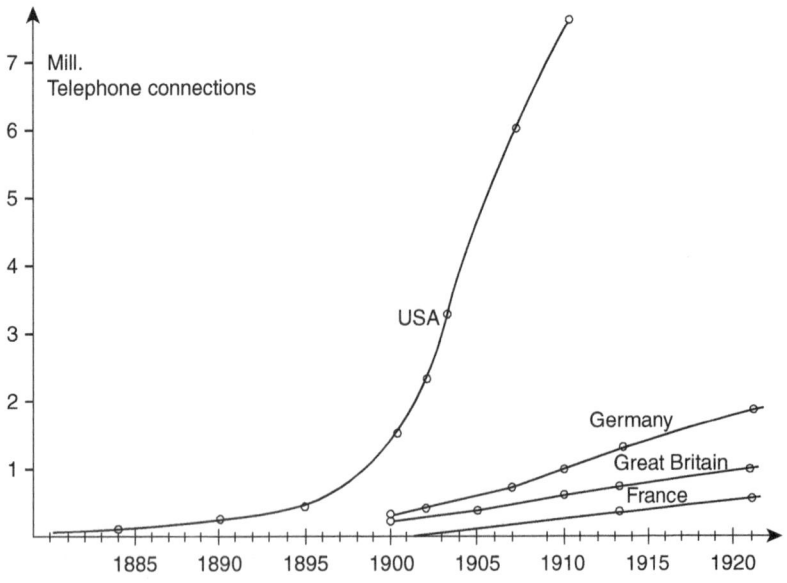

Figure 6.1 The diffusion of telephony from 1885 to 1920 in four different countries (Rammert, 1993, p. 249)

patterns within a society that can shape a technology's diffusion and integration into the social field. In the case of telephony in the USA, Rammert identifies a kind of open and pragmatic culture of communication and information-orientated social practices (Rammert, 1993, p. 262) that promoted the adoption of the technology in everyday life. In Europe, where it was primarily used as a business tool, we can recognize certain communication patterns within society inhibiting the adoption of telephony as a dialogically oriented communication technology. Rammert argues that, in France, a largely monologic and state-orientated culture of communication – having its origins in the days of early optical telegraphy – turned out to be a suppressing force against the rapid adoption of the new communication technology. In Great Britain, the strong impact of hierarchically orientated communication styles led to low adoption rates for telephony within the business world compared with the USA (Rammert, 1993), and telephony also turned out to be a technology for status differentiation between the upper and lower classes. In Germany, two major constraints seem to have hindered a rapid diffusion process. On the one hand, deep-rooted authoritarian communication patterns within society dominated the communication culture of everyday life; on the other hand, the industrial sector seemed to have underestimated the potential for the new technology. Therefore, Rammert identifies predominantly cultural patterns to be at work 'where the directness and the lack of distance between the communication partners came into conflict with a society that was dominated by formal, hierarchic and class-distinguished models of communication' (Rammert, 1989, p. 86). These social-shaping arguments are advanced by Marvin, who pointed out that 'it is clear that the impact of net technologies is as various as the social structure itself. [...] They may strengthen the forms of both liberation and repression, and often in unexpected ways' (Marvin, 1990, p. 150).

Although we may find strong arguments for the idea of the social shaping of a technology at this stage of development, one should not forget the differences between Europe and the USA in the field of actors and industry. The differences on that level determined the external preconditions for the diffusion of telephony and the specific constellations of institutional players, while at the same time the restrictions set in place in the business field shaped the diffusion process as well. Besides that, we also have to take into account the specific technological and economic actors and their potentials for unfolding their power, whether for state welfare or for economic reasons. Therefore, we are faced with an interplay of techno-economic and cultural forces that finally corresponds with the model of a mutual shaping of technologies as proposed by Boczkowski (1999), among others. Processes of mediatization in society, as set in place by the integration of a new communication technology, therefore have to be interpreted as the interplay of techno-economic forces with appropriation processes on the level of the social shaping (Lievrouw, 2002) or social construction (Pincher and Bijker, 1989) of a technology.

By looking at the further development of telephony, we additionally have to broaden the field of analyses and take into account processes of social change addressing factors of mobility and the relationship between private and public life within transformations of industrialization and the rise of new media like radio and television. Integrated into that development, telephony established a new social network by connecting units of private homes and places of business in public life, which had been separated up to that point.

From place-to-place to person-to-person

The next major stage of innovation within the technological system of telephony led to a mobile communication infrastructure that established person-to-person networks in addition to place-to-place connections, a development that was based increasingly on the economic rationalities of expanding markets. 'A society in constant touch was partly created by this economic rationale to squeeze ever higher levels of productive work' (Agar, 2003, p. 83). Thus, mobile communication technologies were predominantly pushed by techno-economic rationalities to expand profit rates (Carey and Elton, 2010). We might, therefore, address the process of commercialization in conjunction with technological innovation that clearly dominated that next level of the diffusion of telephony within society.

In contrast to the adoption processes of fixed-line telephony, the integration of mobile communication technologies showed different patterns of integration into the social field, 'so that the impact of the adoption of mobile phone on telephone adoption (or its abandoning) has been more significant in Europe than in North America, whereas the adoption of the internet as an additional medium of virtual mobility has been more extensive in North America' (Kellerman, 2006, p. 122). Besides the business sector, mobile communication technologies became extremely important for younger people, as those born between 1990 and 2000 turned out to be the 'first mobile generation' (Carey and Elton, 2010, p. 331). Accompanied by the meta-trend of individualization and the establishment of new forms of virtual mobilities within global communication infrastructures, a new kind of mediatization process emerged within society. As Kellerman notes,

> European countries have presented past direct and full governmental involvement in the provision of telephone services, and indirectly in personal physical mobility through the controlling of urban sprawl and the construction of efficient and extensive public transportation systems. Currently, with the privatization of telephone services and the introduction of mobile phones, households in major European nations show higher preferences for personal virtual mobility, whereas North American

ones adopt equally, or close to equally, media for both physical and virtual personal mobilities. These trends are coupled with growing shares of household expenditures to communications, compared with declining shares of expenditures on physical mobility.

(Kellerman, 2006, p. 126)

Within the communication structures of this most successful machine of all time (Nyíri, 2002, pp. 11f.), now 'the person – not the place, household or workgroup – [has] become even more of an autonomous communication node' (Wellman, 2001, p. 230) – or, more succinctly, 'the person has become the portal' (Wellman, 2001, p. 238). At this level of development, a new infrastructure of communication has established a new communication environment within society that should lead to major changes of communication and sets preconditions for further innovations, which we are currently facing within the dynamic processes of ubiquitous and permanent connectivity.

3. Towards a theory of mediatized connectivity

At the present stage of development, a new paradigmatic shift is once again transforming the techno-social system of communication in a fundamental way. After the turn towards mobile communication, the ongoing process of convergence between mobile communication, the internet and applications for ubiquitous computing is producing a new technical and social form of communication that unfolds new dynamics of mediatization in society. By establishing a status of communication that culminates in what we can describe as the permanent connectivity of the individual within a global network, we can identify that structure as a new dispositive of communication as it gets ever more integrated into the routines of everyday communication.

The dispositive of mediatized connectivity

Referring to the theoretical foundations of Foucault's post-structural thinking, a dispositive can be defined as a system or a network of discourses, an order of knowledge or a technical constellation as well as a formation of actions and modes of behaviour that unfolds certain power structures in society (Foucault, 1991). With reference to Foucault's theoretical concepts, Jean Louis Baudry (1993) theorized cinema to be a dispositive with ideological effects, and Knut Hickethier, among other scholars, has identified television as a medium with a dispositive structure (Hickethier, 1992). Following that line of argument, we might now conceptualize the new evolving system of communication within that theoretical framework in order to open up ways for critical reflections on that techno-social system. Hickethier, for instance, asks how dispositives of communication are shaping patterns of consumption or how subjects are dealing with certain media experiences (Hickethier, 1992, p. 28).

Conceptualizing structures of the current systems of permanent connectivity as a new dispositive of communication allows us, for example, to address questions of surveillance or changing structures of privacy. Likewise, we may be able to detect power structures among the global players and the ways they are unfolding their hegemonic positions on the markets and within the communication structures of the 'fabric of everyday lives' as well. Following Bührmann and Schneider (2008, p. 71), we might additionally discuss questions of constraints faced by users in constructing their identities within a connected environment, or how to engage in oppositional modes of action. Besides the historical angle, this theoretical approach opens a holistic conceptual framework that raises questions about techno-economical dominances as well as strategies of adoption within the routines of everyday life. Additionally, structures on the micro level of the individual as well as broader insights on the macro level of society can be addressed. In conjunction with theoretical approaches of mediatization, the concept of the dispositive allows useful insights into specific levels of development and opens ways of combining different theoretical conceptions within a greater framework of critical reflection.

From mobile privatization to mobile individualization

Within the aforementioned broader framework, certain processes have to be taken into account as they are exposed to dynamics of change. First, the meta-process of individualization (Beck, 1992) can be considered an essential social process closely connected to mobile communication. According to Beck's sociological concept of individualization, we find ambivalences in the field of mobile communication as new possibilities of flexibility meet constraints and restrictions. By referring to Raymond Williams' socio-cultural approach of a 'mobile privatization' (Williams, 1975), we can now speak of a 'mobile individualization' to address contemporary developments of ever more mobile and individualized communication processes. Wellman (2001, p. 169), therefore, calls this new form of individualism within digital networks 'networked individualism', and Wilken (2005) suggests the term 'network mobility' to describe the status of integration of mobile individuals into networks of communication.

As Williams once argued in the context of mobile privatization, we also have to observe processes of transformation from a critical perspective by raising questions of power within these specific structures. Kellerman, therefore, speaks of a 'politics of mobility' that focuses on the social implications of mobility and communication. 'Thus, "it does seem that mobility and control over mobility both reflect and reinforce power". [...] One implication of such power relations is the growing number of people who have to be immobile at any given time in order to serve the seemingly growing virtual and physical mobilities of others' (Massey in Kellerman, 2006, p. 31). The whole socio-technical system of mobile and connected communication is characterized by ambivalent tendencies as we face problems of fragmentation and power as well as new opportunities for participation, such as 'smart mobs' (Rheingold, 2002), and new forms of reintegration within social structures that might occur on the level of mobile social networks. In any case, we have to take into account that all of these processes are integrated into infrastructures dominated by commercial interests. New business models working on the basis of tracing the mobile individual on his or her way through the geography of everyday life raise questions of privacy as well as problems of surveillance. Particularly the younger generations, or what we call the 'digital natives', who participate 'in LBSNs (Location-Based Social Networks) and LBMGs (Location-Based Mobile Games) [...] are generally willing to share their location with others, and they normally opt in to use the service' (de Souza e Silva and Frith, 2012, p. 146). In a related development, we are observing new modes of self-exposure in social networks and a decreasing awareness of the need to safeguard private spaces or data, especially among younger users within networks. Transformations like that indicate new ways of adopting and integrating technologies of communication into the routines of everyday practice.

Domestication going mobile

In light of this, we have to reconsider our approaches to the ways new technologies are integrated into everyday social lifeworlds. As already argued by Hartmann (2008), the domestication of technology approach developed by Silverstone and Haddon (1996) needs to be adopted for the currently changing processes in the field of mobile and connected communication. Hartmann argues that we have to abandon the home as the exclusive base for domestication processes and instead accept it as one place alongside others (Hartmann, 2008, p. 413). And, as Höflich and Hartmann (2007, p. 213) stated, it is no more the place but, in fact, the types of interactions that have to be addressed when we talk of new forms of domestication. Considering the emerging new forms of mobile or connected communication infrastructures, we might, therefore, call this a process of 'mobile domestication'. This concept still regards the household as a place providing 'ontological security' (Silverstone, 2006), but also considers the fact that the appropriation strategies for media technologies are increasingly connected to the mobile individual rather than to the family as an entity that decides how media are to be incorporated into everyday life routines. In the context of a 'liquid modernity' (cf. Bauman, 2006), we have to understand the individual's position within a condition of a permanent adjustment of his or her position within a social network or within an 'ongoing stream of renegotiations, reconfigurations involving the constant rescheduling of all obligations and commitments' (Morley, 2007, p. 224). Morley, therefore, calls this configuration 'privatized mobility' and concludes 'that domesticity itself has now been dislocated' (Morley, 2006, p. 36). Nevertheless, it makes sense still to regard the home as an important place for safeguarding the individual's personal integrity in an ever more unstable society, because

> if the human condition requires a modicum of ontological security for its continuing possibility and its development, home – technologically enhanced as well as technologically disrupted – is a sine qua non. We cannot do without it, within or without the household. To be homeless is to be beyond reach, and to be without identity.
>
> (Silverstone, 2006, p. 243)

In addition, Röser (2007) argues in favour of continuing to uphold the concept of the private sphere and the household as an important entity. Evidence confirming this assumption can be seen in the fact that mobile communication technologies are strengthening rather than disintegrating family ties (Feldhaus, 2005). Feldhaus highlights the different functions of mobile communication for families when he speaks of the benefit of those technologies for promoting security and stabilizing emotional ties. Furthermore, these technologies might serve as tools for organization and education. On the other hand, these positive developments for upholding family ties might encounter problems when, for example, children – embedded in a network of 'remote mothering' (Rakow and Navarro, 1993) – claim their 'right to be left alone' (Sennett, 1977). In these contexts, mobile technologies of communication may also strengthen the flexibility of the individual and create new ways of adopting or appropriating media technologies on the level of the mobile individual.

Hybrid spaces

Reflecting the ongoing changes in mobile and connected technologies for communication within the social field, we also have to take into account the changing notions of place and space and how these concepts get transformed in the contexts of ubiquitous and continuous access to communication networks on the level of the mobile individual. In this respect, spaces of communication have to be seen as socially constructed entities (Soja, 1989) and as the results of strategies based upon changing communication practices. So notions of place change within the 'spaces of flows' (Castells, 1996) of networked communication. We are facing hybridizations of spatial structures, as individuals in connected communication structures increasingly have to deal with different spatial representations (within an offline and an online world, or of real and virtual communication spaces) and incorporate them both into a more or less consistent practice of everyday life. Referring to these transformations, the notion of 'hybrid multilocalities' could be seen as a fruitful concept for incorporating the transformations in that field of mediatization.

Within the transition from 'stabilitas loci' to 'mobilitas loci' (Wilken, 2005), we have to be aware of the fact that processes like these might lead us to unrealistic assumptions. Although ' "placelessness" became a popular concept, [...] media use is always situated. We have to look closely at the complex microphysics of the ways in which media take place and claim space' (Löfgren, 2006, p. 299).

Even if Morley speaks of a 'death of geography' (Morley in Wilken, 2005), we should be aware of the fact that social action is always somehow bound to physical space and that spatial structures are, therefore, represented within patterns of social action. Especially in the field of mobile connectivity, we should assume not so much an annihilation or a complete deterritorialization of spatial structures but a reterritorialization (cf. Döring and Thielmann, 2008, p. 14) arising from a hybridization of the social experiences of real geographical spaces within mentally represented structures of space. In this context, Wilken talks of a 'physical and wirelessly co-present context' in which 'networked mobility' is realized as 'a heavily mediated engagement, where place is experienced via a complex filtering or imbrication of the actual with the virtual' (Wilken, 2011, pp. 168–169). Insofar as we may assume that 'place persists and does not remain unchanged', it follows that 'networked mobility in general, and mobile phone use in particular, lead to altered or transformed understandings of place and place-making' (Wilken, 2011, p. 172).

Crucial in that context are Lefèbvre's considerations that presume space to be a politically and ideologically shaped entity, 'as it is a product literally filled with ideologies' (Lefèbvre in Ek, 2006, p. 57). Thus, spaces have to be seen as areas in which the communication activities of users can be exploited for commercial reasons. Practices like these are realized within applications that are based on exploiting the geographical traces of the users and integrating them within network solutions of ubiquitous computing. Users are producing data by simply acting and communicating within networks, but they are excluded from the economic utilization of their 'products'. By involving the mobile individual in network solutions with commercial interests, we can observe an integration of communicative activities into the commercial interests of profit-taking providers (Krotz and Schulz, 2006, p. 65). At this stage of mediatization, processes of commercialization play a central role and are deeply incorporated into technological configurations, as software and hardware solutions are setting the pathways in which users are allowed to 'behave'. In addition, problems of privacy illustrate the fact that spaces of communication must be seen as dominant spaces – as opposed to those spaces that serve people's interests and are orientated towards users' needs and requirements (Lefèbvre, 1994, pp. 164ff.). In the macro perspective of global 'informational capitalism', the 'spaces of flow', in Castell's terms, should be seen not as homogeneous spaces, but as massively affected by the digital divides that separate spaces of digital flows into centres and peripheries.

4. Conclusion: The dispositive of mediatized connectivity in mediatized worlds

By summing up at that point, we might conclude that the process of convergence between mobile communication technologies and the global infrastructure of the internet, combined with applications of ubiquitous computing, has established a new dispositive of communication within society that is at the same time deeply integrated into the structures of everyday life. New interfaces of communication provide a new status of 'communicative connectedness' (Hepp, 2011, p. 77) for the individual and establish a 'completely new communicative figuration' (Hepp, 2013, p. 13) (pre-)configuring modes for new mediatized worlds. These figurations are characterized by the establishment of new modes of access to networks of communication with major changes concerning the structuring of identities, social networks and general modes of communication on a micro as well as on a macro level.

Within this context we have to raise not only questions about the status of new structures but also questions of power and dominant influences. The possibility of detecting constellations of power within these new mediatized worlds is offered by the way of theorizing structures of mediatized connectivity as a dispositive of communication. The model proposed here illustrates some important aspects of the dispositive of mediatized connectivity framed by the relevant changes related to it (Figure 6.2).

By focusing on this model, we can first of all identify the basic aspects that are supposed to impact transformations in the context of mediatized connectivity. In referring to dispositive structures and without overemphasizing techno-deterministic forces, we should be aware of the predetermining parameters that emerge out of the interplay of technological and economic

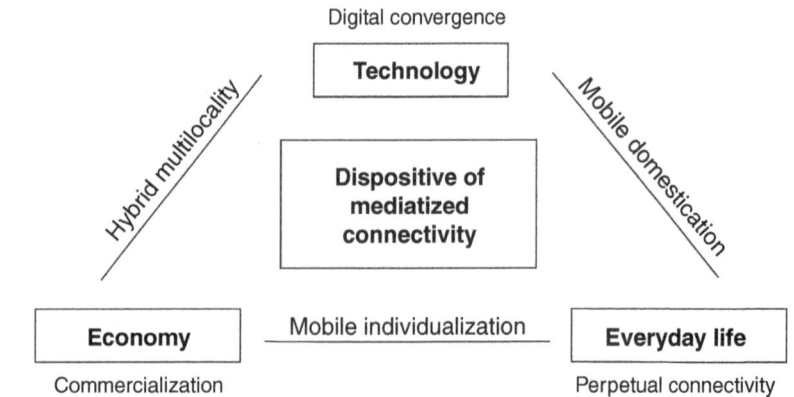

Figure 6.2   The dispositive of mediatized connectivity in context

impact forces. They come into play when certain software applications are strictly integrated into specific hardware platforms, or when proprietary value-added chains are connected to only one provider or major player, as we are currently witnessing on the global market. They are setting constraints of usage, allowing only a certain spectrum of usage and, in so doing, predetermining the range of impact that might evolve out of a specific social-shaping process of a technology. In these cases, the power is only in the hands of dedicated or well-skilled users, or is controlled by strategies beyond legal ability to reopen the spectrum of open access to network technologies. We are meeting a field of socio-technical change and mediatization in which the meta-process of commercialization can be assumed to have a strong impact on modes of social action, on culture and on society as a whole (Krotz, 2008).

When suggesting such a conceptual framework, one has to keep in mind that models like these are abstractions and therefore bear the risk of certain shortcomings or oversimplifications. As a consequence, the present model should draw attention to the aspects that have been taken into account when we speak of mediatization in contexts of mobile connectivity. Furthermore, we have to concede certain accentuations that make no claim to comprehensiveness in terms of the phenomena to be addressed. And, finally, we have to highlight the fact that the addressed processes must be regarded as non-linear but ambivalent phenomena of change, as technologies of connected networks and transformations on the level of social action are facing both constraints and opportunities for flexibility at the same time. In addition, the addressed processes have to be seen as non-static in character because of their tendency to be embedded into a continuously changing interplay of media-technological and social change.

So, in addition to the question of changing structures of place, we have to add that we are observing transformations of notions of time as well, which indicate an ever more accelerating speed within communication processes combining with the effects of multitasking on the level of usage. In addition, we are observing an increasingly closer linkage of communication technologies as material products on the level of the human body and the identity of the users that raises questions of media anthropology: 'The body is assimilated to the machine, objects become technological, technologies become "intelligent". The tendencies to mechanize human beings and anthropomorphize objects intermingle with one another' (Fortunai, 2003, p. 81).

Taking all this into account, we can claim the dispositive of mediatized connectivity as a new dispositive of communication that is already deeply integrated into the 'fabric of everyday life' with a strong impact on social change (Bührmann and Schneider, 2008, p. 74) on both the micro level of the individual and the macro level of society. Further research efforts will be challenged by questions of whether we can expect to see the effects of integration and participation on the level of mediatized connectivity or whether we have to deal with an ongoing fragmentation of society. Concerning the individual, we should also be interested in altering the structures of usage patterns on the level of changing habits of attentiveness, implicating questions of ever shorter attention spans. Transformations like these might also be relevant for the way people are exposed to (media) content on mobile platforms and the extent to which patterns of communication are transformed on the level of the perpetually connected individual in 'mediatized worlds'.

References

Agar, J. (2003) *Constant touch. A global history of the mobile phone* (Duxford: Icon Books).
Baudry, J.-L. (1993) 'Ideologische Effekte am Basisapparat'. In: *Eikon, Internationale Zeitschrift für Fotografie und Medienkunst*, 5, pp. 34–43.
Bauman, Z. (2006) *Liquid modernity* (Cambridge: Polity Press).
Beck, K. (1989) 'Telefongeschichte als Sozialgeschichte: Die soziale und die kulturelle Aneignung des Telefons im Alltag'. In: Forschungsgruppe Telefonkommunikation (ed.) *Telefon und Gesellschaft. Band 1: Beiträge zu einer Soziologie der Telefonkommunikation* (Berlin: Volker Spiess), pp. 45–75.
Beck, U. (1992) *Risk society. Towards a new modernity* (London: Sage).
Becker, G. (1989a) 'Telefonieren und sozialer Wandel'. In: Becker, J. (ed.) *Telefonieren, Hessische Blätter für Volks- und Kulturforschung, Band 24* (Marburg: Jonas Verlag), pp. 7–30.
Becker, G. (1989b) 'Die Anfänge der Telefonie. Zur Industrie- und Sozialgeschichte des Telefons im ausgehenden 19. Jahrhundert'. In: Becker, J. (ed.) *Telefonieren, Hessische Blätter für Volks- und Kulturforschung, Band 24* (Marburg: Jonas Verlag), pp. 63–76.
Boczkowski, P. J. (1999) 'Mutual shaping of users and technologies in a national virtual community'. In: *Journal of Communication*, Spring 1999, pp. 86–108.
Bührmann, A. D. and Schneider, W. (2008) *Vom Diskurs zum Dispositiv. Eine Einführung in die Dispositivanalyse* (Bielefeld: transcript Verlag).
Carey, J. and Elton, M. C. (2010) *When media are new. Understanding the dynamics of new media adoption and use* (Michigan: The University of Michigan Press and the University of Michigan Library).
Castells, M. (1996) *The information age: Economy, society and culture. Volume 1: The rise of the network society* (Oxford: Blackwell).
De Souza e Silva, A. and Frith, J. (2012) *Mobile interfaces in public spaces. Locational privacy, control, and urban sociability* (New York, London: Routledge).
Döring, J. and Thielmann, T. (2008) 'Einleitung: Was lesen wir im Raume? Der Spatial Turn und das geheime Wissen der Geographen'. In: Döring, J. and Thielmann, T. (eds) *Spatial Turn. Das Raumparadigma in den Kultur- und Sozialwissenschaften* (Bielefeld: transcript Verlag), pp. 7–45.
Ek, R. (2006) 'Media studies, geographical imaginations and relational space'. In: Falkheimer, J. and Jansson, A. (eds) *Geographies of communication. The spatial turn in media studies* (Göteborg: Nordicom), pp. 45–66.
Feldhaus, M. (2005) 'Mobile Kommunikation in der Familie: Chancen und Risiken'. In: Höflich, J. and Gebhardt, J. (eds) *Mobile Kommunikation. Perspektiven und Forschungsfelder* (Frankfurt am Main u. a.: Peter Lang), pp. 159–77.

Fortunai, L. (2003) 'The human body: Natural and artificial technology'. In: Katz, J. (ed.) *Machines that become us: The social context of personal communication technology* (New Brunswick: Transaction Publishers), pp. 71–87.

Foucault, M. (1991) *Die Ordnung des Diskurses* (Frankfurt am Main: Fischer Taschenbuch Verlag).

Genth, R. and Hoppe, J. (1986) *Telephon! Der Draht, an dem wir hängen* (Berlin: Transit Buchverlag).

Hartmann, M. (2008) 'Domestizierung 2.0. Grenzen und Chancen eines Medienaneignungsprozesses'. In: Winter, C., Hepp, A. and Krotz, F. (eds) *Theorien der Kommunikations- und Medienwissenschaft. Grundlegende Diskussionen, Forschungsfelder und Theorieentwicklungen* (Wiesbaden: VS Verlag), pp. 401–16.

Hepp, A. (2011) *Cultures of mediatization* (Cambridge: Polity Press).

Hepp, A. (2013) *The communicative figurations of mediatized worlds: Mediatization research in time of the 'mediation of everything'*. Research network 'Communicative figurations', working paper no. 1, http://www.kommunikative-figurationen.de/fileadmin/redak_kofi/Arbeitspapiere/CoFi_EWP_No-1_Hepp.pdf.

Hickethier, K. (1992) 'Kommunikationsgeschichte. Geschichte der Mediendispositive'. In: *Medien & Zeit*, 2, pp. 26–8.

Höflich, J. and Hartmann, M. (2007) 'Grenzverschiebungen – Mobile Kommunikation im Spannungsfeld von öffentlichen und privaten Sphären'. In: Röser, L. (ed.) *MedienAlltag. Domestizierungsprozesse alter und neuer Medien* (Wiesbaden: VS Verlag), pp. 211–21.

Katz, J. E. and Aakhus, M. (2002) *Perpetual contact. Mobile communication, private talk, public performance* (Cambridge: Cambridge University Press).

Kellerman, A. (2006) *Personal mobilities* (London, New York: Routledge).

Krotz, F. (2008) 'Media connectivity: Concepts, conditions and consequences'. In: Hepp, A., Krotz, F., Moores, S. and Winter, C. (eds) *Connectivity, networks, and flows. Conceptualizing contemporary communications* (Cresskill, New Jersey: Hampton Press), pp. 13–33.

Krotz, F. and Schulz, I. (2006) 'Vom mobilen Telefon zum kommunikativen Begleiter in neu interpretierten Realitäten. Die Bedeutung des Mobiltelefons in Alltag, Kultur und Gesellschaft'. In: *Ästhetik & Kommunikation*, 37, pp. 59–65.

Lefèbvre, H. (1994) *The production of space* (Oxford: Blackwell).

Lievrouw, L. A. (2002) 'Determination and contingency in new media development: Diffusion of innovations and social shaping of technology perspectives'. In: Lievrouw, L. A. and Livingstone, S. (eds) *The handbook of new media. Social shaping and consequences of ICTs* (London, Thousand Oaks, New Delhi: Sage), pp. 183–99.

Löfgren, O. (2006) 'Postscript: Taking place'. In: Falkheimer, J. and Jansson, A. (eds) *Geographies of communication. The spatial turn in media studies* (Göteborg: Nordicom), pp. 297–307.

Marvin, C. (1988) *When old technologies were new* (New York, Oxford: Oxford University Press).

Marvin, C. (1990) 'When the telephone was new: Lessons from past voices'. In: Forschungsgruppe Telefonkommunikation (ed.) *Telefon und Gesellschaft. Band 2: Beiträge zu einer Soziologie der Telefonkommunikation* (Berlin: Volker Spiess), pp. 144–56.

Morley, D. (2006): 'What's "home" got to do with it? Contradictory dynamics in the domestication of technology and the dislocation of domesticity'. In: Berker, Th.,

Hartmann, M., Punie, Y. and Ward, K. (eds) *Domestication of media and technology* (Berkshire: Open University Press), pp. 21–39.

Morley, D. (2007) *Media, modernity and technology. The geography of the new* (London, New York: Routledge).

Nyíri, K. (2002) 'Einleitung: Unterwegs zur Wissensgemeinschaft'. In: Nyíri, K. (ed.) *Allzeit zuhanden. Gemeinschaft und Erkenntnis im Mobilzeitalter* (Vienna: Passagen Verlag), pp. 11–23.

Pincher, T. J. and Bijker, W. E. (1989) 'The social construction of facts and artifacts: Or how the sociology of science and the sociology of technology might benefit each other'. In: Bijker, W., Hughes, Th. and Pinch, T. (eds) *The social construction of technological systems* (Cambridge, MA, London: MIT Press), pp. 11–44.

Rakow, L. F. and Navarro, V. (1993) 'Remote mothering and the parallel shift. Women meet the cellular phone'. In: *Critical Studies in Mass Communication*, 10, pp. 144–57.

Rammert, W. (1989) 'Wie das Telefon in unseren Alltag kam ... Kulturelle Bedingungen einer technischen Innovation und ihre gesellschaftliche Verbreitung'. In: Becker, J. (ed.) *Telefonieren, Hessische Blätter für Volks- und Kulturforschung, Band 24* (Marburg: Jonas Verlag), pp. 77–90.

Rammert, W. (1993) *Technik aus soziologischer Perspektive. Forschungsstand, Theorieansätze, Fallbeispiele – ein Überblick* (Opladen: Westdeutscher Verlag).

Rheingold, H. (2002) *Smart mobs. The next social revolution* (Cambridge, MA: Perseus).

Röser, J. (2007) *MedienAlltag. Domestizierungsprozesse alter und neuer Medien* (Wiesbaden: VS Verlag).

Sennett, R. (1977) *The fall of public man* (New York: Knopf).

Silverstone, R. (2006) 'Domesticating domestication. Reflections on the life of a concept'. In: Berker, Th., Hartmann, M., Punie, Y. and Ward, K. (eds) *Domestication of media and technology* (New York: Open University Press), pp. 229–48.

Silverstone, R. and Haddon, L. (1996) 'Design and the domestication of information and communication technologies: Technical change and everyday life'. In: Mansell, R. and Silverstone, R. (eds) *Communication by design. The politics of information and communication technologies* (Oxford: Oxford University Press), pp. 44–74.

Soja, E. (1989) *Postmodern geographies. The reassertion of space in critical social theory* (London, New York: Verso Press).

Wellman, B. (2001) 'Physical place and cyberplace: The rise of personal networking'. In: *International Journal of Urban and Regional Research*, 25, pp. 227–52.

Wilken, R. (2005) 'From stabilitas loci to mobilitas loci: Networked mobility and the transformation of place'. In: *Fibreculture*, 6, http://www.journal.fibreculture.org/issue6/issue6_wilken_print.html.

Wilken, R. (2011) *Teletechnologies, place, and community* (New York, London: Routledge).

Williams, R. (1975) *Television. Technology and cultural form* (London: Routledge).

Winston, B. (1998) *Media technology and society. A history: From the telegraph to the internet* (London, New York: Routledge).

7
Intensifying Mediatization: Everyware Media

James Miller[1]

> The map of the world shows no country called Technopolis, yet in many ways we are already its citizens. If one observes how thoroughly our lives are shaped by interconnected systems of modern technology, how strongly we feel their influence, respect their authority and participate in their workings, one begins to understand that, like it or not, we have become members of a new order in human history... [O]ne begins to comprehend a distinctively modern form of power, the foundations of a technopolitan culture.
>
> (Winner, 1986, p. ix)

1. Introduction

The notion of mediatization, as recent as it is – still taking shape, in fact, with competing definitions – is nevertheless a concept that labels what are fast becoming past developments. Other terms already push beyond it. Roger Silverstone's mediapolis (2006) and Mark Deuze's media life (2011 and in this volume) imply another step in the mediatization process. Mediatization recognizes the emergence of the media as a full-fledged, independent institutional realm, while other institutions necessarily operate interdependently with the media. The ontology of mediapolis or media life, however, grows out of intensifying conditions of media ubiquity, portability, personalization and, most of all, invisibility. When the media are everywhere and used for nearly everything, they lose their familiar distinctiveness as material devices, discrete services and social practices. Instead, they become embedded, intertwined and increasingly hidden. And their use begins to surpass simulation to become an extended social reality and augmented sensory and cognitive experience.[2]

This chapter makes a case for the systematic inclusion of technology as a central element of the media logic – or perhaps one of several strands of logic – at work in mediatization. The need for its conceptual inclusion is pressing because of the steady emergence of new media whose features are already accelerating and intensifying the process. To under-appreciate the influence of technology, to fail to integrate it into larger mediatization theorizing, to neglect what many scholars see as a unique and perhaps pivotal moment in new-media innovation and adoption will only put distance between the concept and the social practices it wishes to explain. The chapter shows how fear of technological determinism ought not to constrain the consideration of technology in mediatization; it explores the intense, often highly personal relationships people form with media devices; and it presents ubiquitous computing as offering a way of thinking about the emerging environments of newest media.

2. Imagining advanced mediatization

Precisely what comes next, in this movement from mere mediation to mediatization to something more intensified, is difficult to say.[3] It may be helpful to look backwards in order to see ahead. Fifty years ago, two quite different writers made remarkably similar forecasts that bear on mediatization and its successors. More than forecasts, really, even more than urgent interpretations: these men were advocates of an unexpectedly shared point of view, insisting that their contemporaries recognize a world being transformed by communication technologies in a very particular way.

In a 1960 article published in a journal of the Institute of Radio Engineers, the American computer scientist J. C. R. Licklider, shortly afterwards a key figure in the eventual invention of the internet,[4] predicted 'man-computer synthesis', by which he meant that 'human brains and computing machines would be coupled together very tightly, and that the resulting partnership will think as no human brain has ever thought' (Licklider, 1960, p. 4). Licklider saw two reasons to seek this synthesis. First, he believed that problem-solving could be more effective, especially if there were 'an intuitively guided trial-and-error procedure in which the computer cooperated, turning up flaws in the reasoning or revealing unexpected turns in the solution'. Even more useful would be if the machine could play a role in the 'formulative parts of technical questions', or in helping people to ask the right question. Licklider's second aim was speed: 'To think in [real-time] interaction with a computer in the same way that you think with a colleague whose competence supplements your own' (Licklider 1960, p. 5).

The second writer was a previously little-known Canadian literary theorist, Marshall McLuhan. His 1964 bestseller *Understanding Media*, importantly subtitled *The Extensions of Man*, begins with this dramatic, metaphorical assertion:

Today, after more than a century of electric technology, we have extended our central nervous system itself in a global embrace [...] Rapidly, we approach the final phase of the extensions of man – the technological simulation of consciousness, when the creative process of knowing will be collectively and corporately extended to the whole of human society, much as we have already extended our senses and our nerves by the various media.

(McLuhan, 1964, pp. 3–4)

The influential computer scientist and the scholar of European literature, the latter transformed by his startlingly unorthodox 'probes' of media futures into such a popular culture reference that he appeared in a Woody Allen movie as himself, may have had little in common but this one shared view: that the development of information machines was on course – fully a half-century ago – to blur the boundaries between them and the human mind and body and the built environment in which social life takes place. In retrospect, this prescient observation can be seen to have leaped over generations of communications research, and to articulate what might be called the advanced mediatization perspective of mediapolis or media life.

3. Mediatization and beyond

As with any new concept, the definition of mediatization is contested ground. It makes few original claims, instead reconfiguring familiar ones and arguing mainly for their collectively novel significance. It may even have 'so far not been properly defined' (Hjarvard, 2004, pp. 47–8). Its proponents seem most comfortable calling it a meta-process, operating perhaps on the scale of modernity's other transformations, individualization, globalization and commercialization (Krotz, 2007). In this way, the idea of mediatization has potentially profound implications.[5]

Mediatization, as it is used here, labels a complex of processes that makes increasing amounts of social action, knowledge and experience available through and in terms of the media. Media are understood to be constant, material companions in everyday life. They are used as instrumental devices and they exist as nearly unavoidable background in public and private spaces. Media themselves are changing, becoming portable, interactive, multimodal and personalizable. Traditional content boundaries dissolve under mediatization, just as the role of producer becomes expanded to include amateurs. A variety of actors – formal organizations like corporations, institutions like the government as well as individuals – arrange their behaviour to conform to 'media logic' so as to achieve a desired representation or simulation, since this is how many others will know them. (It follows that such regular behaviour will shape how they actually are, and experience themselves, and that media logic itself will be altered in the process.) In other words, and allowing for a dynamic, unfolding process that is experienced unevenly across a given society, let alone globally, mediatization is a condition in which social life without media becomes a near impossibility. It is a process by which media representations and simulations become the chief means for people to encounter the larger world. Equally, they are the means by which the world, so to speak, chooses to present itself to most people, most of the time.

4. Media logic and technology

The successful deployment of a media 'logic' across societal domains is a theme fundamental to discussions of mediatization. Some theorists, like Nick Couldry (2008 and in this volume), resist the possibility of a single, over-arching logic, one that is not differentiated by medium, occupational field (like journalism) or content type, let alone historical period. David Altheide and Robert Snow (1979), who originated the term more than 30 years ago, were fairly cavalier in their use of it. They seem mostly to have meant content formats, the genres of broadcast programming or the typologies of news stories.[6] Because the notion is so central to the understanding of mediatization, it is worth worrying over. At this moment in the history of the idea, however, perhaps the most reasonable approach is the one taken by one of mediatization's more vigorous proponents, Stig Hjarvard. For him, the term 'media logic' operates as shorthand for media practices and their integration into larger society. It is, Hjarvard says, a convenient label for the practical and conceptual complexities of media organization, technology and aesthetics, describing the 'modus operandi' of the media (Hjarvard, 2009, p. 160, see also in this volume).

Thinking about 'media logic' from the double perspective of Couldry's critique and Hjarvard's appreciation of it as an umbrella term invites consideration of the individual constituents that make up the larger composite logic of the media. It may be that each of these individual elements, like the material ingredients of engineered composite materials, has its own 'logic'. But when moulded into a whole, to stay with the metaphor, they combine in ways that forge something new, stronger and systemically distinctive.

One constituent logic of mediatization is technological. And yet technology has been mostly neglected by mediatization theorists, or they have taken a contradictory approach to it or, most often, they have actively avoided it, for fear of implying technological determinism. An example of this uncertainty about technology can be found even in Friedrich Krotz's attentive nurturing of the concept of mediatization. Krotz wishes to relegate technology to a minor role (see also Rothenbuhler, 2009, p. 288). First, he characterizes it merely as a tool available for the social behaviour of media users: 'Mediatization is *not* a technologically driven concept, since it is not the media as a technology that are causal, but the changes in how people communicate...' Then Krotz says the examination of technology may be justified, but only as an industrial artefact of a particular political economy:

'The technological evolution is also relevant for mediatization, especially as technologies are not merely a neutral means but are produced, modified and developed by industry for capitalist purposes' (Krotz, 2009, p. 25). Soon, his argument grows bolder, asserting that 'there is no (technically based) media logic' (Krotz, 2009, p. 26, his parentheses). Krotz seems to have dispatched technology as a relatively insignificant mediatization dynamic. But then, unexpectedly, in closing his discussion and looking towards the future, Krotz abruptly reverses himself, though not explicitly saying so, when he correctly observes that 'we will increasingly live in a world where all objects react "intelligently". It may then become more and more complicated to differentiate between an inner dialog and a dialog with such "living" objects' (Krotz, 2009, p. 37). This is precisely the sort of observation that should lead mediatization theorizing not to the avoidance or diminution of technology, as has been its tendency, but to the full incorporation of technology as a central media logic.[7]

Such a conceptual move is not an embrace of technology's independent power. In fact, there is a substantial literature that consistently stresses the powerful role of users in influencing the biography of technology. Technologies and their users, Nelly Oudshoorn and Trevor Pinch say, are the two sides of mutual co-construction (Oudshoorn and Pinch, 2005, pp. 2–3). Roger Silverstone, with his collaborator Leslie Haddon (Silverstone and Haddon, 1996), showed how future users are imagined, imperfectly, in the design process – possibly guided by the designer's provision of user manuals – and are central to the 'culture of the household' where the 'career of the technology' is strongly influenced (see Boddy, 2004 for a critical, cultural analysis of the introduction of media technologies in the USA).[8] The range and depth of these approaches to media technology put to rest concerns about the inevitability of technologically deterministic analysis (see also Thorburn and Jenkins, 2004).[9]

5. Living in polymedia[10]

People live their lives in a material world, and their relations with material objects go well beyond the instrumental. Much of the time, Daniel Miller says, objects even go unnoticed, deriving their power from acting like frames around paintings. Objects 'guide us towards the appropriate way to behave and remain unchallenged since we have no idea that we are being so directed' (Miller, 2010, p. 155).

From a psychological perspective, one's possessions are, as Mihaly Csikszentmihalyi and Eugene Rochberg-Halton argue, a part of one's self.

> People make order in their selves [...] by first creating and then interacting with the material world [...] [T]he things that surround us are inseparable from who we are. The material objects we use are not just tools we

can pick up and discard at our convenience; they constitute the framework of our experience that gives order to our otherwise shapeless selves.
(Csikszentmihalyi and Rochberg-Halton, 1981, p. 16)

They go on to say that this is especially true of domestic objects, which both help shape one's personality and express the most valued aspects of it.

Media objects are distinctive for their 'double articulation', as Roger Silverstone and Leslie Haddon famously put it (Silverstone and Haddon, 1996, p. 50). They argue that the meanings of the medium-as-technology develop out of its design, marketing and actual use. The device-as-medium produces cultural meanings through its content, which they say follow from the technology (Silverstone and Haddon, 1996, p. 62). In life, these features are inseparable. When a new medium is introduced, its materiality and content can seem excitingly different from existing media. But this is to some degree an illusion. Designed-in attributes of the new technology may aim to appear to have a natural relationship to established media, and content forms like programme genres usually borrow directly from what already exists – what Roger Fidler (1997, pp. 15–17) calls 'bridges of familiarity'. The historian of the printing press Elizabeth Eisenstein makes a strong case against 'the doctrine of supersession'. She says that new and old media tend to coexist, like the architectural styles of a great city (Eisenstein, 1997, p. 1056), not one medium eliminating another, the new wholly unlike the old.

These observations imply the very ordinariness of media and the regularity and depth of their integration into contemporary existence.

What people gain from engaging in this artifice is evident in studies of radio. Harold Mendelsohn (1964) discovered that listeners found companionship in their radio and used the rhythm of its programmes to bracket their day; it accompanied or changed their moods, and counteracted feelings of loneliness or boredom; they felt vicarious participation in distant events and acquired incidental knowledge that aided them in later social interaction. David Hendy (2010) daringly speculates that there may be a kind of magic available in the media, especially the experience of an aural medium heard in the darkness of night, when sound and time seem to flow together, creating what he calls 'deep radio'.[11]

Perhaps the relationship between people and media is fundamentally an unusual one. Research from a time when information machines were novel, awkward by today's standards, reveals that even then people experienced computer use as social interaction with implications for the user's own subjectivity. Byron Reeves and Clifford Nass (1996) say that people unconsciously perceive computers as social actors, and behave towards them in ways that Reeves and Nass characterize as politeness of the kind that would be appropriate when dealing with fellow humans. Based on her ethnographic work, Sherry Turkle argues that 'contemporary computational objects are increasingly *intimate machines'* (2004, p. 18; emphasis in the original), and that *'we often feel at one with our objects'* (2007, p. 9; emphasis in the original). She makes the strong claim that children today learn to expect emotional attachments with the devices they grow up with, and not in the way that people might feel warmly about their car – but 'in the way we have expectations about our emotional attachments to people' (Turkle, 2004, p. 26). Turkle (2005) believes that today information machines 'are experienced as both part of the self and of the external world' (p. 5), socially liminal, provoking an anxious 'permanent existence on the edge of things' (p. 15) between the material and the digitally virtual.

Significantly, and highly relevant to notions of intensified mediatization, her analysis of 'evocative objects' locates such things and the subjective practices they promote in terms of Donald Winnicott's object relations theory. She stresses Winnicott's view that they are the means of creating a transitional space, a playful, 'privileged zone in which outer and inner realities can meet' (Turkle, 2007, p. 315). And Turkle (2007, p. 314) underscores that this is a life-long enterprise, not limited to the developmental stages of childhood. In her most recent work, Turkle (2011) finds that

> Our new [digital] devices provide space for the emergence of a new state of the self, itself, split between the screen and the physical real, wired into existence through technology [...] The technology has become like a phantom limb [...] [Y]oung people are among the first to grow up with an expectation of continuous connection: always on, and always on them.
>
> (pp. 16, 17)[12]

Researchers term the process of bringing new media into everyday life 'domestication'. People adopt a device, and adapt themselves to it and it to their lives, especially at home. Today, however, as David Morley (2006, p. 206) points out, devices tend to arrive not individually but as 'ecosystems of technology' (Darrah, English-Lueck, and Freeman, 1998, p. 4). And, with the built environment increasingly integral to the digital infrastructure, 'the domestic realm itself is mediated and made fully electronic [...] the technologies are no longer supplementary to, but constitutive of, what the home itself now is' (Morley, 2006, p. 215). This new, increasingly pervasive sociotechnical condition poses basic challenges to conventional theories of media change. It demands thinking that goes beyond bridges of familiarity and supersession. It requires addressing what Mark Hansen (2006) calls the growing experience of 'mixed reality' in physical and virtual spaces, which, he contends, is increasingly a 'perceptuomotor' experience. Literature on digital games offers a model of what might be required. Introducing a MacArthur Foundation-funded collection of work on 'the ecology of games', Katie Salen, a graphic artist, game designer and academic, describes the conceptual lay of the land by simply defining her subject.

Gaming constitutes the sum total of activities, literacies, knowledge and practices activated in and around any instance of a game [...] It requires players to be fluent in a series of connected literacies that are multimodal, performative, productive and participatory in nature. It requires an attitude oriented toward risk taking, meaning creation, non-linear navigation, problem solving, an understanding of rule structures and an acknowledgement of agency within that structure, to name but a few.

(Salen, 2008, p. 9)

Substituting 'new media' for 'games' begins to suggest the complex analytical approach required to understand the developing features of polymedia and to incorporate technological considerations into mediatization theorizing.[13]

6. Everyware in 'mediatized worlds'

Visual technologies, from the earliest photography and film, have attempted to achieve the 'externalization of the mind', according to Lev Manovich (n. d.). The psychologist Hugo Munsterberg claimed in 1916 an isomorphic relationship between motion pictures and mental life; for example, the close-up was a direct display of focused mental attention. 'The mind', says Manovich, 'was projected on the screen; the inside became the outside' – all of this a literal attempt to 'objectify the psyche'. Manovich believes this general tendency has persisted with the introduction of each new visual medium, and that present-day cognitive science largely accepts the significance of mental imagery in the thinking process.

Perhaps the most extreme example of externalizing the mind can be found in the post-human literature, which foresees hybrid life forms (Fukuyama, 2003; Pepperell, 2003; Seidel, 2008; Smith and Morra, 2005).[14] Katherine Hayles' well-known book foresees the post-human environment as one that 'supplies synthetic sentience on demand, human consciousness would ride on top of a highly articulated and complex computational ecology in which many decisions, invisible to human attention, would be made by intelligent machines' (Hayles, 1999, p. 287). She speaks of 'extending embodied awareness in highly specific, local and material ways that would be impossible without electronic prosthesis' (p. 291). Something of the latter is now being attempted with human augmentation, or prosthesis-like intelligent attachments to the body that can, for instance, restore the functions of a missing limb or enhance natural abilities. Books written for general audiences introduce laboratory work on 'brain-machine interfaces' (Nicolelis, 2011), conferences report on the state of the field,[15] while the military funds a wide range of performance-enhancing technologies (Schachtman, 2007).

Ubiquitous computing envisions a world of globally networked, electronic intelligence that is integrally a part of the everyday world, but whose presence is scarcely noted. The term was coined in the late 1980s by Mark Weiser, a computer scientist at Xerox PARC (Palo Alto Research Center). He proposed the idea by observing how literate access to text had gone historically from the guarded capacity of a skilful few to what it is today: words on objects and surfaces in all corners of life. Weiser foresaw that eventually 'computing access will be everywhere: in the walls, on wrists, and in scrap computers (like scrap paper) lying about to be grabbed as needed'. Ubiquitous computing, or ubicomp, Weiser said, 'has as its goal the enhancing of computer use by making many computers available throughout the physical environment, but making them effectively invisible to the user' (Weiser, 1993, p. 71).[16] Other terms are also used to describe this phenomenon, including pervasive and ambient computing.[17] Physical and tangible computing are related, but emphasize the 'graspability' of objects with computing power and their responsiveness to human touch. The 'internet of things' has become a popular way of connecting the two general ideas (Naughton, 2011). Gregory Abowd and Elizabeth Mynatt (2000, pp. 42–6) use the phrase 'everyday computing' to characterize the terms of daily life that challenge both the conceptualization and design of ubiquitous computing. Mundane activity, into which ubicomp is embedded, is continuous, often without clear-cut beginnings and ends, and is frequently interrupted by the multiple activities that people as a matter of course engage in simultaneously. Adam Greenfield's *Everyware* (2006) cleverly renames the field and appropriately shifts attention away from computing machines and onto the environmental pervasiveness of a mediatized world. Much of this is already familiar territory. Mark Shepard calls it the sentient city, and describes a typical day living in it:

> [W]e pass through transportation systems using magnetic strip or Radio Frequency ID (RFID) tags to pay a fare; we coordinate meeting times and places through SMS text messaging on the run; we cluster in cafes and parks where WiFi is free; we move in and out of spaces blanketed by CCTV surveillance cameras monitored by computer vision systems. Artefacts and systems we interact with daily collect, store and process information about us, or are activated by our movements and transactions.
>
> (Shepard, 2011, pp. 18, 20)

In its intellectual gestation and application, the concept of ubiquitous computing has come to have several elements. It is, first, a way of describing readily available instruments that are quite task-specific, whose computational or communicative power is intended to make human actions more effective and efficient. It underscores, second, the widespread dispersal, or near universality, of these tools. Third, the concept recognizes that they are linked together, not only instruments of like kind, but across categories of devices. And, lastly, ubiquitous computing understands the instruments' intelligence to include a capacity for self-regulation and learning (see Poslad, 2009 for a thorough review of nearly every technical aspect of ubiquitous computing).

Analysis outside the strictly engineering literature has increasingly tended to explore the intertwining of built-in, seamless technological services and the spaces of social life. The architect and urbanist William Mitchell (2005) offers a knowledgeable example in his compelling account of the construction material that will realize the abstract qualities of ubiquitous computing:

> It now seems clear that the miracle material of the future will be a complex, fine-grained composite. It will consist of a substrate providing electrical power and digital networking, together with varying mixes of specialized, embedded particles that provide sensing capability, memory and processing power, communication, mechanical actuation and controlled variation in optical, thermal and acoustic properties. It will suck into the wallboard many of the current functions of lights, televisions and computer monitors, computing and communication devices, cleaning systems, thermostats and interior climate control systems. Its functionality will only be skin-deep, but that will be enough. (p. 97)

Human encounters with information technology are not merely an instrumental moment of 'using' a device to 'get' or 'do' something. Tools they are, but ever more an 'aesthetic event', as Lev Manovich (2007) puts it. The recent minimalist design of Apple products, Manovich thinks, seeks to make the device 'to want to disappear, fade into the background and become ambient'. This, he says, is an historically intermediate design position, 'between the stage of technology as a designed lifestyle object [...] and its future stage as an invisible infrastructure implanted inside other objects, architectural forms and human body'.

7. Conclusion

At the heart of the concept of mediatization is the notion that not only have media come to constitute an independent institutional sphere, but, in doing so, they have made other institutions dependent on them. This situation is characterized by unprecedented, constantly renegotiated and consequential interdependencies. Theories of mediatization generally claim that the media are powerful due to the deployment of their particular logic, or the forms and practices the media employ in creating representations and simulations. It can hardly be doubted that the technologies of media production, distribution and consumption are central to this process. Despite the obviousness of this observation, most mediation theorizing minimizes or avoids sustained discussion of technology, and has failed to incorporate it adequately into the developing concept.

This chapter has sought to begin a conversation on how to do just that, with an emphasis on living with new media technologies. This step is essential to the mediatization project because the theory is in danger of falling behind the unfolding of the very process it hopes to describe and explain. That is, the experience of mediatized worlds is intensifying – due to the rapid innovation of new media, which so far theory has neglected. Various terms describe the intensification of mediatization: mediapolis, media life, polymedia, ubiquitous computing, everyware, the sentient city, mediascapes. They all share the insight of Licklider and McLuhan: that humans will increasingly live in a world of intelligent (digital) devices where the boundaries among the social, the machinic and the biological will grow less distinct.

Incorporation of technology into mediatization theory-building would do well to focus on the new-media practices of young people. While it is too soon to know whether their behaviour is generational, related to their temporal position in the course of life or a function of the particular media of this time, it is clear that the way they use and relate to new media is distinctively different from other age groups. This may offer a partial view of what is to come for everyone in the near term. Attention to the introduction of innovative media need not stop at the conventional study of domestication. The psycho-social relationships that people create and sustain with the newest media, and their cultural implications, require ethnographic investigation. Other literatures can help. The growing study of gaming and simulation is different from most media analysis. But, because of the technological nature of emerging media, this research has much to contribute to the development of mediatization theory. Probably the best overall way to conceive of new media environments is suggested by ubiquitous computing. Taking steps of these sorts will only strengthen the analytical power of mediatization.

Notes

1. My thinking about the issues addressed in this chapter benefited from the appointment as visiting professor at the MIT Media Laboratory. I thank Christopher Csikszentmihalyi, then director of its Center for Future Civic Media, and his colleagues for that invigorating experience.
2. These are tendencies common to the larger system of technologies that Kevin Kelly calls the technium. He sees technology as having evolutionary characteristics, one of which is ever-growing intangibility and immateriality (Kelly, 2010, p. 67).
3. Nick Couldry (2008) and Sonia Livingstone (2009b) closely examine the analytical differences between the terms 'mediation' and 'mediatization' and their conceptual implications.

4. Licklider was the first head of computer research for DARPA (the US Department of Defense Advanced Research Projects Agency), whose ARPANET was the direct predecessor of the internet. Immediately before joining DARPA, while at MIT in 1962, Licklider is credited with writing memos that proposed a 'galactic network' of interconnected computers (Internet Society).
5. The ambition of mediatization as an idea is an open question. While still very much in its formative stage (Schulz's foundational, English-language article dates only from 2004), its conceptual boundaries are unclear; at times they seem quite far-reaching. As long ago as the mid-1980s, Quentin Skinner (1985) noted 'the return of grand theory in the human sciences'. The resistance of critical thinkers to 'all overarching theories and singular schemes of explanation', Skinner says, paradoxically resulted in the re-emergence of large-scale intellectual models (Skinner, 1985, p. 12). Skinner has in mind particularly Foucault, Feyerabend and Derrida, but his book includes chapters on Habermas, Levi-Strauss and others. Skinner also argues that still other analysts were quite explicitly taking broad approaches to 'the most pressing evaluative issues of the day', while others embraced the tradition of normative system-building (p. 14). Because of its rather large claims and its still formative nature, could mediatization take on the qualities of grand theory? Sonia Livingstone introduces the first collection of mediatization research by acknowledging that 'These are grand claims we are making [...] that the media mediate everything [...] ushering in historical changes' (Livingstone, 2009a, p. xi).
6. Much more recently, Altheide (2009, p. 21) takes a more conceptually diffuse view, saying:

> This logic, or the rationale, emphasis and orientation promoted by media production, processes and messages, tends to be evocative, encapsulated, highly thematic, familiar to audiences and easy to use...This is all consistent with a grand theory of the mass media and social change, an "ecology of communication", which refers to the structure, organization and accessibility of information technology, various forms, media and channels of information.

See Knut Lundby's (2009) critique of Altheide and Snow's use of Simmel's understanding of form. His position on media logic is similar to Couldry's.
7. Scott Lash (2005) says that present-day 'second modernity is one of generalized mediatization', which 'always involves technologization'. Interactive media, Lash asserts, promote life unavoidably lived within a mediascape. He also argues that new media disassemble classical forms and reassemble them into 'technological and information content', which people may experience as the flows which constitute a mediascape (that term is presented in Appadurai, 1990).
8. Though not widely known, it might be said that e-mail was invented by users. ARPANET was established to transmit data files between computers located at distant sites. But computer scientists quickly discovered the possibility for messaging (Hafner and Lyon, 1996, p. 189). The feature was not a central design element in field trial versions of Minitel (Vedel and Charon, 1989, p. 105). One of the American versions of (unsuccessful) videotex, Viewtron, found many of its users more drawn to messaging than to information databases (Fidler, 1997, p. 155).
9. Actor network theory goes further, destabilizing the innovation process to the extent of granting agency to a range of factors (actants), some material and non-human, along with intentional human ones, making what is 'social' problematic (Latour, 2005). For an early example of the shift from 'internalist' to contextual

to interactive, or systems or network approaches to the history of technology, see Thomas Hughes (1986). Making innovation a participatory process that directly and regularly involves users is the aim of Eric von Hippel's (2005) research.

10. This term is Mirca Madianou and Daniel Miller's (2011; 2013), who use it to describe the myriad interpersonal media choices that confront international migrants.

11. A group of British academics has recently explored the psychodynamics of radio listening (Media and the Inner World).

12. Mizuko Ito and her colleagues (2010, p. 1) underscore the scope and recency of this relationship by observing:

> Digital media and online communication have become a pervasive part of the everyday lives of youth in the United States. Social network sites, online games, video-sharing sites and gadgets such as iPods and mobile phones are now well-established fixtures of youth culture; it can be hard to believe that just a decade ago these technologies were barely present in the lives of US children and teens.

13. Another realm with implications for understanding the features of new media is simulation and serious games, which includes training applications. Much of its development, testing and use involves the military. For a primer, see Smith, 2009.

14. John Johnston (2008) reviews developments in cybernetics, artificial intelligence (AI) and artificial life (ALife), appreciating their differences through his notion of computational assemblage.

15. For the programme and some video of presentations at *H 2.0: New minds, new bodies, new identities*, a 2007 Media Lab symposium on 'technologies at the neural-digital interface', see MIT Media Lab, 2007. This gathering examined high-technology prostheses and their capacity to augment human bodily activity. An MIT press release summarizes the event (MIT News 2007).

16. Michael Dertouzos (2001, p. 17) says: 'When the computers "vanish," as motors did earlier, we'll know the Information Revolution has finished!'

17. In June 2010, the Santa Fe Complex presented a three-day event featuring 'an "ambient computing" environment that completely maps the complex in digital projection'. The event included a project in 'immersive projection technologies' (Ambient Pixel Project Review).

References

Abowd, G. D. and Mynatt, E. D. (2000) 'Charting past, present and future research in ubiquitous computing'. In: *ACM Transactions on Computer-Human Interaction*, 7(1), pp. 29–58.

Altheide, D. L. (2009) *Terror, post-9/11 and the media war* (New York: Peter Lang).

Altheide, D. L. and Snow, R. P. (1979) *Media logic* (Beverly Hills: Sage).

Ambient Pixel Project Review, http://sfcomplex.org/index.php?s=ambient, date accessed 5 July 2012.

Appadurai, A. (1990) 'Disjuncture and difference in the global cultural economy'. In: *Public Culture*, 2(2), pp. 1–24.

Boddy, W. (2004) *New media and popular imagination: Launching radio, television and digital media in the United States* (Oxford: Oxford University Press).

Couldry, N. (2008) 'Mediatization or mediation? Alternative understandings of the emergent space of digital storytelling'. In: *New Media and Society*, 10(3), pp. 373–91.

Csikszentmihalyi, M. and Rochberg-Halton, E. (1981) *The meaning of things: Domestic symbols and the self* (Cambridge: Cambridge University Press).

Darrah, C. N., English-Lueck, J. A. and Freeman, J. M. (1998) 'Living with technology'. In: *Anthropology News*, 39(9), pp. 1–4.

Dertouzos, M. L. (2001) *The unfinished revolution: Human-centered computers and what they can do for us* (New York: HarperCollins).

Deuze, M. (2011) 'Media life'. In: *Media, Culture and Society*, 33(1), pp. 137–48.

Eisenstein, E. (1997) 'From the printed word to the moving image'. In: *Social Research*, 64(3), pp. 1049–66.

Fidler, R. (1997) *Mediamorphosis: Understanding new media* (Thousand Oaks, CA: Pine Forge Press).

Fukuyama, F. (2003) *Our posthuman future: Consequences of the biotechnology revolution* (London: Profile Books).

Greenfield, A. (2006) *Everyware: The dawning of ubiquitous computing* (Berkeley: New Riders).

Hafner, K. and Lyon, M. (1996) *Where wizards stay up late: The origins of the internet* (New York: Simon and Schuster).

Hansen, M. B. N. (2006) *Bodies in code: Interfaces with digital media* (New York: Routledge).

Hayles, N. K. (1999) *How we became posthuman: Virtual bodies in cybernetics, literature and informatics* (Chicago: University of Chicago Press).

Hendy, D. (2010) 'Listening in the dark: Night-time radio and a "deep history" of media'. In: *Media History*, 16(2), pp. 215–32.

Hippel, E. v. (2005) *Democratizing innovation* (Cambridge: MIT Press).

Hjarvard, S. (2004) 'From bricks to bytes: The mediatization of a global toy industry'. In: Bondebjerg, I. and Golding, P. (eds) *European culture and the media: Changing media – changing Europe* (Bristol: Intellect Books).

Hjarvard, S. (2009) 'Soft individualism: Media and the changing social character'. In: Lundby, K. (ed.) *Mediatization: Concept, changes, consequences* (New York: Peter Lang).

Hughes, T. P. (1986) 'The seamless web: Technology, science, etcetera, etcetera'. In: *Social Studies of Science*, 16(2), pp. 281–92.

Internet Society, www.isoc.org/internet/history/brief.shtml#JCRL62, date accessed 5 July 2012.

Ito, M.; Baumer, S., Bittani, M., boyd, d., Cody, R., Herr-Stephenson, B., Horst, H. A., Lange, P. G., Mahendran, D., Martínez, K. Z., Pascoe, C. J., Perkel, D., Robinson, L., Sims, C. and Tripp, L. (2010) *Hanging out, messing around and geeking out: Kids living and learning with new media* (Cambridge: MIT Press).

Johnston, J. (2008) *The allure of machinic life: Cybernetics, artificial life and the new AI* (Cambridge: MIT Press).

Kelly, K. (2010) *What technology wants* (New York: Viking).

Krotz, F. (2007) 'The meta-process of "mediatization" as a conceptual frame'. In: *Global Media and Communication*, 3(3), pp. 256–60.

Krotz, F. (2009) 'Mediatization: A concept with which to grasp media and societal change'. In: Lundby, K. (ed.) *Mediatization: Concept, changes, consequences* (New York: Peter Lang).

Lash, S. (2005) *Intensive media – modernity and algorithm* (Draft). http://roundtable. kein.org/node/125, date accessed 5 July 2012.

Latour, B. (2005) *Reassembling the social: An introduction to actor-network-theory* (Oxford: Oxford University Press).

Licklider, J. C. R. (1960) 'Man-computer symbiosis'. In: *IRE Transactions on Human Factors in Electronics*, HFE-1, 4–11.

Livingstone, S. (2009a) 'Foreword: Coming to terms with "mediatization"'. In: Lundby, K. (ed.) *Mediatization: Concept, changes, consequences* (New York: Peter Lang).

Livingstone, S. (2009b) 'On the mediation of everything: ICA presidential address 2008'. In: *Journal of Communication*, 59(1), pp. 1–18.

Lundby, K. (2009) 'Media logic: Looking for social interaction'. In: Lundby, K. (ed.) *Mediatization: Concept, changes, consequences* (New York: Peter Lang).

Manovich, Lev (n. d.) *From the externalization of the psyche to the implantation of technology.* http://www.manovich.net/TEXT/externalization.html, date accessed 5 July 2012.

Manovich, L. (2007) 'Interaction as an aesthetic event'. In: Keynote address *Softspace: contemporary interactive environments* (London: Tate Modern Museum), http://manovich.net/articles/, date accessed 5 July 2012.

McLuhan, M. (1964) *Understanding media: The extensions of man* (New York: McGraw Hill).

Madianou, M. and Miller, D. (2011) *Migration and new media: Transnational families and polymedia* (London: Routledge).

Madianou, M. and Miller, D. (2013) 'Polymedia: Towards a new theory of digital media in interpersonal communication'. In: *International Journal of Cultural Studies*, 16(2), pp. 169–87.

Media and the Inner World, http://www.miwnet.org/Website/ date accessed 16 November 2013.

Mendelsohn, H. (1964) 'Listening to radio'. In: Dexter, L. A. and White, D. M. (eds) *People, society, and mass communication* (Glencoe, IL: Free Press), pp. 239–49.

Miller, D. (2010) *Stuff* (Cambridge: Polity Press).

Mitchell, W. J. (2005) 'Elegy for a G-4'. In: *Placing words: Symbols, space and the city* (Cambridge: MIT Press).

MIT Media Lab (2007) http://h20.media.mit.edu/, date accessed 5 July 2012.

MIT News (2007) http://web.mit.edu/newsoffice/2007/medialab-h20.html, date accessed 5 July 2012.

Morley, D. (2006) *Media, modernity and technology: The geography of the new* (London: Routledge).

Naughton, J. (2011) 'The internet of things: It's big but it's not always very clever...' In: *The Observer*, 20 March, www.guardian.co.uk/technology/2011/mar/20/the-internet-of-things-john-naughton, date accessed 5 July 2012.

Nicolelis, M. (2011) *Beyond boundaries: The new neuroscience of connecting brains with machines – and how it will change our lives* (New York: Times Books).

Oudshoorn, N. and Pinch, T. (2005) 'How users and non-users matter'. In: Oudshoorn, N. and Pinch, T. (eds) *How users matter: The co-construction of users and technology* (Cambridge: MIT Press).

Pepperell, R. (2003) *The posthuman condition: Consciousness beyond the brain* (Bristol: Intellect).

Poslad, S. (2009) *Ubiquitous computing: Smart devices, environments and interactions* (Chichester: John Wiley and Sons).

Reeves, B. and Nass, C. (1996) *The media equation: How people treat computers, television and new media like real people and places* (Cambridge: Cambridge University Press).

Rothenbuhler, E. W. (2009) 'Continuities: Communicative form and institutionalization'. In: Lundby, K. (ed.) *Mediatization: Concept, changes, consequences* (New York: Peter Lang).

Salen, K. (2008) 'Toward an ecology of gaming'. In: Salen, K. (ed.) *The ecology of games: Connecting youth, games and learning* (Cambridge: MIT Press).

Schachtman, N. (2007) 'Be more than you can be'. In: *Wired*, http://www.wired.com/wired/archive/15.03/bemore.html, date accessed 5 July 2012.

Schulz, W. (2004) 'Reconstructing mediatization as an analytical concept'. In: *European Journal of Communication*, 19(1), pp. 87–101.

Seidel, A. (2008) *Philosophical explorations of posthumanity* (Lanham, MD: Lexington Books).

Shepard, M. (2011) 'Toward the sentient city'. In: Shepard, M. (ed.) *Sentient city: Ubiquitous computing, architecture and the future of urban space* (Cambridge: MIT Press).

Silverstone, R. (2006) *Media and morality: On the rise of the mediapolis* (Cambridge: Polity).

Silverstone, R. and Haddon, L. (1996) 'Design and the domestication of information and communication technologies: Technical change and everyday life'. In: Mansell, R. and Silverstone, R. (eds) *Communication by design: The politics of information and communication technologies* (Oxford: Oxford University Press).

Skinner, Q. (1985) 'Introduction: The return of grand theory'. In: Skinner, Q. (ed.) *The return of grand theory in the human sciences* (Cambridge: Cambridge University Press).

Smith, M. and Morra, J. (eds) (2005) *The prosthetic impulse: From a posthuman present to a biocultural future* (Cambridge: MIT Press).

Smith, R. D. (2009) *Military simulation and serious games: Where we came from and where we are going* (Orlando, FL: Modelbenders Press).

Thorburn, D. and Jenkins, H. (2004) 'Introduction: Towards an aesthetics of transition'. In: Thorburn, D. and Jenkins, H. (eds) *Rethinking media change: The aesthetics of transition* (Cambridge: MIT Press).

Turkle, S. (2004) 'Whither psychoanalysis in computer culture?' In: *Psychoanalytic Psychology*, 21(1), pp. 16–30.

Turkle, S. (2005) *The second self: Computers and the human spirit*, 20th ann. ed. (Cambridge: MIT Press).

Turkle, S. (2007) *Evocative objects: Things we think with* (Cambridge: MIT Press).

Turkle, S. (2011) *Alone together: Why we expect more from technology and less from each other* (New York: Basic Books).

Vedel, T. and Charon, J. M. (1989) 'Videotex in France: The invention of a mass medium?' In: Schneider, V.,Thomas, G. and Vedel, T. (eds) *Pathways to telematics: The politics of videotex in Britain, France and the Federal Republic of Germany*. Unpublished.

Weiser, M. (1993) 'Ubiquitous computing'. In: *Computer*, 26(10), pp. 71–2.

Winner, L. (1986) *The whale and the reactor: A search for limits in an age of high technology* (Chicago: University of Chicago Press).

8
From Mediation to Mediatization: The Institutionalization of New Media

Stig Hjarvard

> We shape our dwellings, and afterwards our dwellings shape us.
>
> Winston Churchill (1944)

1. Introduction

Within both scholarly research and wider public debate, profound influence on contemporary cultural and social affairs – positively and negatively – is attributed to new media, such as the internet and mobile phones. New media are regarded as either revolutionizing or significantly transforming culture and society, at both the level of global political power and the level of intimate human relationships. At the macro level of social affairs, Castells (2009) suggests that the internet allows a historically new form of 'mass self-communication' that may reconfigure the distribution and exercise of power in the network society. At the micro level of social affairs, Turkle (2011) provides a very critical view of new media and emphasizes that social relationships suffer in an online world: 'The ties we form through the internet are not, in the end, the ties that bind. But they are the ties that preoccupy [...] We defend connectivity as a way to be close, even as we effectively hide from each other' (pp. 280–1). New media are also transforming older forms of mass communication, such as broadcasting and journalism, to the extent that we are witnessing a paradigmatic shift in mediated communication. Deuze (2007) prophesies that 'journalism as it is, is coming to an end. The boundaries between journalism and other forms of public communication [...] are vanishing, the internet makes all other types of news media rather obsolete' (p. 141).

There is little doubt that new media influence and transform cultural and social affairs, including older forms of media, in a variety of ways, yet there are disagreements concerning the degree and character of this influence and even more mixed opinions about the positive or negative consequences of new media. The aim of this article is not to discuss new media's level of influence or to enter into a normative assessment of this influence. Instead, the article seeks to consider theoretically *how* we can account for the ways in which new media may influence culture and society and in *what ways* this influence differs from that of old media, that is, mass media. Taking our point of departure in recent discussions of new media in mediatization theory, we provide a sociological framework for discussing new media's influence – relative to old media – on culture and society. The notion of 'mediatized worlds' proposed by Hepp (2013) and Krotz and Hepp (2013) (see also their introduction to this volume) stresses the need for a grounded approach considering the media practices of smaller lifeworld contexts. The institutional perspective put forward in this article shares the ambition to ground the study of mediatization empirically (Hjarvard, 2013; Hjarvard and Petersen, 2013) and the need to consider human agency as co-constitutive of social change. It may, however, depart from the bottom-up perspective of 'mediatized worlds' by insisting on the duality of structure and agency and by placing the long-term institutionalization of media-influenced patterns of social interaction at the heart of the theory of mediatization.

The spread of new media may not only call into question key propositions of mediatization theory but also provide evidence for a more pronounced and complex mediatization of cultural and social phenomena. Schulz (2004) asks whether the growing prominence of new media means 'the end of mediatization?' (p. 94). Early studies of mediatization have concerned the role of mass media and their control over communicative resources. Such centralized media control is clearly challenged by new media's capacity to allow almost anyone to enter the media and bypass traditional gatekeepers. Schulz (2004) provides a preliminary answer to his own question by stating that 'mediatization' may remain a useful term in the study of new media, assuming that one looks beyond particular forms of media and instead considers their various basic functions: 'Explicating mediatization with reference to basic performances and functions of the medium in communication processes, as I have suggested, makes the concept applicable to all kinds of media, old and new' (Schulz, 2004, pp. 98–9). We will take this approach in the following discussion and will consider *key characteristics and social functions* of media rather than focusing on particular types of media. We will, however, not only consider such media characteristics and functions in relation to the communication process itself but will also take into account how the uses and functions of both old and new media become institutionalized in various social and cultural contexts.

Finnemann (2011) provides a critical examination of existing conceptualizations of new media within mediatization research. He claims that none of the existing accounts offer a satisfactory definition of digital media and that they therefore fail to recognize the epochal shift to a new 'media matrix' in which interrelations between media and society are spelled out differently than in the mass media era. As an alternative to the prevailing concept of media logics (Hjarvard, 2008; Strömbäck, 2008), he puts forward the concept of a 'specific grammar of the internet and mobile devices' (Finnemann, 2011, p. 86). Jensen (2013) also criticizes mediatization research for having paid too little attention to digital media and the material aspects of technologies. Furthermore, Jensen questions the extent to which new media operate according to similar institutional characteristics as mass media have done in the past (for instance, journalism as the fourth estate). In the following analysis, we will address these critical interventions in a constructive manner as a means of building a more coherent framework for understanding how new media may influence culture and society. Before doing so, however, we will clarify our notion of mediatization relative to other contributions to the field and will specify our theoretical approach in analyzing digital media.

2. From mediation to mediatization

In general, media and communication studies have been preoccupied with the study of *mediation*. By mediation, we usually understand the use of a medium for communication and interaction. Politicians may mediate political messages through newspapers in order to influence their constituencies, and individuals may use Facebook to both communicate and interact with their 'friends' on a continual basis. The choice of medium and the particular way in which it is put to use may have a considerable impact not only on the form and content of the message but also on the relationship between senders and receivers and the ways in which they are influenced by the communicative encounter. The study of mediation looks for media's impact on specific communicative situations situated in time and space. Meanwhile, the study of *mediatization* considers the long-term structural transformations of media's role in contemporary culture and society. The study of mediation may provide extensive information about media's influence on communicative practice. Nevertheless, since the process of mediation itself does not alter the relationship between media, culture and society, we must shift our attention to the process of mediatization in order to understand how media, culture and society are mutually implicated in processes of change. The media influence not just the communication circuit of senders, messages and receivers but also the changing relationship between media and other cultural and social spheres. The distinction between mediation and mediatization is theoretically and analytically important, but the actual processes of mediation and mediatization are not empirically distinct, since the accumulated effect of changing mediation practices can represent an instance of mediatization. Take, for instance, the introduction of internet banking and the subsequent transformation of a practice of doing banking business through face-to-face encounters in a physical location to a predominantly mediated activity. This is part of a general mediatization of the financial sector in which digital media have come to constitute an important element of this business sector's technological and institutional infrastructure.

Due to terminological differences between various traditions of media research, the distinction between mediation and mediatization is somewhat blurred. The term 'mediatization' has been used for several decades within continental European research to denote structural transformations in the relationship between media and wider society, for instance, in studies on the mediatization of politics (Mazzoleni and Schulz, 1999; Strömbäck, 2008). The concept of 'mediatization' has been widely used within Scandinavian and German media research in particular (Asp, 1990; Hepp, 2012; 2013; Hjarvard, 2008; 2013; Krotz, 2009). In an Anglo-American context, 'mediation' has primarily referred to mediated communication, but Altheide and Snow (1988) and Silverstone (2007) have also used the term 'mediation' in ways resembling the meaning of 'mediatization' within the continental European research tradition, that is, as the long-term structural influence of media on society. Until recently, Anglo-American research has – with a few exceptions, such as Thompson (1995) – preferred a single term to denote several meanings, ranging from the isolated act of communication via a medium to structural changes in society. Recent international discussions seem to have settled the terminological disagreements in favour of a continental European distinction between 'mediatization' (denoting the long-term structural dimension) and 'mediation' (signifying the use of media in communicative encounters) (see also Lundby, 2009).

3. Definition

More specifically, we use the term 'mediatization' to denote the intensified and changing importance of the media in culture and society. By the mediatization of culture and society, we mean the processes whereby culture and society become increasingly dependent on the media and their modus operandi or media logic. These processes exhibit a *duality*, in that various forms of media have become *integrated* into the everyday practices of other social institutions and cultural spheres while also acquiring the status of a semi-independent institution *in its own right*. The media are simultaneously 'out-there' in society, comprising an institution with a certain momentum of its own, and 'in-here' as part of the lifeworld practices of family, workplace and so on. As a result, social interaction – inside institutions, between institutions, and in society at large – increasingly involves media. By a 'media logic', we do not mean a single or unified logic behind all forms of media; this is, rather, a conceptual shorthand for the institutional, aesthetic and technological modus operandi of media, including the ways in which media distribute material and symbolic resources as well as operating with the help of formal and informal rules. In this light, institutions are characterized by different logics. For instance, the institution of politics is governed by various formal and informal rules that may, in some respects, be at odds with media's modus operandi. Since politics and media are mutually dependent, these institutions must adjust their internal functioning to one another's logics, allowing various types and degrees of mediatized politics and politicized media.

In order to understand how the media, including new media, come to influence various social institutions and cultural domains, we must combine two levels of analysis: (1) the structuring influence of the media in situated social interaction and (2) the institutionalization of the media, both within other institutions and through the development of the media as a semi-independent institution in themselves. Media co-structure communication and interaction (i.e., the level of mediation), but mediatization occurs through the institutionalization of particular patterns of interaction (formal and informal rules) and allocation of interactional resources within a particular social institution or cultural sphere. The media should not be considered an external factor to either social interaction or social institutions but have, on the contrary, become integral to the structuration of both. In the following, we consider new media's role in processes of mediatization by combining several theoretical perspectives. Structuration theory provides the overall theoretical framework for understanding the mutually constitutive role of social interaction and institutions (Giddens, 1984). This 'meta-theoretical' perspective is combined with the analytical framework of 'institutional logics' from organizational theory (Thornton, Ocasio and Lounsbury, 2012). The structuring influence of media on social interaction is developed through a combination of Gibson's (1979) theory of affordances and Goffman's (1956; 1972) theory of social interaction, with particular emphasis on his notion of 'territory'.

4. The limits of linguistic metaphors

According to Finnemann (2011), the importance of digital media as a whole far exceeds the role of their component parts individually. While the majority of the 20th century's media system was structured around television as the dominant medium, the media system – or media matrix – of the 21st century is structured around the internet as the dominant medium. Due to the universal character of the digital alphabet (the binary code), all other media are transformed and digitalized, becoming part of a fifth media matrix dominated by the specific 'grammar' of the internet. Finnemann rejects the notion of a media logic, partly because this notion was first developed in the era of the fourth media matrix, that is, mass media like the press, radio and television. Digital media allow three unique communicative features (hypertext, multimodality and interactivity), yet these features do not in themselves constitute a digital media grammar, says Finnemann. Such a grammar depends on the instantiation and utilization of these unique features within a cultural, social and political context. The combination of digital affordances and their social utilization allows Finnemann to stipulate a 'grammar' of the internet consisting of five elements: (1) it is a medium for both public and private communication (and mixtures thereof); (2) it allows variation of reach, from the local to the global; (3) it is a medium for differentiated communication in terms of possible connections (one-to-one, few-to many, etc.); (4) it offers constant availability; and (5) it unites corporations, individuals and public institutions on the same platform (Finnemann, 2011, pp. 83–4).

Finnemann's (2011) critical intervention is useful because it stresses the need to reconsider our notion of 'media' and media affordances in light of digitalization, and his characterization of digital media is insightful in many ways: hypertext, multimodality and interactivity are key features of the new media system. His preference for linguistic metaphors ('grammar' and 'alphabet') does, however, bestow on his argument a sense of stringency that it does not possess. In linguistics, 'grammar' usually denotes a body of structuring principles and rules governing the use of a language, but none of Finnemann's five elements of a grammar for new media suggest such a regulating or structuring function. They provide an apt description of the almost endless diversity of communicative possibilities that new media may support, but they do not suggest how new media may come to structure, regulate or even limit communicative encounters or influence other cultural and social institutions. For instance, being a medium of both public and private communication does not entail any structuring function of a 'grammar'. In a similar vein, communicative features like multimodality and interactivity do not suggest regulating or rule-governing mechanisms but signal, rather, an ever-growing diversity and complexity of communicative possibilities.

Finnemann's description of the fundamental 'alphabet' of the digital media – the binary code – points to the distinct formal feature of new media, which makes possible an integration of all media on a common platform. However, we cannot – even from a linguistic point of view – reduce either old or new media to such a fundamental linguistic alphabet. The new media system is, as Finnemann himself notes, multimodal. In other words, it comprises a variety of modes of expression such as oral speech, written texts and pictures as well as a variety of genres and forms of media, including audiovisual narratives, news and so on. Digitalization permits new ways of using and recombining these modes of expression, genres and forms of media, yet, in order to study how these may influence communication and social interaction, we can infer but little from simply referring to the fundamental digital binary code itself. News, audiovisual narratives and social network media are influenced by digitalization, but they are also communicative genres or forms of media of a *higher order* and *possess a structure of their own.*

These characteristics cannot be reduced to their elementary binary composition. Media and genres are simultaneously communicative formats with particular affordances and institutionalized forms of social interaction. The study of their possible imprint on culture and society must primarily consider these levels of analysis. Digitalization is a key process in the ongoing restructuration of the media system itself, but the interaction between new and renewed 'old' media, on the one hand, and wider culture and society, on the other hand, is not structured by a digital binary alphabet.

Finnemann's (2011) concept of a fifth 'media matrix' centred on the internet is inspired by Meyrowitz's (1986) use of the term to describe the 'media matrix' of radio and television. Such a categorization is certainly a useful means of gaining an overview of major historical stages or transformations in the media environment, but it may also prove misleading in the study of mediatization. Finnemann's (2011, p. 86) emphasis on the 'unique properties shared only by digital media' suggests that mediatization is predominantly caused and structured by media's own development and the advent of a new media matrix dominated by a new medium with a unifying 'grammar' rather than by a co-development or interaction between media and culture and society. Here, media's influence is attributed to either the distinct features of a macro-level media matrix or the micro level of digital media's inner linguistic features (i.e., the binary code). The framework, however, has little to say concerning the role of media at the level of social interaction or the institutionalization of media practices within culture and society.

The theoretical framework suggested by Finnemann (2011) tends to be media-centric in two ways. For one thing, it does not allow us to consider how culture and society structure the development of (new) media: the development of new media may, for instance, be partly spurred and structured by processes of globalization, neoliberal deregulation and commercialization. Furthermore, it suggests that all forms of media have been remodelled relative to one particular medium, the internet, and thus does not take into account the considerable continuities and differences that also exist within the media system. For instance, despite the advent of new media, the field of political communication remains focused on mass media and the formation of public opinion. Political blogs, political fundraising through micro-donations via the internet and so on have to some extent changed patterns of political communication, but the mass media are still important, and interpersonal, network and mass media serve many similar political functions. As Schulz (2004) suggests, we should not merely consider particular types of media when studying mediatization but should also study communicative functions and performances.

Instead of opting for linguistic metaphors to describe the modus operandi of new media, we will develop the notion of media logics from an institutional perspective. Finnemann (2011) correctly specifies a range of new communicative characteristics and features made possible by new media, but, in order to also consider how new media may be implicated in (formal and informal) rule regulation and allocation of resources for social interaction, we must situate our analysis at a different analytical level than those suggested by linguistic metaphors. More precisely, we consider the co-structuring of social interaction and the institutionalization of patterns of interaction across various domains.

5. Institutions and institutionalizations

When applying an institutional perspective, it is important to consider how we might think of the various media – particularly new media – as institutions. Institutions should not be confused with organizations, which are specific and empirical entities that may be part of an institution but that also interact with wider society. In this sense, CNN and Amazon are media organizations, not institutions. From a sociological perspective, an institution is an identifiable domain or field of social life that is governed by a particular set of formal and informal rules, displays a particular structure, serves certain social functions, and allocates resources for action in various ways. Family, politics and religion can be considered institutions from this perspective. Historically, mass media advanced in order to create and sustain public spheres of either political, cultural or commercial nature, or mixtures thereof. Across individual organizations, the media developed common practices, professional standards and regulatory frameworks. In the past, mass media were controlled primarily by other social institutions. For instance, the political press was significantly influenced by the logics of the political institution. Similarly, many journals and magazines were partly controlled by religious, cultural or scientific institutions. Today, various mass media have lost some of their dependency on other institutions and have acquired a higher degree of control over important resources in society, including public information and attention. We may, therefore, think of these media as comprising a semi-independent institution in society, controlling to some extent the ways in which other institutions access communicative resources and the public spheres.

Jensen (2013) recognizes the institutional character of the old mass media, but is sceptical of the extent to which we can also consider forms of new media as institutions in the same sense, inasmuch as they operate according to different principles:

> Certainly, classic mass media – from newspapers to broadcasting – could be seen to follow legal, professional, and market-based *rules* that made for a comparatively centralized media logic assigning *resources* – attention, legitimacy and, in time, material benefits – to other cultural, political, and economic institutions. But, such a central perspective hardly applies

to the totality of communicative uses to which either telephones or the internet are put across private and public settings.

(Jensen, 2013, emphasis in original, pp. 209–10)

The spread and integration of new forms of media, such as the internet and mobile phones, into the daily practices of nearly all social contexts, including family, work, politics, economics and so on, certainly makes it difficult to regard all practices and uses of these types of media as governed by comparable rules and similar ways of allocating resources. This is true not only of new media in contrast to old media but also of some forms of new media compared with other forms of new media. The use of the internet in the financial sector is governed by quite different rules and patterns of resource allocation than is the case for the use of the internet in workplaces or the use of mobile phones in the family. These three examples demonstrate another common characteristic of new media compared with mass media, namely, their integration in a variety of private and semi-private institutional settings. New media enable, as Finnemann (2011) stipulates, both private and public forms of communication and mixtures thereof, and, as far as non-public uses are concerned, they are less likely to operate according to the logics of a semi-independent media institution. Here, the institutional dimension is less concerned with the media as part of a media institution governing access to public information and attention than with the *process of institutionalization* of patterns of social interaction within other social domains. This process of institutionalization is not only – and perhaps not even predominantly – influenced by the media, yet it may very well be chiefly informed by the logics of practices within a particular institution such as the family or workplace. Ling (2008), for instance, demonstrates how the mobile phone is used primarily to solve practical tasks and maintain social ties between family members and a limited number of friends, and its patterns of use are, thus, influenced by existing patterns of interaction in the household. The initial impetus to acquire and make use of (new) media in various contexts may initially be prompted by the authority of a more generalized media institution promising innovation, efficiency or sociability. The media will, however, gradually be integrated within various contexts and influenced by the particular institution and contexts in question.

In the process of institutionalizing patterns of social interaction, the media may be put to a variety of uses, but the media's affordances – that is, the communicative possibilities enabled by the media's technological, aesthetic and social characteristics – influence *which* patterns of social interaction become more dominant than others and *how* they are spelled out. E-mails may be put to a variety of uses, but the e-mail's affordances suggest that some uses are more likely to occur than others. In general, the affordances structure the way in which e-mails are used. We will consider the *enabling*, *limiting* and *structuring* features in more detail below. Generally speaking, however, the main point is that the influence of media used for private forms of interaction stems more from the media's affordances and less from a semi-independent media institution's modus operandi. New media serve a variety of public communicative functions, and their uses are often intertwined with mass media. For instance, journalistic forms of news media comprise a wide range of new media types and genres, such as websites, mobile phones, blogs and so on; and advertising is a similarly cross-media activity. In the case of public communicative functions, new media may not necessarily work according to different social rules or allocate resources in different ways compared with mass media. In these cases, new and old media converge not only technologically but also in terms of professional standards, claims to public legitimacy, social functions and so on. In the process of convergence, the affordances of new media do not, of course, leave old media untouched. For instance, the internet has generally created an economic crisis for the news media industry, because advertising revenue is increasingly produced in other media and not reinvested in journalism to the same extent as previously (Picard, 2008). The distinction between media use for private and public communication is not absolute, particularly because both old and new media transgress the private–public distinction and create new forms of semi-public or semi-private arenas. The distinction may, nevertheless, be useful, since the media's modus operandi tends to converge relative to particular communicative functions. Public communicative functions tend to be embedded within a semi-independent media institution, whereas private communicative functions tend to be influenced by the affordances of the media outside the realm of a media institution.

6. Media as material technology

More generally, Jensen (2013, p. 215) posits that 'mediatization research has given relatively little attention to the concrete physical structures conditioning and, in some sense, causing mediatization'. This is an apt critique and can, at least partly, be explained by the fact that discussions of mediatization have been promoted by media scholars with social sciences and humanities inclinations and have gained only limited ground within studies of new technology. It may also be partly explained by the efforts of mediatization scholars to distance themselves from the more technologically deterministic and McLuhan-type versions of medium theory or media ecology, whereby they have come to stress the cultural and social components of media developments at the expense of their material and technological dimensions.

Whatever the reasons for this may be, it is important to consider the media as technologies and material objects. Users and audiences cannot simply use or interpret media in any way they like; media's material and technological characteristics (as well as their social and symbolic features) enable, limit and structure communication and interaction in various ways. Hutchby (2001; 2003) suggests that Gibson's (1979) concept of affordance offers a way out of the existing theoretical dichotomy between technological determinism, on the one hand, and radical social construction of technology, on the other:

> I will argue that affordances are functional and relational aspects which frame, while not determining, the possibilities for agentic action in relation to an object. In this way, technologies can be understood as artefacts which may be both shaped by and shaping of the practices humans use in interaction with, around and through them.
>
> (Hutchby, 2001, p. 444)

By affordances of a medium, we understand the possibilities of communication and interaction that a particular medium affords a potential user. The user may or may not use these affordances, and may end up taking advantage of some affordances that were not anticipated by the developers of the medium. A medium, however, may also constrain certain forms of interaction and make particular forms of interaction much easier compared with existing forms of mediated or non-mediated interaction. Furthermore, as Norman (1990) stresses in his study of technological designs, affordances are not only functional aspects of a material artefact but are also relationally defined, and should thus be labelled as 'perceived affordances'. A media technology's affordances must be recognized by users as both possible and useful ways of communicating and interacting, otherwise the technology will fail regardless of its numerous technical features.

Parallel to structuration theory's insistence on the co-constitutive relationship between agency and social structure (Giddens, 1984), we should also consider media technologies as both *shaped by* humans and society and *shaping* human interaction and society. The balance between the media technology as shaped by and shaping human interaction and society may, however, differ over the course of technology's life cycle. Hughes (1994) argues that a technology gains a momentum of its own accord as it passes from the developmental stage and becomes fully implemented in society. In the initial stages of technological development, the notion of the social shaping of technology may provide the best explanatory framework for the ways in which the technology becomes shaped by various social factors, such as economic considerations, cultural values, existing institutional frameworks, research priorities and so on. These stages also include the initial uses of a media technology, in which the users may experiment in various ways in order to make use of and make sense of the new medium. However, once the phase of shaping a technological prototype is complete, and the technology has been put to use on a wider scale within various societal institutions, it acquires a momentum that makes it less malleable by the actions of individual users. Here, a moderate sense of technological determinism may be more appropriate for describing how a media technology can enable, limit and structure the ways in which we use various types of media (Hughes 1994; cf. Jensen 2013). It is not only the presence of a fully developed material technology in itself that is responsible for this momentum; the institutionalization of a medium also makes it more difficult for individual users to transform the medium. Institutionalization involves a more permanent allocation of resources, in terms of both financial investment and social learning of how to use the medium. For instance, once radio had developed as a national broadcast medium in the 1920s and had been bought and installed in most households during the 1930s, it shaped social interaction by, through and around the medium, and the individual user had few opportunities and little encouragement to put the radio to significantly alternative use. Similarly, a social network application like Facebook is initially shaped by particular developers' ideas and outlooks as well as by the wider cultural environment and media system. Once it has achieved a dominant position, however, it structures social interaction in ways that are difficult for individual users to circumvent. The influence of media, both as an artefact and as a material infrastructure, may thus resemble that of buildings and the geographical environment. In the words of Winston Churchill: 'We shape our dwellings, and afterwards our dwellings shape us.'

7. Mediated territories

In order to discuss how new media may influence social interaction and thereby institutionalize new patterns of social behaviour, we will consider the concept of affordances within Goffman's (1956; 1972) theatre model of social interaction and his notion of territory. According to Goffman, social interaction is steered by role-playing, in which the individual actors perform particular social roles appropriate to the particular social situations at hand. In addition to verbal and non-verbal communication and the use of various 'props' (costumes, tables, etc.), the use of territory is an important structuring component of any social interaction. Goffman's fundamental distinction between 'on stage' and 'backstage' demarcates two territories with different situational properties, possible participants, and sets of appropriate behaviour. In Goffman's theatre model, the use of territory also includes the individual's performative control of territory extending from the body. The individual self seeks to influence the course of interaction by exposing or hiding information about the performing self. As Meyrowitz (1986) has argued, Goffman's model of interaction fundamentally concerns information access in different territories: it concerns the kinds of information available to participants on stage, backstage and – in the case of mediated interaction – to audiences and users of communication media who are not present on the physical stage of interaction but who are nevertheless connected with one another on a virtual stage.

Meyrowitz (1986) demonstrates how mass media – particularly television – have been instrumental in modifying the norms of public social interaction by connecting various hitherto disconnected and partly private domains into a unified public space. A general effect of these transformations, Meyrowitz (1986) argues, was the spread of a middle-region behavioural norm encompassing elements of both private and public norms of behaviour. New media push these territorial transformations a step further by allowing every individual to communicate and interact across various social territories. In contrast to mass media, new media do not necessarily establish public forms of communication but can, rather, establish new configurations of private and semi-private forms of communication, connecting participants at one-to-one, one-to-many or many-to-many levels. From a superficial viewpoint, we may imagine that new media 'dissolve' the role of territory by facilitating a virtual common space potentially connecting everyone to everybody and allowing access to all kinds of information. Neither old nor new media, however, render physical location superfluous, since participants are located simultaneously in a physical territory and in the media's virtual space. Furthermore, most virtual encounters are not about sharing information with everyone on the planet but are about interacting with particular people concerning particular issues for particular purposes, for instance, playing games, keeping contact with friends, organizing meetings at work, finding a new partner and so on.

Instead of dissolving the role of territory, new media *complexify* the ways we use territory in social interaction, since they enable new configurations of the extension of the territory, the access of participants to the territory, the level of information distributed to different parts of the territory and so on. New media allow actors to perform on several social stages at the same time and, thus, alternate between being on stage and backstage in any one encounter. Furthermore, new media enable actors to optimize social interaction to their own advantage by allowing actors to hide or highlight particular aspects of their performances vis-à-vis others. These territorial transformations become components of the situational properties governing social interaction, including the exercise of social control. For instance, the introduction of computers and the internet in the classroom has not only changed the availability of information in the classroom but has also challenged the teacher's authority to exercise control in the classroom. Students can discuss the teacher's performance through various social network media or find alternative information that can challenge the teacher's argument through the web. Alternatively, students can opt out completely and do something entirely different (playing, e-mailing, reading news, etc.) while still being present in the classroom. What looks like an enabling media technology from one point of view may look like an obstacle from another point of view. Considered from a structural perspective, the affordances end up modifying the social roles and behaviour of all participants involved. New media not only allow new uses for territory but also allow the flexible manipulation of time and representational modalities (pictures, text, audio and combinations thereof). A medium's particular affordances in terms of time and modality may similarly complexify behavioural patterns and the control of social interaction.

8. Institutional logics

The theoretical framework of institutional logics (Thornton, Ocasio and Lounsbury, 2012) may be useful for our final consideration of how media are implicated in processes of institutionalization. This framework posits that society is made up of an interinstitutional structure in which social actors, organizations and sectors are influenced by several institutions. There is a limited set of institutions in society, including family, education, market, state, religion and so on, but none of these is a priori more important than the others, and all are subject to historical change. As historical and contingent entities, institutions are also subject to change vis-à-vis other institutions: for instance, family values and practices may change due to changes in religious faith, state legislation or new demands from the labour market. In order to analyze how various forms of media are institutionalized within a particular context, we must consider how the practices and overall structure of the domain in question are influenced not only by the media but also by various institutional logics, that is, particular configurations or clusters of formal and informal rules and the allocation of resources within a given domain. Logics may have both material and cultural origins and may also possess a cognitive dimension, since they inform the cognitive categorization of a particular practice and expectations concerning appropriate actions in particular situations. To study these logics we need empirically grounded research into the lifeworlds of human interaction, a perspective also stressed by the notion of 'mediatized worlds' (Hepp, 2013; Krotz and Hepp, 2013). Structures in the form of institutional logics are not above or outside human agency in smaller lifeworlds. On the contrary, resources and rules enable agency, and they may be creatively used, reproduced and altered through agency.

The media are institutionalized in several ways within the overall interinstitutional structure of society. In their capacity for creating public spheres of a political, cultural or commercial nature, they have become important connecting nodes between all institutions in society, allowing them to comprise a semi-independent institution to which others must accommodate in order to access the public realm. By the same process, media have needed to accommodate to the demands of other institutions, for instance, by developing rules of objectivity and fairness in political journalism (accommodation to the political institution), moral considerations regarding children and general society in entertainment (accommodation to the family institution and religion), transparent business principles in advertising (accommodation to the market) and so on. In their capacities for personal and private communication and interaction, the various forms of media have become institutionalized within other social domains and have required integration into the prevailing configuration of institutional logics of the domain in question. This integration is a reciprocal process in which the affordances of a particular form of media may challenge some of the prevailing institutional logics. As suggested above, in the educational system new media may challenge existing role expectations and change patterns of informational control in the classroom.

Finally, media may be implicated in processes of institutional change due to their very nature as media of communication. The institutional logics perspective suggests that institutional change is often stimulated by 'importing and exporting cultural symbols and practices from one institutional order to another' (Thornton and Ocasio, 2008, p. 105). Such import and export may, for instance, take place in the workplace when other professionals with different professional norms and skills are hired. When political parties hire professionals with expertise in new media, they not only acquire the ability to project political messages through social network media but also introduce other kinds of logics into the political realm. Furthermore, since media may convey information and cultural values from almost every institution in society, they can potentially make all institutional practices more fragile and open to change. This argument is in line with Meyrowitz's (1986) observation of television's ability to bridge social contexts, but, with the advent of new media, this has become a radicalized reality. Institutional practices increasingly acquire a virtual dimension, as they may be performed not only in physical settings but also through various types of media. Visiting the library, conducting bank business or doing office work can all be performed virtually, regardless of one's physical location. This introduces a kind of institutional bricolage in a variety of physical settings, prompting existing institutional practices to coexist and in some cases blend with one another. For instance, the school system must take into account that parents may be in online contact with their children throughout the day, and the family may increasingly need to accommodate the presence of work-related tasks on weekends and during vacations. The development towards ubiquitous media has already caused a variety of institutions to change their existing practices. This trend will probably accelerate in the future as various forms of media introduce not only media logics but also other institutional logics into a multitude of settings.

The new media also display institutional properties, though somewhat differently compared with the old mass media. Because new media encompass a variety of communicative and social functions, we should not consider institutional logics in relation to the individual types of media or to a particular media organization. A global media company like Google is involved in a variety of media types and genres, each of which relates to different social functions embedded within various institutional logics. Google operates public media services involving news, library and scholarly work yet also conducts services for private and personal purposes, such as general information search, geographical location services, e-mailing, photo editing and so on. In the case of public media operations, Google may to some extent behave along the lines of similar public mass media organizations and, as such, be part of a semi-independent media institution. In the case of private and personal media services, Google may influence other institutional practices in their respective domains through the various affordances of the media types and genres in question. New media differ from old media in various ways, but they are similarly embedded in processes of mediatization through which media come to influence the institutionalization of social interaction in culture and society.

The author wishes to thank Professor Knut Lundby, University of Oslo, for helpful comments on the article.

References

Altheide, D. L. and Snow, R. P. (1988) 'Toward a theory of mediation'. In: Anderson, J. A. (ed.) *Communication yearbook*, vol. 11, pp. 194–223.

Asp, K. (1990) 'Medialization, media logic and mediarchy'. In: *Nordicom Review*, 11(2), pp. 47–50.

Castells, M. (2009) *Communication power* (Oxford: Oxford University Press).

Deuze, M. (2007) *Media work* (Cambridge: Polity Press).

Finnemann, N. O. (2011) 'Mediatization theory and digital media'. *Communications: The European Journal of Communication Research*, 36(1), pp. 67–89.

Gibson, J. J. (1979) *The ecological approach to visual perception* (Boston: Houghton Mifflin).

Giddens, A. (1984) *The constitution of society* (Cambridge: Polity).

Goffman, E. (1956) *The presentation of self in everyday life* (Edinburgh: University of Edinburgh).

Goffman, E. (1972) *Relations in public. Microstudies of the public order* (New York: Harper & Row).

Hepp, A. (2012) 'Mediatization and the "moulding force" of the media'. In: *Communications*, 37(1), pp. 1–28.

Hepp, A. (2013) *Cultures of mediatization* (Cambridge: Polity).

Hjarvard, S. (2008) 'The mediatization of society, a theory of the media as agents of social and cultural change'. In: *Nordicom Review*, 29(2), pp. 105–34.

Hjarvard, S. (2013) *The mediatization of culture and society* (London: Routledge).

Hjarvard, S. and Petersen, L. N. (2013) 'Mediatization and cultural change'. Special issue on mediatization and cultural change. In: *Media Culture*, 29(54), pp. 1–6.

Hughes, T. P. (1994) 'Technological momentum'. In: Smith, M. R. and Marx, L. (eds) *Does technology drive history? The dilemma of technological determinism* (Cambridge, MA: MIT Press), pp. 101–13.

Hutchby, I. (2001) 'Technologies, texts and affordances'. In: *Sociology*, 35(2), pp. 441–56.

Hutchby, I. (2003) 'Affordances and the analysis of technologically mediated interaction: A response to Brian Rappert'. In: *Sociology*, 37(3), pp. 581–9.

Jensen, K. B. (2013) 'Definitive and sensitizing conceptualizations of mediatization'. In: *Communication Theory*, 23(3), pp. 203–22.

Krotz, F. (2009) 'Mediatization: A concept with which to grasp media and societal change'. In: Lundby, K. (ed.) *Mediatization: Concept, changes, consequences* (New York: Peter Lang), pp. 21–40.

Krotz, F. and Hepp, A. (2013) 'A concretization of mediatization: How mediatization works and why "mediatized worlds" are a helpful concept for empirical mediatization research'. In: *Empedocles*, 3(2), pp. 119–34.

Ling, R. (2008) *New tech, new ties: How mobile communication is reshaping social cohesion* (Cambridge, MA: The MIT Press).

Lundby, K. (2009) 'Introduction: "Mediatization" as key'. In: Lundby, K. (ed.) *Mediatization: Concept, changes, consequences* (New York: Peter Lang), pp. 1–18.

Mazzoleni, G. and Schulz, W. (1999) ' "Mediatization" of politics: A challenge for democracy?' In: *Political Communication*, 16, pp. 247–61.

Meyrowitz, J. (1986) *No sense of place: The impact of electronic media on social behaviour* (New York: Oxford University Press).

Norman, D. (1990) *The design of everyday things* (New York: Doubleday).

Picard, R. G. (2008) 'Shifts in newspaper advertising expenditures and their implications for the future of newspapers'. In: *Journalism Studies*, 9(5), pp. 704–16.

Schulz, W. (2004) 'Reconstructing mediatization as an analytical concept'. In: *European Journal of Communication*, 19(1), pp. 87–101.

Silverstone, R. (2007) *Media and morality: On the rise of the mediapolis* (Cambridge: Polity).

Strömbäck, J. (2008) 'Four phases of mediatization: An analysis of the mediatization of politics'. In: *International Journal of Press/Politics*, 13(3), pp. 228–46.

Thompson, J. B. (1995) *The media and modernity: A social theory of the media* (Cambridge: Polity Press).

Thornton, P. H. and Ocasio, W. (2008) 'Institutional logics'. In: Greenwood, R., Oliver, C., Sahlin-Andersson, K. and Suddaby, R. (eds) *The Sage handbook of organizational institutionalism* (Thousand Oaks, CA: Sage), pp. 99–129.

Thornton, P. H., Ocasio, W. and Lounsbury, M. (2012) *The institutional logics perspective. A new approach to culture, structure, and process* (Oxford: Oxford University Press).

Turkle, S. (2011) *Alone together. Why we expect more from technology and less from each other* (New York: Basic Books).

Part III
Mediatized Communities

9
Benedict in Berlin[1]: The Mediatization of Religion

Hubert Knoblauch

1. Introduction

For a long time, it has been known that, when studying religion, one must consider the role of the media. In fact, one could argue that the science of religion started with the insight made into the difference between orality and literacy in the 19th century. As the science of religion and its literate objects have been more congruent, it took some time for the role of the electronic mass media to be accounted for. However, within the last decade, we have witnessed a rapid increase of studies in the media. Such studies include 'electronic' mass media but, recently, also consider 'internet' and digital media (Hoesgard, 2005; Krüger, 2012).

However, while most studies focus on the representation of religion in the media, on the use of media by religious organizations and on the inter-action between religion and media as social systems, some even claiming a 'religious quality' of the media themselves, the mediatization of religion has only rarely become the subject of scientific inquiry. As the term 'medi-atization' has only been coined in the last decade, it is subject to persistent debate, unsurprisingly, with regard to its definition in comparison with other terms. Given the current knowledge available regarding the relation between religion and media, focusing on the role of media may help to empirically define what is meant by mediatization.

There is no doubt that clarification and refinement of the notion of mediatization in theoretical terms is necessary. Though I will draw on a general notion of mediatization, as it is defined in international discussion and in a theoretical and conceptual frame I have sketched in another article (Knoblauch, 2013), I do not want to apply this notion to an empir-ical field in a deductive way. Instead, I want to start with an account of an empirical phenomenon: the visit of Benedict XVI to Germany, with a particular focus on the service that took place in the Olympic Stadium in Berlin, where we undertook extensive data collection, including video recording, interviews and organizational ethnography. Undoubtedly, the decisive role of the media in the Catholic Church has already been discussed during the reign of John Paul II, particularly during his journeys and services (Bergmann, Luckmann and Soeffner, 1993). The fact that these services have been documented on video, investigated ethnographically (also by the author) and subjected to analysis does not only allow us to compare both 'styles' of communication but, as I shall argue in this article, we can see that they demonstrate a substantial change in the role of the media, and an even more substantial change in the structure of communicative action which may be called religious. As this difference can be firmly understood by the notion of mediatization, a detailed analysis of video-recorded practices during the services allows us to refine what is meant by mediatization. Mediatization not only refers to a particular representation by media (medialization) or the technical mediation of action or social action, but to the mediation of communicative action. As mediatization is a basic feature of communicative action, the forms that this mediatization can take differ. I argue that the use of interactive and digital technology results in new structures of communicative action, which consequently transform religious communication and religion in toto. Elsewhere, I have tried to sketch this transformation towards 'popular religion' in an encompassing way. In this article I want to exemplify this transformation with respect to one specific event.

After having outlined the most relevant aspects of the discussion of media and religion, I then reference the most important aspect of the notion of 'mediatization' in order to provide a link to those few studies that focus on religion and 'mediatization'. Then, I want to briefly outline the empirical basis and procedure of my analysis, before I turn to the event itself, the visit of Pope Benedict XVI to Berlin in 2011. After having described the data and methods of analysis in the empirical part of the article, I shall then present some results drawn from video analysis of this visit, focusing on various aspects of mediatization. In the conclusion I want to summarize these aspects and indicate the transformation of the forms of communicative actions within one specific mediatized symbolic world: religion.

2. Media, religion and mediatization

As indicated above, the modern study of religion is connected to an understanding of the role of the media, particularly the difference between orality and literacy in Bible studies (as well as the study of the written documents of other religions). Although most studies focus on the way in which religion is represented in the media (Arthur, 1993), the role of the media as a way of shaping social action and experience in the field of religion has also been highlighted, for example, by Eisenstein (1979). She demonstrated that the 'Gutenberg revolution' of print was a prerequisite for the Protestant reformation, since it allowed access to individual (and silent) reading of the

Holy Scripture, weakened the institutional (Catholic) monopoly of the transmission of knowledge, and accelerated the dissemination of these practices. Moore (1994) added the observation that, until the 18th century, the market for printed books (at least in the USA) was dominated by religious literature. The rise of new genres (science, literature, newspapers) was countered by the creation of huge religious non-profit organizations producing up to 300,000 bibles a year. Religious organizations in the USA were also among the first to adapt to the new 'electronic' media, such as radio and television. As Hoover (1988) stresses, since the 1940s we have witnessed the rise of an 'electronic church' that makes use of electronic communication, particularly of radio and television. This electronic church created new 'media formats' and a new organizational structure. While less developed in Europe, in the USA it comprised more than 220 television stations in 1987, with a regular audience of some 130 million people (claimed by the providers; critics refer to about 30 million). The electronic church then expanded, especially in areas with strong religious dynamics. The Catholic Church in Brazil, for example, owns more than 122 radio stations. Increasingly, media also allowed global communication. By 1995, Billy Graham's 'World Mission' was transmitted by satellite to 165 countries and some 10 million people.

Since the notion of the 'electronic church' was coined under the reign of mass media, one might ask whether the new digital media can be subsumed under this category. However, it can be claimed that the possibility of individual access and, simultaneously, interactivity offered by digital media distinguishes it from mass media (Knoblauch, 2009). It would, however, be misleading to assume that the difference is 'caused' or constituted by the medium of dissemination, as Luhmann (1997) seems to suggest. As, for example, Meyer and Moors show, the role of pre-digital media, such as radio, records or video in Ghana, Egypt or Nigeria, depends upon 'what forms of mediation and communication [...] these more diversified audiences employ and what styles of communication [...] they use' (Meyer and Moors, 2006, p. 12). Instead of focusing on the media solely as a structure for representation, the study of contemporary religion allows us to observe the use of media in action. The incorporation of media in action has been referred to as 'mediatization'. Since the relevance of the media to the forms of social action and society in toto has been acknowledged by a range of authors (for example, Meyrowitz, 1994; Thompson, 1994), recent dramatic changes in digital and interactive media have prompted a new wave of debate on what is now called mediatization (Schulz 2004). Indeed, as Krotz (2001, p. 23) states, the 'starting point [of the analysis of mediatization] must be communication or communicative action'. The relevance of mediatization for religion has already been emphasized by Hepp and Krönert (2009) and Hjarvard (2009). Hepp and Krönert, for example, convincingly demonstrate the transformation of religion by its mediatization, characterized by fragmentation, pluralization, deterritorialization and a new form of immediacy.

Just as Hepp and Krönert based their analysis on qualitative and quantitative data collected at the Catholic Pope Benedict's visit in 2006 to the World Youth Day in Cologne, Germany, this study will concern the 2011 visit to Berlin. In addition to the data used by Hepp and Krönert, this study is based on a large corpus of video data. By analyzing this data, I will not only attempt to define the notion of mediatization suggested by Hepp and Krönert but, in addition, I would also like to empirically 'ground' the notion of mediatization adumbrated in a theoretical article published elsewhere (Knoblauch, 2013). This notion differs substantially from what has been suggested by Hjarvard (2009). By mediatization I do not mean the subsumption of religion to the 'logic of the media' in terms of institutional regulation, symbolic content and individual practices. Rather, in accordance with Couldry (2012), I would suggest that the technical media are integrated into new forms of communicative action. These new forms of communicative action do not result in a 'banal religion' constituted by 'banal religious representations', such as figures from fantasy film, as Hjarvard claims. Rather, the new forms of communicative action constitute what I would call a popular religion. As I have elaborated the notion of popular religion in extenso elsewhere, I want to back my thesis with a study of a religious event par excellence: the pope's mass. On this basis I want to show that mediatization does not only consist of the transformation of an event into the 'centred performance' of a 'media event', as Couldry (2012, p. 79) rightly suggests, but, in addition, mediatization consists of the integration of new media technologies into the communicative action of the participants in such a way as to transform their religious practice. The mediatization of religion, in this way, empirically supports the development towards 'mediatization' (Krotz, 2009); at the same time it demonstrates the heterogeneity of mediatized worlds (Hepp, 2013), since the new forms of mediatization affect religion in a particular way by transforming the religious forms of religious action, that is, rituals.

3. The Pope in Berlin: Data

The visit of Pope Benedict to Berlin was a global media event. As opposed to the visit of John Paul II in Berlin 1996, this was a German pope visiting the German capital – an event which had not happened for centuries. In fact, while John Paul II met large numbers of Catholics from Poland who travelled across the border to Berlin, in 2011 the German audience dominated and the whole journey was framed as the pope visiting Germany. In addition to Berlin, he also went to a Catholic area in East Germany which had survived Socialism, and to one of the core regions of Catholicism, the city of Freiburg in the southwest of Germany. While being in Berlin for a day and a night, he visited a holocaust memorial, met with representatives of the Jewish community, gave a speech in the German parliament and celebrated a mass at the Olympic Stadium.

As Berlin is a Catholic diaspora, the location, as well as the dimension, of the mass had been quite uncertain for a long time. After it became clear that the numbers of participants interested would exceed 10,000–20,000 persons, the planners in the Vatican, the German bishops' council and the local archdiocese accepted the suggestion to move into the Olympic Stadium. Although recently refurbished as a modern sports stadium, the location is quite controversial since it still retains traces of its fascist origins. While the events in the predominantly Catholic areas integrated open spaces, such as the main market place in Freiburg, the preference for the Olympic Stadium demonstrated the insular atmosphere of the Berlin visit, as opposed to John Paul II visiting Vienna or Benedict's visit to the 'Catholic cities' of Freiburg and Cologne (or Madrid earlier). Benedict was appearing in public only in built spaces, triggering some of the most draconian security measures seen over the last few years, despite the city's familiarity with state visits.

Together with a team of students and a team of documentary film-makers, we have collected data on various aspects of Benedict's visit to Berlin. While one student, Sezgin Sönmez, collected data in the local organization team, another student collected data on the media coverage of the visit. Together with a number of students, we have also visited the Olympic Stadium, conducted interviews and recorded videos and film of the event. The multi-method procedure we pursued attempted to replicate an earlier study of Benedict's visit to the Catholic World Youth Days in Cologne in 2006 (Forschungskonsortium WJT, 2007). In addition to the methods used there, we collected video recordings and photographs produced by ourselves, the documentary film team and the local television station (which was aired worldwide). Finally, we had access to video recordings of earlier public services by Pope Benedict (Cologne) as well as video recordings of John Paul II in Vienna 1998 and in Berlin 1996 (also in the Olympic Stadium).

As the title suggests, the focus here is not so much on the entirety of the papal visit to Berlin. Rather, I want to focus on one aspect: mediatization, particularly with respect to the public service in the Olympic Stadium. For this reason, the video recordings of the services provide the most important data. The data has been subjected to the now commonly used method of 'videography': that is, the analysis of video data collected as part of a focused ethnography (Knoblauch, 2011; Knoblauch and Schnettler, 2012).

4. Mediatization and medialization: Silence

Media coverage of church services is a very common genre on television. Therefore, the pope's services are typically televised. In fact, television coverage is a crucial issue not only for the local organizers but also for the national Catholic episcopal conference. Since the service is often broadcast internationally, even the Vatican's communication department is aware that, by televising events, Catholicism is presented globally and therefore presents itself as a global player. For this reason, the forms of the service as well as the kind of televised presentation are the subject of heated debates between the Vatican, the national and the local organizers: not only Catholic institutions but also local event organizers and, of course, television stations. The latter are in charge of the production of the 'global picture' through control of what is aired by the television editor (as mentioned, the regional television station had produced a 'live' picture for simultaneous global transmission). The global relevance of this event to regional or national television stations is quite obvious: for example, when John Paul II visited Vienna in 1998, Austrian TV (ORF) put up the largest number of cameras ever in use for any local event, including cameras mounted on a huge special crane at the central 'Heldenplatz'.

As with most televised events, the papal service features a live commentary by a TV host. In the following sequence, the event, the media coverage and the TV host have a role to play, rendering the relation between religion and media very explicit.

After the communion, a speaker announces on the stage that the audience may 'venerate this great mystery for a moment' by being silent for a minute. After five seconds, while the camera is fixed at the top of the stadium roof providing a view of the entire stadium, the TV host starts to talk and comments that silence is a crucial element of the service here, particularly desired by Pope Benedict XVI. During her first sentence, the automatic camera starts to move and, as is frequent in football stadiums, to 'fly' down from the stadium roof, zooming in on the 'selected' audience seated on the playing field. As the television presenter continues to discuss silence and its role in the service, the camera moves to about 20, then five and finally up to about two metres from the audience, revealing an incongruous reaction from audience members. The subjects of the camera start to smile and wave their hands and talk to one another. This reaction was not universal, but the pictures are rather dominated by people waving, looking and laughing into the camera (Figure 9.1).

The editors appear to swiftly realize the incongruity, as the automatic camera suddenly moves up as if to look for a distant picture. Not very successfully, however, for even the bird's eye perspective from about ten metres high shows first one, then two and finally several seating blocks (still on the sports field) in which many people visibly wave their hands. The editor seems quite aware that this does not fit with the sentiment of the TV host: 'It is unusual for us here on First German Television to show pictures of silence.' Consequently, the 'global picture' is cut and shows two men on the field, one with closed eyes while the second, just as he starts to close his eyes and lower his head, grins broadly. The presenter herself now falls silent and the picture shifts to show various clerical personnel. In fact, we see the profile of the local archbishop bowed and pensive, but in the focus of the camera we see a priest who, obviously aware of the camera, is smiling from ear to ear. Again the camera moves, now into a safe haven, focusing on

Figure 9.1   Audience during one minute of 'silence'

the row of bishops who sit opposite the stage and successfully 'concentrate' without gazing into the camera or even smiling.

Leaving aside the ironic contrast between the speaker's text and the pictures, the example neatly demonstrates the 'effect' that the camera has on the audience and, simultaneously, the reaction of the audience to the media. In quite an explicit way, the camera is transforming the situation from something which at least resembles 'silence' and 'concentration' to something akin to joy, liveliness and an almost Warholian lust for a few seconds of fame. Of course, this phenomenon is common, and it is not unseemly for audience members of a huge religious event to be sensitive and receptive to the media and their immediate 'live' global reach. As common as the phenomenon may seem to us now, however, in earlier papal services it is almost totally absent. By comparison, let us take a look at the Vienna service by John Paul II, which happened only 14 years earlier and was also extensively covered by the media. In our systematic comparison of both events, we find that, in the latter, the audience was very rarely visible: we could see faces only for 16 minutes per hour, as opposed to 48 minutes per hour in Berlin, close-ups rising from 17 per hour to 79 per hour. While the camera recorded only one audience reaction in Vienna, in Berlin we find 29, that is, 17 per hour. The media transformation is expressed in the ratio between representations of the audience as a whole and from a distance to the representation of individual audience members. From Vienna to Berlin, this ratio changed from 2:1 to 2:6.[2]

As a result, the rather trivial fact that we see audience members reacting to the camera is, in fact, a demonstration of a transformation from the presentation of the mass in which the audience features only to frame the action at the front. It is one of several justifications for the basic thesis that, in the interval between these case studies, the televised mass has changed from an event that is merely represented by audio-visual media to an event which is constructed through practical usages of audio-visual media. It also shows that television not only triggers reactions but also provides a way to showcase them. Although, in the case of silence, joyful reactions seem to contradict the meaning of the speech, in all other cases audience reactions are not cut. Instead, cameras and editors leave time for the audience members to show their reactions in such a way as to represent their interaction with the medium.

The changing role of the audience is even more conspicuous if one looks at the structure of the event. While the audience of John Paul II in Vienna in summer 1998 focused on the stage, the band and the choir as well as the pope and the altar, including the clerical personnel, in Berlin, the band, the choir and most clerical personnel formed part of the audience. While in Vienna the mass was performed by the front, including special songs with melodies unknown to the audience which mostly engendered applause, the Berlin mass was participative in a very intense way. It was a mass *with* the audience.

5. Two communicative styles and the marking-off of real religion

While many commentaries assume Pope Benedict somehow follows the popular pattern set by John Paul II, the Berlin service, much more than any other event before (such as the service in London or in Madrid), demonstrated the differences between the two. There is some evidence that Benedict gave personal instructions per ritual regulations in the capital of his home country. It seems that these regulations address the fundamentals of how the service should proceed and, as mentioned above, the service contained an interesting element. Shortly after the pope came onto the stage, which had been built in the western curve of the stadium, an official in suit and tie went to the microphone set at the front corner of the stage and, to a chorus of cheers from the audience, announced that this Eucharistic mass was the highlight of the event: The 'holy mysteries in which we are included by coming here are commemorating the celebration of Easter by Our Lord and strongly linked to our heartfelt belief and our deep prayer. We are invited to participate in this gracious event and to make our devotions. Everything which could disrupt the focus on this "mystery" should therefore be avoided. We pray not to hold up banners and not to disrupt the proceedings by cheering' (Figure 9.2).

In quite an explicit way, this announcement introduced what Hochschild (1979) calls a 'feeling rule'. As the example of 'silence' shows, this rule could be seen to extend to an 'emotional regime' in which concentration, devotion

Figure 9.2   Announcement on the stage to respect the mystery of the mass

and solemnity predominate, as opposed to cheering and banner-waving. The emotional regime is related to a communicative style (Herbrik, 2012; Knoblauch, 2009) which is, at least on the negative side, explicit: cheering, clapping and waving banners was a pattern of audience action when the pope entered the stadium and drove the 'papamobile' on the track. This style of communication is quite common at other popular events, for example, when celebrities of other kinds, such as film stars, sports celebrities or pop musicians, meet appreciative audiences.

The solemn style of the mass, which seems in accordance with the 'mysterium fidei' emphasized by Benedict XVI as the core of Catholicism, is also represented in forms of communication. As in typical Catholic masses, it demands that the audience participate in various activities, such as singing the hymns, praying in unison and moving their bodies (sitting, kneeling down, standing up) according to the ceremonial patterns of the particular service. As in many Catholic masses, the audience had been provided with a leaflet which not only contained the songs to be sung, which are normally also provided by the church as service books, but also the text of prayers (such as the Credo). Given the clear announcement, the participants distinguish between two styles of communication, one which may be called the 'popular' style and a solemn 'high church' style.

The distinction between the two styles of communication delineates quite an important boundary. While the popular style may be seen to correspond to the 'celebrity', the solemn style of high church allows us to 'mark' a difference between this and what, in a narrower sense, can be considered religious communication.[3] Note, however, that this strategy does not claim to define the essential difference between the two forms of communication. Rather, it helps the actors to draw a line. The distinction between the two styles, for example, corresponds strongly to Benedict's theology: Catholic 'mystery' is embedded in, represented by and enacted in the authentically performed rituals of the congregation. In this respect, he differs theologically from his predecessor, and, for that matter, from popular forms of Protestantism. At the Vienna mass of John Paul II, for example, the role of the audience was quite different. As mentioned above, the audience was not only facing the pope and his stage, the artistic performers, a band, an orchestra, a choir and various singers, but the mass drew on less-known songs from the service book. The artists performed in such a way that the audience was only a spectator and listener, and even the 'Credo' was sung (by an opera singer) in a high art version unknown to the audience, who only listened to the event. Their major form of reaction, therefore, was clapping – a form which seemed to be suppressed by the verdict of the Berlin mass.

One should, however, not mistake the theology of Benedict XVI as an imposition of behavioural rules for the audience. Leaving aside the huge variety of ritual participation, at any given moment even the core audience exhibited quite diverse ritual actions at the same time, such as kneeling down, sitting, standing up during consecration; the distinction between the two styles was empirically not as rigid as theory claims.[4] Clapping and cheering occurred at various points and was even initiated by Benedict XVI when he departed from the stage at the end of the mass. Moreover, the mass was not strictly kept in the 'solemn' style, particularly during the many rituals that did not feature speech or music sung by the audience (supported by a huge choir) that occur in the Catholic mass, which were filled by a singer and a pop band. Despite these concessions to the 'popular style', the audience seems to have kept the original rule. This orientation became particularly salient when the pope had left the stage (and was no longer visible in the stadium), as the 'prohibited' forms of communication started immediately, such as cheering, waving banners and shouting ('Benedetto') – forms which were continued by some Catholic groups intensively outside the stadium until after the mass.

6. Veneration and mediatization: Entering the stadium

The triumphant entry of the pope into the Olympic Stadium was met with an ecstatic reaction by the audience. It began with loud cheering, clapping and, wherever the 'papamobile' passed by, standing ovations. Given that the stadium was mainly filled with Catholics, one could ascribe these audience reactions to the pope's charisma and the 'charisma of the office', as Weber (1978 [1921]) calls it. Yet a series of interviews conducted with participants yields the information that charisma is, at best, ascribed to the office of the pope, rather than to the person of Benedict XVI.[5] If one were to compare the observed audience reactions with a vocabulary of typical reactions, one might find a striking correspondence to the typical form of a celebrity encounter (Turner, 2004). As we analyze our data regarding audience reaction, we must not be limited to conjecture but may scrutinize what can be called their 'communicative actions'. In the face of the magnitude of the audience here, there is, of course, a huge variety of such actions to be observed. Those audiences that are active and share some common knowledge among themselves are able to easily coordinate their actions in such a way as to establish themselves as members of an audience. This does not only relate to the official ceremony of the Catholic mass, such as the songs sung by the congregation, kneeling down, standing up, praying and responding – or keeping quiet – all of which occur in quite some variety during the mass observed, but also relates to those kinds of actions which are more spontaneous and dependent on the situation. As an example, we have scrutinized the entry of the pope into the stadium, an event which many Catholics may experience as unique, exceptional and extraordinary. In fact, in film material of 'masses' confronting John XXIII on his visits, one can discern that many bow, make the sign of the cross or perform other actions of reverence, presenting themselves as 'believers'. Therefore we have achieved a greater insight into the ways in which the audience 'reacted' to the pope's entrance. Since the 'travelling pope' John Paul II may have already had effects on the habits of believers, it seemed to us especially interesting to watch the conduct of clerical personnel. This focus is supported by the fact that most of the 'core' members of the church and the clerical personnel were based on the stadium's ground floor on, or close to, the field. As the 'papamobile' enters the stadium and starts to drive around the track, we watch many audience members moving to create a cordon of onlookers well before the pope comes close. As soon as the security officials, behind the pope's personal photographer, enter into sight, the onlookers become excited. Many get their digital cameras out, many others the Vatican's white and yellow flag. The two nuns who are standing on the right side of the still below do the same: one carrying a Polish red and white flag, holding the camera, the other holding the white and yellow flag in her hands (Figure 9.3).

Note that, at the moment captured here, the nun to the right, after having shown her joy with a broad smile and bouncing impatiently, turns her gaze upwards to the left – this is where one of the big screens is located and where the pope can be seen. Shortly after, however, she realizes that the papamobile is coming so close that she can see it herself. When the pope is almost in front of them, the former keeps her camera, which she holds in front of her face, on the pope while the second nun starts to wave one hand. As the pope passes from the right side in front of them both, the camera is also moved into the field of view of the waving nun. This movement is continued so that the first nun now shows the camera to the second one

Figure 9.3   Papamobile approaching

Figure 9.4   The pope passes by

who, joyfully, acknowledges what she is watching – at the very moment that the pope himself is passing by (Figure 9.4).

Although this sequence was chosen at random, it almost perfectly exemplifies what may be called mediatization. Mediatization here not only refers to the fact that the mass medium, represented by the stadium screen, forms part of the event so as to turn it into a medially reflected event, but also refers to the fact that the medium becomes part and parcel of the very action performed by the actors on the scene. It is clear that the two actors here consider the scene exceptional – it may be that they will never get closer to the pope than now. The camera is, therefore, not only an additional element in the veneration of the pope. While the pope is welcomed by one of the two nuns, through gesture, the second nun turns this bodily appreciation into a technical recording procedure in such a way that the very moment of the experience of the pope's presence becomes a moment in which both concurrently experience a technical record of the moment. The situation, however, does not turn into a simulation of the moment, as Baudrillard (1978) so farsightedly admonished. To the nuns (as to us observers) it is, rather, a very real situation which is, however, characterized by the fact that the media, their technology and the representations produced by these technologies form an integrated part of the action performed by the two nuns. They do not have any doubt that the action is addressed to a venerated person but, simultaneously, they demonstrate that veneration takes a form which differs significantly from those performed by believers who knelt before John XXIII.

7. Conclusion: On mediatization and popular religion

Mediatization does not mean the substitution of an action by the media. It refers, instead, to the transformation of the forms and structures of actions or rituals (as actions defined by religious legitimation are called). In his way, mediatization resembles what Knorr Cetina (2009) calls a scopic situation. While in her view 'scopic' means to visualize what is invisible in a face-to-face situation, here it means the integration of the absent world – full of people, images, sounds and things – into situations. In this sense, mediatization, I would argue, does not lead to the dissolution of the social. Rather, it intensifies the social world (Knoblauch, 2013). Although, in the empirical data presented, mediation, medialization and mediatization are difficult to disentangle, analytically they refer to different aspects of communicative action: while mediation refers to what may be considered the instrumental aspects of action, medialization refers to the representations involved (which, I would argue, are always also part of instrumental action).

As mediatization forms part of any communicative action, its transformation also affects institutions such as churches, and, in our case, Catholicism with respect to papal visits and masses. As Bergmann, Luckmann and Soeffner (1993) rightly stress, earlier mass services in Rome could subject the camera to their requirements and demands, while the travelling pope, John Paul II, has been subjugated under the camera. 'Media logic' prevails in John Paul's service in Vienna in 1998. However, Benedict's Berlin service exhibits yet another striking difference. While in Vienna the mass was an event performed in front of an audience and shown in front of TV cameras, the Berlin service casts the audience in the role of actors. The audience was not only shown on television; it was also made to participate in ways which are not only medialized as an audio-visual motive. The audience actively participated in the very essence of the service. Although the participation of the audience is a feature of the Catholic mass and a concern of Benedict's theology, it fosters the mediatization of the event as highlighted by Hepp and Krönert (2009): audience members do not only participate and are not only shown, but are shown participating, and thus provide what may be understood as a mediated 'model' for the media audience. 'Model' should not be understood in a cognitivist sense. As our preliminary analysis of the use of photos and videos by participants of the mass shows, it is the audience's action, much more than the staged event, which is taken to represent the specific 'emotions': the 'awe' or 'turmoil' of the situation.[6]

In changing communicative action, mediatization changes religious rituals and what used to be called 'religious participation', this being controlled and selected by mediated action, and, thence, 'religious membership'. It turns religious services into increasingly mediatized events. However, it does not turn religion into 'banal' religion, as Hjarvard (2009) claims, or into a 'common culture' only 'represented by the media', as Hoover (2006, p. 284) suggests. Since it allows lay members, even in Catholicism, to become part and parcel of the event, mediatization supports a transformation into 'popular religion', allowing both access to the marked forms and transgression of these marks.

Notes

1. I am grateful to Regine Herbrik for her comments on this text, as well as for her contributions at the sessions on the video data, in which Meike Hellmuth, Sezgin Sönmez and Rene Tuma have also been participating.
2. I am grateful here to Sezgin Sönmez for his research contribution.
3. As to the role of such marks of religious communication, cf. Knoblauch (2009).
4. The ground for this difference had been prepared when Benedict XVI chose a new 'master of ceremonies' in 2007 (cf. Schlott, 2008).
5. I am grateful to Iris Eckhardt for the interviews and their analysis.
6. I am grateful to Mathias Blanc, who accompanied some French pilgrims to Benedict's mass at Freiburg and visited them at home afterwards. 'Turmoil' above has been called 'Ergriffenheit' by one participant, a notion which resonates with mystical experiences.

References

Arthur, C. (ed.) (1993) *Religion and the media* (Cardiff: University of Wales Press).
Baudrillard, J. (1978) *Critique of the political economy of the sign* (St Louis: Telos).
Bergmann, J., Luckmann, Th. and Soeffner, H.-G. (1993) 'Erscheinungsformen von Charisma – Zwei Päpste'. In: Gebhardt, W., Zingerle, A. and Ebertz, M. N. (eds) *Charisma – Theorie, Religion, Politik* (Berlin: de Gruyter), pp. 121–55.
Couldry, N. (2012) *Media, society, world: Social theory and digital media practice* (London and New York: Routledge).

Eisenstein, E. (1979) *The printing press as an agent of change: Communications and cultural transformations in early modern Europe* (Cambridge: Cambridge University Press).

Forschungskonsortium WJT (2007) *Megaparty Glaubensfest. Weltjugendtag: Erlebnis – Medien – Organisation* (Wiesbaden: VS).

Hepp, Andreas (2013) *Cultures of mediatization* (Cambridge: Polity Press).

Hepp, A. and Krönert, V. (2009) *Medien – Event – Religion. Die Mediatisierung des Religiösen* (Wiesbaden: VS).

Herbrik, R. (2012) 'Analyzing emotional styles in the field of Christian religion and the relevance of new types of visualization'. In: *Qualitative Sociology Review*, 8(2), pp. 112–28.

Hjarvard, S. (2009) 'The mediatization of religion'. In: *Northern Lights*, 6(1), pp. 9–26.

Hochschild, A. (1979) 'Emotion work, feeling rules, and social structure'. In: *American Journal of Sociology*, 85(3), pp. 551–75.

Hoesgard, M. T. (2005) 'Cyber-religion. On the cutting edge between the virtual and the real'. In: Hoesgard, M. T. and Warburg, M. (eds) *Religion and cyberspace* (London and New York: Routledge), pp. 50–63.

Hoover, S. M. (1988) *Mass media religion. The social sources of the electronic church* (Newbury Park: Sage).

Hoover, S. M. (2006) *Religion in the media age* (London and New York: Routledge).

Knoblauch, H. (2009) *Populäre Religion. Auf dem Weg in eine spirituelle Gesellschaft* (Frankfurt a. M.: Campus).

Knoblauch, H. (2011) 'Videography'. In: Stausberg, M. and Engler, S. (eds) *The Routledge handbook of research methods in the study of religion* (London: Routledge), pp. 433–44.

Knoblauch, H. (2013) 'Communicative constructivism and mediatization, In: *Communication Theory* 23, 297–315.

Knoblauch, H. and Schnettler, B. (2012) 'Videography: Analysing video data as "focused" ethnographic and hermeneutical exercise'. In: *Qualitative Research* 12(3), pp. 334–56.

Knorr Cetina, K. (2009) 'The synthetic situation: Interactionism for a global world'. In: *Symbolic Interaction*, 32(1), pp. 61–87.

Krotz, F. (2001) *Die Mediatisierung sozialen Handelns* (Wiesbaden: VS).

Krotz, F. (2009) 'Mediatization: A concept to grasp media and societal change'. In: Lundby, K. (ed.) *Mediatization: Concept, changes, conflicts* (New York: Lang), pp. 21–40.

Krüger, O. (2012) *Die mediale Religion. Probleme und Perspektiven der religionswissenschaftlichen und wissenssoziologischen Medienforschung* (Bielefeld: transcript), pp. 377–417.

Luhmann, N. (1997) *Die Gesellschaft der Gesellschaft* (Frankfurt am Main: Suhrkamp).

Meyer, B. and Moors, A. (2006) 'Introduction'. In: Meyer, B. and Moors, A. (eds) *Religion, media and the public sphere* (Bloomington and Indianapolis: Indiana University Press), pp. 1–29.

Meyrowitz, J. (1994) 'Medium theory'. In: Crowley, D. and Mitchell, D. (eds) *Communication theory today* (London: Polity), pp. 50–77.

Moore, R. L. (1994) *Selling God. American religion in the marketplace of culture* (New York, Oxford).

Schlott, R. (2008) 'Der Papst als Medienstar'. In: *Aus Politik und Zeitgeschichte*, 52, pp. 16–21.

Schulz, W. (2004) 'Reconstructing mediatization as an analytical concept'. In: *European Journal of Communication*, 19(1), pp. 87–101.

Thompson, J. B. (1994) 'Social theory and the media'. In: Crowley. D. and Mitchell, D. (eds) *Communication theory today* (London: Polity), pp. 27–49.

Turner, T. (2004) *Understanding celebrity* (London: Sage).

Weber, M. (1978 [1921]) *Economy and society. An outline of interpretive sociology* (Los Angeles: University of California Press).

10
Technology, Place and Mediatized Cosmopolitanism

Miyase Christensen

1. Introduction

The past two decades of media and communication studies have been dominated by a research agenda marked by an overwhelming attention paid to two phenomena: technological change and globalization. The study of digitalization and personalization of technology, particularly in its earlier phase, focused primarily on the emancipatory potential of information and communication technologies, or ICTs (e.g., Plant, 1997; Splender, 1995). While later research incorporated a more down-to-earth appreciation of technology, technological determinism continues to be reinvoked by way of casting new media tools as powerful agents of social change. This leads to the production of reductionist visions, particularly during times of perceived technological breakthrough (such as the Arab Spring and the case of Wikileaks), and a narrow conception of the *mediatized worlds*, which we find ourselves in today. Likewise, earlier theories of globalization foregrounded mediated and imagined dimensions (e.g., Appadurai, 1996; Beck, 2004; Castells, 2012; Rantanen, 2005) as well as cultural fusion and flows, with material aspects and complexities of 'the everyday' often overlooked or underplayed. One reason for this is cookie-cutter approaches to both globalization and technological change. Another is lack of empirical studies to support grand theoretical claims.

Over the past ten years, attempts have been made to counter-balance deterministic or single-logic-based considerations of both globalization and media penetration with more context-specific paradigmatic interventions such as *transnationalism* (Khagram and Levitt, 2008; Vertovec, 1999; 2009) and *mediatization* (Hepp, 2010; Krotz, 2007), highlighting the meta-character of both processes. In various fields of the humanities and social sciences, the volume of research that addresses how socio-political and personal life are continuously transformed due to media saturation has been expanding steadily. Everyday communication technologies such as mobile applications and online social networking have been the focus of many recent studies producing new insights. My own research on global mobility, space and mediatized worlds in Sweden revealed tensions ensuing from increased transnationality and migration. Such tensions manifest themselves in the form of both cultural interconnectivity and recognition, and closure and distrust in urban centres (Christensen, 2011; 2012).

With the aim of further nuancing ongoing debates on mediatization and globalization by way of contributing empirically based insights, in this chapter I will argue for a research agenda for a close study of mediatized lifeworlds. My analyses of globally mobile groups of people (e.g., labour and professional migrants) residing in Sweden, as well as of segments of the general population, point to the existence of social dynamics that yield a *mediatized cosmopolitanism* (or mediatized cosmopolitan worlds) that is simultaneously connected and divided. More specifically, I draw upon qualitative fieldwork conducted in Stockholm, independently and as part of research projects,[1] on urban populations and transnational migrants since 2008.

The projects and my individual studies have raised over-arching and specific questions, such as: what does the perspective of cosmopolitanism (Clifford, 1998; Stevenson, 2002; 2003) offer for the purposes of theoretically grasping both the constraints and opportunities offered by increased transnationality and mediated connectivity? Do intensified mediatization, mobility and connectivity with distant others translate into a normative change in our ethical horizons (that is, making us *either* more *or* less cosmopolitan), as has been suggested in literature (e.g., Rantanen, 2005; Robertson, 2010)? Where do we practically and epistemologically locate 'communicative practice' and 'networked sociality', and 'place' and 'technology'?[2]

It is impossible to conceive of cosmopolitanism(s) today without accounting for mediatized lifeworlds. Yet, while the intense mediatization of our worlds brings with it a *de facto* openness to and the possibility of connectivity with the *other* (cosmopolitanism), it also makes it possible to create mediated bubbles of closure, clash, monitoring and exclusivism as extensions of offline reality. This, in turn, necessitates considering both the *actual* and *virtual* dimensions (Morley, 2011), such as place and technology, of the meta-processes of globalization and mediatization. These processes produce various sorts of concord and dissonance, which are part and parcel of the open-ended futures brought about by cosmopolitanization.

The approach promoted here brings together Bourdieu's field theory and social phenomenology with the aim of achieving a more holistic understanding of the 'mediatized everyday'. While field theory helps to relate mediatization to certain sets of social practice and both intra-/inter-group relations, phenomenology helps to bring it down to the personal and interpersonal levels. Further, in order to account for both macro and micro dimensions, a categorical distinction between *mediatization* and *mediation*, although they are conceptual products of the same epistemology, is utilized. Mediatization, in this context, denotes a socio-cultural meta-process whereby the media in their totality (forms, texts, technologies and institutions) saturate all spheres of life (cf. Krotz, 2007; 2008; Schulz, 2004), regardless of whether one uses a particular form of media (say, social media) or not. I take mediation, in a more confined sense here, to refer to specific everyday processes of media use, communicative practice and sociality, which bring with them both unity and cultural openness as well as division and *distinction*.

This volume is dedicated to exploring, from varied perspectives, how 'mediatization is interwoven with a changing social process of *constructing* the world'. Close scrutiny of mediatized life conditions in our societies today reveals how sociality and identity processes are unthinkable without considering both the material and symbolic dimensions of networked social connectivity and communication. While the materialistic basis of Bourdieuian sociology makes visible the internal and external group dynamics and power geometries that are *reconstructed* by transnationalization and mediatization, a phenomenological approach helps to generate an *inside view* (Berger and Luckmann, 1967) to grasp current modes of communication and sense-making in certain settings in order to reveal positional particularities which are otherwise lost in the Bourdieuian model. Thus, phenomenology is instrumental in reminding us how social reality is not neutral or external, but continuously produced within the highly mediatized worlds of groups and individuals. Supported by an empirical backbone, this two-tiered framework allows a more rounded view of *mediatized cosmopolitanism* as it crystallizes in the everyday cultural realm of mediatized lifeworlds. Through this approach, the role of key components such as *technology* and *place* can also be better explicated rather than left implicit, and techno-determinism alleviated.

The discussion is put forward in two steps. In the first part, I seek to highlight the importance of thinking media change and the so-called transnational condition together with place and technology. I introduce cosmopolitanism as an analytical tool to account for institutional and spatial transformations that ostensibly cosmopolitanize social life, on the one hand, and identity processes, subjective positionalities and moral outlooks which are presumed to have gained a cosmopolitan character due to intense mediatization, on the other. Following from this, the second part offers reflections on the value of using Bourdieu's field theory and phenomenology (Berger and Luckmann, 1967; Ihde, 1990) together in understanding the interrelations between mediatization and the cultural vision of cosmopolitanism (*mediatized cosmopolitanism*). In the final part, I return to the prospects and challenges of addressing the cultural dimensions of mediatization from a non-media-centric but technology- and place-conscious perspective.

2. Media and cultural cosmopolitanism in a transnational context

In considering the rapidly and radically diversifying nature of society and politics of the late 1980s/early 1990s, the globalization paradigm provided a discursive tool to frame the transformations in institutional, technological and cultural domains. The grandiose discourses, such as deterritorialization, borderless economy and cultural fusion, which ensued from this paradigm of change often glossed over continuities and socio-cultural particularities. The massive transformations in the media environment at this time (technological as well as economic convergence) and a mediated saturation of everyday life with global forms and content had clear linkages with the overall process of globalization. Media penetration was seen as both fuelling and emerging as a product of the spatialization of capitalism, making mediatization and globalization profoundly linked processes. While accurately capturing certain dimensions of institutional and technological change, *the real* and *the virtual* were dichotomized in some earlier discourses of globalization, producing a disconnect between the rhetoric of progress and the material reality of late capitalism. Such framings characterized by either instrumental or substantive understandings of technology to which I return, however, were also marked by determinism.

Over the past decade, to counter-balance the limitations of globalism, there has been a marked increase in references made to the 'transnational condition' and transnationalization of the media across social sciences and humanities. Unlike the generalistic rhetoric of the globalization paradigm, then, spatio-temporal and contextual specificity and 'difference' remain integral to social analysis in transnationalism (cf. Christensen, 2013b; Christensen and Jansson, 2011). The same is true for the non-deterministic theoretical interventions of 'mediatization' where it has been historically contextualized and construed as a complex meta-process rather than a singular logic (Hepp, 2010; Krotz, 2008).

Against this backdrop, there has been a noted increase in the publications that address various forms of cosmopolitanism (Brown and Held, 2011; Held, 2010, to name but a few). While transnationalism cannot be equated with cosmopolitanism, the increased interest in cosmopolitanism is, in many ways, linked with heightened mediatization and trans-border flows. In its simplest sense, cultural cosmopolitanism implies an openness towards the *Other* and ethically oriented self-reflexivity articulated as boundary-crossing and questioning of dominant categories. There are many different takes on cosmopolitanism, ranging from cultural to political cosmopolitanism(s) (see, e.g., Delanty, 2009), from Beck's (2004) visionary and philosophical accounts to Hannerz's (1990) cosmopolitan competences; from Habermas' (2006) normatively defined cosmopolitan democracy and to more vernacular, practice-oriented cosmopolitanisms (e.g., Bhabha, 1996; Nava, 2007; Nowicka and Rovisco, 2009; Werbner, 1999).

Despite the fact that there are ideological/epistemological 'fault lines' (Hannerz, 2005) that divide cultural and political cosmopolitanists (see also Robertson, 2010), there are common questions born of mediatization which are closely linked with increased digitalization and individualization of media technologies (cf. Krotz, 2007; 2008) and the intertwining of technological connectivity and tradition (cf. Morley, 2007). At the ontological everyday level, a mediatized perceptiveness of the declining roles of historicism (in understanding and predicting social and natural forces) and distrust in institutional governance brings with it a *de facto* acceptance of open-endedness. As Beck and Willms (2004) rightly note, 'not only is the future indeterminate, but its indeterminacy is part of the meaning of present' (p. 34). Assuming we have passed beyond the linear historicism and positivism of the modern towards an inevitably open-ended late modernity, phenomena such as growing transnational economic connections, migration and global financial crises, environmental destruction and consumption of global media and commodities remind us that we share a global future – however glum or bright one can envision it to be in the face of climate change and resource scarcity. This adds to the relevance of cosmopolitan ideals, reviving the debate around global citizenship and mediated cultural processes in enabling shared visions.

On the flip side, such open-endedness and the cosmopolitan emphasis on the universals also engender reflexes of protectionism, racism and parochialism and a mediated search for ontological security through formations of new 'home territories'. As such, and against a transnational backdrop, cosmopolitanization of social life and mediatization then need to be seen as yielding both acceptance of, and resistance to, the moral and ethical ideals of openness. I invoke cosmopolitanism here vis-à-vis mediatization, as there is clearly a need for (and a gap to be filled by) critically oriented and empirically supported analyses that intervene in the debate and address cultural dimensions of cosmopolitanism. One can ask, among other questions, what heightened connectivity translates into in everyday realities of cultural lifeworlds.

3. Thinking fields and mediatized lifeworlds together

Following from this discussion, and to further narrow down the scope, we should note here the accentuated role the individual/individualization and consumption have gained in parallel to globalization and mediatization. A research agenda that specifically addresses the sociology of mediatization and cosmopolitanization, then, needs to be further nuanced by considerations of location and technology in situated contexts (*de facto* engaging with the individual, and his/her networks and consumptive practices) in order to capture particularities. Such an agenda would involve discussing the role of both structures and subjective positionings in mediatized lifeworlds to address the simultaneously connecting and constraining forces of mediatization and trans-border flows. As a case in point, our study on various segments of the Swedish population of both migrant and native origin living in Stockholm revealed that place and technology factor heavily into both how fields and habitus are shaped and how agency is steered (Christensen, 2012; 2013a).

The overall discourse of globalization underscores deterritorialization and downplays place and borders. The mediatization debate, in general, has understandably avoided emphasizing architectural variations in technology in order not to reproduce the techno-determinism of earlier accounts such as those generated by 'Internet Studies'.[3] While at its meta-level I would argue against framing the longitudinal process of *mediatization* as a fragmented phenomenon and as singular sets of practice (as in consumption of Media A vs. Media B), the qualitative interviews are illustrative of the significance and persistence of both locational elements and increasingly complex variations of technological features (among other important factors) that condition everyday mediations. On the whole, how individuals and groups are socially positioned, the accumulation of capital, and the development of a Bourdieuian 'feel for the game' are clearly intertwined with geographic markers and the extent to which an expressive capacity is afforded by dominant technological applications.

Offline space, such as place of origin and the urban environment where one lives (in addition to class, gender, education and moral-political orientation), has a significant role in influencing perceptions of selfhood and *Otherness* and global mobility. The interviews revealed ambivalence and distrust (about/of both technology and changes in society) when it comes to personal views of media saturation of everyday life and mobility. A German female, aged 42, who moved to Sweden 13 years ago commented on global mobility and cosmopolitanization of cities:

> I almost don't dare answer honestly. I'm critical about borders, I don't think you should have open borders because of criminality. I see immigration critically because of criminality and other things, but I think it's important that we as Europeans can move freely, so there are two sides.
>
> (personal interview, 2012)

Views regarding state-regulated control of borders and movements differed from one individual and group to another. Self-regulation and self-monitoring were often pointed to as means to take advantage of the open connectivity that technology and globalization bring, while avoiding the pitfalls (cf. Christensen, 2013a). On the whole, some of the informants displayed reflexivity and awareness along with acceptance (even if not moral approval) of the 'control' dimension of mediatized societies and human/cultural flows. Some were more critical. One inner-city resident, a 30-year-old British female who migrated from the UK, noted:

> It's a double-sided question. For me personally I have absolutely no problem with being photographed or registered. I can see for some people that they would feel it was Big Brother checking up on them, but on the other side it's a safety measure, a way of protecting property such as schools. In an ideal world you wouldn't need it but we're not in an ideal world.
>
> (personal interview, 2012)

A native Swedish female aged 69, from Stockholm, reflected on the ambivalent nature of mediatized life (in response to the question of 'future trends' and penetration of technology) by commenting: 'In one way it's a reduction of freedom and it becomes more of a surveillance society. But at the same time it gives opportunities; I wouldn't say freedom, but opportunities to be used in positive ways' (personal interview, 2012).

While mediated communication, in some cases, was seen as an alternative to the restrictions and exclusivism of actual space and mobility, borders and enclaves also exist in online domains in numerous ways for numerous reasons. To give a few examples from my interviews with Turkish and Kurdish migrants, a young Turkish man in his twenties described how he created different groups and sets of personal data such as photos (practically producing different data-doubles of himself) on his Facebook page. He maintained differentiated personal profiles among his relatives, friends and family in Sweden and Turkey to protect his privacy about his sexual preference and prevent his lifestyle from being monitored (personal interview, 2009). Young Turkish and Kurdish women, in particular, noted how social media made possible alternative ways of connecting and arranging meetings to circumvent offline spatial closures and 'neighbourhood monitoring' (personal interviews 2008–11). I should briefly note here that Turkish migrants form neighbourhoods based on the geographic region in Turkey they originate from and live in close proximity to each other, making monitoring an everyday routine, which troubled many of the younger individuals interviewed. Swedish metropolises such as Stockholm, Gothenburg and Malmo are highly segregated areas where a great majority of the migrants live in suburban parts.

A young woman living in a student flat in Uppsala noted that, while she avoids dedicating her evenings to watching popular Turkish soaps on television, she time-shifts and quickly watches segments online and reads chats and information pages on the web before visiting family and relatives 'to have something to talk about'. She explained that she preferred

Swedish and international channels but did not want to give the impression to her family that she is alienated from her culture or has become too much of a Swede – potentially leading to the diminishing of symbolic capital in certain contexts (personal interview, 2008). Online constellations using place-based resignification that both reclaim presence in the centre and maintain home-oriented ties provide another example of strategized mediation and how Bourdieu's (1990 [1980]) *social field* constitutes an intermediary position between actual territories and virtual flows (sometimes affording resistance and power, and sometimes the reproduction of existing hegemonic categories or new forms of segregation and parochialism). 'Isvecli Turkler (Swedish Turks)', 'Isvec Turkleri (Turks of Sweden)', 'Turkar i Stockholm (Turks in Stockholm)', 'Isvec'teyiz (We are in Sweden)', 'A Group for the Swedish Turkish' and 'Isvecli Konyalilar' (Swedes from Konya) constituted some of the popular Facebook groups at the time of the fieldwork (Christensen, 2011; 2012). As was revealed during the interviews, some of these groups rivalled with each other, displaying forms of symbolic violence such as deleting messages/announcements posted by the administrators of other groups.

While it is not possible to follow Bourdieu to the depths of his analytical vision in this short chapter, it should be noted that the incorporation of Bourdieuian theory (1984 [1979]; 1990 [1980]) has dual relevance here. First, habitus and social field (and accumulation of capital and power) provide an intermediary analytical tool between the macro realm of political economic analysis and everyday cultural dimensions. His conception of field is based on an understanding of power, its unequal distribution and the forms of domination/subordination it enables. Such a material configuration of power and power relations remains key in understanding societal order, social relations and mediated communicative practice. Second, his reflexive sociology allows taking globalization and mediatization beyond their abstract levels and addressing their complexities in empirical contexts, ultimately producing them as 'theories of practice' (see also Bourdieu and Wacquant, 1992). As Bourdieu (1990 [1980], p. 25) argues, this 'presupposes a critical objectification of the epistemological and social conditions that make possible both a reflexive return to the subjective experience of the world and also the objectification of the objective conditions of that experience'. The entangled meta-processes of mediatization and cosmopolitanization of social fields and everyday lifeworlds clearly necessitate such a dialectical view and reflexivity.

Bourdieu himself did not address 'the transnational' as a category in which non-nation-state-centric fields and habitus take shape. Taking it a step further here, his notion of the field allows a construction of transnational social formations as fields with both porous and rigid boundaries. While the construct of field is directly associated with class-based professional and cultural domains, if we are to take fields, akin to Jenkins (1992, p. 85), as social arenas defined by 'the stakes that are at stake', then the similarities between differentiated fields and the particular geographies and practices of being/becoming (Hall, 1996) generated by transnational dynamics become obvious. Although there are marked differences in economic, social and cultural capital across the members of transnational groups, they also constitute stakeholders, within the host-country context they live in, with common aims and inclinations towards (1) acquiring representation and recognition in the larger social arena and (2) engaging in collective and individual pursuits of symbolic power accumulation as well as resistance within the field itself (creating intra-group tensions).

What we discussed earlier in broader terms in relation to cultural cosmopolitanism and cosmopolitanization of fields and the everyday is also at play in transnational contexts. In many ways, migrant groups develop various forms of adaptive sensibilities and a vernacular repertoire of resources to cope within and across cosmopolitanized fields. Yet, it should be importantly noted here that transnationalism and cosmopolitanism cannot be conflated. For instance, the general absence of transnational *others* in the cultural imagination and civic realm of the host countries also engenders cultural reflexes towards seeking belonging through marginal expressivity. In some cases, individuals and groups find refuge in mediated rearticulations of home and nation in larger-than-life forms, turning home-bound symbolism into a site of worship. Similar reflexes of rejection, hostility and racism are present among native populations, simultaneously creating cosmopolitanized zones of contact and exclusivism alongside each other in urban centres.

The roles of communication and mediation, symbolic accumulation, and the complexities of capital conversion (which Bourdieu does not elaborate in depth) beyond class boundaries constitute areas in need of fresh inquiry in order to fully grasp 'mediatized everyday lifeworlds' in specific contexts today. Theoretically, the incorporation of the trope of transnationalism is complementary to the Bourdieuian transhistoricity and lack of attention to epochal, spatial and cultural particularity in his discussion of fields and capital. Empirically, the *inside view* of social phenomenology (Berger and Luckmann, 1967; Berger, Berger and Kellner, 1973; Schütz and Luckmann, 1973) and Ihde's (1990) phenomenology of technology further complement Bourdieu's sociology by way of allowing a more honed appreciation of the role of geography and technology – or, 'the subjective geography of technology' (Morley, 2007, p. 250). Such an approach would solidify *mediatized cosmopolitanism* as a grounded approach that rests upon both structural/institutional and agentic/experiential considerations. It would also offer a theoretically and empirically meaningful ground to regard the dual forces of cosmopolitanization and mediatization in their complexity and contradictions. As Atkinson (2010) elaborates, Bourdieu's epistemology is compatible with the individual lifeworld to 'adequately handle the heterogeneity and subtlety of human lives' (p. 5).[4]

In relation to transnational groups, which we took as a case in point here, there is already a rich body of literature exploring the linkages between digital communication use and migrant communities (cf. Adams and Ghose, 2003; Nakamura, 2002) in relation to both the place of mediation in the everyday lives and political deliberation and cultural expression. My fieldwork is illustrative of how mobility runs parallel to significant and complex forms of boundedness. Fixity of field/s (*strategies*) is challenged, if not eliminated, through mediations of place and technological intervention (*tactics*).[5] At the same time, mediated communication opens the door for the creation of new borders. Ethnographic analysis and a phenomenological perspective (both phenomenological geography and phenomenology of technology and media) provide a framework to understand how individuals engage with the world via media technologies.

To continue with phenomenology of geography, as noted in my analysis of the migrant groups in Sweden (cf. Christensen, 2012), the city of residence and the city of origin have significant material and symbolic meanings that impact upon patterns of sociality, communication and cultural practice. Through mediated (technologically and otherwise) signification, space becomes place and its meaning is continuously contested and reinvented. Rather than detaching, mediations of place reattach. Moores (2006; 2007) and Moores and Metykova (2010) also advocate a phenomenological approach to the study of transnational groups and mediation. As Moores (2006, emphasis added) notes:

> How are time-space routines and dwellings – at different geographical scales – reconstructed, with the possibility that experiences of at-homeness could be modified and multiplied? Is there a reorganization of senses of reach and experiential horizons that accompanies this process? *Crucially, from my perspective, do media sometimes figure significantly in those transformations?*

Phenomenological geography provides a useful conceptualization of place whereby the latter is 'understood as more than simply a spatial location. It is location that has been transformed by the routine practices and feelings of its inhabitants' (Moores and Metykova, 2010). While this perspective, as Moores and Metykova argue, allows for an individual's 'environmental experiences' to develop and change over time, it makes visible historical and cultural specificities.

Don Ihde's (1990) experimental phenomenology (or, postphenomenology) is useful in further nuancing the debates around mediatization and cosmopolitanization. Mediatized culture (parallel to global mobility and market forces) figures as the common cultural denominator of late modernity and is deeply entrenched in everyday lifeworlds and meaning-and sense-making processes (cf. Christensen and Jansson, forthcoming). Social life and communicative practice rest upon collective sense-making and meaning-production through negotiation and contestation of ideas and visions. Through this process, both practices and habits (e.g., uptake, over time, of technological artefacts as necessity rather than luxury items or capital value of certain acts and symbolic exchanges over others) and fields and habitus are shaped and reshaped.

Mediatization, both in scalar terms and in relation to the textural density of the forms it assumes, has reached a level (Christensen and Jansson, forthcoming) where it is impossible to think of the structural and the everyday realms without taking into account technological modifications. As Ihde (1990) frames it, media and accompanying technologies are themselves embedded in culture (just like other historical technologies, such as papyrus). They do not distantiate human mind and body from reality, but they reconstitute them in it. Cultural positionality and the sorts of morality and normativity (such as cosmopolitanism) produced in mediatized lifeworlds, in return, are not merely 'affected' by technology and media use. Rather, the 'technologically textured ecosystem' or the 'technosystem' (Ihde, 1990, p. 3) is generative of particular modes of belonging/identity and spatial morality. Such an understanding of technology and mediation underlines the redundancy of dichotomizations, as in real vs. virtual. Phenomenology of technology, then, allows a vision that exceeds the limitations of instrumental and substantive theories of technology, where the former regards technology as merely manufactured and subservient to politics and culture, and the latter attributes to it autonomy above all competing processes and norms (as in dystopic scenarios of destruction by technological agents).

4. Mediatized worlds – mediatized cosmopolitanism

The role of the media, particularly in relation to cultural globalization, has been explored extensively in media studies. Media-centrism, inadequate contextualization and lack of empirical studies have been commonly pointed to as problems. In the mediatization literature, less attention has been paid to critical considerations of place, power dynamics and technology. While it is virtually impossible to do justice to such questions in a short chapter, taking the provocative and inspiring scope afforded by this edited volume as a starting point, I sought to offer some reflections and point to further questions to which the current mediatization debate leads us.

Combined, Bourdieu's reflexive sociology and social phenomenology have a high degree of relevance for grasping how the structural and everyday experiential dimensions of our media-saturated worlds are yielding a mediatized cosmopolitanism. Culture, for Bourdieu, is a contested realm through which the social order of hierarchies and power is reproduced. His vision reveals the complexities of the ways in which class and culture are intertwined and explicates the material dimensions of mediatization and social reproduction. Yet, the modernist bend in his understanding of the collective and individual realm and his collapse of cultural signification and class into a singular model of reproduction of dominant status through capital accumulation make it difficult to account for the particularities of space, technology and experience. In different but complementary ways, phenomenology and transnationalism open up discursive and empirical possibilities for regarding communication and persons (or communicating persons) and for better grasping the inherent contradictions (i.e., openings and closures) that underlie mediatized cosmopolitanism.

In this framework, geography/place and technology remain as interfaces (in both actual and rhetorical senses) that mediate, generating both nearness and distance, and both proximity and alienation (Bauman, 1989; Silverstone, 2007). Mediated 'place-making' and the persistence of *territoriality* in the technological realm have significance here. While the discourses of globalization and networked connectivity commonly emphasize deterritorialization and placeless flows, mediated modes of sociality and visibility, akin to offline place and social relations, are governed as much by a logic of divisions, borders and control as they are by a technologically enabled openness and inclusions. Mediatized cosmopolitanism is distinct from earlier conceptualizations linking media to cosmopolitanism, roughly put, on a cause–effect axis (cf. Rantanen, 2005). We need not only be concerned with *whether* individuals can/have become true cosmopolitans or the extent to which mediated imaginary fosters genuinely cosmopolitan dispositions.

What needs further attention within the mediatization debate is the resulting tension fields due to the cosmopolitanization of everyday lifeworlds. Both the mediated and physical broadenings of our reach and possibilities are accompanied by a new 'feel for the game' and new social–cultural aspects to consider. This necessitates keeping checks and balances on our paradigms and toolboxes. While mediatized cosmopolitanism and extension of the *self* correspond to 'the erosion of distinct boundaries dividing markets, states, civilizations, cultures, and not least of all the lifeworlds of different peoples' (Beck, 2007), it also brings new possibilities for bounding, controlling and reifying hegemonic roles. As we argue elsewhere, the theoretical interrogation of cosmopolitanism vis-à-vis mediatization, then, finds itself caught up between the impossibility of thinking of cosmopolitanism without actual and virtual forms of encapsulation and the paradoxical nature of the moral–ethical compromise such encapsulation entails for the cosmopolitan vision (Christensen and Jansson, forthcoming). One way of generating deeper understandings of these ambiguities is to look closely into everyday lifeworlds through the lens of nuanced theoretical and empirical frameworks.

Notes

1. 'Secure Spaces: Media, Consumption and Social Surveillance' (2008–12), research project funded by Riksbankens Jubileumsfond (Swedish National Bank);

preliminary work as part of 'Cosmopolitanism from the Margins: Mediations of Expressivity, Social Space and Cultural Citizenship' (2012–15), research project funded by the Swedish Academy of Sciences; and, 'Kinetic Élites: The Mediatization of Social Belonging and Close Relationships among Mobile Class Fractions' (2012–15), research project funded by the Swedish Academy of Sciences.
2. This chapter does not directly address these questions, but they inform the general discussion presented here.
3. By 'Internet Studies' I mean the body of uncritical, celebratory scholarship that has been produced on media use from the 1990s onwards.
4. Bourdieu himself acknowledges that he drew insights from phenomenology. Yet, that field-activity always leads to reproduction in Bourdieu's sense, and actual reflexivity is merely a feature of habitus (rather than an individual agentic attribute), occurring during times of crisis and movement between fields, remains problematic – hence the need for incorporating phenomenology.
5. In the sense of de Certeau (1984).

References

Adams, P. C. and Ghose, R. (2003) 'India.com: The construction of a space between'. In: *Progress in Human Geography*, 27(4), pp. 414–37.

Atkinson, W. (2010) 'Phenomenological additions to the Bourdieusian toolbox: Two problems for Bourdieu, two solutions from Schutz'. In: *Sociological Theory*, 28, pp. 1–19.

Appadurai, A. (1996) *Modernity at large: Cultural dimensions of globalization* (Minneapolis and London: University of Minnesota Press).

Bauman, Z. (1989) *Modernity and the Holocaust* (Ithaca: Cornell University Press).

Beck, U. (2004) 'Cosmopolitical realism: On the distinction between cosmopolitanism in philosophy and the social sciences'. In: *Global Networks*, 4(2), pp. 131–56.

Beck, U. (2007) 'A new cosmopolitanism is in the air', In: *Sign and Sight*. http://www.signandsight.com/features/1603.html (Date accessed 1 May 2010).

Beck, U. and Willms, J. (2004) *Conversations with Ulrich Beck* (Cambridge: Polity Press).

Berger, P. L. and Luckmann, T. (1967) *The social construction of reality* (New York: Anchor Books).

Berger, P., Berger, B. and Kellner, H. (1973) *The homeless mind. Modernization and consciousness* (New York: Vintage Books).

Bhabha, H. (1996) 'Unsatisfied: Notes on vernacular cosmopolitanism'. In: Garcia-Morena, L. and Pfeifer, P. C. (eds) *Text and nation* (London: Camden House), pp. 191–207.

Bourdieu, P. (1984 [1979]) *Distinction: A social critique of the judgement of taste* (London: Routledge).

Bourdieu, P. (1990 [1980]) *The logic of practice* (Cambridge: Polity Press).

Bourdieu, P. and Wacquant, L. J. D. (1992) *An invitation to reflexive sociology* (Chicago: The University of Chicago Press).

Brown, G. W. and Held, D. (2011) *The cosmopolitanism reader* (Cambridge: Polity Press).

Castells, M. (2012) *Networks of outrage and hope: Social movements in the internet age* (London: Polity).

Christensen, M. (2011) 'Online social media, communicative practice and complicit surveillance in transnational contexts'. In: Christensen, M., Jansson, A. and Christensen, C. (eds) *Online territories: Globalization, mediated practice and social space* (New York: Peter Lang Publishing).

Christensen, M. (2012) 'Online mediations of sociality in transnational spaces: Cosmopolitan re/formations of belonging and identity in the Turkish diaspora'. In: *Journal of Ethnic and Racial Studies*, 35(5), 888–905.

Christensen, M. (2013a) 'Complicit surveillance and mediatized geographies of visibility'. In: Jansson, A. and Christensen, M. (eds) *Media, surveillance and identity: A social perspective* (New York: Peter Lang).

Christensen, M. (2013b) 'Transnational media flows: some key questions and debates'. In: *International Journal of Communication*, 7, pp. 2400–2418.

Christensen, M. and Jansson, A. (2011) 'Fields, territories and bridges: Networked communities and mediated surveillance in transnational social space'. In: Fuchs, C., Boersma, K., Albrechtslund, A. and Sandoval, M. (eds) *The internet & surveillance* (London: Routledge).

Christensen, M. and Jansson, A. (forthcoming) 'Complicit surveillance, interveillance and the question of cosmopolitanism: Towards a phenomenological understanding of mediatization'. In: *New Media and Society*.

Clifford, J. (1998) 'Mixed feelings'. In: Cheah, P. and Robbins, B. (eds) *Cosmopolitics: Thinking and feeling beyond the nation* (University of Minnesota), pp. 362–71.

de Certeau, M. (1984) *The practice of everyday life* (Berkeley: University of California Press).

Delanty, G. (2009) *The cosmopolitan imagination: The renewal of critical social theory* (Cambridge: Cambridge University Press).

Habermas, J. (2006) *Time of transitions* (Cambridge: Polity).

Hall, S. (1996) Cultural studies and the politics of internationalization. In: Morley, D. and Chen, K. H. (eds) *Stuart Hall: Critical dialogues* (London: Routledge), pp. 392–410.

Hannerz, U. (1990) 'Cosmopolitans and locals in a world culture'. In: *Theory, Culture and Society*, 7(2), pp. 237–51.

Hannerz, U. (2005) 'Two faces of cosmopolitanism: Culture and politics'. In: *wStatsvetenskaplig Tidskrift*, 107(3), pp. 199–213.

Held, D. (2010) *Cosmopolitanism: Ideals, realities and deficits* (Cambridge: Polity Press).

Hepp, A. (2010) 'Researching "mediatized worlds": Non-media-centric media and communication research as a challenge'. In: Cammaerts, Bart, Carpentier, Nico, Tomanić Trivundža, Ilija, Pruulmann-Vengerfeldt, Pille, Sundin, Ebba, Olsson, Tobias, Kilborn, Richard and Nieminen, Hannu (eds) *Media and communication studies: Intersections and interventions* (Tartu: University of Tartu Press), pp. 37–48.

Ihde, D. (1990) *Technology and the lifeworld: From garden to earth* (Bloomington, Minneapolis: Indiana University Press).

Jenkins, R. (1992) *Pierre Bourdieu* (London: Routledge).

Khagram, S. and Levitt, P. (2008) 'Constructing transnational studies'. In: Khagram, S. and Levitt, P. (eds) *The transnational studies reader: Intersections and innovations* (New York: Routledge).

Krotz, F. (2007) 'The meta-process of "mediatization" as a conceptual frame'. In: *Global Media and Communication*, 3(3), pp. 256–60.

Krotz, F. (2008) 'Media connectivity: Concepts, conditions, and consequences'. In: Hepp, A., Krotz, F. and Moores, S. (eds) *Network, connectivity and flow: Key concepts for media and cultural studies* (New York: Hampton Press).

Moores, S. (2006) 'Media uses and everyday environmental experiences: A positive critique of phenomenological geography'. In: *Particip@tions: Journal of Audience and Reception Studies*, 3(2).

Moores, S. (2007) 'Media and senses of place: On situational and phenomenological geographies', *Media@lse Electronic Working Paper 12*, Department of Media and Communications (London School of Economics and Political Science), http://www.lse. ac.uk/collections/media@lse (date accessed 1 July 2010).

Moores, S. and Metykova, M. (2010) ' "I didn't realize how attached I am": On the environmental experiences of trans-European migrants'. In: *European Journal of Cultural Studies*, 13(2), pp. 171–89.

Morley, D. (2007) *Media, modernity and technology: The geography of the new* (London: Routledge).

Morley, D. (2011) 'Afterword: Electronic landscapes: Between the actual and the virtual'. In: Christensen, M., Jansson, A. and Christensen, C. (eds) *Online territories: Globalization, mediated practice and social space* (New York: Peter Lang), pp. 273–90.

Nakamura, L. (2002) *Cybertypes: Race, ethnicity, and identity on the internet* (New York: Routledge).

Nava, M. (2007) *Visceral cosmopolitanism: Gender, culture and the normalisation of difference* (Oxford: Berg).

Nowicka, M. and Rovisco, M. (2009) 'Introduction: Making sense of cosmopolitanism'. In: Nowicka, M. and Rovisco, M. (eds) *Cosmopolitanism in practice* (Farnham: Ashgate), pp. 1–16.

Plant, S. (1997) *Zeroes and ones. Digital women and the new techno culture* (London: Doubleday).

Rantanen, T. (2005) *The media and globalization* (Thousand Oaks, CA: Sage).

Robertson, A. (2010) *Mediated cosmopolitanism. The world of television news* (Malden and Cambridge: Polity Press).

Schulz, W. (2004) 'Reconstructing mediatization as an analytical concept'. In: *European Journal of Communication*, 19(1), pp. 87–101.

Schütz, A. and Luckmann, T. (1973) *The structures of the life-world* (Evanston: Northwestern University Press).

Silverstone, R. (2007) *Media and morality: On the rise of mediapolis* (Cambridge: Polity Press).

Splender, D. (1995) *Nattering on the net* (Toronto: Garamond Press).

Stevenson, N. (2002) 'Cosmopolitanism, multiculturalism and citizenship'. In: *Sociological Research Online*, 7(1), http://www.socresonline.org.uk/7/1/stevenson.html.

Stevenson, N. (2003) *Cultural citizenship: Cosmopolitan questions* (Maidenhead: Open University Press).

Vertovec, S. (1999) 'Conceiving and researching transnationalism'. In: *Ethnic and Racial Studies*, 22(2), pp. 447–62.

Vertovec, S. (2009) *Transnationalism* (London: Routledge).

Werbner, P. (1999) 'Global pathways: Working-class cosmopolitans and the creation of transnational ethnic worlds'. In: *Social Anthropology*, 7(1), pp. 17–35.

11
Mediatized Worlds of Communitization: Young People as Localists, Centrists, Multi-localists and Pluralists

Andreas Hepp, Matthias Berg and Cindy Roitsch

1. Introduction

The role of the media in 'communities' and 'community-building' has been a fundamental question since the beginning of media and communication research. However, the focus of this research had mainly been the single community as such. To take some examples, one line of investigation has been the role of the media in building up the imagined community of the nation; another, the media as a reference point of fan cultures or certain scenes. More recently there has been increasing research on new forms of community-building in the internet and social web.

While this investigation of communities and their media use has produced an important contribution to knowledge, which we will also refer to later, this chapter positions two kinds of arguments against this orientation as such: a 'radical argument' and an 'anti-futurologist argument'. At first glance, the two seem to be contradictory. However, taken together, they reflect how we might position our investigation of 'media and community' in the frame of mediatization research. In core, our 'radical argument' is that it seems to be increasingly inappropriate to focus on only one community and the role of media in its constitution. Rather, if we really want to capture the changes of recent mediatization, we have to grasp the 'mediatized totality' of different communities within which human beings position themselves. To investigate this, we will develop the concept of the 'mediatized horizon of communitization'. At the same time – and here our 'anti-futurologist argument' comes in – we must be very careful with any projection that the emergence of digital media would have resulted in a complete change of communitization (*Vergemeinschaftung*).[1] This is also the case if we analyze the communitizations of young people, who, as 'digital natives', are very often understood as being highly different in their mediatized way of building up social relations and communities. Taking these two arguments as a starting point, this article first introduces our fundamental theoretical concepts. Based on this, we explain our methodology of a qualitative, ethnographic research on the communicative networking and mediatized communitization of young people. This research brings us to four types of mediatized horizons of communitization: the horizons of the 'localists', 'centrists', 'multi-localists' and 'pluralists'. Such an empirical analysis offers us the chance to make some more general observations on mediatization and the changing forms of communitization.

2. Horizons of communitization: Rethinking 'community' in the context of mediatization research

In sociology, questions of community are fundamental for the constitution of the discipline as such: Ferdinand Tönnies, for example, located the 'general classification of key ideas' (Tönnies, 2001, p. 15) in the field of tension between 'community' (*Gemeinschaft*) and 'society' (*Gesellschaft*). Max Weber – working more with a process approach – understood 'communitization' and 'socialization' as being much more intertwined, but nevertheless as fundamental processes of building up social relationships (Weber, 1978, p. 40). A reflection of the ongoing constitution and change of community in (post-)modern times still continues within sociology, as present concepts of 'communitarianism' (Etzioni, 1996, p. 16), fluid 'aesthetic communities' (Bauman, 2001, p. 65) or 'post-traditional communities' (Hitzler and Pfadenhauer, 2010) indicate. We can grasp this sociological discussion as the implicit reference point for investigating the relation between 'media' and 'community' within media and communication research. However, here, 'community questions' (Wellman, 1979) are understood in a more focused way, analyzing the role of the (transforming) media for communitization. Therefore, when we use the term 'communitization' in contrast to 'community', we emphasize the subjective perspective of feeling as a part of a 'community' instead of the more structural perspective of a 'community' as a social entity.

In recent years, a core focus of this research has been to investigate the role of the internet in our changing communitization and, in so doing, to analyze how far it is, alternatively, a 'driving force' or a 'manifestation' of this change. We can refer here, for example, to Sherry Turkle's most recent book, *Alone Together*. Researching the changes of our lives, which, through digital media, become 'networked lives', she also reflects how far this is related to so-called online communities. Referring to this concept, Turkle emphasizes that we should not ' "broaden our definition of community" to include [...] virtual places' (Turkle, 2011, p. 238). For her, these places, rather, build up 'worlds of weak ties' (p. 239) that do not comprise communities, as the latter are 'constituted by physical proximity, shared concerns, real consequences, and common responsibilities' (p. 239). Rather, our 'networked lives' with their (weak) 'always on' (p. 17) connectivity are a manifestation of the loss of real community experience.

While such an understanding reduces communitization to the level of local communities – something that is not substantial if we consider our own research – Turkle's arguments are, nevertheless, characteristic of the idea that communitization changes with digital media. Here she is very much in line with research conducted by Barry Wellman and his team (Wellman, Quan-Haase, Boase Chen, Hampton, Díaz and Miyata, 2003), who, however, come to a completely different evaluation. They argue that the internet supports what they call 'networked individualism', that is, 'the transformation of interpersonal social structures from "door-to-door" or "place to place" to "person to person", and (even more specialized) "role to role" relations' (Hua and Wellman, 2010, p. 1164). For them, this is not so much a decline, more a transformation that is characteristic of the present (western) cultures and societies. This conforms to the position of Manuel Castells, who emphasizes that the internet supports a networked individualism but does not cause it (Castells, 2001, pp. 130–1). In his ethnographic research, Andreas Wittel refers to considerations like these, but places more emphasis on the emergence of a new form of 'network sociability' (Wittel, 2008, p. 157). For him, this 'network sociability' should not be understood as a communitization in the original sense of the word, as these (new) social relations would not be based on a shared narration of belonging, but, rather, on an informational organization.

Analyses like these are very often linked to what we might call 'digital natives narrative'. This expression reflects the very often implicit (and not further considered) argument that the above-mentioned changes – however they are evaluated – are much more characteristic of the generation that grew up with digital media, that is, the 'digital natives' (Prensky, 2001). This link exists in a double way. On the one hand, generational concepts are very often an implicit reference in the work of academics who focus on our present changes of communitization (cf., for example, Turkle, 2011, p. xii). On the other hand, publications on the generation of so-called 'digital natives' discuss the change of social relations and communities as one characteristic moment of these generations' identities (cf. Palfrey and Gasser, 2008, p. 17–38).[2]

Reflecting on this scholarly work in the perspective of mediatization research, it is important and problematic at the same time. It is important, as it gives us an impression of the phenomena's complexity. The research indicates that the internet or the social web does not have just 'one effect' on communitization. Rather, we are confronted with a circular phenomenon, as Manuel Castells tried to comprehend with his concept of the internet as a 'material basis' of a 'networked individualism': The change of social life-forms goes hand in hand with the establishment of an appropriate communication environment that, in turn, stabilizes the present change. However, at the same time the aforementioned research is problematic insofar as it remains an analysis of digital media (the social web, mobile phones, etc.), mainly in terms of generational change. Phenomena of digital media and communitization are researched in isolation from their further contexts as well as from other kinds of media, and quite often an over-homogeneous image of the generation of 'digital natives' is constructed.

At this point, the mediatization approach offers a different kind of paradigm for conceptualizing the role of 'old' and 'new' media for communitization. Summarizing present understandings of mediatization (cf. Hjarvard, 2013; Krotz and Hepp, 2013; Lundby, 2009; Schulz, 2004), we can argue that mediatization is a concept for analyzing the interrelation between media-communicative and socio-cultural change (Hepp, 2013, p. 31). Thereby, mediatization refers at the same time to quantitative as well as to qualitative aspects. Quantitatively, the concept of mediatization reflects the increasing spread of technical communication media in spatial, temporal and social contexts. However, this is related to qualitative aspects, that is, to a 'communicative construction' (Knoblauch, 2013) of socio-cultural entities that alter with changing media environments. At this point, the concept of 'mediatized worlds' is related to the argument for investigating not only the influence of one kind of medium[3] on a certain entity but also how different kinds of media altogether are constitutive for the presently changing processes of the communicative construction of 'small life-worlds' (Luckmann, 1970) and 'social worlds' (Shibutani, 1955; Strauss, 1978). When we call them 'mediatized worlds', we are referring to this approach (cf. Hepp, 2013, pp. 75–83).

Taking such a perspective on communitization, we inevitably have to reflect the following question: what, then, is the 'mediatized world' we might refer to? A first approximation might be to answer this question by arguing that we are currently confronted with 'mediatized worlds of communitization'. To explain this phrase in more detail, we have to consider the term 'communitization' (*Vergemeinschaftung*), which refers back to Max Weber.[4] For Weber, communitizations are social relationships in which the orientation of social action rests 'upon a subjectively *felt* (affectual or traditional) *mutual sense of belonging* among those involved' (Weber, 2013, p. I, §9, original emphases). This classical definition is helpful in answering our question for two reasons. First, it does not assume a particular territorial foundation of community, but locates communitization in the character of a social relation. Communitizations can, therefore, be local (something Turkle has in mind when speaking about the neighbourhood as a community), but can also be widely scattered (if we think about the communitization of a certain fan culture, for example). Second, Weber's definition places emphasis upon the manner in which this sense of belonging is 'felt', something that is not simply associated with traditional forms of communitization. He thus draws attention to the fact that we also need to consider forms of communitization that are *non*-traditional but which, nonetheless, involve a strong sense of belonging (cf. Hitzler and Pfadenhauer, 2010; Knoblauch, 2008). Both are related to an individual perspective, that is, a communitization is a belonging *felt subjectively* in a social relationship.

If we take this understanding of communitization as a starting point, 'mediatized worlds of communitization' can be seen in two ways. The first is in relation to one specific communitization, that is, in the perspective of a defined social relation as such. As emphasized above, this has been the typical starting point in media and communication research which has investigated various forms of communitization as mediated phenomena. Examples for this would be the research on nations as 'imagined communities' (Anderson, 1983) being constructed by, among other things, mass media discourses (cf., for example, Billig, 1995; Madianou, 2005). In addition, this kind of research can also focus on communities of certain places or interests articulated by different kinds of community media (Bailey, Cammaerts and Carpentier, 2008; Howley, 2010; Jankowski, 2006). Other examples might be the different kinds of 'interpretative communities' (Lindlof, 1988), especially in the form of fan communities (cf., for example, Baym, 2010, pp. 73–90; Jenkins, 2006). In all of these cases, we might investigate these communities as 'mediatized worlds', focusing on how these communities as certain social worlds are articulated across a variety of different media.

However, taking original reflections from Weber, the more interesting second way might be to take the subjective perspective more seriously. In such a view, we do not focus on the social entity of one community as a mediatized world but on an individual and the totality of his or her mediatized world of communitization. In this sense, the idea of the mediatized world refers to the 'everyday life-world' (Schütz and Luckmann, 1973) of this individual. This said, we do not investigate the mediatization of this whole lifeworld – a venture that would hardly be possible. Rather, we take communitization as one important aspect of the 'everyday life-world' and research its mediatization across a variety of different kinds of media. If we adopt such an approach, we do not focus on one single kind of communitization (within a neighbourhood, fan culture, nation, etc.) but on how the individual positions himself or herself in the variety of these different communitizations and how this positioning might change with mediatization.

For such an undertaking we need a concept to theorize this totality of communitizations in a subjective perspective. This is exactly what the concept of 'mediatized subjective horizons of communitization' has been developed for (see Hepp, 2013, pp. 122–6). In our view, the above-mentioned social phenomenological approach of Alfred Schütz and Thomas Luckmann is particularly powerful in understanding what a subjective view on communitization means.[5] They characterize the experience of the everyday lifeworld of an individual as being taken for granted. Consequently, actions in the everyday lifeworld are initially regarded as being unproblematic. However, this lack of questioning is hedged around with uncertainties:

> One experiences that which is taken for granted as a kernel of determinate and straightforward content to which is cogiven a horizon which is indeterminate and consequently not given with the same straightforwardness. This horizon, however, is experienced at the same time as fundamentally determinable, as capable of explication. [...] [W]hat is taken for granted has its explicatory horizons – horizons therefore of determinable indeterminacy.
>
> (Schütz and Luckmann, 1973, p. 9)

It is now possible to transfer this kind of reasoning to communitization mediated by the media. What people experience as taken for granted are – besides the communitization of local groups based on direct communication – moments of translocal communitization articulated by reciprocal communicative exchange via media, such as phone calls or the exchange of e-mails with friends at different places. Communitizations characterized by more far-reaching translocal horizons of meaning, however, are 'determinable indeterminacies', as they do not rely on direct or reciprocal (communicative) experience, but on 'imaginations' with a probable origin in produced media communication.

If we consider this from a subjective point of view, we can say that for each individual person there is a complex whole of 'meaning horizons for communitization' in which that person is situated, with, of course, situational variation. This whole can be termed the subjective horizon of communitization. For an individual, this horizon poses a 'determinable indeterminacy' since it is experienced as an unproblematic reference framework of communitization in the everyday world. Through various experiences, single moments within this horizon of communitization may become problematic, especially when it comes to translocal communitizations based on processes of media communication. At this point, direct local experience and mediated translocal experience are related.

For today's 'mediatized worlds', we can assert that subjective horizons of communitization are sustained by diverse networks of (media) communication. They are, thus, comprehensively mediatized, meaning that they are 'moulded' by the specifics of various media. This refers, to begin with, to all moments of translocal communitization. The various horizons of meaning profoundly refer back to different forms of media communication, as has been frequently argued before. One can even assume that an intensively translocal-oriented subjective horizon of communitization is imaginable only in media cultures, that is, cultures being marked by mediatization.

This said, the appropriate starting point for analyzing the 'mediatized worlds of communitization' is, in our view, researching 'mediatized horizons of communitization'. The reason for this is that only if we focus on the individual horizon in its totality are we able to answer the question of how communitization changes with present mediatization: otherwise, our research would stick to the change of one community as such but not to the (possible) transformation of communitization.

3. Methodology: Contextualized qualitative network analysis

To research this complexity of community horizons, we want to use a methodology we call contextualized network analysis. The idea of this methodology is to combine media ethnography with a more structured way of ascertaining the communication networks of people and analyzing both within the frame of an approach which is oriented to theory development. For us, media ethnography is not an 'ethnography proper' in the sense of a long-term stay and 'thick description' (Geertz, 1994) of the (media) life of a certain group. Instead, we use an approach that works with 'ethnographic miniatures' (Bachmann and Wittel, 2006, p. 200), that is, short-term stays in certain contexts in which we conduct our data grouped around a binding research question. This is, in our case, the question of how the totality of belonging is constructed in the lives of young people and how this is related to their communication networks, being built up as forms of 'reciprocal media communication' ('personal communication') and forms of 'produced media communication' ('mass communication' or 'public communication'). All data was collected in two German cities (Bremen and Leipzig) and the surrounding rural areas; it comprises 60 cases of young people aged between 16 and 30. In more detail, our methodology is based on a three-level approach (for the different kinds of data sources, see the figures in Section 4).

Meaning dimension: On the level of meaning, we work with typical methods of qualitative and ethnographic media research. In summary, our investigation is based on interviews of between 90 and 230 minutes (on average 130 minutes), focusing on the topics of media appropriation and connectivity, (media) biography and felt belonging/communitizations. Additionally, the interviews include a half-standardized part in which we asked our interview partners about their personal and financial situation and their outlay on media use, and to sequence the various communitizations they feel a belonging to in relation to their subjective relevance. If possible, these interviews were conducted at the homes of the interview partners, which gave us the chance to document the domestic places of media use that are protocolled and, if possible, photographed. Doing this, we also asked our interview partners to show us their main communication media and – if they are active – their social network sites. The idea is that this rich data provides a deep insight into the practices of media appropriation, of media connectivity and of communitization, reflecting the meaning these practices have in the everyday lives of the young people.

Structural dimension: With respect to the structural dimension, we work with 'free network cards'. By this we mean drawings made by our interview partners. More concretely, we asked them to sketch, on the one hand, their networks of personal communication in relation to their feelings of belonging ('reciprocal media communication') and, on the other hand, the networks of so-called mass communication ('produced media communication'), if they are relevant for their communitization. Both network cards are explained by our interview partners as part of the above-mentioned interviews to get an understanding of the meaning these different forms of media connectivity have for them. The idea of this approach is twofold. First, we use this instrument as a form of data collection that makes a different kind of remembering possible. By focusing on drawing communication networks in the interview situation, more aspects of media appropriation become accessible than in the (discourse-centred) interview on its own. Second, this form of data collection offers us a subjective representation of the structural dimension of media connectivity the person sees himself or herself positioned in. Both offer us a deeper insight into the structural dimension of networks of communitization than a single interview would allow.

Process dimension: Finally, we are also interested in the process of communicative networking and communitization. To represent this in our data, we asked our interview partners to keep a half-standardized media diary over one week in which they made a note of each form of media use, its reason and – in the case of reciprocal media communication – the communication partners involved. This data was analyzed using self-developed software that visually represents the types of media used across the seven days of the week (social web, television, newspaper, etc.) in relation to the forms of communitization they are relevant to. The idea of this approach is to get an insight into the processes of communicative networking over one week as far as they are relevant to (mediated) communitization. However, the problem with media diaries is the great effort it takes to complete them properly. Because of that, only 27 of our 60 interview partners submitted their media diaries, which is why we use this kind of data as purely supplementary to the data we could obtain for all cases.[6]

These various kinds of data were analyzed based on a categorization in the tradition of grounded theory (cf. Glaser and Strauss, 1999; Strauss and Corbin, 1998). This means a multi-step process, first an 'open coding' of the data, then an 'axial coding' that searches for the interrelation of the analytical categories, and finally a 'selective coding' that rounds off the theory. In all, we developed 70 categories, which are structured into three subgroups: communitization (first core category), communicative networking (second core category) and problem areas (communicative demarcation, communicative mobility and communicative participation). This coding was software-based. Our aim with this analysis is to build up step by step a 'formal theory' (Glaser, 2007; Hepp, 2013, pp. 128–32) of communitization in times of present-day mediatization. This means that we understand the study presented here as a first step towards developing a more general theory of the present changes of communitization in times of increasing mediatization – a theory that will also focus on other generations.[7]

4. Four types of mediatized horizons of communitization: Localists, centrists, multi-localists and pluralists

The main result of our research is that, across our data from young people, we can distinguish four types of mediatized horizons of communitization: the horizons of the 'localists', 'centrists', 'multi-localists' and 'pluralists'. This typology is built across our two core categories, that is, on the one hand 'communitization' and on the other hand 'communicative networking', while reflecting at the same time the thematic orientation of this 'communitization' and 'networking'.[8]

To structure the variety of different communitizations we are confronted with, it was helpful to differentiate two kinds of communities in relation to questions of mediatization (cf. Hepp, Berg and Roitsch, 2011).[9] The first are communities that exist in principle independently of technical media but that are constructed *in their present form* through various kinds of media. We can call them 'mediatized communities'. One example for this is the family, which is originally founded in direct communication but in the present form articulated in various forms of media use: discourses in the media on how the family should be, shared television reception, the organization of the family by e-mail and smartphone, the exchange of digital family photographs in the social web, and so on. Other forms of communitization refer to 'mediatizing communities', namely, communities that cannot exist beyond the media. Again we can take one typical example for this: a film fan culture. The core of this community is already media-related: a certain kind of film or film series like StarTrek. In addition, media are the instruments for building up such a communitization, for instance, by using fanzines or internet forums.

These two kinds of communities can differ in their reach, by a more or less strict local focus ending with various forms of translocal scope. This scope goes hand in hand with the different practices of networking that are either locally orientated or have a more translocal reach. As an intermediating concept between both core categories, we are confronted with different kinds of 'thematic foci' of communitizations and communicative networking. When it comes to questions of communitization, we either have no striking thematic concentration or spread at all, a concentration on a

Table 11.1   Four types of mediatized horizons of communitization

Type	Communitization	Thematic focus	Communicative networking
'Localist'	Dominance of mediatized communities	No striking thematic concentration or spread	Strong local communicative networking, partly national
'Centrist'	Mediatized and mediatizing communities side by side	Dominant thematic concentration	Strong local communicative networking, additionally strong thematic translocal
'Multi-localist'	Mediatized and mediatizing communities side by side	No striking thematic concentration or spread	Local communicative networking, translocal in relation to selected persons and topics
'Pluralist'	Plurality of mediatized and mediatizing communities	Spread of different thematic foci	Extremely strong local and translocal communicative networking

dominant topic (like, for example, a certain religion or popular culture), or a distinct thematic spread (a high multiplicity of themes is important).

Taking 'communitization', 'thematic focus' and 'communicative networking' together, we have criteria to differentiate the above-mentioned four types of mediatized horizons of communitization: the 'localists', 'centrists', 'multi-localists' and 'pluralists' (see Table 11.1).[10] Our aim in the following is to discuss these types of mediatized horizons of communitization in more detail by explaining their characteristics based on two selected cases of young people that are characteristic of each type. When we present these persons, it is important to keep in mind that they are selected as typical representatives of their cases. Therefore, we present no 'thick descriptions' of the 'media life' (Deuze, 2012) of these persons. Instead, our focus is only on one certain moment of their lives, namely, the overall orientation of the young individuals in relation to their feelings and forms of belonging. All the names are pseudonyms to secure anonymity.

1. The most characteristic moment of 'localists' is their strict orientation to mediatized communities. This becomes manifest, first of all, in a highly local communication network, a network that is related to the direct surroundings. In the following, we want to present two cases to exemplify this horizon of communitization. The first is Yessica Nullmair, a 23-year-old retrainee from Bremen, and the second, Felicitas Franke, a 17-year-old schoolgirl from Leipzig. Yessica trained originally to be a nurse, but at the

time of our interview she was attending a vocational retraining course to become a businesswoman in public health. She makes her local orientation very clear when she says: 'I am rather the country girl. I love the countryside [...].' Born in the area around Bremen, she moved into the city for financial and pragmatic reasons, nonetheless already planning the move back to her parents' home municipality. On the basis of her personal communication network card (see Figure 11.1), it becomes manifest that five groups of people are important for her communitization: 'family' (*Familie*), 'friends' (*Freunde*), colleagues at 'work' (*Arbeit*) and her 'retrainee' programme (*Umschüler*) and further 'acquaintances' (*Bekannte*). Nearly all of them live in the direct surroundings. However, besides direct communication, she uses various means of reciprocal media communication with them, especially the mobile and fixed-line phone, Facebook and StudiVZ (a German social network platform for students and young people). Thus, we can say that Yessica's communicative networking of local communitizations happens in a transmedial manner, something that can also be recognized in the visualization of her media diary (see Figure 11.2). Only as part of the group of 'acquaintances', Yessica mentions some contacts to persons with whom she 'came in contact with via StudiVZ, whom I did not know and who are not from my region'.

The second case we want to discuss here as an example of 'localists', the 17-year-old pupil Felicitas from Leipzig, also has a comparably local orientation. Again, we can find locally centred communication networks with reference to the family, friends, classmates and a local aerobic sports group – all groups she feels a deep belonging to. Besides that, she articulates a certain belonging to Saxony, the federal state she lives in, and especially Leipzig, her place of residence: 'Leipziger – yes, exactly, I understand myself as a Leipziger!' This emphatic orientation to a certain city demonstrates that 'localists' are not necessarily country folk. In contrast, we can find a local orientation also with reference to a certain city, a city district or an urban region. Felicitas has more translocal relations than Yessica; however, their relevance for her horizon of communitization is limited. Via Skype, she keeps in touch with her cousin, who at the time of the interview was staying for six months in Northern Ireland. In addition, she comes into contact with formerly unknown persons via social web sites like YouTube, and especially via online games on social network sites like Facebook and Habbo. But she considers these kinds of social relations as 'practically not so intensive' and therefore of no deeper relevance in her subjective horizon of communitizations.

Therefore, in the tension between locality and translocality, 'localists' have a clear tendency towards the local: their typical horizon of communitization is centred around local groups; translocal extensions are rather seldom, of lower everyday relevance, or they refer back to the experience of local communitizations. There are two reasons for a slight translocal reach. On the one hand, there can be personal relations with family

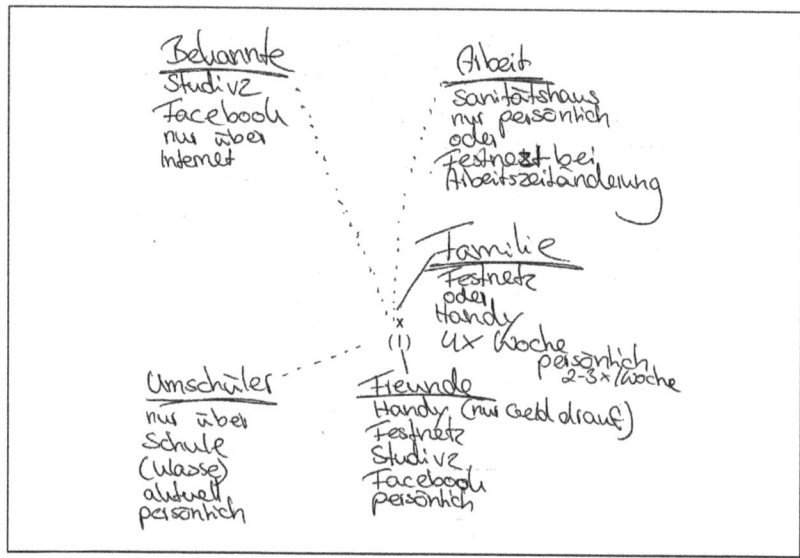

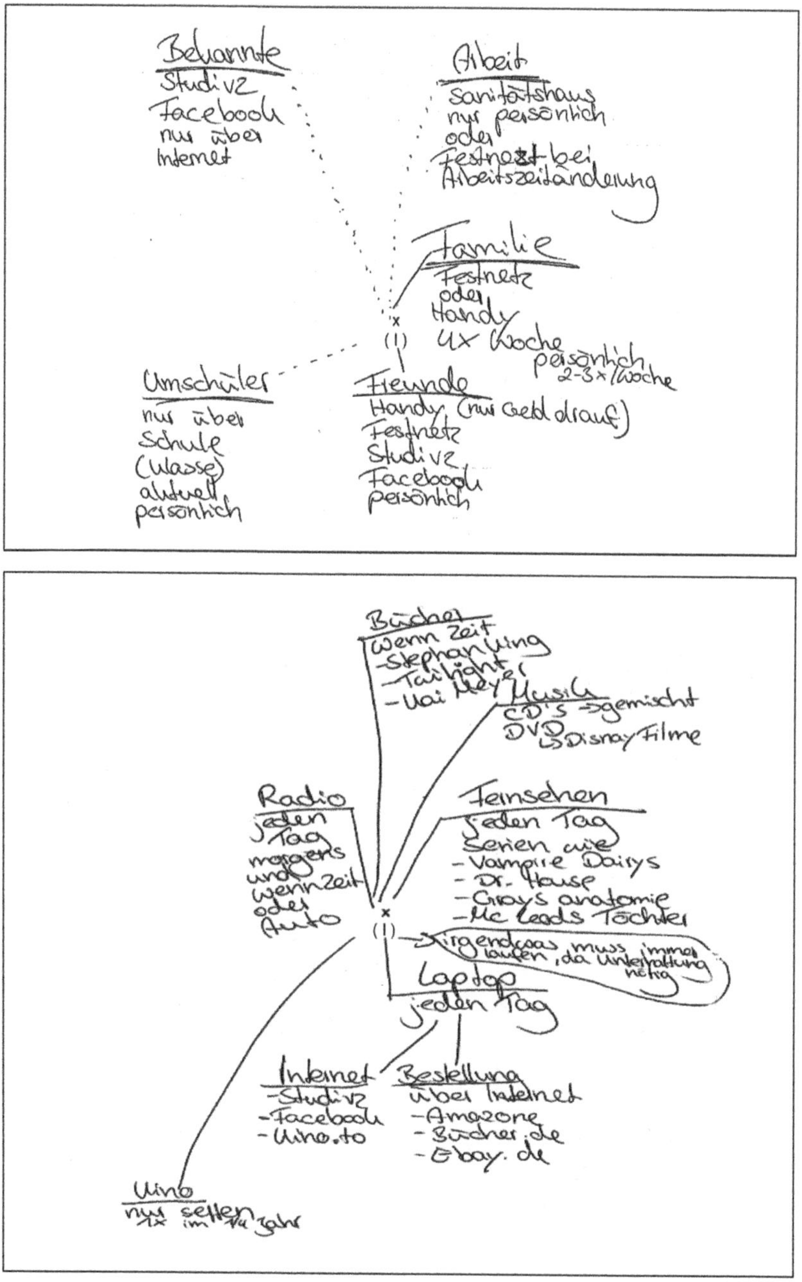

Figure 11.1 Yessica's reciprocal and produced media communication network cards

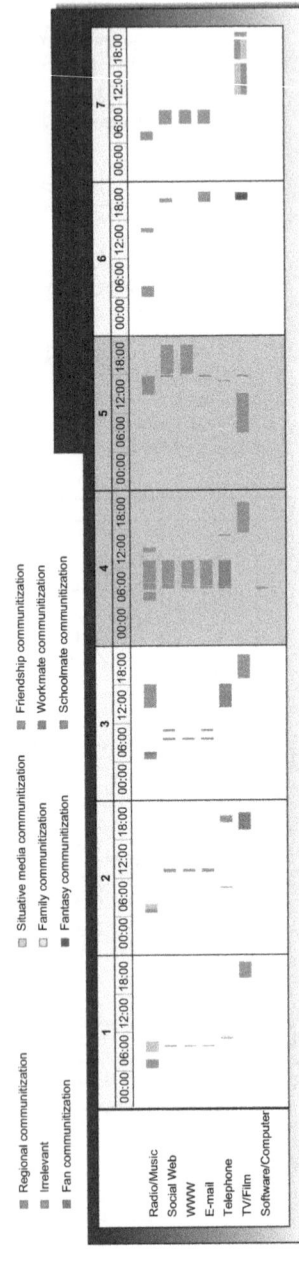

Figure 11.2 Visualization of Yessica's media diary

members or friends who move away and live (for a certain time) at another place. On the other hand, 'localists' are involved in various forms of reciprocal or produced media communication and, based on this, build up certain forms of further translocal feelings of belonging. Besides regional or national communitizations, the latter can also include fantasy communities. As Felicitas says: 'I love to empathize in other worlds, in films, that is really cool.' We find comparable aspects in Yessica's produced media communication card (see Figure 11.1) and when she speaks about the fantasy world of vampires. She avidly reads corresponding novels, watches vampire films and soaps, and understands herself as a fan of the *Twilight* series. Therefore, she sympathizes with this translocal fan community.

This demonstrates that 'mediatizing communities' – for which media communication is constitutive – also play a role in the community horizons of 'localists'. However, they are a rather weak counterpart to the local 'mediatized communities' that dominate this horizon. The direct family surroundings and the local friends are, as the cases of Yessica and Felicitas demonstrate, striking examples of 'mediatized communities' which build the all-dominating core of this horizon and are articulated in an interweaving of direct communication and reciprocal media communication. Accordingly, Yessica talks about her parents' spontaneous telephone calls in the following manner: 'Well, we plan to go to an Asian or Chinese restaurant. Do you want to join us? – Yes, of course, I do!' Or she portrays evenings when she feels 'just absolutely groovy', which is the reason why she has a look 'if there is somebody online in StudiVZ I can join to go out with'. In addition, communication media are important for local communitizations beyond making appointments, as the following section of the interview with Felicitas demonstrates:

First of all I have the idea: Let's watch a DVD. [...] And then I talked before that with another girl, she said, she bought a DVD like mine and liked it – then I asked her: Do you lend it to me? This was not via Facebook, this was now normal for once. And then we agreed on that. And then we wrote, I think, an SMS in-between [...] and [the girlfriend] called me of course back and said 'I come later', yeah, right, and then we are sitting around at my place, maybe eating something, watching that film and chatting of course at the same time.

This quote illustrates the number of different media that are (potentially) used to build up relationships of local friends and communitizations within them. Beside that, it demonstrates how far the communitization in the joint reception of various kinds of media content is part of building up these forms of local relationships.

As already emphasized, the community horizon of 'localists' has neither a distinctive thematic centring nor a decentring. This does not mean that their communitizations are not also marked by certain interests: both Yessica and Felicitas, for example, have an interest in vampires and Hollywood films. Also they are interested in certain forms of pop music, television soaps or novels. However, none of these interests dominate their horizon of communitization, nor is the variety of different topics striking.

2. In contrast to all other types, the core characteristic of 'centrists' is the striking thematic concentration of their horizon of communitization. This concentration can refer to various topics, starting with religion and ending in the sphere of popular culture. The main aspect is that one topic dominates the community horizon. We want to discuss this by introducing two persons, namely, Kerstin Faber, a 27-year-old educator from Bremen, and Dirk Hermann, a 26-year-old self-employed person from Leipzig.[11]

In the case of Kerstin Faber, the horizon of communitization is dominated by her religious orientation. Typical of this is the central position of the religious community she feels a belonging to. This community is, for her, not only the congregational of the Protestant church – which is, however, the main reference point – but it also includes further groups and institutions. Kerstin Faber is engaged in her congregation on various levels. For example, she is engaged in youth work by participating as a supervisor in youth camps, and she supports the confirmation classes. This corresponds with her formal position as a youth leader and member of the parish church council.

This is in clear contrast to the thematic domination of Dirk Hermann's horizon of communitization. Since Dirk was a teenager he has been active in various music bands in the town of Leipzig. At the time of the interview he was in the process of building up an artist agency. This business engagement is closely related to his own interests and feelings of belonging in the field of music, which is the reason that Dirk Hermann refuses to make a clear distinction between work and leisure: 'Also if you attend a concert just to listen it comes to a point when it is relaxed work, because somebody you know comes to you and then chats about work.' With respect to this thematic orientation, different communitizations merge with each other: the communitization with his business partners (*Kunden* and *Geschäftspartner*), his friends (*Freunde*) and former band colleagues (see Figure 11.3). All this happens with a strong connection to the local arts and music scene, to which Dirk Hermann feels a strong belonging.

As already emphasized, in the case of 'centrists' these thematic concentrations dominate the whole horizon of communitization, as this thematic interest is action-guiding for different forms of belonging. More precisely, this means that communitizations with, at first glance, no direct relation to the dominating topic are dominated by, or at least related to, this over-riding 'topic' of communitization. In the case of Kerstin Faber, we can substantiate this by focusing on her workmate communitization, which is deeply

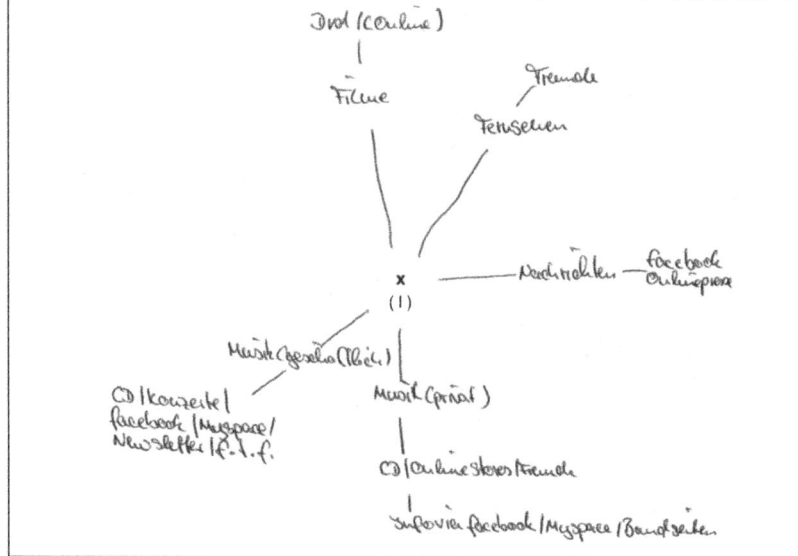

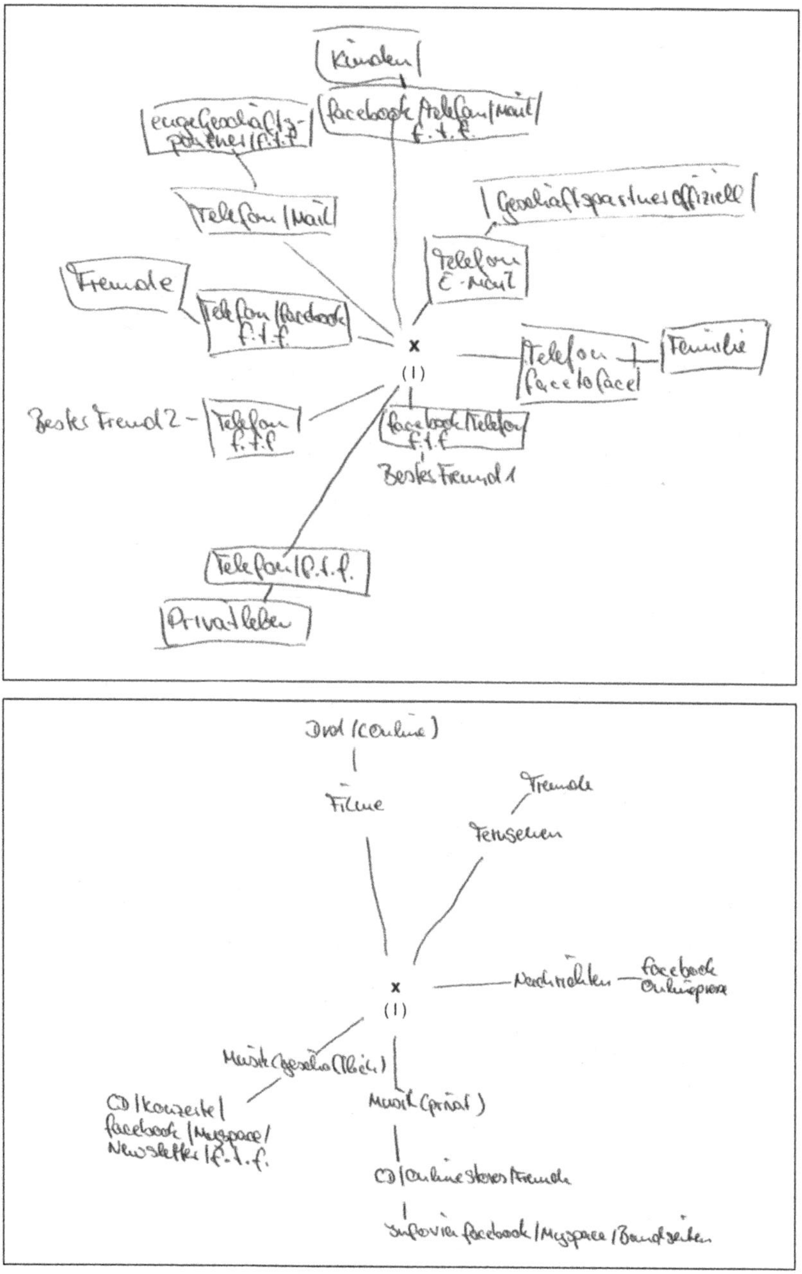

Figure 11.3 Dirk's reciprocal and produced media communication network cards

related to religion because she chose to work in a Protestant kindergarten. And when it comes to imagined moments of communitization – for example, in the sphere of fantasy narrations – she especially feels a belonging to imaginations with links to religion. One example of this is the *Lord of the Rings* film series, which she became interested in when she realized its relation to religion: 'At a certain moment I came to notice that [...] everything has a relation to the bible. That is really thrilling, that there are people who somehow think these things up.' In his interview, Dirk Hermann says himself that he focuses more and more on social relations that have a link to his engagement and activities in the music and arts world, privately as well as beyond. However, this is not only a process of losing former relations but also a process of winning new ones: 'There are many new circles of friends because of the music – with them you are more active.'

All this is related to a certain communicative networking in which the local very often remains a strong point of reference. If we take the example of Dirk, the relevance of the local becomes evident in his narration of situative communitizations at music gigs, but also when he speaks about the status of the whole local music scene. At the same time, this 'being artist' also opens translocal moments within his horizon of communitization, and this is the point where again the media come in.

Kerstin's example also brings to mind the importance of the local in many centred horizons of communitization. With reference to her parish council, she says the following: 'I have always been in the parish, well, the Protestant church. [...] I attended the confirmation classes as many people did [...] and I got stuck there.' As it comes to her corresponding communicative networking, not only media of interpersonal communication (telephone, e-mail and social web) but also produced media (print, radio and music) reflect her religious orientation. This is, on the one hand, indicated in the visualization of Kerstin's media diary (see Figure 11.4) and, on the other hand, when she talks about her interests in TV and film series like 'Hand auf's Herz', 'Alles was zählt' or 'Immenhof'. All of them are German productions, dealing with local life and partly also with questions that interest her in relation to religion. This interest becomes an additional push when it is related to her personal experiences. For example, Kerstin argues that she is interested in the film series 'Immenhof' (produced from the 1950s to the 1970s) because she has a personal link to the film location: 'Our parish has a youth holiday home on the coast there.'

This said, in contrast to 'localists', mediatizing communities have a much greater relevance for 'centrists', especially if they are related to the dominating life topic. The imagined character of these communitizations can even become 'fantasy communitizations', like the 'boarding school community' in the case of Kerstin: while she has never attended a boarding school, she still has a deep interest in the community life there and imagines herself as being linked to this. Such an imaginative situation is totally based on media

191

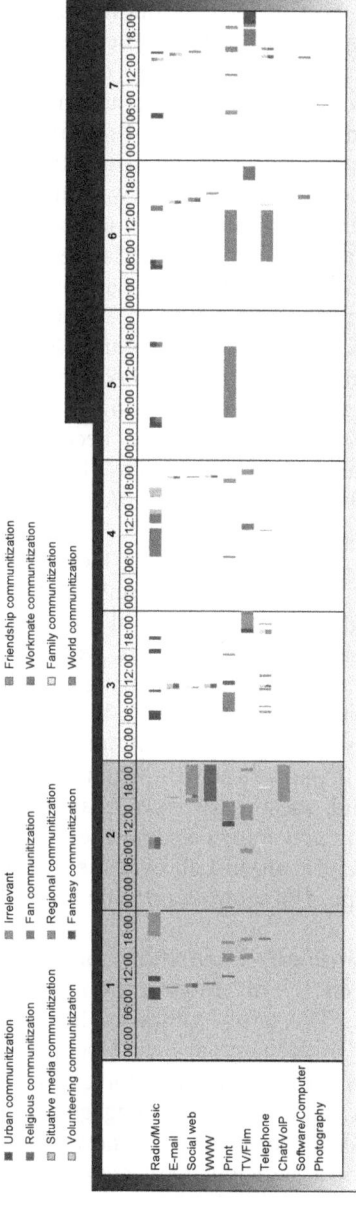

Figure 11.4 Visualization of Kerstin's media diary

texts, like, for example, Enid Blyton's 'St Clare's' books or the 'Harry Potter' narration.

3. 'Multi-localists' have a horizon of communitization that is marked by communitizations built up through translocal communicative networking in relation to selected persons and topics. To discuss this type, we want to focus on two persons, namely, Sebastian Schulmeister (26) from Bremen and Jeffrey Löbig (28) from Leipzig. Sebastian Schulmeister, who works as a customer service employee, moved some years ago from Saxony-Anhalt to Bremen to start as a trainee. He built up a new group of friends, exercises in a fitness studio and is involved in a community of workmates as well as local scenes (HipHop, Graffiti) to which he also feels a translocal belonging. Simultaneously, he maintains intensive relationships with friends and family members living in his home town. In addition, his girlfriend was studying abroad in Austria at the time of the interview. Against this background he keeps up a multi-layered translocal communication network via different media (see Figure 11.5). When referring to his partnership during the interview, he said: 'She doesn't live here, because of that we simply Skype, basically at least about one hour a day.' Those conversations take place on an almost daily basis in the afternoon/evening, as his media diary strikingly indicates (see Figure 11.6).

Jeffrey Löbig – a computer scientist – is not locally mobile: he grew up in Leipzig, still lives there and leaves the city only when on holiday. Therefore, we are confronted with a remarkable local foundation underlying his horizon of communitization. Family members, workmates and friends all live at the place he feels an emotional belonging to, Leipzig, where he is also engaged in an orchestra. It is not so much his own local mobility that explains his 'multi-localist's' horizon of communitization; it is more the mobility of friends who left Leipzig and with whom he stays in close contact via digital media. This said, social network sites are important for him to 'keep contact to people you now meet personally less often'. This can be old school friends 'who are jetting around all over the world' and with whom he communicates via Skype. The same can be said for family members, like his siblings.

In addition, the translocal orientation of Jeffrey's horizon of communitization is driven by his interest in media technologies and his political engagement. The latter comprises his union activities and his belonging to a social movement against Fascism. Both engagements are primarily related to local practices like, for example, participation in demonstrations. However, in relation to his engagements Jeffrey builds up communicative contacts with persons he only knows via the internet. Therefore, local mobility is not a sufficient explanation for a 'multi-localist's' horizon of communitization. Such a horizon can also be driven by certain interests that stimulate building up contacts with people at other localities

193

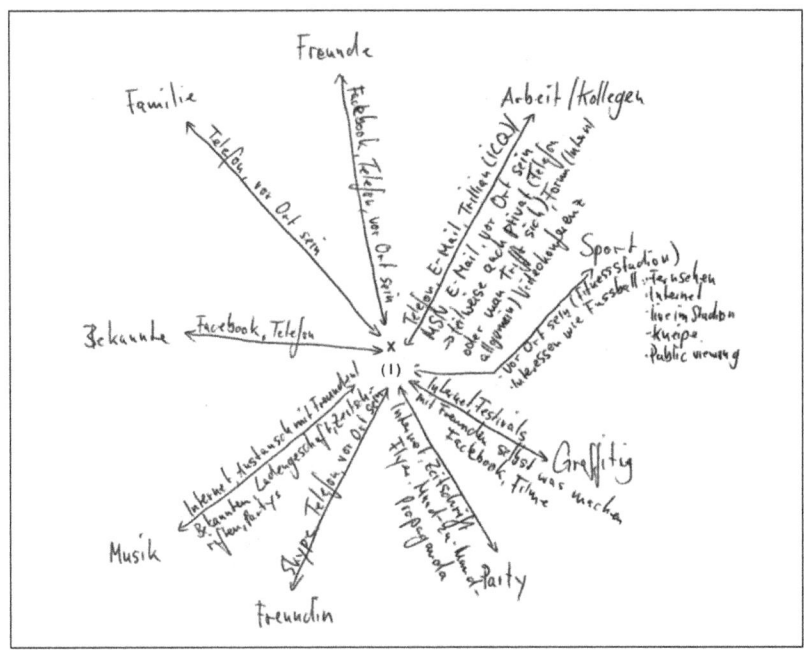

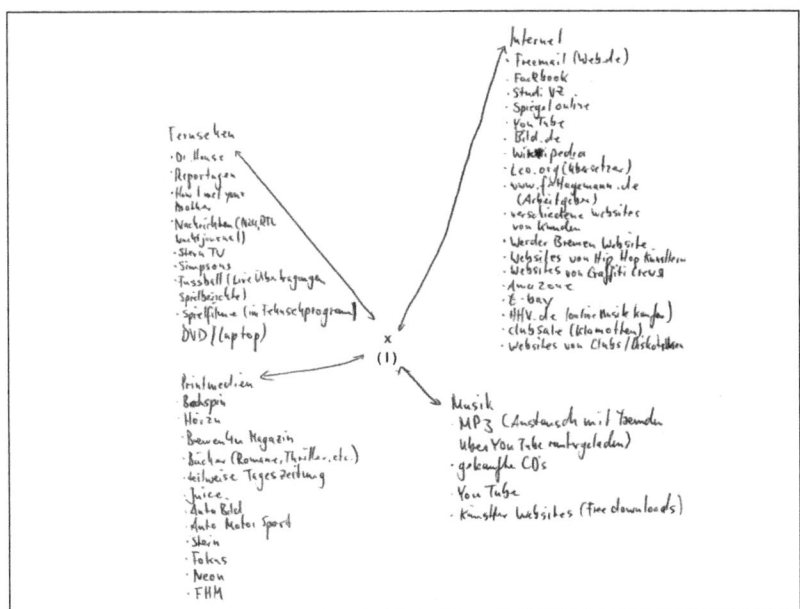

Figure 11.5 Sebastian's reciprocal and produced media communication network cards

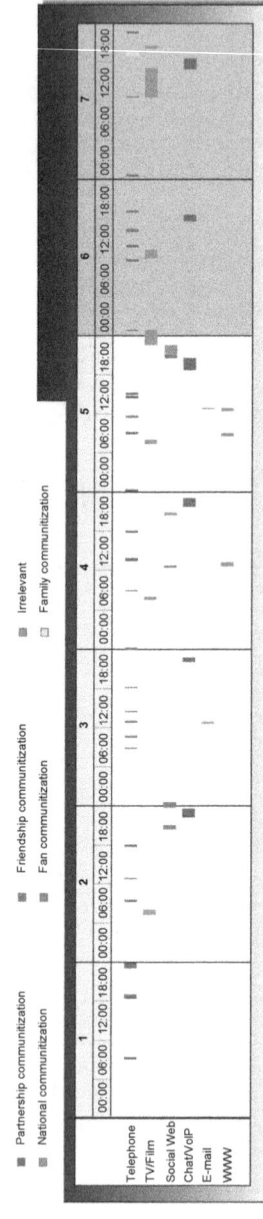

Figure 11.6 Visualization of Sebastian's media diary

alongside the shared interest. For Jeffrey, for example, his 'purely online-friends' are persons he 'contacted via Twitter or via Facebook, namely people you do not know personally but who have certain interests that you share, about which you can exchange and you come into contact with via online forums'.

Comparing a 'multi-localist's' horizon of communitization with the horizon of 'localists' and 'centrists', we can argue that – while the local remains an important point of reference – an extension to the translocal also takes place. Additionally, we can also discern an increasing variability of topics that are of relevance to communitization.

4. A further move in such a direction is characteristic of 'pluralists'. A striking feature of this group is an extensive local as well as translocal communicative networking across a high variety of different topics. As in the case of 'multi-localists', a higher local mobility can be a driving force for this; however, this is an insufficient explanation. We take Sara, a 16-year-old schoolgirl with a migrant background, as the first example.[12] Her father is originally from the Lebanon, her mother from Turkey, and her own biography is marked by an ongoing long-distance mobility: 'In Turkey I was in kindergarten and later we sometimes lived there during the summer [...] I have Turkish friends, all sorts of things.' She still regularly visits her relatives in Turkey during the summer holidays. This has resulted in various further friendships with Turkish migrants across Germany. In addition, Sara built up contacts across Europe when she was in France and the UK as an exchange student. In Brighton she met 'Italians and Frenchmen and Spaniards and, yes, nations from all over Europe and they just have only Facebook and keeping in contact with them is very important for me'. All these translocal communitizations are represented in her personal communication media network card (see Figure 11.7).

However, as said above, this local mobility is again an insufficient explanation for a 'pluralist' horizon of communitization. This becomes obvious when we focus on our second example, Claas Kuhnert, a 29-year-old retrainee who moved to Bremen some years ago but maintains a personal communication network not only across Europe but also across various other parts of the world like Asia, North America, Australia and New Zealand. Although he visited some of the countries on holidays, these contacts are mainly a result of his previous job as a language tutor and teacher for international students: 'Then I made many international acquaintanceships and some of them turned into real friendships.' He keeps these worldwide friendships alive via the social web, e-mail and internet telephone calls – together with occasional visits.

At the same time, a 'pluralist's' horizon of communitization should not be confused with a detachment from the local. In Sara's case her local family, friends and classmates (*Schule, Freunde*) remain a central reference point

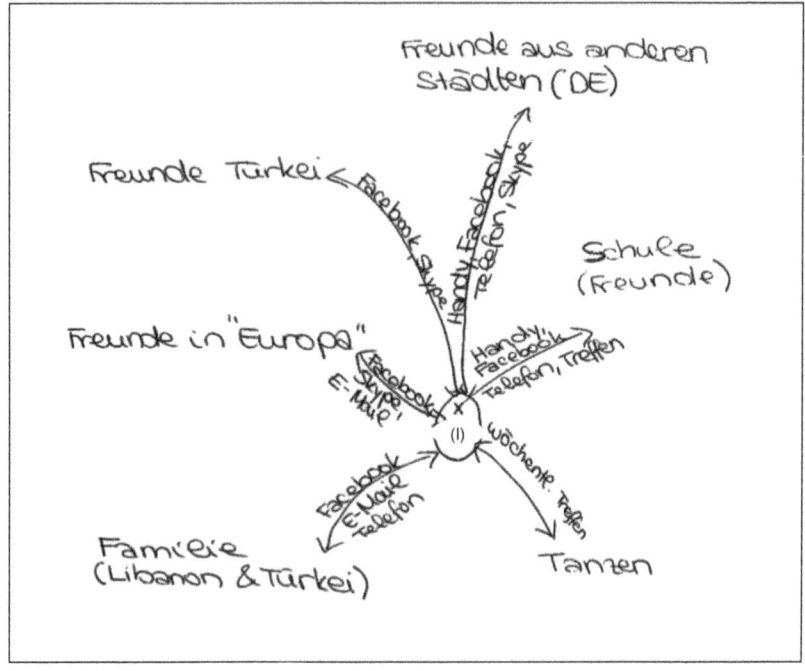

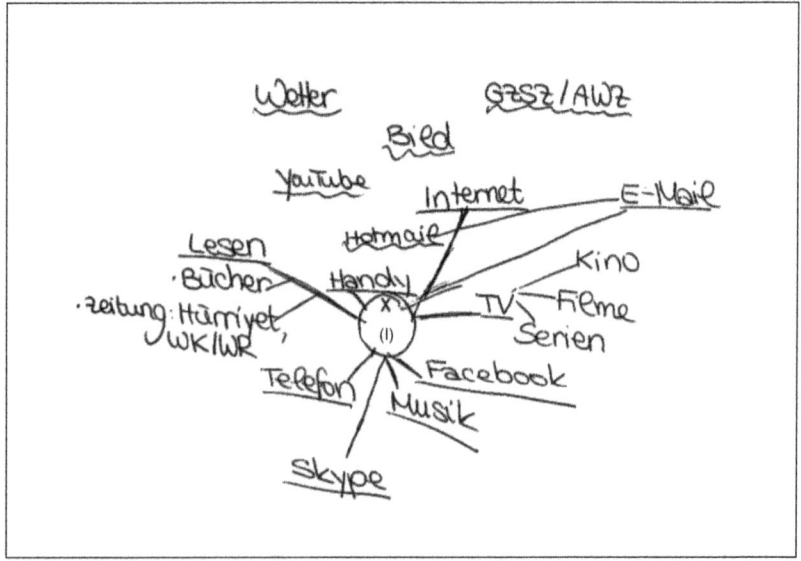

Figure 11.7 Sara's reciprocal and produced media communication network cards

of communitization, but also her dancing club (*Tanzen*; see Figure 11.7). However, all these local communitizations are also articulated by media communication, especially by fixed-line and mobile phone and the social web. The latter is also the kind of media Sara uses to extend her communication network by building up contacts with the Lebanon and her (father's) family there: 'You might laugh now, but I only have contact with my family, the Lebanese family, via Facebook.' Further moments of communitization build on her standardized media communication (see her produced media communication network card in Figure 11.7), through which she became involved in a television serial fandom of 'Gute Zeiten, schlechte Zeiten', a German adaption of 'The Restless Years', and 'Alles was zählt', a German soap. She watches both of them daily, partly together with her sister. In addition, she watches Turkish series together with her mother and sister via satellite television, and American series like 'Desperate Housewives', which is 'an absolute must-do each Wednesday'. In addition, Sara informs herself about series via the internet to have additional information sources for talks with her friends – along with their communication via Facebook: 'Then you also write on Facebook – yes, especially when watching Desperate Housewives – and, oh no, she and she did that, and so on.' Besides that, she is interested in different kinds of music and feels belonging to various music scenes.

Examples like this give us a hint of how to grasp a further aspect related to the 'pluralist's' horizon of communitization: it is typical that various interests are related to different forms of communitization which partly stand unconnectedly next to each other. In Sara's case this has partly linguistic and cultural reasons – for example, she cannot discuss the Turkish series with her school friends – which is partly a result of the incompatibility of the communitizations as such.

Here, we can discover the first moments of a thematic decentring, something that is much stronger in the case of Claas Kuhnert. Claas is involved in a high number of interest-related communitizations, which are articulated in a highly transmedial manner of communicative networking, as his media diary shows (see Figure 11.8). However, they are positioned in his community horizon without any connection with each other. There is his community of football fans, the graffiti and street-art scene, communities of music and film fandom, the gay community and his distinct belonging to Europe. For sure, there are certain overlaps, especially when it comes to the communitization of his city district, the local football team and the local gay community. However, it is typical of his horizon of communitization that these different forms of communitization refer to different communication networks and groups of people who only overlap with him as a person. As he describes this with relation to his friends: 'Partly, my friends do not know each other at all.' He explains this with his social character: 'A clique is nothing for me anyway because I don't like being in groups at

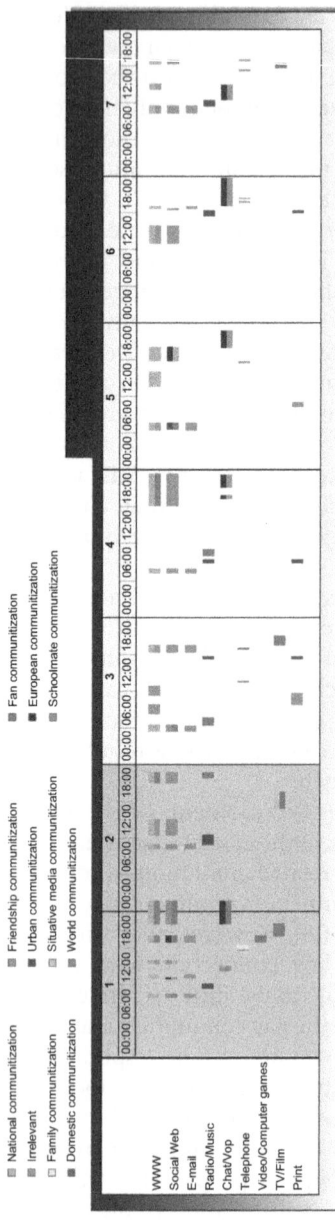

Figure 11.8 Visualization of Claas' media diary

all.' While we must be careful here with this statement – in other parts of the interview he expresses how much he is involved in various groups – we can read this quote as evidence for the partial separation of different aspects of communitization within his horizon of communitization. This kind of partial unconnectedness is typical of 'pluralists'.

5. Conclusion: Mediatized horizons of communitization

As discussed so far, we can detect at least four types of young people's mediatized horizons of communitization, namely, the horizons of 'localists', 'centrists', 'multi-localists' and 'pluralists'. Altogether, our data indicates that individual cases can be a certain mixture of different types. However, this typology gives us an insight into the fundamental orientations of young people's communitization horizons. But does this research allow a more general conclusion on the mediatization of communitization?

If we pose this question it might be helpful to come back to the two arguments that defined the starting point of this article, the 'radical' and the 'anti-futurologist' argument. Referring to the 'radical argument', our analysis demonstrates that mediatization is also related to the emergence of what we called 'mediatized communities', that is, communitizations which were originally not related to the media – like families, local friendship groups, and so on – but are increasingly articulated by the use of various media. In addition, 'mediatizing communities' that constitutively rely on technical communication media play an important role in the lives of the young people we interviewed. In conclusion, we cannot describe the present horizons of communitization without reflecting the role of media communication across all of these levels. We have to detect how far their present communicative construction pre-supposes various kinds of media.

However, and referring to our 'anti-futurologist argument', this does not mean a complete change of our everyday worlds of communitization. Rather, we are confronted with impressive results: in the generation of young people who all grew up with digital media, 'localists' are still common – and also other horizons of communitization are marked by the relevance of local experiences. We can see this as evidence for the ongoing relevance of direct communication and local experience, even in times of increasing mediatization – despite communication and experience taking place in mediatized environments. Beyond this, our research does not indicate a decline of communitization, for example, in the sense that a 'network sociability' or a 'loneliness' would take over its role; nor does it indicate the breakthrough of completely different forms of communitization. Rather, we have a slow but general move into an increasing mediatization of all horizons of communitization – at least in the European context on which our research was focused.

If we reflect this in a wider frame, we can argue that such a mediatization of communitization horizons is tied to certain moments of institutionalization and reification of media communication. As our analysis demonstrates, we are, for example, confronted with institutionalized communication relations of 'localists' and 'multi-localists', in the sense that certain persons at their own or another locality are communicatively contacted via media in a specific way at habitualized moments of time. Or in the group of 'centrists', with reference to standardized media communication, we find institutionalized thematic selections and forms of media use. Besides that, some 'pluralists' partly have a tendency towards an institutionalized 'always-on' communication style, being accessible to (digital) media anywhere and at any time. All this is related to a technological reification of communitization. This does not only mean the reification of communicative spaces in which the 'localists', 'centrists', 'multi-localists' and 'pluralists' position themselves. It includes, for example, the reification of the social web as a technological environment to represent each other's horizon of communitization in a technologically pre-figured way.

However, examples like these demonstrate that the recent mediatization of communitization is not incorporated in one single kind of institutionalization and reification: depending on which type of communitization horizon you are confronted with – 'localists', 'centrists', 'multi-localists' and 'pluralists' – as well as the various hybridizations of these types, one and the same kind of medium – social web, mobile phone, television, newspaper and so on – is related to different forms of institutionalization and reification. If we take this as a core result, this means that mediatization research has to focus more deeply on further factors that play a role in the constitution of these mediatized horizons of communitization. This is a point where we can expect notable differences between (media) generations. Therefore, we have to continue our research on young people's mediatized horizons of communitization by focusing comparatively on other generations – especially on the elderly, as we plan to do.

Notes

1. In the following, we will use the term 'communitization' to refer to Weber's understanding of *Vergemeinschaftung*. See Section 2 for more detail.
2. In our view it is striking that we are confronted with this 'digital natives narrative' as a transcultural pattern, that is, as a narration we find in research in various cultural contexts.
3. This was mainly the approach in researching the mediatization of politics (cf. Altheide and Snow, 1979; Mazzoleni, 2008; Strömbäck, 2011; Strömbäck and Esser, 2009).
4. In the present English translation of Max Weber's work, this term is rather vaguely translated as 'communal relationship' (Weber, 1978, p. 41) – a form of translation that misses the original character of the German *Vergemeinschaftung*, which

also reflects the process character of this kind of social relationship. For a new translation of this classical sociological work, see Weber (2013).

5. For the relevance of a Schützian approach to media and communication research, compare also Bakardjieva, 2005; Bakardjieva and Smith, 2001.

6. To achieve a better response rate in the future, we are in the process of developing an application for mobile devices that will make keeping the media diary easier.

7. At present, we are researching retired persons, in contrast to the young people between 16 and 30 years presented here.

8. The 'problem areas' of mediatized communitization are not further reflected in this table and discussed in this chapter; however, they are, of course, related to this typology. For example, 'communicative demarcation' is something different for a person being localist and for a person being pluralist; or questions of 'communicative mobility' and 'communicative participation' are different for multi-localists than for others.

9. Hubert Knoblauch (2008) has a quite similar approach when he distinguishes 'communities of knowledge' and 'communities of communication', but he understands this difference as a historical transformation. In contrast to this, we emphasize, rather, that 'communities of knowledge' (which are based on direct communication) are increasingly also becoming mediatized.

10. In a response note, Sigrid Baringhorst kindly gave us important hints on how to structure this table more systematically, something we are deeply thankful for.

11. The example of Kerstin Faber demonstrates very well how general aspects of the mediatization of religion (as described in the chapters by Hubert Knoblauch and Knut Lundby in this volume, the latter with a relation to digital storytelling) become concrete in an individual mediatized horizon of communitization.

12. In relation to her diaspora, we might also characterize Sara as being 'world-oriented', in contrast to 'origin-oriented' and 'ethno-oriented' members of the mediatized diaspora (cf., for this typology of identity orientations and communicative networking within diasporas, Hepp, Bozdag and Suna, 2012).

References

Altheide, D. L. and Snow, R. P. (1979) *Media logic* (Beverly Hills: Sage).

Anderson, B. (1983) *Imagined communities: Reflections on the origins and spread of nationalism* (New York: Verso).

Bachmann, G. and Wittel, A. (2006) 'Medienethnografie'. In: Ayaß, R. and Bergmann, J. (eds) *Qualitative Methoden der Medienforschung* (Reinbeck b. Hamburg: Rowohlt), pp. 183–219.

Bailey, O. G., Cammaerts, B. and Carpentier, N. (2008) *Understanding alternative media* (Berkshire: Open University Press).

Bakardjieva, M. (2005) *Internet society: The internet in everyday life* (London, Thousand Oaks, New Delhi: Sage).

Bakardjieva, M. and Smith, R. (2001) 'The internet in everyday life'. In: *New Media & Society*, 3, 67–83.

Bauman, Z. (2001) *Community. Seeking safety in an insecure world* (London: Polity).

Baym, N. K. (2010) *Personal connections in the digital age* (Cambridge, Malden: Polity).

Billig, M. (1995) *Banal nationalism* (London: Sage).

Castells, M. (2001) *The internet galaxy. Reflections on the internet, business, and society* (Oxford: Oxford University Press).

Deuze, M. (2012) *Media life* (Cambridge, Malden: Polity).

Etzioni, A. (1996) *The golden rule. Community and morality in a democratic society* (New York: Basic Books).

Geertz, C. (1994) 'Thick description: Toward an interpretive theory of culture'. In: Martin, M. and McIntyre, L. C. (eds) *Readings in the philosophy of social science* (Cambridge, MA: Massachusetts Institute of Technology), pp. 213–31.

Glaser, B. G. (2007) 'Doing formal theory'. In: Bryant, A. and Charmaz, K. (eds) *Grounded theory* (Los Angeles, London, New Delhi, Singapore: Sage), pp. 97–113.

Glaser, B. G. and Strauss, A. L. (1999) *Discovery of grounded theory: Strategies for qualitative research* (New Brunswick: AldineTransaction).

Hepp, A. (2013) *Cultures of mediatization* (Cambridge: Polity Press).

Hepp, A., Berg, M. and Roitsch, C. (2011) 'Mono-thematic and multi-thematic horizons of mediatized communitization: Patterns of communicative networking and mediated belonging'. In: *Studies in Communication and Media*, 2, pp. 1–34.

Hepp, A., Bozdag, C. and Suna, L. (2012) 'Mediatized migrants: Media cultures and communicative networking in the diaspora'. In: Fortunati, L., Pertierra, R. and Vincent, J. (eds) *Migrations, diaspora, and information technology in global societies* (London: Routledge), pp. 172–88.

Hitzler, R. and Pfadenhauer, M. (2010) 'Posttraditionale Vergemeinschaftung: Eine "Antwort" auf die allgemeine gesellschaftliche Verunsicherung'. In: Soeffner, H.-G. (ed.) *Unsichere Zeiten, Verhandlungen des 34. Kongresses der Deutschen Gesellschaft für Soziologie in Jena 2008. Band 1* (Wiesbaden: VS), pp. 371–82.

Hjarvard, S. (2013) *The mediatization of culture and society* (London: Routledge).

Howley, K. (2010) 'Introduction'. In: Howley, K. (ed.) *Understanding community media* (Thousand Oaks, London, New Delhi, Singapore: Sage), pp. 1–14.

Hua, W. and Wellman, B. (2010) 'Social connectivity in America: Changes in adult friendship network size from 2002 to 2007'. In: *American Behavioral Scientist*, 53, pp. 1148–69.

Jankowski, N. W. (2006) 'Creating community via media: History, theory and scientific investigations'. In: Lievrouw, L. A. and Livingstone, S. M. (eds) *The handbook of new media* (London, Thousand Oaks, New Delhi: Sage), pp. 55–74.

Jenkins, H. (2006) *Fans, bloggers and gamers: Essays on participatory culture* (New York: New York University Press).

Knoblauch, H. (2008) 'Kommunikationsgemeinschaften. Überlegungen zur kommunikativen Konstruktion einer Sozialform'. In: Hitzler, R., Honer, A. and Pfadenhauer, M. (eds) *Posttraditionale Gemeinschaften. Theoretische und ethnographische Erkundungen* (Wiesbaden: VS), pp. 73–88.

Knoblauch, H. (2013) 'Communicative constructivism and mediatization'. In: *Communication Theory* (in preparation).

Krotz, F. and Hepp, A. (2013) 'A concretization of mediatization: How mediatization works and why "mediatized worlds" are a helpful concept for empirical mediatization research'. In: *Empedocles. European Journal for the Philosophy of Communication*, 3, pp. 137–52.

Lindlof, T. R. (1988) 'Media audiences as interpretive communities'. In: *Communication Yearbook*, 11, pp. 81–107.

Luckmann, B. (1970) 'The small life-worlds of modern man'. In: *Social Research*, 37, pp. 580–96.

Lundby, K. (2009) 'Introduction: "Mediatization" as a key'. In: Lundby, K. (ed.) *Mediatization: Concept, changes, consequences* (New York: Peter Lang), pp. 1–18.

Madianou, M. (2005) *Mediating the nation* (London: Routledge).

Mazzoleni, G. (2008) 'Mediatization of politics'. In: Donsbach, W. (ed.) *The international encyclopedia of communication*, VII (Oxford: Blackwell Publishing), pp. 3047–51.

Palfrey, J. and Gasser, U. (2008) *Born digital. Understanding the first generation of digital natives* (New York: Basic Books).

Prensky, M. (2001) 'Digital natives, digital immigrants'. In: *On The Horizon*, 9(5), pp. 1–6.

Schulz, W. (2004) 'Reconstructing mediatization as an analytical concept'. In: *European Journal of Communication*, 19, pp. 87–101.

Schütz, A. and Luckmann, T. (1973) *The structures of the life-world*. 2 Volumes (Evanston: Northwestern UP).

Shibutani, T. (1955) 'Reference groups as perspectives'. In: *American Journal of Sociology*, 60, 562–9.

Strauss, A. (1978) 'A social world perspective'. In: *Studies in Symbolic Interactionism*, 1, pp. 119–28.

Strauss, A. C. and Corbin, J. (1998) *Basics of qualitative research: Techniques and procedures for developing grounded theory* (Thousand Oaks, New Delhi, London: Sage).

Strömbäck, J. (2011) 'Mediatization of politics'. In: Bucy, E. P. and Holbert, R. L. (eds) *Sourcebook for political communication research* (London, New York: Routledge), pp. 367–82.

Strömbäck, J. and Esser, F. (2009) 'Shaping politics: Mediatization and media environmentalism'. In: Lundby, K. (eds) *Mediatization: Concept, changes, consequences* (New York: Peter Lang), pp. 205–23.

Tönnies, F. (2001) *Community and civil society* (Cambridge: Cambridge UP).

Turkle, S. (2011) *Alone together. Why we expect more from technology and less from each other* (New York: Basic Books).

Weber, M. (1978) *Economy and society. An outline of interpretative society. Volume I* (Berkeley, Los Angeles, London: California UP).

Weber, M. (2013) *Economy and society*, trans. Tribe, K. (in preparation).

Wellman, B. (1979) 'The community question'. In: *American Journal of Sociology*, 84, pp. 1201–31.

Wellman, B., Quan-Haase, A., Boase, J., Chen, W., Hampton, K., Díaz, I. and Miyata, K. (2003) 'The social affordances of the internet for networked individualism'. In: *Journal of Computer-Mediated Communication*, 8(3), pp. 0.

Wittel, A. (2008) 'Towards a network sociality'. In: Hepp, A., Krotz, F., Moores, S., and Winter, C. (eds) *Connectivity, network and flow. Conceptualising contemporary communications* (Cresskill: Hampton), pp. 157–82.

Part IV
Mediatization and Private Life

12
Media Life and the Mediatization of the Lifeworld

Mark Deuze

1. Introduction

In 20th-century discussions about the colonization of the lifeworld by the systemworld (and vice versa), the ongoing mediatization of everyday life has gone barely noticed, to the extent that media are so pervasive and ubiquitous that they disappear. It is exactly the invisibility of media – their disappearance into natural user interfaces, the vanishing of concrete uses through convergence and portability, and their evaporation as the infrastructures of everyday interactions – that alerts us to their profound prominence. In this chapter, I will trace the unseen disappearance of media into the lifeworld, and explore how we can still 'see' media even if they have become invisible, turning the lifeworld into a lived experience of a completely mediatized, multisensory, two-way interactive environment. This is not the Star Trek holodeck, nor is it The Matrix – as such habitats still pre-suppose a way out. It is argued that the mediatization of the lifeworld does not have an exit, nor does it inevitably lead to social cohesion or solitude. Instead, I like to argue that the mediatization of the lifeworld does pose a more or less new ethical and aesthetic challenge considering our being in the world.

2. Together alone

As people's lives are experienced inseparably fused with media, a mediatized life – a *media life* (Deuze, 2012) – can be understood as a spatial form within which people are alone together in often (but not necessarily) meaningful ways. The supposedly anti-social outcome of the lonely togetherness of mediated intrapersonal and interpersonal relationships is expressed forcefully by Sherry Turkle (2011), who in her aptly titled book *Alone Together: Why We Expect more from Technology and Less from Each Other* introduces what she considers less-than-ideal consequences of a life completely immersed in media. In this ever-increasing intimacy between people and machines, Turkle argues, we use media to defend against (p. 13) or even defeat (p. 3) loneliness – which she considers 'failed solitude' (p. 288), if it means that without constant connectivity people cannot be meaningfully alone with themselves anymore. The notion of being together and generally having a great time, yet still being alone in one's experience of reality, captures the notion of a media life, where people are more connected than ever before – whether through common boundaryless issues such as global warming, terrorism and worldwide migration, or via internet and mobile telecommunications – yet at the same time on their own, securely secluded in a personalized mediasphere. This reality, however individualized, is also inevitably shared. Media artefacts, their uses, and how they fit into the daily lives of people around the world amplify media life's complexity in two directions at the same time. On the one hand, today's ubiquitous, pervasive, personalized and networked media can be seen as 'intrinsically solipsistic' technologies (Morley, 2007, p. 211), enabling an ongoing retreat of people into quasi-autonomous personal information spaces that can be kept free from the noise of others. Seen in examples such as the Arab Spring and Planet Occupy, people can affect a social reality without necessarily being there. On the other hand, such individualized immersion at-a-distance instantly and haptically (considering today's touchscreen technology) connects people with people anywhere else, thus stretching their personal social bubbles into a fully mediated space of global coexistence where we seek a common humanity (if only because we are biologically wired to do so). This space is what Peter Sloterdijk calls a *mediasphere* (2004), forming an invisible electronic shell around us whereby our entire experience of others becomes mediated. Sloterdijk seems convinced that life in a bubble of media leaves people blind to coexistence.

In an attempt to bridge the false dichotomy between social isolation and connection as implied in media life, it is important to recognize that the same media that isolate and divide also heighten people's awareness of others, potentially fostering social participation and collective action. Thus, when it comes to who we are as individuals *together alone* in media life, another boundary needs to be dissolved: between solitude and solidarity.

The individual in media life is perhaps best described as more or less acutely aware of her own private and personal experience while at the same time living through an involvement with distinct others – with the added unique perspective of being together alone with endless versions of themselves – avatars, online profiles, digital dossiers, tracking systems and archival databases – at the same time. In a way, media make visible the intense interconnectivity between people, social institutions, technologies and the world at large. A monadological metaphysics – as proposed by Gabriel Tarde (2012 [1893]) based on Gottfried Leibniz' work (1714[1]) – works in practical terms if people do indeed *see* themselves and their environment as affected by each other's actions. In media life, the monadic hypothesis (as formulated by Tarde) may offer the most important element of being together alone: that of seeing, and being seen. In media, people can see themselves live, which in theory allows us to take responsibility for what we witness in (and want of) the world.

Zizi Papacharissi (2010) considers this kind of ethical engagement, powered by 'the technological architectures of the private sphere' (p. 166), as establishing autonomy together with collective action. Seen as such, a mobile phone, for example, is not an instrument of either isolation or solidarity – it is a device in which our solitude and togetherness is embodied, gets meaning and provides purpose. A Facebook profile, Twitter account or YouTube channel can enable, but is not required for, political revolution. Beyond *charismatic*, our media are *aspirational*, and, thus, constituent of collective action as well as social solitude.

Bruno Latour (1993) argues that our proclivity for neatly separating the natural, technological and social worlds is a particular feature of the modernist project, disempowering us from making sense of (or effectively taking responsibility for) phenomena such as global warming and biotechnologies. Instead, Latour advocates a 'nonmodern' Constitution, premised on a 'nonseparability of the common production of societies and natures' (p. 141). In our growing awareness of the fused relations between technology, body, environment and social role, one can find pleasure or seek solace in the opportunities and problems of the mediatization of everyday life. The fusion Latour reintroduces from pre-modern times can be articulated to media life with specific reference to the lifeworld, as it is in this most direct experience of the world that mediatization comes to full fruition.

3. Systemworlds, placeworlds, wikiworlds, mediaworlds

To contextualize the various ways in which we, as human beings, make sense of ourselves in the world in media life, one has to do so without making distinctions between mind and matter (including, quite specifically, technology), or between the individual and society (and nature). The purpose here is to do justice to the fact that people generally make sense of whatever happens in a particular context (including where they are, what they are doing, what their history is, what people and things they share the moment with), and that this mode of being should be included in any attempt to articulate what life is really like. One of the first attempts to articulate such a point of view comes from Edmund Husserl (1970 [1936]), who in 1936 argued how every single individual is part of the world 'as living with one another in the world; and the world is our world, valid for our consciousness as existing precisely through this "living together"' (p. 24). Without directly referencing media, Husserl stresses the intersubjectivity at play when making sense of the world. Regardless of what they do and how they go about doing it, people are always connected to other people (e.g., through a shared history and cultural memory), to things (including any and all technologies that facilitate or prevent communication) and nature.

A more deliberate attempt to connect such an understanding of how people are both *in* and *of* the world to the formation and development of modern society as a whole comes from Jürgen Habermas, whose theory of communicative action is an expression of his concern with an ongoing colonization of the lifeworld by the systemworld. With the *lifeworld*, Habermas (1985 [1981]), in somewhat similar terms to Husserl, alludes to the background of everyday life and giving life meaning without people being overtly aware of it: our values and beliefs, the influence of (and over) others, shared understandings, desires and aspirations, motives and goals, sense of identity and personality. This realm of everyday experience is something to which no one can take up an extramundane position (p. 125): it is always familiar, and immediate. The *systemworld* is the area of society that translates people's values, beliefs, wants and needs into services and institutions that make society work – in a nutshell, these would primarily be the domains of economy (money) and politics (power). What keeps a society together, according to Habermas, is a regular, open and free exchange between systemworld and lifeworld as the two key aspects of existence – which explains why communication is key to the philosopher's ideas. At the moment when this *public sphere* of communication becomes dominated by money and power, social institutions lose their legitimacy. Sure, market forces and bureaucracies are important for a society to survive and reproduce itself over time – but if that were all there is, it would drain the lifeblood out of society. When the systemworld colonizes the lifeworld, Habermas warns us, people are reduced in their identities to mere citizens and consumers whose communication is only heard as long as it prolongs the instrumental rationality of political and economic power. As long as we shop and vote, our *affect* – including who we think we are or could be – does not really matter.

Habermas' take on society – regardless of his many detractors and critics, especially regarding the reductionist normativity implied by his conceptualization of a public sphere (and how it should work in practice) – seems rather bleak and does serve as a word of warning. Several prominent scholars noted at the end of the 20th century a similar, but paradoxical, concern: a *recolonization* of the systemworld by the lifeworld. At the forefront are social theorists such as Ulrich Beck, Anthony Giddens, Karin Knorr Cetina, Robert Putnam and Zygmunt Bauman, who invariably note that the hyper-individualized and post-social character of contemporary society (as, for example, expressed in conspicuous consumption, an increasingly unpredictable shifting of political affiliations and an over-reliance on technology and machines, as well as a gradual decline in amateur league bowling) shifts the burden of making sense of the world almost entirely onto the shoulders of the individual. Mark Elchardus (2009) puts forth a pointed argument that all this emphasis on the self should be seen not as a new-found individual autonomy vis-à-vis the systemworld, but, rather, as a new form of social control mainly exercised through media. What we learn from advertising, in school and by reading self-help books (or going through psychotherapy) are lessons towards the formation of what Elchardus calls an *amenable self* that can take care of itself without relying too much on society's institutions. Social problems thus become problems of the self. The continuing emphasis on the self as a typical modern and rather pitiful phenomenon additionally positions the individual favourably towards media, concludes Elchardus, as 'a self that sees itself as a center of decision making [...] is likely to interpret the influence of schooling, media, the world of goods and therapy as forms of self-expression' (p. 155).

As the lifeworld becomes subject to our constant questioning of it – who am I, what should I do, how should I be – it runs the risk of trumping any and all concern we may have for others – including issues of shared and common concern. A fully individualized society, argues Bauman (2000), is one in which 'the way individual people define individually their individual problems and try to tackle them deploying individual skills and resources is the sole remaining "public issue" and the sole object of "public interest"' (p. 72). With specific reference to media, Andreas Wittel (2001) similarly sees the ongoing individualization of society as a key feature of network sociality, as people seem to make their way in life 'defined by a multitude of experiences and biographies' (p. 65) rather than relying on shared histories and cultural memories. As the lifeworld colonizes the systemworld, suggests Henk Vinken (2007), people feel forced to take their life into their own hands, and are thus going to lead a more 'biographized life course' (p. 46), making sense of their lives primarily in their own terms. For Vinken, as for Elchardus, media are crucial in this process, forming a powerful mix.

What I would argue in the context of the mediatization of everyday life is that the Habermasian systemworld (the world of rules) and lifeworld (the world we experience) are not just colonizing or being colonized, but, rather, can both be seen as collapsing into media. In order to appreciate the ramifications of this, one could consider Don Ihde's (1990) key work 'Technology and the Lifeworld', in which he proposes a de-essentialization of nature, society and technologies, while building an overall argument that, throughout history, human cultures and societies have been technologically embedded and that those technologies transform the human lifeworld. Although Ihde, unlike Latour, implicitly keeps media and life at some distance from each other, he does emphasize how their relations are mediated through a *technological intentionality* (p. 141). Jos de Mul (2010) makes a similar point with specific reference to media in that 'every medium carries with it its own distinctive worldview or metaphysics' (p. 89). For de Mul, the essential worldview we get from our current media mix is based on their key characteristics of being multimedial, interactive and capable of virtualizing reality.

Considering media as technologies and institutions of social integration, and as providers of a shared lifeworld (rather than instrumental to alienation and social isolation), is a powerful trope in scholarly work. Directly inspired by Don Ihde, Terje Rasmussen (2003) states how people's wide range of media uses can both reproduce and disintegrate the lifeworld. As media become pervasive and ubiquitous in everyday life, the voguish verbosity on how this may impact the lifeworld – the world taken for granted, every person's horizon of experiences – ratchets up. In the field of game studies, the potential of emerging genres of gaming that deliberately blend real-world environments with various forms of mediated gameplay – such as alternate reality games, live action role-playing games, location-based and pervasive games – can be seen as similarly benchmarking a fused lived and mediated experience. Virtual worlds scholars Eric Gordon and Gene Koo (2008) introduce the concept of *placeworlds* in this context, suggesting that the integration of an online living environment such as *Second Life* with offline activities (such as urban planning involving community feedback) may empower individuals and allow people to form new alliances. As Gordon and Koo argue, '[i]f a lifeworld comes into being when a group of people arrives at a mutual understanding of something, a placeworld arises when people come to a mutual understanding of some*place*' (p. 206; italics in original).

Using a socio-technical perspective on media life to stretch arguments about mixing media and lifeworlds even further, Juha Suoranta and Tere Vadén (2008) look forward to the emergence of what they call a *wikiworld*:

> [t]he Wikiworld is built through the 'collaborative turn', or what is called participatory culture, which includes relatively low barriers to civic engagement and activism, artistic and other sorts of expression, easy access for creating and sharing one's outputs with others, peer-to-peer relations and informal mentorship as well as new forms of socialization, social connections, collectivism and solidarity. (p. 1)

For Suoranta and Vadén, it is up to each and every one of us to take responsibility for the interactive and co-creative opportunities new media seem to promise. In Paul Taylor's (2009) critical analysis of the literature on digital media and society, the suggestion is made that the wikiworld point of view is one among many rather one-dimensional takes on the conditions of everyday experience in 'a new mediated lifeworld' (p. 95). Often, Taylor laments, people cannot help but see media as either empowering or enslaving, without thinking through the implications of a lifeworld as affectively expressed and experienced in media. Interestingly, he points to hackers and hacktivists (conjoining political activism and computer hacking) as embracing a more fluent and imaginative engagement with media, in that hackers take media apart, re-engineer and repurpose them. Taylor's critical, yet at the same time hopeful, account represents a distinctly normative take on what otherwise can be considered a fairly mundane observation particular to the mediatization perspective as explored in this volume: individuals, communities and any other social groups can (and, indeed, should) be seen as living in a world of ubiquitous and pervasive media, where every act of media production or consumption also constitutes that world. What the point of these and other scholars invariably comes down to is that media, as they enter and become fused with the lifeworld, add certain *qualities* to our individual and shared experience of life, and in the process dissolve any meaningful distinction between reality (noumena) and representation (phenomena). Considering the nature of contemporary media's multiple and mutual implications in all aspects of everyday life, I would like to connect these points and extend that line to its logical end-point: considering the lifeworld as completely mediated, unable to self-actualize in any meaningful or distinctive form outside media.

4. The mediatized lifeworld

Göran Sonesson (1997) offers a far-reaching, yet at the same time grounded, take on what life must be like in a mediatized lifeworld, suggesting that as media 'transform secondary interpretations into significations taken for granted [they] may already be colonizing the lifeworld' (p. 71). Starting from a consideration of people's lifeworlds as working a bit like magic, in that we apply all kinds of rules in our dealings with the world without necessarily being aware of them, Sonesson maintains that our media work in much the same way. Even if we uncover the many rules, rituals and routines that govern the generally taken-for-granted understanding of our living environment, many (if not most) of these processes would not necessarily make a lot of sense – just as the inner workings and protocols that govern media (as artefacts, as activities and as social arrangements) tend to remain unseen and often escape our grasp. All of this 'should force us to realize how deeply mediated is our ordinary, unreflected life in the questioned, sociocultural lifeworld' (Sonesson, 1997, p. 71). Within the emerging field of mediatization studies, Andreas Hepp (2013) expounds such a point of view to postulate the concept of mediatized worlds, 'since the resort to communications media is constitutive for the articulation of [...] social worlds in the present form' (p. 78).

Departing from an ongoing mediatization of the lifeworld, it is exactly the increasing invisibility of media – their disappearance into natural user interfaces, the vanishing of concrete uses through convergence and portability, and their evaporation as the infrastructures of everyday interactions – that should alert us to their profound prominence. As the ultimate case study of a complete *multimediatization* of the lifeworld, Sonesson considers the uncanny virtual system proposed in Argentinian writer and journalist Adolfo Bioy Casares' 1940 novel *The Invention of Morel*.

Casares (2003 [1940]) writes *The Invention of Morel* as the diary of a young man who, while trying to escape a life sentence (apparently due to an error of justice), crashes his ship on the beach of a 'lonely island' (p. 10). Yet,

214 Mediatization and Private Life

for all its loneliness, the island is not empty. In fact, it features a museum (as the protagonist notes, the building could also be a fancy hotel or sanatorium), a swimming pool and a chapel. The basement of the museum even features a working power plant, hidden in a doorless, azure-blue-tiled room. And then, all of a sudden, the island is not uninhabited either, as its grassy hillsides become crowded with cheerful tourists – even though no form of transportation has arrived that could have taken them there. The fugitive, afraid that these people might have come to turn him in, observes them from the marshlands where he has been living for exactly 100 days and nights:

> I suppose someone might attribute their mysterious appearance to the effect of last night's heat on my brain. But there are no hallucinations or imaginings here: I know these people are real – at least as real as I am. (p. 11)

He wonders how they do not notice him – as he sometimes takes great risks to get close to them. At times the dancing of the sharply dressed men and women even goes on during the torrential downpours that are quite common on this island. After observing these people for a while, he falls desperately in love with one beautiful woman – whom others in the group call Faustine. She walks down to the beach near his hideout every day to sit on the rocks and watch the sunset. He is afraid to approach her – although he secretly hopes she will not judge him by his now less than impeccable appearance. So he remains in his hiding place, trembling at the mere sight of her 'as if she were posing for an invisible photographer' (p. 26). Even when she suddenly stands up and walks towards him, it seems as if Faustine does not see him at all, and her complete detachment from reality frightens the fugitive. At some point, he thinks he has figured out what is the matter: she is trying to steer clear of another man who is seeking her attention, a beardy fellow called Morel, who pressures Faustine to accept his advances because – as the fugitive overhears him saying – '[w]e have only a short time left – three days, and then it will all be over' (p. 36).

At this moment in the story, something eerie happens. We take note of the fugitive's account of days passing – and after four days go by without meaningful changes to the situation with the people, the buildings, the music and dancing, he again overhears a discussion Morel and Faustine have on his beach, where Morel asks for her understanding as there are only three days left. The fugitive suspects that they are mocking him, putting up a performance just to make him look ridiculous. He stands up and shouts at them – but they completely ignore his presence. Outraged, he storms up the hill – and finds all the buildings empty, as if no one was ever there. To verify this incredible discovery, he goes down to the basement to turn on the power plant so that all the lights in the museum will go on. Once he is back upstairs, the people have returned – but still ignore him. Even as he moves among them, lies down next to them, stands in front of them: no response. At this point in his diary, the fugitive starts thinking through every conceivable explanation for what is going on. Nothing seems to make sense. With direct reference to the magical nature of our lifeworld's operations now uncovered through his experiences with the intruders, he ponders how '[t]he habits of our lives make us presume that things will happen in a certain foreseeable way, that there will be a vague coherence to the world. Now reality appears to be changed, unreal' (p. 65).

In the end, the fugitive witnesses a dinner party with all the tourists present as Morel stands up and formally announces the explanation of everything that is happening. As it turns out, Morel is a scientist obsessed with the idea of overcoming mortality. Considering how various media – radio, television, phonography and the telephone – extend the senses of sight and hearing, Morel has proceeded to develop new technologies that receive and transmit the senses of smell and touch. He collapsed all these media into a singular device that records a complete and authentic image of a certain person and their reality:

> With my machine a person or an animal or a thing is like the station that broadcasts the concert you hear on the radio [...] if you turn all the dials at once, [the recorded person] will be reproduced completely [...] When all the senses are synchronized, the soul emerges.
>
> (pp. 69, 70, 71)

After testing his machine, Morel indeed finds that people cannot distinguish his recordings from real human beings anymore – raising the possibility of capturing people *forever*. He picks an uninhabited and almost impossible to reach island in the middle of nowhere, invites his best friends and closest relatives, and reduces them – without ever telling them what is going on – to 'living transmitters' (p. 71). No matter how hard he tries, the people in the room do not seem to believe him. 'Don't you see that there is a parallelism between the destinies of men and images?', Morel cries out – but it is in vain. Trembling with anger and disappointment, he asks his friends for forgiveness. Because, like him, they are all dead.

It is for this spine-chilling story that Casares can take credit for inventing immersive virtual environment technology (commonly referred to as virtual reality) decades before the first computers arrived. More specifically, Morel's invention seems a precursor to a StarTrek holodeck. The holodeck, as a virtual reality simulator, has an edge over the island machine: its virtual constructs – people as well as objects – are tangible, and they see you, get to know you. Today's technologies make such completely immersive and multisensory environments quite feasible, combining the ability of media to project any kind of sensory information (sight, sound, smell, touch and taste) in three-dimensional space with software algorithms that would allow someone to interact with a physical environment (e.g., by manipulating a floor to resemble different surfaces: sand, water or rocks). In computer engineering, game design and robotics communities there is considerable excitement about the possibility of building true lifelike and massively inhabitable environments – which does not seem a far-fetched notion, given the availability and popularity of 3D cameras and projection systems, augmented reality applications for personal media devices, natural user interfaces (including touchscreens and motion-sensing technologies) and the rapid wiring of the planet for broadband media access.

The lifeworld as a *project* that is at once immediate and mediatized raises all kinds of interesting questions about the nature of reality, the essence of self-identity and our experiences of each other. It is perhaps not surprising in this context that Casares' unsettling story also functioned as one of the key inspirations for the popular American television series 'Lost' (2004–10). The book features quite literally in episode four of season four, in which one of the characters can be seen reading it.[2] The series follows the lives of more than 40 individuals who survived a plane crash on a tropical island. Their survival is hampered by all kinds of mysterious events – including encountering a mysterious woman (named Danielle) who was shipwrecked on the island 16 years prior to their crash. After six seasons and 121 episodes, the show ends with the suggestion that all survivors have died and reunite, perpetually, in some form of limbo (represented by gathering in a church), where everyone is able to see, recognize and remember everyone else and their lives together.[3] In Casares' original story, the fugitive in the end realizes that he cannot stand the idea of witnessing the same week of images repeat forever – especially given his enduring love for the 'artificial ghost' (p. 85) Faustine. As she lives in an image for which he does not exist, his love is tragically impossible. In the end, he does the only thing he can do: he faithfully records a week of his experiences on the island into Morel's machine, inserting himself in every scene next to Faustine, appearing as if she is interacting with him. The machine then projects the week eternally – and they all live in media forever.

I could be callous by concluding how all of us are like the tourists on Morel's island, living a mediatized version of our lives. This is not the point of Sonesson's argument, nor does it offer much help in ethically and aesthetically navigating a media life. The key to understanding the significance of media to the lifeworld can be found in what Sonesson (1997) considers lacking in Morel's invention: a 'double-sided permeability to all senses', which would indeed 'break down the limits between the worlds' (p. 80). Given the developments in media, it is perhaps safe to say that these limits have indeed broken down – our lives in media do not exist independently of the actual (or real) world.

Considering the collapse of media and the lifeworld as a potent peda-gogical concept, Norm Friesen and Theo Hug (2009) postulate that media become epistemology – the grounds for knowledge and knowing itself – and therefore call on educators and educational researchers to take seriously what they call the *mediatic a priori*: 'The contention that media play an important role in defining the epistemological preconditions or characteristics of cog-nition, such as the perception of time, space, and the shaping of attention and communication' (p. 73). Friedrich Kittler (2009) raises the stakes to an even higher level of abstraction in this debate, forcefully arguing that media must be considered in ontological terms, for there is nothing we can say about what is without using some form of media to do it – hence, all our expressions of the world are essentially of media. Thinking about media in these terms, the various placeworlds, wikiworlds, media(tized) worlds and multimediated lifeworlds can be seen as more or less distinct ontological bubbles or spheres that exist next to each other, intersect and overlap.

As Nigel Thrift (2011) suggests, the existence of multiple ontologies is not necessarily problematic if we accept that this introduces opportunities for us to understand things differently and to come up with new or alternative con-ceptualizations of how worlds work or should work. In other words, instead of having to settle with a timeless and complete, one and only world, a series of incomplete and permanently-under-construction worldviews 'can live tolerantly side-by-side' (p. 6). What needs to be emphasized here is that an ontologically adventurous perspective is afforded by social worlds that are mediatized, allowing what John Hartley (2000) describes as a *redac-tional* sense of society: the experience or expectation of living in a world that can be edited. Don Ihde's (1990) perspective on the increasing interde-pendency between technology and the lifeworld additionally outlines how contemporary mediating technologies of the information age make possi-ble an 'essential pluricultural pattern' (p. 156) in people's understanding of themselves and each other. According to Ihde, our global pluriculture gets established through the various ways in which media expose us to ideas, beliefs, cultures and rituals, up to and including culinary and architectural traditions different from our own. In media we cannot help but see and experience the lives of others (and they can see us). In media life, our world seems intrinsically open to intervention, thriving on our constant remixing and over-sharing of it. This plasticity inevitably extends to our sense of self.

5. Who am I and who are you?

In a series of interviews with Benedetto Vecchi on the topic of identity, Zygmunt Bauman (2004) remarks that 'asking "who you are" makes sense to you only once you believe that you can be someone other than you are' (p. 19). Pondering the same issue, Hans-Georg Gadamer (1997 [1973]) high-lights a further problem of asking this, as '[a]ll understanding presupposes an answer to this question, or better, a preliminary insight superior to the formulation of the question' (p. 68). Assuming for a moment that a life as lived in media brings with it an inevitable multiplication of selves with whom we are dancing in our very own silent disco, who is it that we are looking for in media when we want to answer the question of who we really are? In his engagement with the dilemma, Gadamer (1997 [1973]) suggests that the 'I' in the question 'who am I?' is a fisherman who casts a net, over and over again, expecting to catch something (pp. 83–4). Like the fisherman, we do everything we can to cast the net the right way and in the right place, but ultimately just have to wait and see whether something is caught – and, whether we catch something or not, we will always have to do it again. Additionally, we have to carefully weigh our options with everything we catch, as we cannot load the net on our lifeboat too lightly or too full – or else it will tip over. Furthermore, the catch of the day is always intended for someone – a real or imaginary friend, perhaps, an audience, guests at the dinner table, or just for you. Either way, 'what lends reality to the I is the interplay between I and You that promises a catch' (Gadamer, 1997 [1973], p. 85). Rather than jumping overboard or solely focusing on building more and better contraptions to catch fish (such was the intent of Morel's invention), Gadamer challenges you to consider every confrontation with You as situating you in a space of indeterminacy. Instead of aiming towards controlling all these versions of ourselves into an, at best, temporary illusion of a final and complete mould, we should strive to create as many different versions of ourselves as possible, thus cultivating a sense of respect for the multiplicity and (therefore) messiness of the identities and ideals of the people around us.

It can thus be said that the malleability and endless virtualization of the self in a media life is not so much a function of our media, but, rather, the expansion and enhancement of a possible (and intentional) way of thinking about who we are as human beings in conjunction with each other, with nature and with technology. This perspective can certainly lead to more or less solipsistic, scatterbrained and lonesome attitudes or behaviours. Yet the link between individualization and contemporary society is not made in media – in media, the relationship between the self and any kind of social cohesion is just another version of society. Slavoj Žižek (2008) engages most explicitly the link between our being together alone and the omnipresence of networked computers and cyberspace, suggesting that media are a 'directly universalized form of sociality which enables us to be connected with the entire world while sitting alone in front of a screen' (p. 34). The life we find in media is, therefore, just as real and otherworldly unreal as any other life. The mediatization of everyday life offers, in this context, a way to take responsibility for being (on our own, yet completely connected) in the world. It is not a technological, or a social challenge – mediatization is an ethical and aesthetic challenge.

Notes

1. See: http://www.marxists.org/reference/subject/philosophy/works/ge/leibniz.htm. Date accessed: 11.11.13.
2. See: http://en.wikipedia.org/wiki/Eggtown. Date accessed: 11.11.13.
3. Source: http://en.wikipedia.org/wiki/The_End_(Lost). Date accessed: 11.11.13.

References

Bauman, Z. (2000) *Liquid modernity* (Cambridge: Polity).

Bauman, Z. (2004) *Identity* (Cambridge: Polity).

Casares, A. B. (2003 (1940]) *The invention of Morel* (New York: NYRB Classics).

De Mul, J. (2010) *Cyberspace odyssey* (Newcastle upon Tyne: Cambridge Scholars Publishing).

Deuze, M. (2012) *Media life* (Cambridge, UK: Polity Press).

Elchardus, M. (2009) 'Self-control as social control: The emergence of symbolic society'. In: *Poetics*, 37, pp. 146–61.

Friesen, N. and Hug, T. (2009) 'The mediatic turn'. In: Lundby, K. (ed.) *Mediatization* (New York: Peter Lang), pp. 64–81.

Gadamer, H.-G. (1997 [1973]) *Gadamer on Celan* (Albany: SUNY Press).

Gordon, E. and Koo, G. (2008) 'Placeworlds: Using virtual worlds to foster civic engagement'. In: *Space & Culture*, 11(3), pp. 204–21.

Habermas, J. (1985 [1981]) *Theory of communicative action, Vol. 2: Lifeworld and system* (Boston: Beacon).

Hartley, J. (2000) 'Communicational democracy in a redactional society'. In: *Journalism*, 1(1), pp. 39–47.

Hepp, A. (2013) *Cultures of mediatization* (Cambridge: Polity Press).

Husserl, E. (1970 [1936]) *The crisis of European sciences and transcendental phenomenology* (Chicago: Northwestern University Press).

Ihde, D. (1990) *Technology and the lifeworld: From garden to earth* (Bloomington: Indiana University Press).

Kittler, F. (2009) 'Towards an ontology of media'. In: *Theory, Culture & Society*, 26(2–3), pp. 23–31.

Latour, B. (1993) *We have never been modern* (Cambridge, MA: Harvard University Press).

Morley, D. (2007) *Media, modernity and technology* (London: Routledge).

Papacharissi, Z. (2010) *A private sphere: Democracy in a digital age* (Cambridge: Polity Press).

Rasmussen, T. (2003) 'On distributed society'. In: Liestøl, G., Morrison, A. and Rasmussen, T. (eds) *Digital media revisited* (Cambridge: MIT Press), pp. 445–68.

Sloterdijk, P. (2004) *Sphären* (Berlin: Suhrkamp Verlag).

Sonesson, G. (1997) 'The multimediation of the lifeworld'. In: Nöth, W. (ed.) *Semiotics of the media* (New York: Mouton de Gruyter), pp. 61–78.

Suoranta, J. and Vadén, T. (2008) *Wikiworld* (Tampere: University of Tampere).

Tarde, G. (2012 [1893]) *Monadology and sociology*, trans. by Theo Lorenc (Prahran, Australia: re.press).

Taylor, P. (2009) 'Critical theory 2.0 and im/materiality: The bug in the machinic flows'. In: *Interactions*, 1(1), pp. 93–110.

Thrift, N. (2011) 'Lifeworld Inc – and what to do about it'. In: *Environment and Planning D*, 29, pp. 5–26.

Turkle, S. (2011) *Alone together* (New York: Basic Books).
Vinken, H. (2007) 'Changing life courses, new media, and citizenship'. In: Dahlgren, P. (ed.) *Young citizens and new media* (London: Routledge), pp. 41–54.
Wittel, A. (2001) 'Toward a network sociality'. In: *Theory, Culture & Society*, 18(6), pp. 51–76.
Žižek, S. (2008) *In defense of lost causes* (New York: Verso).

13
Media Love: Intimacy in Mediatized Worlds

John Storey and Katy McDonald

1. Introduction

When we fall in love, we connect to the other person in multiple ways. Many of these connections involve media. We go to the cinema together or we watch television, listen to music or play a computer game; we increasingly have photographs in common; we compare (consciously and unconsciously) our relationship with those we see in literature, film and television; and when we are not together, we use various media technologies to close down the space between us. This use of media allows our connection to intensify, and it is this intensification that in part allows others and ourselves to recognize that we are in love.[1] Although we call this Media Love,[2] we certainly do not think that media have successfully colonized contemporary practices of romantic love. Many aspects of a romantic relationship do not involve a direct connection with media. Nonetheless, our research shows that contemporary romantic practice has become entangled in, and almost unthinkable without, media. There can be little doubt that people increasingly, and actively, use media as part of the architecture and choreography of a romantic relationship.

The aim of our research is to explore media-entangled practices of romantic love. We seek to do this without reverting to media determinism or to the view that romantic love is a simple fact of nature, which people articulate in moments of emotional and sexual intimacy. Stepping between these two temptations, we try to show how people use media to actively make romantic love. We share with actor-network theory (Latour, 2007) what it shares with ethnomethodology (Garfinkel, 1967): the view that our everyday social worlds, including practices of romantic love, are not a given; they have to be assembled and reassembled. We treat media and its uses as existing in networks that materially produce romantic love. Therefore, the use of media is not a supplement to contemporary practices of romantic love;

it is increasingly fundamental and foundational to the construction and maintenance of such relationships.

2. Romantic love and mediatization

The relationship between romantic love and what is sometimes called mass media is, historically speaking, quite new. Although it is not difficult to find examples of stories of romantic love throughout recorded history, it is really only at the end of the 18th century, and expanding rapidly throughout the 19th and 20th, that romantic love becomes in the west an increasingly visible part of a shared public culture and a widely accepted means to emotional happiness and sexual fulfilment. As historian Edward Shorter (1977) points out, 'The romantic revolution [...] began late in the eighteenth century, sweeping across vast reaches of class and territory in the nineteenth to become, in the twentieth, the unassailable norm of courtship behaviour' (152).

The widespread development of this 'unassailable norm', as something socially visible and widely accepted, and as the main social practice of sexual and emotional intimacy, coincided with the development of romantic media. As the historian Lawrence Stone (1977) observes, 'after 1780 romantic love and the romantic novel grew together' (190). The sociologist Anthony Giddens (1992) makes much the same point: 'The rise of romantic love more or less coincided with the emergence of the [romantic] novel' (40). This was also a view shared by contemporary commentators: 'Of all the arrows which Cupid has shot at youthful hearts, [the romantic novel] is the keenest. There is no resisting it. It is literary opium that lulls every sense into delicious rapture' (*The Universal Magazine*, 1772; quoted in Stone, 1977, p. 190). Moreover, as Francois de la Rochefoucauld claimed, writing a little earlier: 'There are some people who would never have fallen in love if they had not heard there was such a thing' (quoted in Stone, 1977, p. 191). This may have been intended as a mocking jibe at those supposedly too stupid to be able to think for themselves, but we do not think that what he identifies implies self-deception; rather, we take it as an unknowing recognition of the fact that we actively learn to do many of the things we assume to be natural. But the real problem with presenting this particular narrative of the relationship between media and romantic love is that it can often imply a one-way flow of influence from media to romantic practice. This is almost certainly what *The Universal Magazine* had in mind when it used the term 'literary opium'. Working from this assumption, the only valid reason to research the relationship between media and romantic love is to explore 'media effects' or to identify a particular 'media logic'. We totally reject this reduction. Instead, our critical focus is on what people do with media, rather than what media make them do. This does not mean a denial of media influence, but recognition that influence is not an inevitable consequence of supposed passivity, but a complex process that almost always involves agency and use.

What is clear from our findings is that people do not passively consume media and then translate this unproblematically and straightforwardly into social practices of romantic love. Instead, we continually encountered a dialogue between media and the active consumption practices of people in love. In Storey and McDonald (2013) we argue that the best way to understand the romantic power of media is to conceptualize it as working like a language; a 'language' we have to work with in order to communicate our romantic feelings to others and to ourselves. To be clear, we do not mean that media literally provide the language of romantic love, although at times they may in fact do this; rather, we are suggesting that the discourses media produce work *like* a language in that they enable and constrain social practices of romantic love. To be in love, therefore, is to locate oneself in a network of meanings and practices (often contradictory) produced and/or circulated by media which establish a system of romantic 'common sense' or what we might call a romantic 'regime of truth'.³ And, because media discourses of romantic love operate like a language, we need to recognize that the performance of a language and language as a system are quite different: the language spoken does not dictate the act of speaking; the speaker actively selects from the resources the language makes available. In this way, then, although media discourses of romantic love both enable and constrain agency, they certainly do not dictate romantic practice as would be assumed by the 'media effects' model. It is like speaking any language; we are situated in a structure that both enables and constrains our ability to understand and to communicate, and, as with language competence generally, there are different levels of media-derived romantic literacy. Umberto Eco's (1985) much-quoted definition of the post-modern attitude, we think, points to this.

> I think of the post-modern attitude as that of a man who loves a very cultivated woman and knows he cannot say to her 'I love you madly', because he knows that she knows (and she knows that he knows) that these words have already been written by Barbara Cartland. (17)

This may or may not identify a post-modern attitude, but for us it certainly identifies people with high levels of media-derived romantic literacy. Media, therefore, do not directly shape romantic practice; rather, they provide the language from which romantic practice is articulated – a structure that both enables and constrains romantic agency. But, and this is a very important but, we have to stay within the romantic 'common sense' or the romantic 'regime of truth' in order to remain romantically intelligible to others and to ourselves. As a result, romantic practice (even in all its contradictory variety) only becomes recognizable as romantic practice through conformity with media-derived standards of romantic intelligibility (to deviate from these standards may cause 'translation' problems).[4]

3. Mediatized love

This does not mean that our experiences of being in love are some kind of pre-scripted 'false consciousness' in which our emotional reactions are simple media creations. What the interviewees made clear is that media do not have the effect of dictating romantic practice. They offer a language; a language people use to articulate the meaning of their own experience of romantic love. Part of the form this agency takes is in the way media discourses are both recognized and negotiated with (see Storey and McDonald, 2013).[5]

Listening romantically to music is a good example of the active use of media. As we expected, many of the interviewees talked about how particular songs had played a significant role in their romantic experiences. Although many of the interviewees identified music as something to relax with or as background to a romantic setting, most suggested that music was almost always used to reactivate a romantic memory; it had an archival function in that it allowed them to return affectively to a romantic situation in the past. Interviewee 6 gave a typical response. 'It's not something that particularly enhances it for me as in when I'm falling in love or if I am in love. I don't think the music is something I think about at the time. For me it has always been afterwards.' Interviewee 4 made a similar point. 'It was playing when I first got together with somebody in a relationship and I always remember that song.' Interviewee 2 talked of how it 'reminded me [...] I'm not going to regret it, it does remind me'. Interviewee 1 told us that 'every time I hear that song it always reminds me of that incident'. He also told us about other songs that made him think of her. It was very clear that these songs had a powerful affective charge in their ability to enable him to rearticulate the past.

> I think of her straightaway. [...] Sometimes it can be a bit sad. You know like, I think it depends on what mood you're in, cos sometimes when I hear that song I think, oh, yeah, that was a really good night, we had a really good time. Then other times I think, oh, I'm never gonna be with her.

Interviewee 6 used music in much the same way.

> I think with music and the emotion of love, I think sometimes when you have been in love and you hear music, you do especially if you're on your own, you relate things that are in that music to yourself. [...] Lately, over the last four or five weeks, since I decided to distance myself from the girl I was telling you about I was in a bit of a situation. I would say

I was probably in a bit of a vulnerable state of mind and I was listening to music. Sometimes, if it was on and I would find it was actually making me more kind of sad and making me think of that person more.

The two most important technologies identified by our interviewees were texting and Facebook.[6] Texting was the media technology mentioned the most. Interviewee 9 gave a typical response: 'I'd say 90% of the communication is by text and then I'd say mobile phone for like a quick ten min phone call here and there.' Sometimes the romantic relationship itself seemed to be held together by texting.

We just got on really well and we saw each other about three or four times I think over about six weeks. [...] [A]nd then we were texting a lot. A lot of it was based on texts and sending messages to each other and the fact that we only saw each other four times out of those six weeks I suppose was kind of irrelevant in the sense because we were texting a lot.

(Interviewee 6)

Many interviewees told us how texting had the effect of speeding up the development of their romantic relationship. 'I think it speeds things up more than anything, because now with phones [for texting] you can constantly be in contact' (Interviewee 10). Interviewee 9 made much the same point.

I think I'm closer to her because you get to know someone quicker cos you're texting them and like we do text quite a bit. And like in the early stages of us getting together that's kind of like how we got to know each other and like we were texting quite a bit and so I think it does help you get to know them a bit closer.

Often it was the extent of texting that produced this effect.

Constantly, it wouldn't stop, it was ridiculous, our phones would be silent if we were together. But if we weren't together then they would be constantly going off. Even if we'd only been together that hour and I'd just come into uni for an hour he'd be texting me making sure I was OK, even though I'd be going back to his after. [...] It was constant. The only reason we would stop is if I was in a lecture or he was in an exam at college.

(Interviewee 8)

Part of the speeding up is in terms of sexual intimacy. 'I think you can be a bit more risky, a bit more rude, a bit more cheeky' (Interviewee 1). 'I think it's easier for people to let themselves get more intimate than what it previously would've been' (Interviewee 10). 'Yeah, I think especially when you're getting to know them, it's easier to be a bit more brash than, say, if you just met them on the street out of the blue. I don't think you'd be like, huh [he makes a noise suggesting sexual excitement]' (Interviewee 9). Interviewee 8 pointed out how, in this context, texting could provide a screen to hide behind.

> Yeah, you've got more confidence to message each other, haven't you. Rather than face to face. [...] I think in a message you can hide behind the words a bit: Oh, I didn't mean to send you that...I was drunk. If you say something stupid, my friend sent it. *You've got a million excuses to not mean what you wanted to say* (our italics).

It is very clear that for Interviewee 8 the ability to be able to deny an intended meaning is very liberating. Interviewee 6 also found texting liberating.

> I try to act the same in texts as I would do in person, but then I think that you do find yourself talking on text, or in fact on Facebook chat, you find yourself saying things that you probably truly wouldn't say in person. [...] [W]hen you're looking somebody in the eye, I think it's sometimes difficult to actually say what you want to say.
>
> (Interviewee 6)

According to Interviewee 13, texting 'helped us seduce each other. [...] It allowed us to express ourselves and say those things which made us feel the urge and need for the other person even more. [...] It was precisely through text messages [...] that very "romantic" and breath-taking things were said between us.' Interviewee 11 gave an example that went beyond the speeding up of sexual intimacy. In her case, texting was a form of sexual intimacy.

> My last relationship [...] began with a (tipsy) text message after not having seen each other in five years, and then largely developed by texting, e-mail and Skype (without video), before we were able to see each other [they were living in different countries]. So in that case, the falling in love part really happened without any face-to-face interaction.

When they eventually met, their technologically enabled sex life continued into their face-to-face relationship. As she explained,

> I also felt that this [their previous text life] influenced how the relationship then actually worked. I remember, for instance, coming to [she names where her boyfriend lived] after months of not having seen each other, and what alienated me was that he immediately verbalized [as in a text] what he wanted to do when I had barely entered the house.

Somehow, having just kissed me passionately and then went on to do what he was talking about would have been different.

Sometimes the speeding up caused by texting can have other negative effects. 'But with texting it happens in fast motion, um, um, really fast, because I had a relationship with someone where we went out for a month and I really liked them, but from texting each other it just went downhill from there' (Interviewee 10). She identified one reason for this negative effect. 'I think cos it's always in contact quite a lot [...] there's not really a lot to say when you've met up afterwards.' Constant texting can reveal too much too soon, or it can simply feel like a prison house. Interviewee 2 complained that it denied him space. 'I wanted space and she wouldn't give it to me, so I just left my phone at home every now and then.' It later became clear that leaving his phone at home meant telling her he had left it at home.

Texting can create other difficulties in a romantic relationship. Interviewee 14, who described her younger self as a 'love detective' always on the look-out for evidence of attraction, had a different experience of texting, one that nevertheless indicates how important it is as a measure of romantic attachment. 'I had the misfortune to fall in love with a very unenthusiastic texter [...] which meant that a low response rate to text was interpreted as evidence of a lack of interest.'

Text messaging also has the potential to create a record of the romantic relationship. It can work like an electronic diary in which comments from both sides of the relationship are stored. As Interviewee 6 explains,

> I think looking back, cos that's one thing you will do with text messages, cos your mobile phone will store a lot of messages. [...] I think when you have a situation like this [the end of a romantic relationship], one of the things you find yourself doing, which is probably more harmful than helpful, is looking back on everything you have said, and I did that and it was actually quite interesting. I don't think it was harmful for me because it was more interesting to see what had happened. [...] It was interesting to try and find out why this individual had made me act differently and had made me feel differently, and how come it upset me and made me generally unhappy when things weren't working.

Many of the interviewees included Facebook when talking about texting. They tended to use it in similar ways and, like texting, thought of it in relation to romantic relationships in both positive and negative terms. Interviewee 3, whose boyfriend was overseas, talked about 'romantic times when we used to instant message each other on Facebook'. When asked what they talked about, she replied, 'The boring things, like what I had done during the day and stuff. [...] I think it's really important to have that sort of contact when someone is away for that long.' It is clear that Facebook allowed them to maintain their romantic relationship in circumstances that put the relationship under great strain. Like Interviewee 3, Interviewee 7 told us that much of the conversation she has with her boyfriend on Facebook is often quite mundane. They would also do other things while they chatted.

I will be doing essays and that when I'm talking to him and I'll say, oh, I'm not in the mood to do this essay and he says, yes, but if you just get it done it's out of the way. If he's had a really bad day at work, I'll say, oh, it'll be fine, it's just another day at work. If I'm watching TV, I'll tell him about it and he'll tell me about the game he's playing and things like that.

Clearly, Facebook allows them to talk and develop their relationship in a way that would normally only be possible in a situation of co-presence. Interviewee 11 used Skype in a similar way.

[We would] Skype very often all day when we are both at home. We then usually go about our own business most of the time but feel that the other is there. [...] We both work [...] but I have the iPad next to me and can glance at him every once in a while; or we leave it on when we go to sleep, and I might sleep already but he is still reading, or we have breaks together or in the end spend the evening together as if we had a proper date.

She then added:

I think that especially in times like these, when everyone is expected to be flexible and mobile in career terms, these media make a huge difference in how close you can feel to each other in spite of the distance, and it can enable at least a variety of everyday life together.

Like texting, Facebook also has the potential to undermine what it has helped to develop. As Interviewee 3 explained, 'you can see on Facebook their ex and their ex e-mailing them cos they still got a house together that they can't get rid of. I think that makes that relationship a bit more complicated.' She told us of further complications when she discovered photographs of her boyfriend's ex-girlfriend in his Facebook album. As she explained, 'she wasn't wearing that much clothes and obviously they upset me'. It became clear that it wasn't just that these photographs existed, but that they existed in a public space: 'If it was printed photos, I kind of understand that he would have photos of his ex around cos they were together quite a while.' So the photographs themselves were not the problem; it was their location that really caused her to feel upset. 'I also felt a little humiliated, cos it's on Facebook so everyone can see that he has still got pictures of his ex, which kind of reflects on me.' Interviewee 5 was also aware of this problem.

> If there is any pictures of me with like ex-girlfriends or girls I used to see, when I break up with them I remove them, cos the last thing you want to do when you're looking at someone's Facebook and saying, oh, that's what their ex looks like. [...] [I]f she meets a lad, he's gonna be like, wow, look at all these things, her and the ex-boyfriend [...] and that's gonna put him under pressure [...] and he's like, shit, he bought her this hotel [a couple of nights in a hotel], they went to London for the weekend. I'm broke, what do I do? If there was no social network and then that lad would know nothing about me, he wouldn't be able to click on profile to see where I'm from or what I do or whatever. He would probably forget about my name after a week.

Without Facebook the situation identified by Interviewees 3 and 5 would not be possible.

Interviewee 5 also told us how Facebook is changing the practical possibilities of romance.

> Thirty years ago when my Dad met Mum, he said when he met her the next day he would phone her. See if you done that now the girl might go, here, I don't remember you. By texts or Facebook, they don't have to reply and if they don't reply you know they are not interested.

Interviewee 6 gave another example of how Facebook is changing romantic practice. 'If you see somebody on a night out and you get talking to them they would probably find it less personally invading to be asked if they could be your friend on Facebook than to ask for their number.' But this may not be as benign as it sounds; it can lead to what he calls 'Facebook stalking'.

> If I know nothing about her I go on their Facebook and I can find out every single thing about her; I can look through her pictures and see what her ex-boyfriend looked like, what her friends are like, what she likes. [...] Like, 'I like a man who holds my hand in the dark', say. You can tell everything they like and that's really scary because when you go on the first date you know everything about them and you're asking them questions that you already know. You're asking them what do you study and it's written on the top of her Facebook.

As a consequence, a first date may seem 'traditional', but it could be prepared for and structured by information that would have been unthinkable to lovers in the past.

4. Conclusion

The concern of our research is with what people do with media, which may in some cases be nothing at all. So we did not begin with media and then examine their use; rather, we began with accounts of everyday experiences of romantic love and then attempted to tease out how these are enabled and constrained by media use. During the interviews we did not seek to define romantic love or what we meant by media. In each interview it was the interviewee who decided what these terms describe and delimit. Our focus, therefore, was not on the media of romantic love, but on how people use media to make romantic love, to make it socially manifest in practice. In this way our study follows a position recently advocated by David Morley (2007a; 2007b; see also Moores, 2012) in which he calls for a non-media-centric study of media. As Morley points out,

> [W]e need to 'decentre' the media [...] so as to better understand the ways in which media processes and everyday life are interwoven with each other. [...] The key issue here, to put it paradoxically, is how we can generate a non-media-centric form of media studies, how to understand the variety of ways in which new and old media accommodate to each other and coexist in symbiotic forms and also how to better grasp how we live with them as parts of our personal or household 'media ensemble'.
>
> (Morley, 2007a, p. 200)

If we are doing media studies, we are doing it refracted through the conscious selection and active use made of media by people whose main concern is the development and maintenance of a romantic relationship.[7] Therefore, while it is true that texting and Facebook enable a new kind of romantic communication and constrain the form this communication may take, they do not determine that we communicate or what we communicate; this is always a matter of agency and use. What is also certain is that more empirical research needs to be done. This may not be a very resounding way to conclude our discussion of media love, but it is the only way to conclude unless, of course, we are willing to be satisfied with incomplete answers or with theoretical speculations untroubled by empirical investigation.

Notes

1. There is a small but important body of work that examines social practices of romantic love. Two of the best are Brown (2006) and Illouz (1997). Illouz's now classic account has had a major influence on our research project. However, we do not believe that this previous work directly addresses the questions that have organized our research.
2. Our chapter presents some of the findings of a research project we call *Media Love*. These findings are based on analysis of 42 discursive questionnaires and 14 semi-structured interviews consisting of almost 20 hours of recorded material.

The aim of the project is to examine how people use media when in romantic relationships.
Interviewees:

Interviewee 1: male, British, straight, aged 19.
Interviewee 2: male, British, straight, aged 19.
Interviewee 3: female, British, straight, aged 25.
Interviewee 4: male, British, gay, aged 19.
Interviewee 5: male, British, straight, aged 23.
Interviewee 6: male, British, straight, aged 21.
Interviewee 7: female, British, straight, aged 19.
Interviewee 8: female, British, straight, aged 19.
Interviewee 9: male, British, straight, aged 19.
Interviewee 10: female, British, straight, aged 19.
Interviewee 11: female, German, bisexual, aged 36.
Interviewee 12: female, Austrian, straight, aged 30.
Interviewee 13: female, Spanish, straight, aged 33.
Interviewee 14: female, Irish, straight, aged 34.

We would like to take this opportunity to thank all those who have taken part in the project.

We have already presented our preliminary research findings in Hong Kong, London, Freiburg, Bremen, Boston, Vienna and York. We would like to take this opportunity to thank all those who made comments on the project and its future direction.

3. See Gramsci (1971) and Foucault (2002). Although Gramsci and Foucault do not talk about romantic love, the way they theorize power can help us to understand the relationship between media and practices of romantic love.

4. See Volosinov (1973) and Butler (1993; 1999). Again, although Volosinov and Butler do not discuss romantic love, their respective concepts of multi-accentuality and performativity help us to understand the relationship between media and practices of romantic love.

5. To paraphrase a famous observation about the making of history: we make romantic love but we do not make it just as we please; we do not make it under circumstances chosen by ourselves, but under circumstances directly encountered, given and circulated (directly and indirectly) by media. For the original quotation, see Marx (1977). For a more general discussion of structure and agency in relation to the politics of signification, see Storey (2010).

6. There are a number of excellent books that examine the use of media technologies in human relationships. None, however, work the same terrain as our research. See, for example, Baym (2010), Gershon (2010), Miller (2011), Turkle (2011).

7. Our chapter also contributes to a long tradition of 'active audience' research in Cultural Studies. For more details, see Storey (1996; 1999). We believe our research extends work in this tradition. Part of our contribution is our insistence that the active audience is always active with something and that this something always both enables and constrains its activity.

References

Baym, N. K. (2010) *Personal connections in the digital age* (Cambridge: Polity).
Brown, J. (2006) *A psychosocial exploration of love and intimacy* (Palgrave: Basingstoke).

Butler, J. (1993) *Bodies that matter: On the discursive limits of sex* (New York: Routledge).

Butler, J. (1999) *Gender trouble: Feminism and the subversion of identity*, 10th anniversary edition (New York: Routledge).

Eco, U. (1985) 'Reflections on "The name of the rose"'. In: *Encounter*, 64(4), pp. 7–18.

Foucault, M. (2002) 'Truth and power'. In: Faubion, J. D. (ed.) *Michel Foucault essential works: Power* (Harmondsworth: Penguin).

Garfinkel, H. (1967) *Studies in ethnomethodology* (Englewood Cliffs, New Jersey: Prentice-Hall).

Gershon, I. (2010) *The breakup 2.0* (New York: Cornell University Press).

Giddens, A. (1992) *The transformation of intimacy* (Cambridge: Polity).

Gramsci, A. (1971) *Selections from prison notebooks* (London: Lawrence and Wishart).

Illouz, E. (1997) *Consuming the romantic utopia* (Berkeley: University of California Press).

Latour, B. (2007) *Reassembling the social* (Oxford: Oxford University Press).

Marx, K. (1977) *The Eighteenth Brumaire of Louis Bonaparte* (Moscow: Progress Press).

Miller, D. (2011) *Tales from Facebook* (Cambridge: Polity).

Moores, S. (2012) *Media, place and mobility* (Basingstoke: Palgrave Macmillan).

Morley, D. (2007a) *Media, modernity and technology* (London: Routledge).

Morley, D. (2007b) 'Rhetorics of the Technological Sublime', paper presented at the Centre for Research in Media and Cultural Studies (University of Sunderland).

Shorter, E. (1977) *The making of the modern family* (London: Collins).

Stone, L. (1977) *The family, sex and marriage in England, 1500–1800* (Harmondsworth: Penguin).

Storey, J. (ed.) (1996) *What is cultural studies? A reader* (London: Edward Arnold).

Storey, J. (1999) *Cultural consumption and everyday life* (London: Edward Arnold).

Storey, J. (2010) *Culture and power in cultural studies: The politics of signification* (Edinburgh: Edinburgh University Press).

Storey, J. and McDonald, K. (2013) 'Love's best habit: The uses of media in romantic relationships'. In: *International Journal of Cultural Studies*, doi: 10.1177/1367877912467274.

Turkle, S. (2011) *Alone together* (Philadelphia: Basic Books).

Volosinov, V. (1973) *Marxism and the philosophy of language* (New York: Seminar Press).

14
The Meaning of Home in the Context of Digitization, Mobilization and Mediatization

Corinna Peil and Jutta Röser

1. Introduction

Arguing for the lasting relevance of the home as meaning-giving sphere of media communications does not seem very popular these days. With the emergence, pervasion and increased centrality of online media and mobile technologies, the research focus of many communication scholars has been aimed at mobility rather than locality, and on networks rather than places. This is mainly due to the liberation of media from their physical restrictions that has characterized the better part of media innovations in the last two decades. As a consequence, the use of media technologies is no longer bound to well-defined settings, as was common for most of the last century when the television had its permanent place in the centre of the living room, and the telephone was considered perfectly placed in the entrance hall. Nowadays, media communications of all different kinds have shifted into the public sphere, permeating a plethora of places and cultural spaces. By using devices such as smartphones and tablet PCs, people can connect to their friends and families and have access to media content and online services from anywhere in the world. This has brought about several changes for the perception and understanding of the outside world which have increasingly become subject to negotiations and customizations by the media users. It is often overlooked, however, that significant changes are also taking effect *within* the home. Media such as the internet and mobile technologies have given rise to a special dynamic that has been unfolding within the domestic realm. Not only have they contributed to a rearrangement of the domestic media ensemble and to a realignment of family interactions, routines and activities within the social fabric of the household: they have also taken part in the further erosion of the already porous boundaries between public and private life, since online media, in particular, are regularly being used to bring into the home what had previously belonged to the outside world. These changes are, without doubt, worth examining in more detail, especially as they are closely connected to the transformation of various socio-cultural fields and are not isolated from larger trends within society.

In light of these developments, it will be argued that the home is today more than ever an important signifier of media technologies and their implications for society. Although developments such as digitization, mobilization and mediatization are currently widely discussed among scholars and have promoted a perspective on instable geographies such as in-between-spaces or virtual and augmented realities, the home has not lost its relevance within media and communication discourse. On the one hand, this is because the processes that are taking place at the macro level are reflected at the micro level of the household. On the other hand, the home is still the place where questions of participation and inclusion are negotiated and where meaning is allocated to the media as part of a broader media ensemble which is deeply rooted in everyday life. Starting out from these assumptions, what follows is the reasoning for upholding the significance of the home as a meaning-giving sphere of media communications. A theoretical approach in media and communication research that has traditionally put emphasis on the home is the concept of domestication, which will be discussed and critically reflected in the context of digitization, mobilization and mediatization. In this sense, the home is considered a field of action which constitutes one out of several overlapping 'mediatized worlds' (Krotz and Hepp, 2012) of changing communication cultures (Section 2). Based on empirical data drawn from an ethnographically oriented panel study with 25 households, we will then elaborate on the crucial role of everyday domestic life in the ongoing process of adoption, appropriation and alteration of media technologies (Section 3). It will be argued that the relevance of the home is expressed in the following processes, as will be illustrated based on our empirical studies: (a) Participation in new media technologies is fostered due to their integration into everyday domestic life; at the same time, inequalities are being reproduced (e.g., regarding gender relations); (b) the coexistence of old and new media is managed at home; it is where their functions and roles within the media menu are negotiated; and (c) the process of mobilization becomes effective within the household; it takes form as something that we call 'the domestic mobilization of media practices'. The chapter concludes with an outlook on the communicative connections between the household and the outside world, which have increased in number, range and complexity. The mediatized home is, thus, to be seen as an ongoing process coined by the gradual transformation of communication cultures both within the domestic sphere and in connection to the world beyond (Section 4).

2. Domestication in the light of digitization, mobilization and mediatization

When it comes to a theoretical understanding of the complex relationship between media and the home, the domestication concept is the theory of choice. Rooted in British and European cultural media studies, the domestication approach describes and analyzes the process in which new media technologies move into the household and become part of everyday life (for example, Berker, Hartmann, Punie and Ward, 2006; Peil and Röser, 2012; Röser, 2007c; Silverstone and Haddon, 1996; Silverstone, Hirsch and Morley, 1992). Essentially, it is about allocating technologies a physical and symbolic place within the domestic sphere by integrating them into the daily routines, social interactions and spatio-temporal structures of the household. The approach has emerged from ethnographic research traditions that sought to analyze media use within the mundane surroundings of everyday life. Instead of creating artificial research settings, domestication theory calls for the consideration of the situations, places and social constellations of media appropriation. In this respect, one of its merits is the 'discovery' of the home as a meaning-giving sphere of media use. Within domestication theory, everyday domestic life represents an important context of media appropriation. On this basis, the approach sheds light on the entanglement of different domestic practices, mediated and non-mediated, and links them back to discourses and changes in society.

The domestication concept was initially developed by Silverstone, Hirsch and Morley (1992) and Livingstone (1992) as an outcome of their *Household uses of information and communication technologies* (HICT) project. Not only did the authors intend to elaborate a conceptual framework for examining the role of information and communication technologies in the home, but they also challenged the idea of a technological determinism by emphasizing the active role of users in the process of media adoption. In their original concept, the authors conceptualized four phases of domestication that account for the dynamics that are stimulated when integrating new media technologies into the domestic sphere: appropriation, objectification, incorporation and conversion. However, rather than succeeding in the order described, these phases mutually shape and interact with one another. In this sense, domestication has to be seen as an ongoing process that is never entirely successful or completed, as Haddon (2001) points out. Unlike mainstream research at that time, which mainly focused on the impact of television and its content, the project shifted analytical attention towards the whole range of information and communication technologies inside the home. It aimed at understanding media use with regard to the household and to family, generation and gender constellations. By considering the 'double articulation' of media technologies (Silverstone and

Haddon, 1996) the researchers introduced another novelty, in that they differentiated between media as material artefacts and media as providers of content-related symbolic meaning. Accordingly, the domestication concept, in theory, claims to take into account both of these dimensions (Livingstone, 2007; Silverstone and Haddon, 1996). However, empirical domestication studies seem to concentrate on the level of the artefact and its integration into everyday life (Hartmann, 2006) rather than on the user's interpretation of the contents.

The focus on the household in ethnographically oriented studies of the 1980s is not surprising, given their interest in the everyday contextualization of media use and, in particular, television use, which was, back then, considered a truly domestic practice. In the understanding of Silverstone, Hirsch and Morley (1992, pp. 16 ff.), the household is a 'moral economy' of shared values and identity. It is seen as an economic, social and cultural unit that is linked to the public sphere in several ways, especially as 'part of a transactional system, dynamically involved in the public world of the production and exchange of commodities and meanings' (Silverstone, Hirsch and Morley, 1992, p. 19). Building on this idea, domestication theory has always been interested in the household's transformative relationship with the external sphere. It thus regards media use and everyday domestic life not as detached from the surrounding world, but as closely related to society at large.

The domestication approach, with its original focus on the domestic sphere as a pivotal context of media use, has been challenged in more recent domestication studies in which the home seems to have become less relevant (e.g., Vuojärvi, Isomäki and Hynes, 2010). By hinting at the importance of social relationships in media use, Haddon (2001), for example, makes some instructive suggestions on how to extend domestication theory outside the home. Morley (2003) follows a different perspective when he argues for a reconsideration of the home as a dynamic space of close social relations that can be experienced anywhere in the world through the use of ubiquitous media (compare Peil, 2011; Peil and Röser, 2012; Röser, 2007a). A shift away from the household as signifying context of media use has become apparent, especially with the emergence of mobile phone research drawing on domestication theory. While some of the respective studies are concerned with mobile phone use in the specific context of the household (e.g., Dobashi, 2005), others underpin the need for a reconceptualization of the domestication concept. Most commonly, however, they just refer to its more general ideas of the social character of media technologies that do not develop to an inner logic, but are related to negotiations, social interactions and changing discourse (e.g., Hjorth, 2009; Ling, 2004).

From our perspective, the home's perceived loss of significance can be associated with the processes of digitization, mobilization and mediatization, which are profoundly interconnected with each other and have been important promoters of social change. The concept of mediatization (Hepp, Hjarvard and Lundby, 2010; Hjarvard, 2008; Krotz, 2007; Lundby, 2009) is concerned with media-related changes in communication that implicate new ways of making sense of the world. The underlying assumption is that social action is increasingly moulded by media communication (Hepp, 2009). Mediatization, hence, refers to the cultural and social change related to the emergence and saturation of different forms of media communications in all spheres of everyday life. Mediatization is not a new phenomenon; for example, the emergence and spread of the television set in the 1950s could already be linked to a mediatization of the home which was, among other ways, expressed in the realignment of domestic family rituals, the mobilization of lifestyles and a transformation of the relationship between the public and the private sphere. Mediatization, therefore, has an history, but no defined endpoint, and it is to be understood as an ongoing, highly heterogeneous meta-process shaping modernity.

Characteristic of the present mediatization of culture and society is its intensification by the digitization and mobilization of media. The term 'digitization' basically indicates a new media standard that helps to store, modify and distribute information, and, thus, describes a form of technical change. It represents the technical side of the current mediatization process and stands for far-ranging implications concerning the activities of media users and society as a whole (Hüsig, 2012). These include the emergence of a variety of new communication facilities, the technological convergence of media and media contents, and the enhancement of existing media devices that are becoming increasingly connected and networked. As a consequence, media uses overlap, and the media's scopes of action and signification have become less distinctive (Krotz, 2007, p. 94). However, even though digitization has resulted in a proliferation of convergent technologies and all-purpose media, this does not mean that older media are being replaced or substituted. Rather, a dynamic coexistence can be noticed, as Jenkins (2006) puts it:

> Each old medium was forced to coexist with the emerging media. That's why convergence seems more plausible as a way of understanding the past several decades of media change than the old digital revolution paradigm had. Old media are not being displaced. Rather, their functions and status are shifted by the introduction of new technologies.
> (Jenkins, 2006, p. 14; see also Morley, 2003)

The process of mobilization points in a similar direction, in that it is not only about technological advancements but also about the accompanying change of culture, society and everyday life. Mobile media, such as the smartphone or tablet PC, play a key role within this process. They are highly personalized and portable technologies that allow the users to access a broad spectrum of communication tools while, at the same time, leaving the well-known contexts of media consumption, such as the home or the office. Instead of referring to an immobile, localized context of media reception, mobile technologies are available on the go, wherever and whenever they are needed. Their liberation from geographical constraints and, in particular, their ability to overcome distances have fed the debate about the sense of place, which is either believed to have become irrelevant or regarded as an ever more crucial condition of everyday life (Morley, 2007, p. 223).

With regard to the growing impact of these ongoing processes, as well as the increasing blurring of boundaries that comes with it, the upkeep of the home as a significant context of media use seems like a difficult undertaking that still deserves greater support. For the social construction of home media have played a major role since the early 20th century. Through the use of media, domestic routines and communicative patterns are established, social interactions are structured and differences within the family are negotiated (Silverstone, 2007, p. 172). At the same time, the home has been and still is an important context of media use, even in times of a growing significance of mobile media that often come into operation within the home. While the boundaries of the home have become more porous and subject to modifications, the home is still crucial for the acquisition of media and their position and function within the media ensemble. Regardless of the consequences one draws from the changes depicted above for the reconceptualization of the domestication approach, it can be concluded that the home is still a special place. It is not just one out of many spheres of everyday life where media are appropriated. Featuring some specific structures and qualifications that provide a unique ground where 'the molding force of the media' (Hepp, 2012) and the communicative actions of the people intersect, the home is a microcosm of mediatization that is closely connected to the macrocosm of society. Even today, with the ongoing processes of mobilization, digitization and mediatization, the relevance of the home has not diminished, as we will demonstrate in the following chapter, based on the findings of our empirical study on the mediatized home and the changes of domestic communication cultures.

3. The mediatized home

The empirical data of the mediatized home project is drawn from a qualitative panel study with examination periods in 2008 and 2011.[1] The underlying concept was the assumption that the domestic use of the internet had contributed to significant changes within the mediatized home which are articulated in the reconfiguration of the media ensemble and in the realignment of domestic interactions and relations. The core interest of the study was, therefore, directed to the domestication and appropriation of the internet (= main focus of the first examination period) as well as to the alteration of domestic communication cultures (= main focus of the second examination period), from a process-oriented perspective. Overall questions addressed the emergence and negotiation of participation, the interplay of media usage patterns and gender constellations, and the media-related construction of fragmentation and community within the home. Another emphasis of the study was the changing relationship between the household and the outside world.

In order to gain insights into the designated research areas, we completed 25 ethnographically oriented household studies with cohabiting heterosexual couples in Germany. In total, 50 men and women were interviewed. We first conducted a written survey with 135 individuals, who were recruited through snowball sampling, to build up the sample. Of these, 25 people and their respective partners were selected with respect to three different age groups (25–35, 36–50, 51–63)[2] and two different educational groups (general/intermediate secondary school, high school graduation or vocational diploma) for the household studies. Certain attributes were also considered, such as the date of internet acquisition, professional affinity and non-affinity to the internet, as well as children, housewives and retirees within the household.

The qualitative household studies included two visits to each couple's household (in 2008 and 2011) with a guided interview, a home site inspection and photographs of the media settings. We interviewed husband and wife together, since our primary interest was not in the individuals but in the social situations, communication practices and gender-related arrangements that shape the daily lives of the couples. According to the shifting emphasis of the study – from the reconstruction of the internet acquisition and domestication process in the first examination period, to the analysis of changing communication cultures in the second examination period – additional instruments were applied. In 2008, the household studies were part of a broader methodological design that additionally comprised the secondary analysis of representative data about the development of online use in Germany.[3] When conducting the qualitative interviews, we made use of a timeline to help the respondents recollect the early days of computer and internet adoption and appropriation. They also had to fill in lists to provide information about the use of online applications and the functions allocated to different media. A new element in 2011 was a drawing, whereby the respondents had to sketch in the media and their position within the household (Morley, 2007, p. 83). On the one hand, these drawings were used to encourage talk about the meanings that were assigned to the media in everyday life. On the other hand, they supported a comparative analysis of the households, since the media setting of each household was comprehensively documented and visualized.

We developed the genre of *ethnographic household portraits* for the data analysis and created a detailed portrait of each household by drawing on interview transcripts and memos (with impressions from the interviews), as well as other empirical material such as questionnaires, lists and photographs, and supported it with interview quotes. After the second examination period, these portraits were complemented by structured summary reports centring on selected interview themes and topics. In this way, we were able to perform a context-oriented analysis of all domestic media activities and preferences. Instead of interpreting the data in an individual-based way, as it is done in most other studies, we put a special focus on social constellations and interrelations of various factors within the household. Based on these portraits and reports, a comparative analysis was carried out, followed by a grouping and typifying of the households according to selected questions.

Media domesticity, participation and persisting inequalities

The idea of the home's ongoing significance is supported by the findings of the household studies in multiple ways. One key aspect is the involvement in new media technologies that is moderated and negotiated within the household. The 2008 study, with its focus on the process of domestication and appropriation of the internet, has already shown that the integration of the new technology into everyday life and its connection to domestic duties, routines and interactions have given a major boost to online participation in Germany (Peil and Röser, 2012; Röser and Peil, 2010a). This was mirrored in the quantitative data by the ARD/ZDF online studies (cf. endnote 3). It became obvious with regard to internet diffusion in the first ten years of the survey (1997–2007) that the expansion of the user community and especially the broadening of user groups – from tech-savvy young men to users of different age, educational background and gender – had largely taken place via the domestic context. Whereas places such as the office or school were the preferred localities of internet use in 1997, the share of home internet users increased from 42 to 91 per cent in the following decade. After 2000, the number of people using the internet exclusively at home rose significantly, totalling some 20 million people in 2007, which accounted for half of all the internet users in Germany at that time. In large parts, this rise was a result of the internet adoption by population groups for whom professional inputs were likely to be lacking, for example, due to maternity leave, retirement or 'deskless' professions. Even though some well-known socio-demographic differences in the composition of internet users were still visible in 2007, these trends clearly indicate that the internet had diffused into different social groups and towards a broadening of the user community. Internet use was considerably fostered through the domestication of the technology, contrary to what was predicted by digital divide theorists at the beginning of online connectivity in Germany. The data speaks for the interplay of various factors, such as the implementation of the internet into the domestic sphere, the broadening of the user community and the integration of the technology into everyday life at home.

Our qualitative household studies point in the same direction, and they shed light on the domestication process from the perspective of the users and their initial motivation to access the internet from their private homes. Based on these findings, we identified two different adoption stages that were linked to specific sets of motives. The early stage of internet adoption refers to the households with online access from the mid-1990s onwards. Their interest in the internet was strongly influenced by work or education. A general interest in technology was also often mentioned as a motive for the adoption. The second adoption stage, which was characterized by households without any professional reference to the internet, began in 2000, with peaks in 2002 and 2003. At that time, the user's motivations to access the internet from home were significantly connected to the domestic sphere and the politics of everyday life. In most cases, either there was a specific private concern that initiated internet adoption (e.g., a hobby) or services that supported daily life attracted people's interest, such as travel planning, online banking or eBay. Some of the later adopters had already experienced some pressure from friends or family members to use the internet, and the fear of being left behind motivated their adoption. Another relevant factor was the availability of friends or relatives with some technical expertise who could help to get the internet started and solve problems. These supporters – who in our sample were all male – had, and still have, an outstanding role in the domestication of the internet.[4]

Both the findings based on quantitative data and those based on qualitative data hint at the importance of the domestication process for the diffusion of the internet. They are theoretically rooted in a second perspective of the domestication approach that has been rather neglected so far, even though it was already part of the original concept. Besides emphasizing the role of everyday-life-related contexts for the appropriation of media, the domestication approach represents an analytical framework for describing and theorizing the diffusion process of new media. By asking to what extent the diffusion of new media technologies is fostered through their integration into the domestic sphere, it provides an appropriation-oriented perspective of analysis which primarily centres on the increase of participation as an implication of domestication (Peil and Röser, 2012). This further perspective of the domestication concept can be underpinned by historical studies about early radio (Moores, 1988; 1993; Morley, 1992; 2000) and the telephone (Fischer, 1994; Rakow, 1988). The alteration of these media from technical artefacts to integral parts of everyday life bears some interesting analogies with the diffusion of computers and the internet in the 1990s. All have in common that they attracted wider audiences in the course of their domestication; social inequalities that usually characterize the introduction phase of a new medium were levelled during this process (Peil and Röser,

2012). Additional insights into the quality of this process were gained in the 2011 interviews that revealed how different forms of digital participation were repeatedly negotiated in the further domestication (and re- and de-domestication; see Peil and Röser, 2007) of the internet. The increase of participation is, thus, not to be understood as a linear process, but as being subject to domestic communication cultures: eventually, it is the activities and relationships in the home that decide over the proliferation of competences, the promotion of interest and the use of social resources that constitute the basis of the involvement with digital technologies.

The domestication-driven dynamics unfolding within the home should, however, not be mistaken for an equal use of domestic media technologies. Some inequalities became evident, especially with regard to gender relations and online uses, that exemplarily shed light on the internal processes of inclusion and exclusion and their potential changes over time. Today, the internet still remains a medium framed by its technical character, despite its increased contextualization and integration into everyday life. As a networked technology with multiple interfaces, it still cannot be as easily handled as media such as the radio or television. This technical dimension of the internet (and computer!) is a major reason for its male coding at the hardware level. Correspondingly, in most households in our sample the male partner was responsible for technical issues around the domestic use of online devices. Even in those households where the women were quite confident about their own technical skills and competently used the internet, they usually delegated the technical responsibility to their partners. Nevertheless, there were some differences pertaining to the two adoption stages: while in the majority of households belonging to the first adoption stage (with the exception of the student couples) the male partner was the dominant or even sole user of the internet, the gender constellations within the second adoption stage were more diverse and the partners lagging behind were more likely to start using the internet shortly after domestic implementation. In a few of these households, the woman initiated the internet purchase and remained in charge of the technology. However, the man held this responsibility in most of the households, whatever his factual expert status. Even men with limited internet knowledge were often constituted as the expert within the male–female relationship. This kind of relative difference points to persisting inequalities that are reflected in the representative data: while a lot of women now have access to the internet, there is still a gap between male and female users in terms of range, intensity and diversity of use. This difference is repeatedly constructed by both partners as part of a doing gender process taking effect within the home.

In summary, everyday life at home plays an ambivalent role in the domestication of media. On the one hand, it fosters participation in new media technologies; on the other hand, it represents a cultural field where inequalities are being reproduced. This is especially true for gender relations, because gender-related divisions of labour and the reproduction and alteration of gender discourse within society are inscribed in the domestic media practices (see Morley, 2000; 2001; Peil and Röser, 2012; Röser, 2007a; 2007b; Röser and Peil, 2010a; 2012).

Coexistence of old and new media

The home is still the place where the coexistence of old and new media is managed. It is the place where their functions and roles are negotiated and where each single medium is allocated its specific position within the media ensemble. The decision over which medium to use at a given moment is made at home, where the whole range of media are set in relation to each other (see Morley, 2003, p. 445). This can be illustrated by assuming people's information needs in times of crisis and their corresponding media usage. When, for example, Japan was devastated by the triple catastrophe in March 2011, media users selectively chose from their set of media in order to meet different interests. Watching television might have helped them to feel part of a national community that simultaneously shared the immediacy and shock of the events; social media, such as Facebook, potentially enhanced this mediatized experience in that they delivered tailored and customized information and allowed direct communicative exchange over what had happened; the radio, with its perpetual flow of news that is deeply embedded in everyday life, possibly served as an additional source of information; again, the connected smartphone might have been used to expand the factual knowledge about the backdrops of the disaster. Envisaging this overall setting, it becomes clear that no medium works completely independently, nor does it establish its own separate space of cultural meaning (Bolter and Grusin, 2000). On the contrary, the interplay of media is crucial to understand what each part stands for and how it is used. The significance and impact of media are, thus, to be assessed against the background of domesticity.

The role of media as part of the domestic media ensemble was critically analyzed in our ongoing household studies. The results provide instructive information about the digital mediatization process currently affecting the home. Rather than a predominance of online media, the findings suggest a dynamic coexistence of old and new media that is deliberately managed by the household members. In most households, the internet was integrated into the existing media repertoire as a discrete element with specific concerns and gratifications. Its use was related to tasks that were not at all or only partially covered by the other media in the home – mainly the management of needs and wants that emerged in the context of everyday life. Hence, instead of substituting the purpose of older media, such as radio, television and newspapers, the internet began occupying a cultural sphere that was previously unoccupied by media communications. This insight is reflected in our typology of domestic media usage patterns, which distinguishes three types of households with regard to the internet's role within the media repertoire: internet as integrated medium, internet as convergent medium and internet as marginal medium. While the latter – referring to households with a strong affinity to a classical media repertoire dominated by radio, newspapers and television – has lost relevance in the last few years, the convergent use of the internet still applies to only a minority of the households, but is likely to gain importance in the future. The large majority, about two-thirds of the households we interviewed, were characterized by the integral nature of the internet, whereby the other media had retained their specific role and meaning. At this level, the data hints at a persistence of everyday life contexts within the home that are not easily overturned by new media, but take a significant part in the shaping of domestic technology.

Domestic mobilization of media practices

One process by which the significance of home is particularly challenged is the mobilization of media. In our view, mobilization should not be considered as the opposite of domesticity, because it becomes effective not only beyond but also within, the domestic sphere. Our empirical data provides evidence of the increased importance and various uses of mobile media within the home. This trend will be referred to as the *domestic mobilization of media practices*. Between 2008 and 2011, quite a few of the couples in our panel had purchased smartphones for their private use, which have now come to infiltrate nearly all rooms of the household. However, domestic mobilization is not founded in the mere availability of mobile technologies that were already present in a fair share of households in 2008. Above all, it is expressed in the more flexible use of laptops and other related media, since in most of the households that owned such a device in 2008 it had expanded into a greater variety of rooms three years later. In fact, mobile uses of the internet with a smartphone or a laptop computer were common in every second household in 2011. The household members connect different rooms and places temporarily to the online world via mobile media technologies; they generate provisional internet spaces, and thus create new media spheres within the home that are subject to a complex management of family relationships, as well as media preferences. In this way, the domestic mobilization of media practices comes with new communicative settings that are actively constructed by the media users. Couples, for example, mostly relied on mobile media when they wanted to share a physical space in the home with their partners without having to share involvement in the same media content. Some form of community was enabled even with diverging media preferences, in that one partner, for instance, watched television, while the other was surfing on the internet. As proved by the household studies, these social situations were clearly connected to the content and kind of online activity that was performed. Some of the respondents reported that they would answer e-mails or administer their social networking profiles in the living room in order to be in the company of their partner or other household members. For work-related internet uses, however, they would rather retreat to a separate room. This is a good example of how domestic media are used to adjust community and individuation within the home.

The domestic mobilization of media practices can be linked to new sociospatial routines and new ways of negotiating interactions at home (Röser and Peil, 2010b). This tendency has been intensified by the increased use of smartphones within the domestic sphere. Permeating more and more domestic localities, mobile media have given rise to a variety of new situations and contexts of mediatized communication in which media uses overlap and interfere in a complex way with daily life. Given the intention to buy a smartphone or laptop in the near future, which was articulated by several of the couples, it is expected that this trend will continue over the next few years. This not only applies to interpersonal mediatized communication, which looks back at a longer tradition of domestic mobilization thanks to the popularity of cordless telephones since the 1990s, but also gradually affects all different kinds of media communications within the home. In the course of this development, face-to-face communication between the household members, as well as other domestic activities, such as cooking, studying or watching television, are augmented – to name but one of the consequences. Most notably, the domestic mobilization of media practices has led, and still leads, to a further dissemination of the internet within the mediatized home that is closely associated with the configuration of community.

4. Conclusion: Grasping the mediatized home in the ongoing decade

Supported by the empirical findings of our qualitative panel study with 25 couples in Germany, we have given evidence of the home's lasting relevance as a meaning-giving sphere of media communications. Current developments, such as mediatization, digitization and mobilization, seem to have promoted a perspective on contemporary societies that is centred on flows and networks rather than on locality and domesticity. However, these processes cannot hide the fact that the home still represents a significant terrain for people to negotiate the impact and meaning of media technologies. This was proven by the household studies, with their insights into the dynamics of digital inclusion and exclusion, as well as the coexistence of old and new media and the mobilization of media practices within the home. As one out of many 'mediatized worlds' (Krotz and Hepp, 2012) within society that overlap and influence each other, the home is currently undergoing significant changes. These changes cannot be solely linked back to the increased pervasion of the domestic sphere with different forms of media communications, but also relate to the alteration of domestic communication cultures which are expressed, among other ways, in new media settings and sites of social interaction, reworked patterns of work and family organization, and innovative socio-spatial arrangements. As these fields of action, in turn, constitute 'small life-worlds' (Krotz and Hepp, 2012, p. 13) of shared belief, knowledge and practice, the mediatized home further represents a local reference for multiple concretions of an encompassing mediatization process.

The domestication approach, with its process and context orientation, helps to analyze the manifestations of cultural change within the mediatized world of the home, as it turns its focus to the media-related routines, interactions and disputes inside the house. Beyond that, the concept has always been interested in the household's transformative relationship with the public sphere. Since the communicative connections between the home and the outside world have considerably increased in number, range and complexity, this field is expected to bring about the most significant changes in the near future. To a great extent, this is a result of different forms of mediatized interpersonal communications that have gained relevance in the last few years, especially e-mailing and participation in online communities. In addition, the management of daily tasks and activities has become more and more mediatized and is regularly performed within the domestic sphere. The constant presence of work inside the home and the virtual proximity of distant friends and peers are likely to have some kind of influence on interpersonal communication between the household members. These processes, in particular, call for a re-evaluation of the mediatized home and its ever more complex relationship with the outside world.

Notes

1. The German Research Foundation-funded project 'The mediatized home: A qualitative panel study on changes of domestic communication cultures' is situated at the University of Münster and is run under the leadership of Jutta Röser. It is part of the German priority programme 'Mediatized World' (Krotz and Hepp, 2012) and will be continued with a third examination period in 2013/2014.
2. The age of the respondents refers to the date of the first examination period in 2008. The minimum age was set at 25 years because of our interest in the domestication process of the internet that commenced in the mid-1990s and was supposed to be recounted from the perspective of adult users.
3. The quantitative data was originally collected for the ARD/ZDF online studies that annually survey the internet usage of the German population over the age of 14. The studies have been commissioned by the media board of the two main public service broadcasters in Germany, ARD (Arbeitsgemeinschaft der öffentlich-rechtlichen Rundfunkanstalten der Bundesrepublik Deutschland) and ZDF (Zweites Deutsches Fernsehen) since 1997, which made the data available to us for secondary analysis. Some, but not all, of the data is regularly published in the journal *Media Perspektiven* (e.g., van Eimeren and Frees, 2010).

4. Bakardjieva (2005, p. 98) also found such helpers in her study and described them as 'warm experts'.

References

Bakardjieva, M. (2005) *Internet society. The internet in everyday life* (London: Sage).

Berker, T., Hartmann, M., Punie, Y. and Ward, K. J. (eds.) (2006) *Domestication of media and technology* (Berkshire, New York: Open University).

Bolter, J. D. and Grusin, R. (2000) *Remediation. Understanding new media* (Cambridge, MA, London: MIT Press).

Dobashi, S. (2005) 'The gendered use of *keitai* in domestic contexts'. In: Ito, M., Matsuda, M. and Okabe, D. (eds.) *Personal, portable, pedestrian: Mobile phones in Japanese life* (Cambridge, MA: MIT Press), pp. 219–36.

Fischer, C. S. (1994) *America calling. A social history of the telephone to 1940* (Berkeley, CA: University of California Press).

Haddon, L. (2001) 'Domestication and mobile telephony'. Paper presented at the conference *Machines that become us*. Rutgers University, New Jersey, 18–19 April 2001. http://members.aol.com/leshaddon/Domestication.html, date accessed 7 November 2005.

Hartmann, M. (2006) 'The triple articulation of ICTs. Media as technological objects, symbolic environment and individual texts'. In: Berker, T., Hartmann, M., Punie, Y. and Ward, K. J. (eds.) *Domestication of media and technology* (Berkshire: Open University Press), pp. 80–102.

Hepp, A. (2009) 'Differentiation: Mediatization and cultural change'. In: Lundby, K. (ed.) *Mediatization: Concept, changes, consequences* (New York: Lang), pp. 139–57.

Hepp, A. (2012) 'Mediatization and the "molding force" of the media'. In: *Communications: The European Journal of Communication Research*, 37(1), pp. 1–28.

Hepp, A., Hjarvard, S. and Lundby, K. (2010) 'Mediatization – Empirical perspectives: An introduction to a special issue'. In: *Communications: The European Journal of Communication Research*, 35(3), pp. 223–8.

Hjarvard, S. (2008) 'The mediatization of society. A theory of the media as agents of social and cultural change'. In: *Nordicom Review*, 29(2), pp. 105–34.

Hjorth, L. (2009) 'Domesticating new media. A discussion on locating mobile media'. In: Goggin, G. and Hjorth, L. (eds.) *Mobile technologies. From telecommunications to media* (New York, Abingdon: Routledge), pp. 143–57.

Hüsig, U. (2012) 'Das neue Fernsehen: Transformationen eines Mediums auf der Ebene seiner Nutzungspraktiken'. In: Ligensa, A. and Müller, D. (eds.) *Re:zeption. Die andere Seite der Medienumbrüche* (Bielefeld: transcript), forthcoming.

Jenkins, H. (2006) *Convergence culture. Where old and new media collide* (New York, London: New York University Press).

Krotz, F. (2007) *Mediatisierung: Fallstudien zum Wandel von Kommunikation* (Wiesbaden: VS).

Krotz, F. and Hepp, A. (eds.) (2012) *Mediatisierte Welten. Forschungsfelder und Beschreibungsansätze* (Wiesbaden: VS).

Ling, R. (2004) *The mobile connection: The cell phone's impact on society. The Morgan Kaufmann series in interactive technologies* (Amsterdam: Morgan Kaufmann).

Livingstone, S. (1992) 'The meaning of domestic technologies: A personal construct analysis of familial gender relations'. In: Silverstone, R. and Hirsch, E. (eds.) *Consuming technologies. Media and information in domestic spaces* (London, New York: Routledge), pp. 113–30.

Livingstone, S. (2007) 'On the material and the symbolic: Silverstone's double articulation of research traditions in new media studies'. In: *New Media & Society*, 9(1), pp. 16–24.

Lundby, K. (ed.) (2009) *Mediatization: Concept, changes, consequences* (New York: Peter Lang).

Moores, S. (1988) ' "The box on the dresser": Memories of early radio and everyday life'. In: *Media, Culture & Society*, 10(1), pp. 23–40.

Moores, S. (1993) *Interpreting audiences. The ethnography of media consumption* (London: Sage).

Morley, D. (1992) *Television, audiences and cultural studies* (London: Routledge).

Morley, D. (2000) *Home territories. Media, mobility and identity* (London: Routledge).

Morley, D. (2001) 'Familienfernsehen und Medienkonsum zu Hause'. In: *Televizion*, 14(1), pp. 20–5.

Morley, D. (2003) 'What's "home" got to do with it? Contradictory dynamics in the domestication of technology and the dislocation of domesticity'. In: *European Journal of Cultural Studies*, 6(4), pp. 435–58.

Morley, D. (2007) *Media, modernity and technology. The geography of the new* (London, New York: Routledge).

Peil, C. (2011) *Mobilkommunikation in Japan. Zur kulturellen Infrastruktur der Handy-Aneignung*. Cultural Studies Series, ed. by Rainer Winter (Bielefeld: transcript).

Peil, C. and Röser, J. (2007) 'Vollendete Veralltäglichung: Die Re-Domestizierung des Fernsehens im dualen Rundfunksystem Deutschlands'. In: Röser, J. (ed.) *MedienAlltag. Domestizierungsprozesse alter und neuer Medien* (Wiesbaden: VS), pp. 89–101.

Peil, C. and Röser, J. (2012) 'Using the domestication approach for the analysis of diffusion and participation processes of new media'. In: Bilandzic, H., Patriarche, G. and Traudt, P. (eds.) *The social use of media. Cultural and social scientific perspectives on audience research*, ECREA Book Series (Bristol, Wilmington, NC: Intellect Ltd), pp. 221–40.

Rakow, L. F. (1988) 'Women and the telephone: The gendering of a communication technology'. In: Kramarae, C. (ed.) *Technology and women's voices. Keeping in touch* (New York: Routledge & Kegan Paul), pp. 207–28.

Röser, J. (2007a) 'Der Domestizierungsansatz und seine Potenziale zur Analyse alltäglichen Medienhandelns'. In: Röser, J. (ed.) *MedienAlltag. Domestizierungsprozesse alter und neuer Medien* (Wiesbaden: VS), pp. 15–30.

Röser, J. (2007b) 'Wenn das Internet das Zuhause erobert: Dimensionen der Veränderung aus ethnografischer Perspektive'. In: Röser, J. (ed.) *MedienAlltag. Domestizierungsprozesse alter und neuer Medien* (Wiesbaden: VS), pp. 157–71.

Röser, J. (ed.) (2007c) *MedienAlltag. Domestizierungsprozesse alter und neuer Medien* (Wiesbaden: VS).

Röser, J. and Peil, C. (2010a) 'Diffusion und Teilhabe durch Domestizierung. Zugänge zum Internet im Wandel 1997–2007'. In: *Medien und Kommunikationswissenschaft*, 58(4), 481–502.

Röser, J. and Peil, C. (2010b) 'Räumliche Arrangements zwischen Fragmentierung und Gemeinschaft: Internetnutzung im häuslichen Alltag'. In: Röser, J., Thomas, T. and Peil, C. (eds) *Alltag in den Medien – Medien im Alltag* (Wiesbaden: VS), pp. 220–41.

Röser, J. and Peil, C. (2012) 'Das Zuhause als mediatisierte Welt im Wandel. Fallstudien und Befunde zur Domestizierung des Internets als Mediatisierungsprozess'. In: Krotz, F. and Hepp, A. (eds) *Mediatisierte Welten: Beschreibungsansätze und Forschungsfelder* (Wiesbaden: VS), pp. 137–63.

Silverstone, R. (2007) *Anatomie der Massenmedien. Ein Manifest* (Frankfurt am Main: Suhrkamp).

Silverstone, R. and Haddon, L. (1996) 'Design and the domestication of information and communication technologies: Technical change and everyday life'. In: Silverstone, R. and Mansell, R. (eds.) *Communication by design. The politics of information and communication technologies* (Oxford: Oxford University Press), pp. 44–74.

Silverstone, R., Hirsch, E. and Morley, D. (1992) 'Information and communication technologies and the moral economy of the household'. In: Silverstone, R. and Hirsch, E. (eds.) *Consuming technologies: Media and information in domestic spaces* (London, New York: Routledge), pp. 15–31.

van Eimeren, B. and Frees, B. (2010) 'Fast 50 Millionen Deutsche online – Multimedia für alle? Ergebnisse der ARD/ZDF-Onlinestudie 2010'. In: *Media Perspektiven*, 7–8, pp. 334–49.

Vuojärvi, H., Isomäki, H. and Hynes, D. (2010) 'Domestication of a laptop on a wireless campus: A case study'. In: *Australasian Journal of Educational Technology*, 26(2), pp. 250–67.

Part V

Mediatization in Organizational Contexts

15

Mediatized Politics – Structures and Strategies of Discursive Participation and Online Deliberation on Twitter

Caja Thimm, Mark Dang-Anh and Jessica Einspänner

1. Introduction

In today's social environments, many activities implying the construction of cultural and social meaning are intrinsically tied to media. It is not only the interpersonal level of communication that has been shaped by technological innovations like e-mail, instant messaging or chat (Thimm, 2008); but so have complex societal processes. Whether in politics, economy or business, media traverse the whole society. They are part of the transformation of the public sphere and interwoven within the differentiation of new communication structures and segments. Consequently, media development and societal changes have to be seen as closely connected processes. The concept of mediatization offers an approach to explain the reciprocal impact of media on groups and persons, but it also sheds light on structures and processes within public, political, secular, institutional and private spheres and in daily life (see the contributions in Lundby, 2009). As Krotz (2001; 2007) points out, mediatization is one of the pivotal 'metaprocesses' by which social and cultural changes can be described and explained: 'Today, globalization, individualization, mediatization and the growing importance of the economy, which we here call commercialization, can be seen as the relevant metaprocesses that influence democracy and society, culture, politics and other conditions of life over the longer term' (Krotz, 2007, p. 257).

This focus on processes over time is one of the main characteristics of the concept of mediatization (Lundby, 2009). Drawing on this processual approach, Strömbäck (2008), for example, develops 'phase models of mediatization' in which he conceptualizes 'mediatization' as multidimensional and inherently process-oriented. The perspective on mediatization as an ongoing development, which can be characterized by specific phases, grasps the dynamics of the overall process, but does not account sufficiently for the specific dynamics in certain *arenas of mediatization*. In this article we want to argue that some sectors, environments or contexts (*arenas*) undergo specific processes of mediatization in respect of categories like intensity, time and societal impact, to name but a few. Certain arenas can be more or less dynamically mediatized than others. Politics, for example, cannot be thought of beyond media any more. As shown by the dynamics of several election campaigns worldwide, for instance, the Obama campaign (Thimm, 2012), as well as the recent revolutionary movements in North Africa and the Middle East, new media especially have become a crucial part of global political developments. Political information and public opinions evolve from various media and are influenced by the corresponding media features. However, it is no longer the mass media or politics that exclusively shape public opinion. Due to the ubiquitous availability of various media technologies, individuals are able to contribute to the public news agenda, for example, through eyewitness reporting or online collaboration. Thus, the political arena can be regarded as one mediatized world (*Lebenswelt*) with a growing variety of actors as well as media channels, both of which are subject to mutual influence.

Apart from the contextual determinations of the mediatization process, it still remains open how exactly the media logic of certain applications, like, for example, Twitter, corresponds to their role, value and function within the mediatization process as a whole. This is to say that technology has to be regarded as a key issue for the mediatization process. As Miller (in this volume) rightly observes, much theorizing has failed to consider technology, so that there is 'an awkward gap in mediatization theory, made worse by limited treatments of technology that are ambivalent and even contradictory'.

Between radical perspectives of technological determinism and technological symptomism, Hepp (2013) put forward his concept of the media as 'moulding forces', describing media usage and development and social and cultural change as mutually shaping processes for social dynamics in mediatized worlds. One of these moulding forces is the technological frame in which communicative actions manifest. The technological frames are enablers and disablers at the same time – they offer, or even create, new ways of communication and interaction with the help of technology, but they restrict options at the same time by setting limiting regulations of usage. These regulations have been discussed more recently under the heading of the 'power of algorithms' (Dang-Anh, Einspänner and Thimm, 2013; Pariser, 2011).

When focusing on the political arena, we want to demonstrate that, due to the rapid changes in internet technologies, the mediatization of politics has gained new momentum. We start with an outline of the internet's potential as a deliberative medium at the interface of e-democracy and participation. By drawing on empirical data from the microblogging system Twitter, it will then be shown how Twitter can be seen as highly relevant for political exchange and public discourse.

2. The mediatization of politics, the internet and online deliberation

There is widespread agreement that one of the most viable forces behind the mediatization of society is the internet (see the contribution by Hjarvard in this volume). Marked by characteristics like ubiquity, produsage (Bruns, 2008), multimediality and, more recently, portability (Chayko, 2008), the internet has gained increasing influence on mediatization processes. In personal routines like online shopping, information seeking, social networking or gaming, online technologies pick up on many human needs and interests by offering online options. But not only are private habits influenced by online cultures; the public sphere is undergoing changes as well. Most notably, citizens all over the world have been taking their protests to the internet. Most prominently during the so-called Arab Spring in 2011 (Tufekci and Wilson, 2012), but also during a political scandal in Italy (Vicari, 2012) and in a local conflict about a traffic project in Germany (Thimm and Bürger, 2012), citizens have used online media to voice their protest. Even in China, online activities on Sina Weibo, the Chinese equivalent to Twitter, have started to gain watchdog functions (Hassid, 2012).

The discussion about the potential of the internet as a tool for networking and democratic discourse is not a new one. Given the ever-increasing pace of political decision-making and the globalized forces of control that seem to dictate much of life around the world, many citizens, whether politically active or not, have a feeling of being alienated from decisions that affect their lives. In these circumstances, the internet in particular has seemed to many a potential antidote. Consequently, the internet raised high hopes as a two-way, many-to-many medium with the potential to open communication to almost everyone in a medium that is not centrally controlled and that is flexible enough to facilitate citizen action (Delli Carpini, Cook and Jacobs, 2004). The increasing socio-communicative functionalities, particularly of social networks like Facebook, Twitter or YouTube, have also spawned new forms of mediatized political communication. As Bohman (2004) points out, 'new technologies are often greeted with political optimism' (p. 131). The new ways of citizens' online participation and political protest mirror the dynamics of the contemporary mediatization of the political sphere. The new vigour of participation can be regarded as one of the major developments in user empowerment, as digital networks and communications were actually developed to meet the desire for interpersonal contact (Baym, 2010; Rheingold, 2000).

However, less optimistic perspectives highlight possible downsides of political communication on the internet, such as the fragmentation or polarization of society (Sunstein, 2001) and the digital divide (Norris, 2001), and thus cast doubt on the internet's deliberative potential (Shapiro, 1999) or even see it as a 'net delusion' (Morozov, 2011). As mentioned, the internet was accompanied with high hopes by politicians and scholars for strengthening processes of 'deliberative democracy' in a Habermasian sense (Habermas, 1989). Correspondingly, this optimistic perspective on the internet as being a more democratic and egalitarian medium gave rise to the concept of 'online deliberation' (Thimm, Einspänner and Dang-Anh, 2012a), which has a close link to ideas of 'e-democracy':

> E-democracy may be the 21st century's most seductive idea. Imagine technology and democracy uniting to overcome distance and time, bringing participation, deliberation, and choice to citizens at the time and place of their choosing. Goodbye, then, to 'attack ads' and single-issue politics – and to dimpled chads. E-democracy will return the political agenda to citizens. Or so the dream goes.
>
> (Culver, 2003)

For designers, scholars and practitioners, the term 'online deliberation' holds many different meanings. Words or phrases like 'consensus', 'participation', 'access to information', 'voting', 'project management', 'learning' and 'collaboration' inflect the vocabularies used by those developing, assessing or disseminating digital technologies that facilitate deliberation (Davies, 2009). For many, talk of online deliberation is synonymous with talk of changing or improving democracy and seeing it work via digital media. For others, online deliberation is concentrated on certain tools, which enable participation online (like Fishkin's online polling tolls; see Fishkin, 1991; 2009).

Deliberatively perceived political communication is inseparably linked to the Habermasian notion of the public sphere (Habermas, 1989). It has been a subject of constant debate, interpretation and reinterpretation. One of the outcomes of such re-evaluation is a belief that the public sphere can and should be a venue for the renewal of public discourses. Public discourse is thereby at the very core of deliberative democracy as a new social order constructed from below, as opposed to the dominant traditional system of political communication constructed from above (Coleman and Blumler, 2009). Habermas' (critical) theories of communicative action, discourse ethics, pragmatic meaning and truth constitute the theoretic and philosophical bedrock for deliberative democracy (Habermas, 1984; 1987). Its aim is to reconsider the role of argumentation, rationality and reasoning by rejecting their metaphysical self-sufficiency, and to make them instead dependent on the unique context of communication practices, including their actors, objectives, rules and so on.

The conceptualization of the virtual character of the public sphere follows the Habermasian tradition of deliberating socio-political communities of equal citizens engaging in public discourse. Digital media can be a new hosting platform, where discursively interactive properties can be constructed and strengthened in order to raise the level of democratic participation. Dahlgren (2005) stresses, for example, that 'the theme of internet and the public sphere now has a permanent place on research agendas and in intellectual inquiry for the foreseeable future' in both the media and political communication research, leading eventually to 'convergences between mass and interactive media' (p. 41). Public deliberation online emerges in the new social context of everyday life, but is independent of the existing social settings and conventions. By going online, civic interaction and deliberation expand and pluralize the existing systems of political communication, allowing the expression of socio-political concerns to everyone, not only to political elites.

But, as we argue elsewhere (Thimm, Einspänner and Dang-Anh, 2012a), there can be no one-to-one adoption of Habermas' ideals to the specific setting of digitally mediatized worlds. Particularly in the open and unstructured digital world of politics, as one example of a mediatized world, the Habermasian ideal might never be achieved: 'There will always be some constraints limiting the full and equal participation of all citizens' (Steiner, Bächtiger, Spörndli and Steenbergen, 2004, p. 19). As Delli Carpini, Cook and Jacobs (2004, p. 318) show, most analyses on political participation exclude the discursive perspective and only count activities like voting, signing petitions, lobbying and so on as political participation. 'But talking in public is a form of participation, one that arguably provides the opportunity for individuals to develop and express their views, learn the positions of others, identify shared concerns and preferences, and come to understand and reach judgement about matters of political concern' (Delli Carpini, Cook and Jacobs, 2004, p. 319).

Reflecting on the idealized ethical principles of a deliberative discourse, Steiner, Bächtiger, Spörndli and Steenbergen (2004) come to the following conclusions:

> No one with the competence to speak and act may be excluded from the discourse. All have the same chances to question and introduce any assertion and to express their attitudes, desires, and needs. No one may be prevented, by internal or external coercion, from expressing these rights; all have the right to question the assigned topic of conversation; and all have the right to initiate reflexive arguments about the very rules of the discourse procedures and the way in which they are applied and carried out.
>
> (Steiner, Bächtiger, Spörndli and Steenbergen, 2004, p. 19)

While these rules were initially only applied to institutionalized discursive procedures, such as parliamentary talk (Steiner, Bächtiger, Spörndli and Steenbergen, 2004) or 'deliberative polls' (Fishkin, 1991), it is necessary to ask whether an allegedly uncontrolled, informal discourse – like the ones on Twitter – shows indications of deliberation on the structural as well as the communicational dimension. Particularly on Twitter, with its flat communicative structures, we see a limited, yet vast, potential for discursive participation in terms of a fundamental publicness, individuality, general freedom of expressing and selecting sources, and eventually (and ideally) reasoning on political issues.

3. Microblogging functions and strategies: Discursive participation on Twitter

Due to its format and technological frame, Twitter can be seen as highly relevant for 'public reasoning around social contention' (Vicari, 2012, p. 291), and thus as a crucial facet of the mediatization of politics or even a constitution of a mediatized world of politics itself. The 140-character format may be seen as a constraint, but it is actually no limitation at all (Boyd, Golder and Lotan, 2010): Tweets can be shortened or modified by their distributors and extended by inserted informational links. Because of being so short, Twitter communication is often regarded as being catchy and comprehensible. Additionally, the user is able to substantiate his statement by adding embedded multimodal content (photos, videos and links to other websites), for instance, uploading a picture as evidence of a particular newsworthy situation (Liu, Palen, Sutton, Hughes and Vieweg, 2008). Inserted hyperlinks to online articles or blogpostings can provide additional background information and help to create a discourse system. This system is based on four operators: @ for addressing or mentioning, # for tagging, http:// for linking and RT for republishing. These operators serve different functions and communicative strategies and can be conceptualized in the 'Functional operator model of Twitter' (see Thimm, Dang-Anh and Einspänner, 2011, Table 15.1).

The relationship between the three levels of operator, text and function can be explained as follows:

@-replies: By @replying, users can address other users on Twitter directly. Using the @-function as an interactional 'cross-turn coherence' (Honeycutt and Herring, 2009, p. 2) gives users more options to take part in political online discourses (e.g., @-initiated interaction between citizens and politicians). On the functional level, these actions serve the strategies of 'direct and indirect addressing'. By @-mentioning, that is, putting the '@' somewhere else than at the beginning of a tweet, users talk about each other, creating attention and raising awareness of the subject in question in two ways. First, the addressed or mentioned user becomes aware of being addressed or mentioned, resulting in a potential response. Second, users following the initial tweeter also become aware of the addressed user being talked about or to. This opens up conversational potential for multi-level

Table 15.1 Functional operator model of Twitter

Operators	Text	Function
@ (addressing, mentioning)	Name of account locational reference, emotions, part of e-mail address	Personal reference, creating attention, dialogicity/interaction, contacting, responsivity, intertextuality, coherence
# (indexing)	Lexeme, key word, occasionalism, abbreviation, acronym, cumulated phrases	Contextualization (cue), discourse organization, topical referencing, tagging, creating ad hoc publics, rhetorical branding
http:// (hyperlinking)	Other websites: internal and external links, pictures/photos (e.g. Twitpics), videos (e.g. You Tube)	Information diffusion, argumentation, illustration, quasi evidencing
RT (Retweet) (redistributing)	Citation, comment	Diffusion, reference, citation, creating attention

interaction with several participants involved. Furthermore, it constitutes @-interactions as genuinely public.

Hashtags: Hashtags (#-symbol) mark topics in tweets and offer one or more categorizations. By checking on hashtags, the user can sort the tweets and can easily obtain an overview over the ongoing discourse. Conversations can be followed and whole lists of contributing tweets accessed. Discussions about specific topics often emerge around specific hashtags. These might be lexemes ('#election'), abbreviations such as acronyms ('#NRA'), cumulated phrases ('#gunsinamerica') or temporarily utilized occasionalisms, that is, neologisms created for a particular situation, event, issue, topic, person and so on. The instantaneous constitution and availability of hashtag-discourses characterize them as 'ad-hoc publics' (Bruns and Burgess, 2011).

Hyperlinks: Hyperlinks extend the limitations of text-based tweets by embedding tweet-external content. Videos from YouTube, photos from Flickr, product links from Amazon, slides from Slideshare, music files from Soundcloud, to name but a few of the most popular examples, can all be embedded in a tweet. Multimodal content can be included in the tweet as a display underneath the related text message (see Table 15.1). Especially audio-visual content might also have a narrative and storytelling function if presented sequentially (Thimm, Dang-Anh and Einspänner, 2011, p. 278), as well as cogency of proof (Liu, Palen, Sutton, Hughes and Vieweg, 2008). The depicted example demonstrates the narrative potential of twitpics, by embedding a whole series of photos (Figure 15.1).

The inserted photos (twitpics 1–4) document the overnight construction of parts of a violently contested construction project in Germany, thereby

@stuttgarter1977
André Dietenberger

Zuerst so http://twitpic.com/2tgfnx
dann http://twitpic.com/3wcvim dann
http://twitpic.com/4025qg zum Schluß
http://twitpic.com/3wqbzp #S21

vor 22 Minuten via web ☆ Als Favorit markieren ♻ Retweet ↩ Antworten
von Stammheim, Stuttgart

Figure 15.1 Twitpic narration on Twitter: storytelling in a political conflict (#S21)

telling the demonstrators about the breach of political promise by the city government not to continue the construction process.

Retweets: The fourth communicative strategy, which offers options for participation in Twitter discourses, is retweeting (RT). With this function the user can resend another user's tweet by clicking the retweet-button. The RT-function is a quick opportunity for sharing and distributing messages and reaches many people at the same time. The RT-operator signifies a fast diffusion of information.

Altogether, the operator model offers an approach to allocating strategic value to Twitter activities and putting them into a conversational context.

4. Political discourse and deliberation on Twitter

Applying the ideal discourse principles to the microblogging system Twitter, specific options but also limitations become evident. Following Steiner, Bächtiger, Spörndli and Steenbergen (2004), we want to focus on five dimensions of discourse: access, contribution, exclusion, topical assignments and discourse procedures.

Access. Twitter can be regarded as a forum, allowing everyone with access to the internet and an e-mail address to sign up and join. However, not everyone has access to the internet, be it for financial or infrastructural reasons. Additionally, mediated discourse demands a certain level of technical competence as well as knowledge of medium-specific conventions and functionalities.

Contribution. Basically, there are no restrictions on the content of tweets. However, expressing voice is not the same as being heard. Depending on various factors, such as the number of followers, the user's reputation offline and online, the number of retweets, the retweeter's reputation, and so on, there is a high variation in getting attention and thus being heard in the Twittersphere.

Exclusion. As stated above, in general, no one is prevented from signing up on Twitter. There have been cases, though, of Twitter closing down accounts that either violated their terms of service (e.g., for impersonation, hate speech) or were accidentally accused of such violations (Masters, 2012).

Topical assignments. In general, any contribution is allowed, except for hate speech or violations of national rights. There are no institutionally assigned topics on Twitter. However, Twitter displays frequently used hashtags, lexical items and phrases as 'trending topics'. These topics are algorithmically promoted. Users cannot alter these automated topical assignments.

Discourse procedures. From a deliberative point of view, there are no elaborated discourse procedures on Twitter fixed by rules. Conversational regularities are created out of certain usage cultures, such as the hashtags referring to other users. For example, follower recommendations can be marked by '#ff'. Regarding the communicative functionalities, Twitter itself sets the rules by its programme code and offers a stable communication environment, but at the same time limits interactive creativity.

When applying these five dimensions to concrete Twitter activities, different perspectives can be taken for text analysis. Subsequently, we present three approaches based on the analysis of a large corpus of tweets collected during the 2010–12 state elections in Germany.[1] Bases of analysis are tweets posted by politicians, citizens ('public sphere') and media accounts during four state elections in Germany. The data is summarized in Table 15.2:

Table 15.2   Twitter usage during four state elections in Germany by selected groups

	Northrhine-Westfalia	Saxony-Anhalt	Baden-Wuerttemberg	Rhineland-Palatinate
	Election day: 9.5.2010 Evaluation period: 18.4.–16.5.2010	Election day: 20.3.2011 Evaluation period: 27.2.–27.3.2011	Election day: 27.3.2011 Evaluation period: 6.3.–3.4.2011	Election day: 27.3.2011 Evaluation period: 6.3.–3.4.2011
Public	8,769	15,089	21,288	21,055
Politicians	3,080	1,833	981	1,610
Parties	1,316	1,109	1,829	1,682
Media	5,496	1,434	1,997	2,749
Total	**18,661**	**19,465**	**26,095**	**27,096**

For analysis, the following categories were chosen:

(a) *Topic frequency*: Depending on topic engagement, intensity and time (frequency over time), certain discourse topics can be regarded as more (or less) influential. Here, agenda-setting functions of Twitter also come into play (Thimm, Einspänner and Dang-Anh, 2012b).

(b) *Discursive participation on the individual level*: From the perspective of deliberation, it is necessary to identify and analyze concrete interactive activities as 'communicative actions' (Habermas, 1984). Here, two perspectives can be taken: the *individual level* (style of tweets) and the *interactive level* (interactive exchanges). At the individual level, our operator model of Twitter allows a systematic approach of operator usage and frequency as markers of individual styles. Especially for politicians interacting with citizens, this perspective becomes relevant.

(c) *Discursive participation on the interactive exchange level*: Direct discursive exchanges between interactants reflect the dyadic approach to deliberation. For this perspective, direct exchanges on Twitter are taken as 'deliberative discussions', which demonstrate the discursive options of microblogging.

For the analysis, a triangulate approach was chosen: a quantitative (1) and a qualitative (2) content analysis as well as a linguistic tweet analysis (3). The quantitative analysis is used in order to evaluate interpersonal interaction (@replies and @retweets) on the basis of the functional operator model (see Table 15.1). Frequency counts of the specific Twitter elements and the analysis of their co-occurrences lead to different types of Twitter communication (activity profiles, tweeting styles). In addition, not only were the most frequently discussed topics during the evaluation periods counted, but all hashtag-based discourses on the interactive level, identifying specific communicative actions and interaction structures (e.g., types of reference, topic management), were assessed. With this multi-method approach, tweets can be analyzed with regard to quantitative and qualitative qualities. In addition, the social exchange between the participants within a politically motivated Twitter discourse can be categorized. The results discussed below were selected to highlight these functionalities in the context of deliberation structures.

(a) *Topic frequency*: The most interesting results were obtained during state elections in Baden-Wuerttemberg. Here, not only #Fukushima (black line) and nuclear power (#akw, dark grey line) but a local traffic project in the state capital of Stuttgart (#s21, light grey line) were the top topics. Particularly on the day of the election (March 27, 2011), the high peak of #s21 shows intense activity. This is important insofar as the Green Party fervently fought against this traffic project and won the election, overthrowing the conservative Christian Democratic Union (CDU) after 50 years of uninterrupted power in this state.

That Twitter can be a platform for local protests and demonstrations is underlined by the high usage frequency of the hashtag #s21 over the whole pre-election period (Figure 15.2). Interestingly, this project received nationwide attention, although it is a strictly local traffic project (construction of a train station). Due to the extensive media coverage

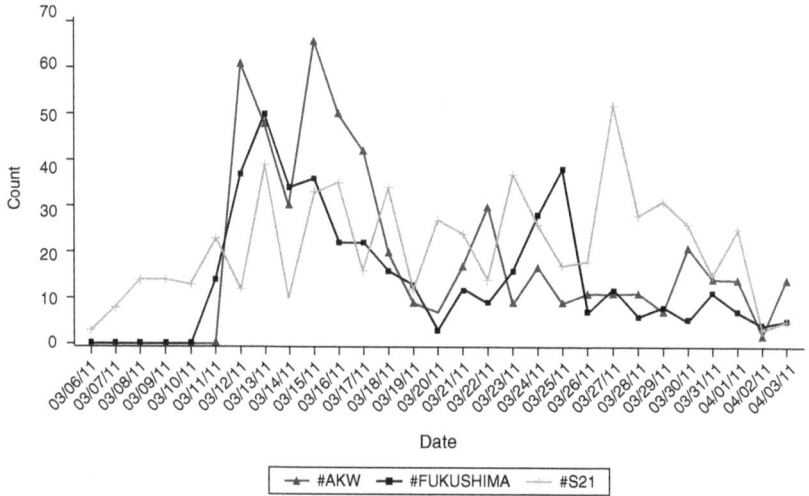

Figure 15.2 Selected hashtag frequency during the state elections in Baden-Wuerttemberg 2011 (election day, 27 March 2011)

and the activities on various social media channels, it became a symbol for citizens' protest against political ignorance. On Twitter, #s21 was used not only by people to virtually support the protesters in the streets but also by protesters themselves to organize and coordinate activities on the ground.

(b) *Discursive participation on the individual level*: For this category, selected politicians from one state were chosen for an analysis on their interactive strategies. Twitter offers a low threshold for direct exchanges between the political establishment and the general public, so that interactions between politicians and the public should yield some typical patterns of distinct exchanges. Based on our functional operator model, types and styles of tweets of the most active politicians per party were assessed (Table 15.3).

The quantitative analysis of the tweets, that is, the frequency count of the occurring signifiers @, RT, # and http//:, reveals two main tweeting styles, both of which are performed by politicians (Thimm, Einspänner and Dang-Anh, 2012b).

When putting these results together, the following results are obtained (Table 15.4).

The 'personal–interactive' style is characterized by a high frequency of @replies and RTs and only a small number of hyperlinks. This tweeting style focuses on the networking aspect of the Twitter communication. The other tweeting style can be classified as 'functional–informative', with a high number of hyperlinks and a rather small number of @replies or RTs. The characterization of this tweeting style is mainly to inform the followers, not so much to engage in dialogue. Overall, the strategies of each politician differ in level of interaction and responsiveness. Whereas some politicians used Twitter in a dialogical manner, others did not participate directly, but, rather, went ahead with their personal agenda ('presentational type').

As can be seen in Table 15.4, most politicians do not engage with the public directly. In particular, Stefan Mappus, at the time head of the state government in Baden-Wuerttemberg, shows a specific Twitter style: he does not use a single interactive or personal element, whether @-operators or retweets, but employs hyperlinks and hashtags only. His strategy can be characterized as strictly informational and non-discursive.

The findings show that politicians were not actively seeking contact and personal interactions with their voters. At least for these (early) years of Twitter in Germany, online deliberation on the level of the politically responsible personnel and the public is rare – the politicians mainly refer to related topics by using hashtags and links. Only a minority address citizens directly or respond to their comments and questions.

Table 15.3 Operator frequencies by most active politicians per party during state elections in Baden-Wuerttemberg

| | Stefan Mappus (CDU) @stefanmappus | | Matthias Tröndle (SPD) @M_Troendle | | Michael Gelb (FDP) @mmgelb | | Barbara Bruhn (GRÜNE) @BJ_Bruhn | | Jan Lüdke-Reißmann (PIRATEN) @Jan_LR | |
| | N (Tweet) 44 | | N (Tweet) 22 | | N (Tweet) 51 | | N (Tweet) 117 | | N (Tweet) 183 | |
	Count	Share of activity	Count	Share of activity	Count	Share of activity	Count	Share of activity	Count	Share of activity
Retweets	0	0%	2	6%	3	5%	19	9%	116	24%
@-Communication	0	0%	2	6%	17	29%	3	1%	60	13%
Hashtags	44	73%	14	39%	4	7%	72	35%	238	50%
Links	13	22%	17	47%	21	36%	112	54%	61	13%
None	3	5%	1	3%	14	24%	1	0%	4	1%

Table 15.4   Twitter styles of the most active politicians during state elections in Baden-Wuerttemberg 2011

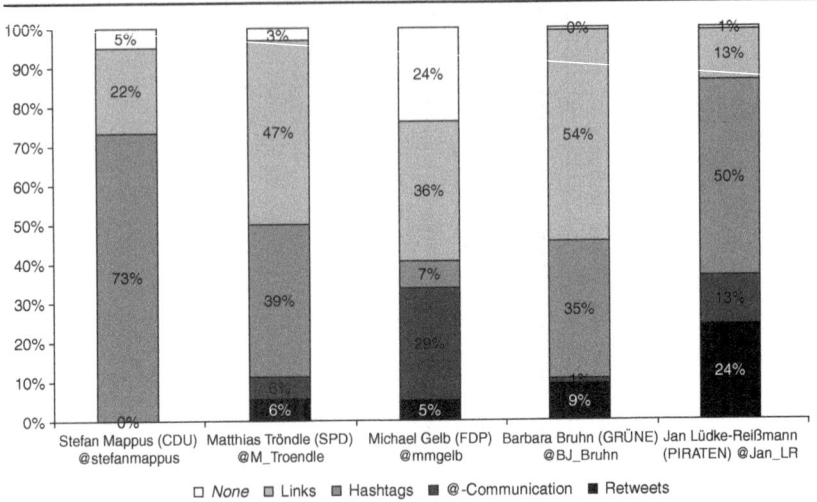

(c) *Discursive participation on the interactive exchange level:* At the beginning of this article, it was argued that mediatization is a process over time. The final example shows how important it is to reflect on the changes of media usage over time. It illustrates a passage of direct exchange between a politician and a citizen in October 2012. This excerpt gives an example of a more recent type of usage of Twitter, in which *argumentation* and *discussion* play a much bigger role. The participants are Volker Beck, a well-known gay MP of the Green party, and a user (user1). They discuss the equal rights bill for gays:

(1) Volker_Beck: How many verdicts do Merkel and the government need until they understand: Anything else than equal rights [for heterosexuals and homosexuals] is discrimination!

(2) User1 (male): How many arguments does @Volker_Beck need to understand that inequality isn't discrimination?

(3) Volker_Beck: 'All are equal before the law.' With all of its diversity. That's what the Basic Law, article III, says @User1 http://[link to Basic Law text]

(4) User1: @Volker_Beck Basic Law, article 6 governs the promotion of marriage as (also biological) foundation of families with children #demography

(5) Volker_Beck: @User1 The Parliamentary Council has already decided differently in 1948/49. Read the protocols! It was governed differently in the Weimar Constitution though

(6) User1: @Volker_Beck I stick to the text of the Basic Law, the comments and verdicts that argument predominantly for today's common juridical practice

(7) User1: @User2 @User3 @Volker_Beck I'll revise my interpretation of the Basic Law only after you're born in a cabbage patch and raised by a cuckoo

(8) Volker_Beck: @User1 I'll leave this circular discussion. Thanks! @User2 @User3

A wide range of communicative functions described above can be found in this interaction between Volker Beck, the gay politician and a user. In this example, a politician expresses himself and responds to a citizen's inquiry and critical comment made possible by the @-operator.

While the interactional sequence starts with Beck's comment on Angela Merkel and the government, several users join (as user1 has the most tweets in this sequence, other posts are not included). Beck's first tweet (1) is a general comment on a contemporary topic he is concerned with. As user1 steps into the conversation (2), he @-mentions Beck and thus creates attention for his comment. As Beck answers (3), user1's @-mention in (2) becomes a 'post facto initiation' (Honeycutt and Herring, 2009, p. 6) for the subsequent conversation. Beck refers to the cited law text via a hyperlink (3) in order to substantiate his argument. The hyperlink leads to a website containing a collection of legal texts. User1 retorts with a reference to another article from the Basic Law of Germany (4). By adding the hashtag '#demography' to his tweet, he implicitly refers to the demographic aspect of gay marriage. With this complex contextualization he deliberately condenses his argument into one hashtag. However, his argument is countered by Beck (5), who refers to the interpretation by the Parliamentarian Council, the founding institution of the German constitution after World War II. The discussion leads further participants to join the conversation. As user1's counter-argument remains unanswered, his multiply addressed argumentation turns non-rational (7). The politician decides to stop the discussion and informs the participants about it (8) by addressing all of them.

As shown in this short excerpt, Twitter can be used not only to inform the public and diffuse information but also to engage actively in online debate. In this case, no solution was reached, but the chance of direct discussion with an MP in a virtual environment can be regarded as a distinctly new option for many voters.

5. Summary and outlook

A diverse set of constellations, types and strategies of political discourse emerge in the public sphere of microblogs. The technical and communicational structure of Twitter enables political discourse between all interested parties, but can also serve as a purely informational tool. By empowering the users all over the world to document, observe, comment or criticize, this social network has the potential to influence political discourse, as was shown by the above examples from the field. Twitter can already be regarded as an establishment within the mediatized world of politics. In a manner of discursive participation, users can share political news and opinions, organize political support or demand more participation from their governments. On the other hand, politicians themselves can address criticism personally and enter public discussion with other users. The global trend towards mobile phones additionally opens up local incidents to the world, as mobile online access enables citizens to immediately report news to the global public (Thimm and Bürger, 2012). Consequently, the dynamics of Twitter usage can be regarded as a pacemaker for the mediatization of politics.

The mediatization of politics is not only one of the most visible and dynamic forms of mediatization but also a very influential one. By changing forms, strategies and structures of access, ubiquity and transparency, this mediatization process is likely to influence political decision-making itself. This is not to say that the deals of the Habermasian concept of 'deliberational democracy' automatically become reality in the online environments. Online deliberation has lots of pitfalls, as was shown for the case of Twitter. So far the microblogging platform is mainly being conceptualized as a 'social news diffusion' medium. But, through the course of media development, it can not only help to organize one's private or – in the case of electoral candidates – political life but also enable citizens to keep track of the political events, share, document and discursively reason on them and thereby influence politics by participating in political discourse online.

Note

1. We thank the German Science Foundation (DFG) for supporting our research project 'Political deliberation and microblogging' in the special research programme 1505 'Mediatized worlds'.

References

Baym, N. (2010) *Personal connections in the digital age* (Chichester: Polity Press).
Bohman, J. (2004) 'Expanding dialogue: The internet, public sphere, and transnational democracy'. In: Shane, P. M. (ed.) *Democracy online* (New York: Routledge), pp. 47–61.
Boyd, D., Golder, S. and Lotan, G. (2010) *Tweet tweet retweet: Conversational aspects of retweeting on Twitter*. Proceedings of HICSS-43. Kauai, HI, 5–8 January.
Bruns, A. (2008) *Blogs, wikipedia, second life, and beyond: From production to produsage* (Digital Formations) (New York: Peter Lang).
Bruns, A. and Burgess, J. (2011) *The use of Twitter hashtags in the formation of ad hoc publics*, 25–27 August 2011, http://eprints.qut.edu.au/46515/ (date accessed 29 August 2011).

Chayko, M. (2008) *Portable communities. The social dynamics of online and mobile connectedness* (New York: SUNY Press).

Coleman, S. and Blumler, J. G. (2009) *The internet and democratic citizenship: Theory, practice and policy* (Cambridge: University Press).

Culver, K. (2003) 'The future of e-democracy – lessons from Canada'. In: *OpenDemocracy.net*, http://www.opendemocracy.net/null-edemocracy/article_1586.jsp (date accessed 23 December 2012).

Dahlgren, P. (2005) 'The internet, public spheres, and political communication: Dispersion and deliberation'. In: *Political Communication*, 22(2), pp. 147–62.

Dang-Anh, M., Einspänner, J. and Thimm, C. (2013) 'Die Macht der Algorithmen – Selektive Distribution in Twitter'. In: Emmer, M., Filipović, A., Schmidt, J.-H. and Stapf, I. (eds) Echtheit, Wahrheit, Ehrlichkeit. *Authentizität in der computervermittelten Kommunikation* (Weinheim: Juventa), pp. 74–87.

Davies, T. (2009) 'The blossoming field of online deliberation'. In: Davies, T. and Gangadharan, S. P. (eds.) *Online deliberation: Design, research, and practice* (Stanford: CSLI Publications), pp. 1–19.

Delli Carpini, M. X., Cook, F. L. and Jacobs, L. R. (2004) 'Public deliberation, discursive participation, and citizen engagement: A review of the empirical literature'. In: *Annual Review of Political Science*, 7, pp. 315–44.

Fishkin, J. S. (1991) *Democracy and deliberation: New directions for democratic reform* (New Haven, London: Yale University Press).

Fishkin, J. S. (2009) 'Virtual public consultation: Prospects for internet deliberative democracy'. In: Davies, T. and Gangadharan, S. P. (eds.) *Online deliberation: Design, research, and practice* (Stanford: CSLI Publications), pp. 23–36.

Habermas, J. (1984) *The theory of communicative action. Vol. 1: Reason and the rationalization of society*, trans. McCarthy, T. (Boston: Beacon).

Habermas, J. (1987) *The theory of communicative action. Vol. 2: Lifeworld and system: A critique of functionalist reason*, trans. McCarthy, T. (Cambridge: Polity Press).

Habermas, J. (1989) *The structural transformation of the public sphere. An inquiry into a category of bourgeois society* (Cambridge: Polity Press).

Hassid, J. (2012) 'Safety valve or pressure cooker? Blogs in Chinese political life'. In: *Journal of Communication*, 62(2), pp. 212–30.

Hepp, A. (2013) *Cultures of mediatization* (Cambridge: Polity Press).

Honeycutt, C. and Herring, S. C. (2009) 'Beyond microblogging: Conversation and collaboration via Twitter'. In: *Proceedings of the Forty-Second Hawaii International Conference on System Sciences* (Los Alamitos, CA: IEEE Press).

Krotz, F. (2001) *Die Mediatisierung des kommunikativen Handelns. Der Wandel von Alltag und sozialen Beziehungen, Kultur und Gesellschaft durch die Medien* (Opladen: Westdeutscher Verlag).

Krotz, F. (2007) 'The meta-process of "mediatization" as a conceptual frame'. In: *Global Media and Communication*, 3, pp. 256–60.

Liu, S. B., Palen, L., Sutton, J., Hughes, A. L. and Vieweg, S. (2008) 'In search of the bigger picture: The emergent role of on-line photo sharing in times of disaster'. In: Fiedrich, F. and van de Walle, B. (eds.) *Proceedings of the 5th International ISCRAM Conference*, http://works.bepress.com/vieweg/11/.

Lundby, K. (ed.) (2009) *Mediatization: Concept, changes, consequences* (New York: Lang).

Masters, S. (2012) '#NBCFail: Backlash as Twitter locks out reporter Guy Adams'. In: *The Independent*, 31 July, http://www.independent.co.uk/news/world/americas/nbcfail-backlash-as-twitter-locks-out-reporter-guy-adams-7987906.html.

Morozov, E. (2011) *The net delusion. The dark side of internet freedom* (New York: Public Affairs).

Norris, P. (2001) *Digital divide: Civic engagement, information poverty, and the internet worldwide* (Cambridge: University Press).

Pariser, E. (2011) *The filter bubble. What the internet is hiding from you* (New York: Penguin Press).

Rheingold, H. (2000) *The virtual community: Homesteading on the electronic frontier* (Cambridge, MA: MIT Press).

Shapiro, I. (1999) 'Enough of deliberation: Politics is about interests and power'. In: Macedo, S. (ed.) *Deliberative politics: Essays on democracy and disagreement* (New York: Oxford University Press), pp. 28–38.

Steiner, J., Bächtiger, A., Spörndli, M. and Steenbergen, M. R. (2004) *Deliberative politics in action: Analyzing parliamentary discourse* (Cambridge: University Press).

Strömbäck, J. (2008) 'Four phases of mediatization: An analysis of the mediatization of politics'. In: *International Journal of Press/Politics 2008*, 13, pp. 228–246.

Sunstein, C. R. (2001) *Republic.com* (Princeton, NJ; Oxford: Princeton University Press).

Thimm, C. (2008) 'Technically mediated interpersonal communication'. In: Antos, G. and Ventula, E. (eds.) *Handbook of interpersonal communication* (Berlin: De Gruyter), pp. 331–54.

Thimm, C. (2012) 'The visuals of online politics: Barack Obama's web campaign'. In: Depkat, V. and Zwingenberg, M. (eds.) *Visual cultures – Transatlantic perspectives* (Publications of the Bavarian American Academy, 12), pp. 185–203.

Thimm, C. and Bürger, T. (2012) *Digitale Citoyens – Politische Partizipation in Zeiten von Social Media. Fallanalysen zur politischen Beteiligung in Deutschland, Ägypten und China* (Bonn: BAPP).

Thimm, C., Dang-Anh, M. and Einspänner, J. (2011) 'Diskurssystem Twitter: Semiotische und handlungstheoretische Perspektiven'. In: Anastasiadis, M. and Thimm, C. (eds.) *Social Media – Theorie und Praxis digitaler Sozialität* (Frankfurt a. M.: Peter Lang), pp. 265–86.

Thimm, C., Einspänner, J. and Dang-Anh, M. (2012a) 'Politische Deliberation online – Twitter als Element des politischen Diskurses'. In: Hepp, A. and Krotz, F. (eds.) *Mediatisierte Welten: Forschungsfelder und Beschreibungsansätze* (Wiesbaden: Springer VS), pp. 95–117.

Thimm, C., Einspänner, J. and Dang-Anh, M. (2012b) 'Twitter als Wahlkampfmedium'. In: *Publizistik*, 57(3), pp. 293–313.

Tufekci, Z. and Wilson, C. (2012) 'Social media and the decision to participate in political protest: Observations from Tahrir Square'. In: *Journal of Communication*, 62(2), pp. 363–79.

Vicari, S. (2012) 'Twitter and public reasoning around social contention: The case of #15ott in Italy'. In: Tejerina, B. and Perugorria, I. (eds.) *From social to political: New forms of mobilization and democratization*, Conference Proceedings (Servicio Editorial de la Universidad del País Vasco, Bilbao), pp. 277–92.

16

The Quantified Listener: Reshaping Providers and Audiences with Calculated Measurements

Jan-Hendrik Passoth, Tilmann Sutter and Josef Wehner

1. Introduction

Various relationships between providers, audiences and other participants of cultural production are changing today. In the case of platforms that offer their users recommendations for pieces of music, formerly unknown artists are providing a fan base detached from the traditional mainstream of the music industry. While these artists were previously only able to establish a niche as an alternative to mainstream distribution, today they are being culturally re-evaluated. We argue that this is due to changing practices when calculating user activities of online services, which we understand as an important, but quite often overlooked, aspect of the complex meta-process of mediatization (Krotz, 2001; 2009). Similarly to the traditional mass-media approach of constructing a dependable audience through statistical measurements, online services rely on complex computer-assisted techniques and methods to construct their specific audiences. But today every single activity on the net is also a quantifiable and measurable piece of data: whoever uses the net inevitably leaves traces, a huge and harvestable amount of data. When services use this, it is really in only the rarest cases for profiling single and individual users. Mostly they form comparisons by looking for similarities and differences between user collectives. These new forms of quantifying the listener do not try to establish an average taste to recommend a compatible range of average mass culture. Instead, they support the automatic recommendation of special interests and help associate formerly mass-incompatible works. These developments are changing conventional music distribution: what an audience is or what it is supposed to be is transforming – in some cases radically, in others incrementally – and so is what it means to distribute and perceive music. The emerging mediatized world of music distribution is informed, affected or maybe even governed by new (and blends of old and new) techniques of quantifying listening and listeners.

The primary goal of this article is to substantiate this observation. First, we will step back a bit and elaborate more generally on the problem of quantification as a modern technique of producing and implementing comparisons. We have long since got used to having relevant events and developments in more and more areas of daily life presented to us in numerical form. From a sociological point of view, it is interesting that such number systems are not restricted to single objects – since they deal with results of measurement techniques, they always deal with several objects that are compared with the aid of respectively selected indicators. Measurements, thus, do not only inform about special numerically representable relations in the world; they also suggest reciprocal observations and relationships.

In a second step, we will discuss the glaringly apparent interference of mass media with ever more deep-reaching and constantly expanding processes and structures of a 'quantification of society'. This may also be regarded as the close connection between cultures of mediatization (Hepp, 2013) and cultures of quantification (Lave, 1986). What role do the media play in processes producing and circulating quantified comparisons? Traditional mass media are involved in these processes in at least two distinct ways. On the one hand, they are obviously a main mediator of reusable forms of quantified comparisons, due to their focus on numeric forms of presenting news, entertainment and commercials in the form of survey results and polls, blockbuster sales or special offers. However, the media do not only support other social sectors with number-based self- and third-party observation. Much more interesting for us is that, on the other hand, providers of media content rely heavily on audience ratings and viewer levels, and therefore organize their internal reproduction on quantified comparisons. Conversely, viewer, listener and reader statistics contribute to media profiling, thus making the media publicly visible and more understandable. Audience measurement also turns stations into competitors for audience approval and offers opportunities for mutual comparison and assessment, which, in turn, have consequences for the formation and the change of the media system.

In a third step, we use current literature on audience measurement on the internet and our empirical research into online music recommendation platforms. New media environments radicalize the process of mediatized quantification, but, in the current state of the art, they do this incompletely and are blended with many old and traditional views. Additional possibilities for data creation and measurement of the media world are gained through the broadened possibilities for intervention and collaboration present on the internet ('web 2.0'). This also enables the participants themselves to observe the various mediatized worlds, as well as to participate in possible mutual comparison and assessment – something the traditional mass media cannot offer.

2. Quantification *and* the media

Statistical methods and models, number systems connected with them and the expectations and objectives justified by them have long been handled in sociology as a fringe phenomenon and remained as topics in niches of small researcher circles over many decades (Miller, 2007). However, there were repeated attempts to counteract this marginalization, indicating just how closely related measures of quantification and social modernization processes were (Mennicken and Vollmer, 2007; Vollmer, 2004; Wagner, 1994). In such a general sociological perspective, methods of quantifying comparison and assessment are fundamentally integrated into the creation and change of modern society. This includes its (worldwide) information and communication relations and the processes connected to them, such as (global) circulation of technical or social innovation and (global) approximation of societal subsystems (Heintz, 2010). However, the role of modern (mass) media in these processes has rarely been examined.

Numbers and their (mass) audiences

Mass media have a strong preference for events that can be quantified (Harcup and O'Neill, 2001; Luhmann, 2000). Readers and television viewers are used to having events and developments from politics, economy or sports dressed up in numbers and figures. It seems that numbers primarily serve the news factors that are common in professional journalism. Quantities are able to express novelties just as convincingly as they simplify complex topics. They enable references to the past, but also to future-related predictions (increasing export rates, increasing gross national product, falling unemployment numbers). This makes quantifications an important raw material of mass-media information processing and circulation. Most of these numbers are usually provided by the corresponding institutions themselves (companies, parties) or by third parties (e.g., survey institutes, advertisement companies, economics institutes, etc.), which pass them on to their clients (e.g., parties) to review and arrange them before passing them on to the media.

What makes quantifications especially interesting is their capability to relate and compare similar events and developments within one thematic field (Siemes, 2009). Changes in one object or situation can be assessed, as well as differences between several objects or situations over longer periods of time: Company financial records, national debt rates or unemployment rates are integrated into reports on economic issues and developments. The results of the latest PISA study (Programme for International Student Assessment, OECD) or university rankings are used to provide information on current developments within the educational system. Such statistics do not just inform about individual current situations and differences, but also present changes of the respective observed units and the ups and downs connected to them. In addition, when these reports are published, the relationships between the representatives of those parts of society about which numbers-based reports were published and their respective audiences also become public (Burzan, Lökenhoff, Schimank and Schöneck, 2008).

Preconditions of counting and reading numbers

Techniques of calculation and measurement are boundless. They seem to overcome the restrictions of all special qualitatively oriented languages and comparative methods and become more of a universal technique of observation and comparison (Heintz, 2010; Manhart, 2008). Apparently, number systems enable us to observe and assess highly complex situations and to become involved in them with others – without having to be a participant or a person directly affected (Porter, 1995). This is only possible, however, because the quantitative perspective focuses only on a few criteria. The technique itself is regarded as being generally impersonal, objective and therefore trustworthy, and the results are understood to be rooted within the matter – not in the technique itself, or even in the particular interests of the facilities involved (Desrosières, 2002).

Another motivation to accept numbers might have to do with their being prepared and published in a way that will make them easier to perceive. Measurement results alone are obviously not enough – they are often accompanied by additional interpretations:

> [Numbers] somehow provide the impression of something preliminarily final. They offer a basis for connecting operations. [...] Unfortunately, however, numbers only have two options: to increase or to decrease. Everything else is an ingredient, an interpretation.
>
> (Luhmann, 1981, p. 327, own translation)

Published financial statements, rankings and rates already embody conversions to special presentation formats, tailored to the public's abilities (Schulte-Holtey, 2001). Such formats preferably contain narrative framings and infographic elements, which present the corresponding quantified events, such as decreasing birth rates or increasing unemployment rates, in such a way that they become understandable for an audience – in the sense of a 'preferred reading' (Hall, 1980). With regard to TV ratings, Thiele (2006, p. 306) also speaks of a 'discoursivation and visualization' of the audience measurement results, whereas Espeland and Stevens (2008, p. 422) use the term 'aestheticization' of the measurement results. This means that numerical data is always dependent on preliminary coding in order to be able to motivate attention.

Without being coded into publicly appealing formats, numbers would remain too complex, inexplicable, not communicatively understandable – unless they have already been converted into visual formats (diagrams, charts, graphs, etc.). Number-based comparisons may facilitate audience relationships as well as connecting operations, for example, when universities make themselves comparable using rankings. Such statistics, however, always create a demand for interpretation and translation (Vormbusch, 2007). These demands are met by results that have been reworked to be reception-oriented, by means of which numerical data can be acquired and translated into different socio-cultural contexts (Cleveland, 1994). Mass media do not only contribute to the circulation of numbers; they also support their reception by circulating corresponding interpretations.

Numeric comparisons and competitive relationships

Performance comparisons such as survey data, financial statements and stock listings do not only provide information about political or economic success and failure. They also provide opportunities to identify and assess other relevant participants and/or competitors in the light of these results. Very complex and diffuse relations – for instance, those of the current financial crisis in Europe – are translated into public events by using statistics and accompanying interpretations. Participants find themselves challenged by their partial responsibility for these events and developments – at least under the public eye. They are also expected to assess their own role and chances in relation to other participants and to take measures in order to improve their own situation (Espeland and Stevens, 2008, p. 412). Published performance measures, therefore, create competitive relationships, informing every participant of respectively assumed positions and initiating processes of self-optimization, competition-stimulated deviation and approximation, and thus of change – and all without the necessity for direct meetings and negotiations (Cohen, 1982; Heintz, 2010).

3. Quantification *of* the media

Mass media do not only use numbers simply as content. They have long since become accustomed to handling their own activities through processing and measuring numeric data. This has not gone unnoticed in the field of media studies. However, media have restricted themselves to interpreting and critiquing the data as a justification to simplify and commercialize media reception (Webster, Phalen and Lichty, 2000). This critical interpretation, however, is countered by the consideration that it is exactly this simplification that is one of the conditions for modern media to work in the first place. Without measurement equipment and techniques, it would not be at all conceivable to measure the sophistication, speed and range of modern mass media – in particular, television. Methods and results of audience measurement are closely connected to the development dynamics of mass media and to the diffusion and spread of mediatization. Competitive relationships have arisen, in particular, from the audience rating system; these relationships represent an important impetus for the circulation of successful media content and forms of organization. Finally, there is some indication that measurements such as viewer ratings do not only help providers to take a peek at the audience; they also allow the audience to peek back at them.

The audience as a numeric construct

The question of why mass media treat their audience as a mere statistic draws attention to a problem which has accompanied the process of mediatization from the very beginning: (mass) media must continuously produce media content without knowing how the audience will receive it. Due to the way mass communication is structured, the audience will always remain anonymous to the media (Luhmann, 2000; McQuail, 1997, pp. 109ff.). Television, in particular, has made the attempt to solve the problem of not knowing its audience with the help of a constantly refined system of statistical analysis, based on several selected parameters like age, sex, television viewing time and preferences for channel selection. Although not the inventor of this solution, television promotes it, because it perceives its audience as statistical aggregates, primarily in the form of the notoriously famous ratings. To speak of individual 'viewers' or 'the audience' is partially possible because of the techniques of making media usage observable and understandable (Meyen, 2004; Schorr, 2000; Schrage, 2001; 2005).

As with statistical methods and quantification in general, methods of audience measurement are highly accepted in the media corporations. This is because, unlike informal knowledge and intuition, these methods are considered to be a much more exact and objective form of observation without any true alternative (Ang, 1991; 1996). Diffuse differences in sociocultural contexts and individual preferences of media reception are reduced: the variety of individuals watching television, listening to radio or reading the newspaper is turned into a homogeneous mass of measurable objects which can then be distinguished by defined criteria. However, the informal, more personal and more contextual knowledge about the audience does not lose its function. It has always played a role in programming decisions of media management, and it has been even more strategically relevant in less measurement-capable media such as radio. It may have lost significance, particularly regarding television, but it remains irreplaceable for interpretation and translation of measurement results into the respective station's concept, and thus also for addressing media contents (cf. Ang, 2001).

Media competition and media transition

Audience statistics use relatively short time intervals to provide information on what type of content appeals to what types of audience(s) in which time slots. Furthermore, trends may be identified regarding ratings of individual shows, formats or programme sections. Thus, audience measurements indicate which programmes and stations are successfully using which show, concept or format. They, therefore, also offer the option of comparing and assessing content according to set criteria, and that may even be their primary function:

> For the communicator, the public is a dark and inaccessible entity which has transformed into the ambiguous and very mysterious 'audience'. [...] 'Audience' measurement does not seem to serve the purpose of getting to know the viewers, it seems more to be offering the producers a self-referential orientation – especially in respect to advertising and its costs.
>
> (Esposito, 1999, pp. 98–99, own translation)

Audience measurement thus allows a shift in perception. It supports the observation of the information and communication habits of the audience, but also provides a glimpse of the competitors and how they deal with the anonymity of their audience. Whoever wants to know how successful the others are in their relevant field only has to look at their ratings, sales figures or circulation.

Viewed in this light, audience statistics introduce a specific kind of competitive relation between content providers by allowing a permanent comparison of their publicly accessible performance. Every actor involved is informed of its own as well as the other's strengths and weaknesses and encouraged to self-optimize, which can lead to the potentially worldwide circulation of successful formats and content. Thus, audience measurement creates a dynamic and responsive (in respect to new ideas, formats and structures) network of relationships, in which positions are not attributed once and for all but have to be newly consolidated over and over again. This all works without the need for direct exchange or cooperation between the participants (Hasse and Wehner, 2005).

Competition created in this way does not lead to complete alignment within the field of actors. Taking over a successful format does not free one from having to adjust it to one's own programme structures, production conditions, audience relationships and available budgets. Just as the audience measurements require corresponding interpretations and translations, adopted media contents have to be adapted to the provider's own special conditions. This facilitates a better understanding of why there are, on the one hand, strong tendencies of alignment between content providers (e.g., reality TV formats or daily soaps) and, on the other hand, subtle differences that might be more clearly recognizable and more significant for the competitors than for the audience.

Station–audience relationships in numbers

Audience measurement is supposed to give providers insights into the habits and preferences of their audience. But it also provides opportunities for the public to inspect the media. Programme reviews and daily tips based on the ratings system and measurement techniques summing up audience approval help to find one's way through the abundance of programmes. They support the development and habitualization of media-related practices of differentiation and evaluation which can be recognized through the 'willingness to tune in' to the different stations (Thiele, 2006, p. 317). In addition, audience measurement and its public-oriented coding also affect relationships between participants. Looking at television ratings, radio station music charts or publishers' bestseller lists, anyone can explicitly decide for or against current trends in media use and for or against 'normal' (in the sense of averaged) media habits – even if the room for this is admittedly relatively small under the conditions of mass media (Link, 1997). Thus, what is perceived as being an audience, how the role of a viewer, listener or reader is assumed, and, finally, how participants become distinguishable from each other – all this apparently also depends on processes of measuring the audience and corresponding interpretations (Wehner, 2010).

4. New media, new quantification

With the internet's expanded potential to engage and participate (Sutter, 2010), new conditions for quantification of media activities are emerging that go far beyond the possibilities of the conventional methods for audience measuring. More and more personal information and communication habits of users are moving into the focus of content providers, and it becomes increasingly possible to customize media content to particular interests. In turn, users' access to media content is becoming increasingly personalized, which also fosters possibilities for comparisons of one's own media use with the habits of others. Media change associated with the internet is, therefore, connected not only to the latest possibilities for interaction and deliberation but also with the new machinery of measuring and analyzing them (Napoli, 2011).

This has been the starting point of the research on platforms that offer their users an online music experience that is built directly or indirectly on techniques of recording and processing usage data. We selected two very distinct case studies to maximize the potential for empirical comparisons: a platform that explicitly developed from traditional 'quality radio' has been contrasted with a platform that describes itself as an algorithmic and automatic recommendation device, a 'personal radio'. Our ethnographic data comes from three months of participant observation,[1] extended content analyses of first- and third-party documents, and a number of long, narrative interviews. These interviews were conducted with current and former members of the respective project teams, with third-party observers and with platform users. Although we are still in the process of evaluating and characterizing the collected data, some preliminary findings shed light on a couple of very interesting features of the use of user tracking and audience quantification in the case of digital, web-based technologies. We are just at the beginning of these developments, and, as our data indicates, things are always empirically more complex than they are in principle. That said, it is very obvious from the cases we studied that the so-called paradigm change from mass media to digital technologies is, in fact, a constant struggle and a set of intertwined transition processes, in which the use of user tracking and audience calculation is one of the main tenets.

From audiences to clusters of users

Under the conditions created by mass media, content and its reception were solidly linked to one another and media usage was predominantly station-ary, almost 'in-house'. This is in contrast to new media technology such as smartphones, netbooks and other multimedia technology that facilitate mobility and flexibility in media usage. However, with relatively inflexible reception settings becoming less relevant, important conditions for classical methods of audience measurements will get lost. This is the case with video streaming services and mobile access to e-books, e-mail and websites, but it is even truer with music distribution. Radio and listening to recorded music has been a background service and an individualized and mobile experience since the invention of car audio in the 1930s and the Sony Walkman in 1972. But, for a long time, radio also used to be a local experience, played in shops, at work or in public spaces.

Individual music consumption has always been hard to track because only sales are countable, not copies or borrowed tapes and CDs. Radio listening has been (and still is) measured mostly by diary-based systems and regu-lar surveys that rely mostly on listeners' perception and memory. In the USA, radio consumption in public spaces has been tracked with the LPM system, a device that records hidden signals in the broadcast programme. This makes radio a great, if not the banner, case to study because radio rat-ings have always been artificial and problematic. Nevertheless, they have been treated as the only way to get a glimpse of the audience. With web radio and mobile, Internet-Protocol-based distribution systems, this radically changes. Platforms know exactly when, where and how long they are turned on. Suddenly there is data – so what can be done with it? This now poses the question of whether and which user measurement techniques will be able to keep up with this development.

One answer to this can be found in studies which point to the general feasibility of measuring any kind of internet activity (Röhle, 2010). Anyone who uses digital media technology will, inevitably, leave data traces which can be numerically coded, measured and analyzed. Every visit to a platform, every download, every entry made into a search engine, every article purchased can be used in order to create patterns of activity and user profiles, which can then be compared (Bermejo, 2007; 2009). Logging and analysis procedures, for example, provide opportunities to evaluate which document was clicked as well as how many times, how strongly they are linked to one another, how often they were assessed and in which way. Participant activity data on mobility, consumption or ascribed interests is collected on a large scale and increasingly consolidated into corresponding profiles and patterns.

This tends to switch the trend to abstract from contextual and incomparable qualitative factors to favour homogenized measuring units in (mass) audience measurement. With the data available in digital media settings, measuring probes can reach increasingly deeper into the information and communication habits of users and create more complex participant profiles and comparisons. There is also, at least in principle, no barrier to connecting temporally, spatially and factually varying activities that previously could not, or could only with great effort, be quantified (e.g., mobile habits, the perception of advertising spaces and subsequent purchases). Contrary to mass media processes of topic filtering and preparation, relatively little is known about how these measuring techniques and/or the algorithms used in them work, and which criteria they use to track, compare and evaluate the participants' contributions. Search engines like Google that make excessive use of automated monitoring, analyzing and ranking often look like black boxes for external parties. Whereas under mass-media conditions it was possible for all participants to acquire some kind of shared knowledge on the relevant inclusive and exclusive criteria of topic selection, this now becomes considerably more difficult due to the use of algorithms.

A first step in remedying this is an explanatory and ethnographic study on the production side of internet developments. Oriented towards research that was done in the field of 'Social Studies of Finance' (Callon, 1988; Callon and Muniesa, 2005; MacKenzie, 2006), we first turned our attention to the machinery of algorithms and techniques used by the platforms we studied. Similarly to the way this research penetrated the depths of construction done on modern financial instruments and algorithms in order to understand the inscribed classifications, ad hoc negotiations and random decisions, our approach would deal with observing the development in measuring techniques in order to understand the ideas and models of users that are incorporated into the machinery of user measurement.

What we found, however, was even more interesting than these simple account details (Akrich, 1993). The construction and assembly of new technologies is never only an act of engineering, but also an act of applied sociology (Law and Callon, 1988): in both cases we studied, there was no one single new way of analyzing user activities that embodied a certain (modified) idea of how that 'quantified listener' would appear. Instead, we found – although in very different ways – that a blend of old and new techniques, practices and ideas is present in both circumstances. Whereas in the case of the renewed 'quality radio' an explicit orientation towards an interested and educable listener is omnipresent, there is, nevertheless, a whole armoury of tracking and quantification techniques in place that inform programming and even human resource decisions.

The case of the 'personal radio' is also very interesting in this respect. Although it presents itself as a paradigm case for algorithmic recommendation systems, and while the hard disks of their web- and streaming-servers are overflowing with activity data, implementing that into an algorithm is extremely complicated. Instead, a team of 'playlist writers', who use contextual knowledge and ad hoc estimations of what the respective listener might like, 'manually' change the similarity lists that the algorithm uses to recommend music.

Calculated connectivity

Calculations of participant activities are extremely useful for searching and finding similarities and differences. Whatever goes (un)seen and (un)heard by an individual also goes (un)seen and (un)heard by others. The more data every individual creates about him- or herself – knowingly and unknowingly – the more precisely the clustering of internet participants can be carried out. It is, for example, only a superficial purpose of search engines and help systems to draw conclusions about individual personal interests and preferences from personal media habits. The creation of personal offers online is, in fact, always preceded by the search for similarities and differences within the behaviour of as many participants as possible (Sunstein, 2008).

A factor that increases feasibility for this is that digital media technologies, media usage and media measurement have become almost the same thing. The previously laborious conversion of media habits into measurement data and the corresponding user statistics becomes redundant. Instead, it is possible to gain insights into what kind of functionalities and what content are more suitable for which assumed user groups or user profiles simply by analyzing the participants' activities in online platforms. Through the comparison and grouping of initially incoherent activities carried out by measurement techniques, preconditions for permanently auto-correcting and mutual addressing between those participating are created 'under the hood' of the pretty interfaces. Programmes that run automatically seem to lend themselves as mediators for this. Their principle of operation is ever-changing yet cannot be questioned or scrutinized (Passoth, 2010).

Such attempts to keep the connection between supply and calculated habit hidden from the participants must be separated from processes that provide insight into preliminary or interim results. Charts, access statistics and rankings provide information on which video was watched, how often, which songs were listened to on a certain platform and which suggestions were rated on a platform. By using such more or less dynamically changing number-based formats, participants can be informed about the (preliminary) results of comparative assessment of their every activity. They can then reflect upon their personal preferences and interests as if they were looking in a mirror; they can intensify or vary their behaviour. Allocation possibilities of self and others, as well as those of mutual relationships, become dependent on measurement processes as well as visual representation possibilities – in completely different application environments (Adelmann, 2006).

For arguments like these, we found evidence in the cases we studied, but, to our surprise, it was not the 'personal radio' that made most use of these techniques. Interestingly, this was also quite the opposite of the impression that the users of the platform had. It was mentioned in the interviews that users assumed using the love and ban buttons to skip a title led to a refined profile of listening preferences. But it did not – love and ban clicks are forgotten as soon as the player is restarted; they are just used in the current session.

However, in the 'quality radio' example, the monitored listening activities are very relevant: although content is not automatically changed in relation to changes in listening habits, the effect is much more direct than in traditional radio. Every access of the music stream is a tracked activity that is turned into a constantly available graph that can be monitored by show hosts and the editor in chief and is used – together with click-statistics – by the management to evaluate shows and schedules. Logged-in customers who have the ability to listen to shows that are not constantly on air are a source of even more data. A feature like amazon.com's 'Customers who bought this item also bought' mechanism is already implemented. Although it is not directly used, the use of this data and the insights gained from the behaviour of logged-in users has been intensively discussed in attempts to switch to a new content management system.

Numeric inclusion

From the onset, new media technologies have been described as a chance for a communicative utopia. Not only could the recipients – formerly condemned to passivity – now become sovereign creators of the media world, but perspectives, interests, topics and problems could be considered that had previously been marginalized by the gatekeeper function of the mass media. In light of the previously discussed literature and our case of online music distribution, this interpretation has to be modified. The view that participants would engage with the media world independently must be changed to one in which measurement and analysis techniques of media activities mediate in such a way that the participants have no influence. The respective collectivities dealt with here would not be possible without the measurements and activity assessments delegated to algorithms and statistical programmes (Passoth, 2012; Wehner, 2008). If, for example, access and evaluation statistics carry out listener comparisons, or proposals are generated for a mutual establishment of contact, then it is already apparent here how computer-based measurement and analysis techniques wedge themselves between the participants – meaning that they initially, in a radical sense, divide them, only to reconnect them again based on a comparison of data and profiles.

In the future these processes of participant inclusion based on calculative techniques may come to mediate between, on the one hand, a world of information and communication habits, consumer and entertainment needs, and political addressability (which are all short-lived, widely spreading and rapidly changing) and, on the other hand, a variety of (so far rather unnoticed) topics, products, events and providers adapting to these conditions (Livingstone, 2003). Computerized measurements that are growing more diverse and microscopic provide insights into the lifeworld, especially of those people whom mass media and other established forms of representation tend to ignore. Thus, one of the important functions of new media pertains to making interests outside the mainstream visible (Adelmann, 2013). And, with the visibility of those special needs, interests and habits, measurements support the development of a larger variety of consumer, articulation and information offers that have also remained invisible for a long time due to their niche existence.

5. Conclusion

Audience measurement techniques have been criticized within media studies for quite some time as being inadequate forms of describing the media world, because these forms had to be simplified. Recently, however, it has become apparent that measurement techniques can support the construction and further development of complex relationships, especially because they represent a mode of observation which focuses only on a few criteria. Mass media circulate numerical data such as financial statements and political survey results, and thus contribute to the creation of observation and communication spaces in which representatives of different sectors of society (parties, companies, universities) establish relationships with their respective audiences. They also foster mutual observations and comparisons, and – since this happens under the eyes of the public – they are urged to take measures to keep or improve the position assigned in the number systems. Mass media thereby fulfil the task of preparing circulation formats for numerical data. This is because number systems such as surveys or rankings do not reliably reach the affected measured units or the interested public without prior reprocessing; this preparation changes them into preferred readings and makes them understandable. Mass media subject not only different sectors of society, but themselves as well, to an increasingly finer measurement system for formal aspects of information and communication habits. In addition, measurement results such as ratings motivate innovative processes and media transition, since opportunities for mutual comparison and assessment (controlled by success criteria) open up between content providers. It is still very unclear how the new digital media can be classified into these developments. In this chapter, several propositions have been outlined that were guided by the literature and by some preliminary results of our own research on audience measurement in the case of online music distribution. Accordingly, it can be presumed that the internet opens new opportunities for measurement which take individual media behaviour more strongly into consideration. Apparently, the results of such calculations are no longer just a basis for decision-making in favour of or against content programming – they enter directly and automatically, as well as indirectly and in a mediated way, into the creation of content. They additionally offer participants opportunities for reflection (insofar as these results are published). Finally, these new measurement techniques seem to have a different task from audience measurement techniques in the case of the mass media. The latter are aimed at average tastes of the masses; the former mediate between a constantly expanding variety of providers and products and a diversifying multitude of participant interests. Processes of media use can be collected in a more sophisticated way due to changed forms of media communication that are rich in feedback. The changes of media production and use that are presently observable are, therefore, closely connected to the change of measurement techniques used – mediatization and quantification are strongly connected. On a more general level, these findings demand from us that, for a deeper understanding of how the media-mediation of variously scaled mediatized worlds might actually work, we might need to 'open the black box' of *the* media and try to get a grasp on some of the inner workings of what otherwise can just be called media logic. The presumed distance between providers and audiences, even the categories of providers and audiences themselves, are effects of historically contingent, only partially stabilized forms of measuring, calculating and sorting media use.

Note

1. The fieldwork was done by two doctoral students, Roman Duhr and Thorben Mämecke. Individual ethnographies are currently being written. For a first report on field access and the very specific form of data available in this field, see Mämecke and Duhr, 2014.

References

Adelmann, R. (2006) 'Schwarm oder Masse? Selbststrukturierung der Medienrezeption'. In: Adelmann, R, Hesse, J. O., Keilbach, J., Stauff, M. and Thiele, M.(ed.) *Ökonomien des Medialen. Tausch, Wert und Zirkulation in den Medien- und Kulturwissenschaften* (Bielefeld: transcript), pp. 283–303.

Adelmann, R. (2013) 'Die Normalitäten des "Long Tail"'. Zur Sichtbarkeit von mobilen Medien und Nischenkulturen'. In: Passoth, J. H. and Wehner, J. (eds) *Quoten, Kurven und Profile*. *Zur Vermessung der sozialen Welt* (Bielefeld: transcript), pp. 89–103.

Akrich, M. (1993) *Inscription et coordination socio-techniques: Anthropologie de quelques dispositifs énergétiques*. PhD thesis (Paris: École Nationale Supérieure des Mines de Paris).

Ang, I. (1991) *Desperately seeking the audience* (London, New York: Routledge).

Ang, I. (1996) *Living room wars: Rethinking media audience for a postmodern world* (London, New York: Routledge).

Ang, I. (2001) *On not speaking Chinese: Living between Asia and the west* (London, New York: Routledge).

Bermejo, F. (2007) *The internet audience: Constitution and measurement* (New York: Peter Lang).

Bermejo, F. (2009) 'Audience manufacture in historical perspective: From broadcasting to Google'. In: *New Media & Society*, 11, pp. 133–54.

Burzan, N., Lökenhoff, B., Schimank, U. and Schöneck, N. M. (2008) *Das Publikum der Gesellschaft. Inklusionsverhältnisse und Inklusionsprofile in Deutschland* (Wiesbaden: VS Verlag).

Callon, M. (ed.) (1988) *The laws of the markets* (Oxford: Blackwell).

Callon, M. and Muniesa, F. (2005) 'Economic markets as calculative collective devices'. In: *Organization Studies*, 26, pp. 1229–50.

Cleveland, W. S. (1994) *The elements of graphing data* (Murray Hill, NY: ATT Bell Laboratories).

Cohen, P. C. (1982) *A calculating people: The spread of numeracy in early America* (Chicago: University of Chicago Press).

Desrosières, A. (2002) *The politics of large numbers: A history of statistical reasoning* (Cambridge, MA: Harvard University Press).

Espeland, W. N. and Stevens, M. L. (2008) 'A sociology of quantification'. In: *European Journal of Sociology*, 49, pp. 401–36.

Esposito, E. (1999) 'Macht als Persuasion oder Kritik der Macht'. In: Maresch, R. and Werber, N. (eds.) *Kommunikation – Medien – Macht* (Frankfurt a. M.: Suhrkamp), pp. 83–107.

Hall, S. (1980) 'Encoding/decoding'. In: Hall, S., Hobson, D., Lowe, A. and Willis, P. (eds.) *Culture, media, language: Working papers in cultural studies, 1972–79* (London, New York: Routledge), pp. 128–38.

Harcup, T. and O'Neill, D. (2001) 'What is news? Galtung and Ruge revisited'. In: *Journalism Studies*, 2(2), pp. 261–80.

Hasse, R. and Wehner, J. (2005) 'Innovation und Wettbewerb im Mediensystem – eine netzwerktheoretische Perspektive'. In: *Medienwissenschaft – Science des Mass Médias Suisse*, 1, pp. 23–33.

Heintz, B. (2010) 'Numerische Differenz: Überlegungen zu einer Soziologie des (quantitativen) Vergleichs'. In: *Zeitschrift für Soziologie*, 39, pp. 162–81.

Hepp, A. (2013) *Cultures of mediatization* (Cambridge: Polity).

Krotz, F. (2001) *Die Mediatisierung kommunikativen Handelns: Wie sich Alltag und soziale Beziehungen, Kultur und Gesellschaft durch die Medien wandeln* (Opladen: Westdeutscher Verlag).

Krotz, F. (2009) 'Mediatization: A concept with which to grasp media and societal change'. In: Lundby, K. (ed.) *Mediatization: Concept, changes, consequences* (New York: Lang), pp. 21–40.

Lave, J. (1986) 'The values of quantification'. In: Law, J. (ed.) *Power, action and belief: A new sociology of knowledge* (London: Routledge), pp. 88–111.

Law, J. and Callon, M. (1988) 'Engineering and sociology in a military aircraft project: A network analysis of technical change'. In: *Social Problems*, 35, pp. 284–97.

Link, J. (1997) *Versuch über den Normalismus. Wie Normalität produziert wird* (Opladen: Westdeutscher Verlag).

Livingstone, S. (2003) 'The changing nature of audiences: From the mass audience to the interactive media user'. In: Valdivia, A. (ed.) *A companion to media studies* (Oxford: Blackwell Publishing), pp. 337–59.

Luhmann, N. (1981) 'Theoretische und praktische Probleme der anwendungsbezogenen Sozialwissenschaften'. In: Luhmann, N. (ed.) *Soziologische Aufklärung. Vol. 3* (Opladen: Westdeutscher Verlag), pp. 321–34.

Luhmann, N. (2000) *The reality of the mass media* (Palo Alto: Stanford University Press).

MacKenzie, D. (2006) *An engine, not a camera: How financial models shape markets* (Cambridge, MA: MIT Press).

Mämecke, T. and Duhr, R. (2014) 'Top-Titel, Top-Alben, Top-Hörer: Zahlenbasierte Musikempfehlungsdienste und die Mediatisierung von Selbstdarstellungen im Internet'. In: Löw, M. (ed.) *Vielfalt und Zusammenhalt. Verhandlungen des 36. Kongresses der Deutschen Gesellschaft für Soziologie an der Ruhr-Universität Bochum und der TU Dortmund 2012* (Wiesbaden: Springer VS), in print.

Manhart, S. (2008) 'Vermessene Kultur. Zur Bedeutung von Maß, Zahl und Begriff für die Entstehung der modernen Kultur'. In: Baecker, D., Kettner, M. and Rustemeyer, D. (eds.) *Über Kultur. Theorie und Praxis der Kulturreflexion* (Bielefeld: transcript), pp. 191–220.

McQuail, D. (1997) *Audience analysis* (Thousand Oaks, London, New Delhi: Sage Publications).

Mennicken, A. and Vollmer, H. (eds.) (2007) *Zahlenwerk. Kalkulation, Organisation und Gesellschaft* (Wiesbaden: VS Verlag).

Meyen, M. (ed.) (2004) *Mediennutzung. Mediaforschung, Medienfunktionen, Nutzungsmuster* (Konstanz: UVK).

Miller, P. (2007) 'Wie und warum das Rechnungswesen in der Soziologie in Vergessenheit geriet'. In: Mennicken, A. and Vollmer, H. (eds.) *Zahlenwerk. Kalkulation, Organisation und Gesellschaft* (Wiesbaden: VS Verlag), pp. 19–42.

Napoli, P. M. (2011) *Audience evolution. New technologies and the transformation of media audiences* (New York: Columbia University Press).

Passoth, J.-H. (2010) 'Sind das deine Daten? Kontemporäre Selbstpraktiken und ihre medientechnische Transformation'. In: Soeffner, H. G. (ed.) *Unsichere Zeiten. Herausforderungen gesellschaftlicher Transformationen* (Wiesbaden: VS Verlag), CD-Rom.

Passoth, J.-H. (2012) 'Not only angels in the cloud. Rechenpraxis und die Praxis der Rechner'. In: Passoth, J.-H. and Wehner, J. (eds.) *Quoten, Kurven, Profile – Zur Vermessung des Sozialen* (Wiesbaden: VS Verlag), pp. 255–72.

Porter, T. M. (1995) *Trust in numbers. The pursuit of objectivity in science and public life* (Princeton: Princeton University Press).

Röhle, T. (2010) *Der Google-Komplex. Über Macht im Zeitalter des Internets* (Bielefeld: transcript).

Schorr, A. (2000) *Ergebnisse der Publikums-und Wirkungsforschung* (Wiesbaden: Westdeutscher Verlag).

Schrage, D. (2001) *Psychotechnik und Radiophonie. Subjektkonstruktionen in artifiziellen Wirklichkeiten 1918–1932* (München: Fink Verlag).

Schrage, D. (2005) 'Anonymus Publikum. Massenkonstruktion und die Politiken des Radios'. In: Gethmann, D. and Stauff, M. (eds.) *Politiken der Medien* (Berlin, Zürich: Diaphanes), pp. 173–94.

Schulte-Holtey, E. (2001) 'Über Kurvenlandschaften in Printmedien'. In: Gerhard, U., Link, J. and Schulte-Hotley, E. (eds.) *Infografiken, Medien, Normalisierung. Zur Kartographie politisch-sozialer Landschaften* (Heidelberg: Synchron), pp. 93–114.

Siemes, A. (2009) *Zahlen in Medienangeboten* (Oberhausen: Athena Verlag).

Sunstein, C. R. (2008) *Infotopia: How many minds produce knowledge* (Oxford: Oxford University Press).

Sutter, T. (2010) 'Der Wandel von der Massenkommunikation zur Interaktivität neuer Medien'. In: Sutter, T. and Mehler, A. (eds.) *Medienwandel als Wandel von Interaktionsformen* (Wiesbaden: VS Verlag), pp. 83–105.

Thiele, M. (2006) 'Zahl und Sinn. Zur Effektivität und Affektivität der Fernsehquoten'. In: Adelmann, R., Hesse, J. O., Keilbach, J., Stauff, M. and Thiele, M. (eds.) *Ökonomien des Medialen. Tausch, Wert und Zirkulation in den Medien- und Kulturwissenschaften* (Bielefeld: transcript), pp. 305–30.

Vollmer, H. (2004) 'Folgen und Funktionen organisierten Rechnens'. In: *Zeitschrift für Soziologie*, 33, pp. 450–70.

Vormbusch, U. (2007) 'Die Kalkulation der Gesellschaft'. In: Mennicken, A. and Vollmer, H. (eds.) *Zahlenwerk. Kalkulation, Organisation und Gesellschaft* (Wiesbaden: VS Verlag), pp. 43–64.

Wagner, P. (1994) *A sociology of modernity. Liberty and discipline* (London, New York: Routledge).

Webster, J. G., Phalen, P. F. and Lichty, L. W. (2000) *Ratings analysis. The theory and practice of audience research* (Mahwah, NJ, London: Lawrence Erlbaum Associates).

Wehner, J. (2008) 'Social Web – Rezeptions- und Produktionsstrukturen im Internet'. In: Jäckel, M. and Mai, M. (eds.) *Medien und Macht* (Frankfurt a. M.: Campus Verlag), pp. 197–218.

Wehner, J. (2010) 'Numerische Inklusion – Medien, Messungen und Modernisierung'. In: Sutter, T. and Mehler, A. (eds.) *Medienwandel als Wandel von Interaktionsformen* (Wiesbaden: VS-Verlag), pp. 183–210.

17
Schools as Mediatized Worlds from a Cross-cultural Perspective

Andreas Breiter

1. Introduction

If we think about education in the 21st century, we can identify a process of continuous change that is happening globally. Schools, in particular, are under constant reform pressure – from the Education Reform Act in the UK (1988), to 'No Child Left Behind' in the USA, (2001) to post-PISA in Germany (Programme for International Student Assessment). Furthermore, these processes are intertwined with meta-processes such as mediatization, globalization or commercialization. In order to understand the transformation of education, we need to understand the complex interplay between organizational reform (devolution, school autonomy and accountability) and changing media and their role in communication. The first is mainly induced by political pressure on the macro level, as well as on the micro level by parents. The second influences, and is influenced by, the way in which children learn and teachers teach, that is, communicate – inside and outside the classroom – and how administrators manage a school on the meso level. Hence, the traditional perspective of the functional distinction between the three levels of educational governance (Altrichter, Brüsemeister and Wissinger, 2007) underestimates the process perspective across the levels, which is described by the meta-process of 'mediatization' (e.g., Hepp, 2013; Hjarvard, 2012; Krotz, 2007; 2009; Lundby, 2009).

Educational reform in the process of mediatization can be framed by looking at schools as 'mediatized worlds'.[1] In this way, patterns of transformation in the 'communicative construction' (Putnam and Nicotera, 2010) of the school as an organization can be linked to the 'moulding forces of the media' (Hepp, 2012). Furthermore, the combination of the three-level model of educational governance and the process perspective of mediatization can help to understand cross-cultural differences in educational reform and development using the example of the UK and Germany.

2. Schools as mediatized worlds

Similarly to individualization, globalization and commercialization, the process of mediatization has been described by Krotz as a meta-process (Krotz, 2007; 2009). This long-term perspective of continuous change is strongly connected to emerging media and the process of institutionalization. Similarly to Moores (2012), Krotz follows a non-media-centric perspective in order to describe social phenomena. Furthermore, 'new' media do not replace 'older' media but, rather, coexist and merge, somewhat as 'moulding forces' (Hepp, 2012).

As the concept of mediatization is based on communication as the basic principle of how people construct the social and cultural world, this can be used to understand different 'social worlds'. Building on Shibutani's (1955) understanding, social worlds can be framed as being continuously communicatively reconstructed. For Shibutani, each social world 'is a culture area, the boundaries of which are set neither by territory nor by formal group membership but by limits of effective communication' (Shibutani, 1955, p. 566). Education can be regarded as an example of a social world, taking into account that this social world represents the core mechanism through which values and relations are passed on from one generation to the next (Bourdieu and Passeron, 1977). It can be defined and measured in different forms in relation to individuals (the educated self based on knowledge and dispositions to learn and to value education), objects (such as books, degrees or computers) and institutions (such as libraries, schools or universities). Hence, we can observe a change of social worlds as they rely heavily on communicative practices. Given this, mediatization can help us to understand the complex transformation processes in education, and in schools in particular as the dominant form of institutionalized education. As digital media technologies become more and more available and communicative processes change, schools can be framed as mediatized worlds.

Education has been subject to intensive research about the changes in teaching and learning, but most of the studies focus on student outcomes. Many empirical studies in schools all over the world show ambivalent results with regard to learning outcomes, student motivation or media literacy (e.g., Kozma, 2003; Pelgrum, 2001). But only limited research can be found examining the increasing relevance of digital media in communicative processes within the school as a social organization. The use of school information systems, educational data warehouses and learning management systems has become a natural element of school-wide internal communication. Empirical research (e.g., Breiter, Welling and Schulz, 2011; Visscher, Wild, Smith and Newton, 2003) suggests that different media are used for different purposes (announcements, information distribution, exchange of teaching material, etc.) and with different stakeholders (teachers, students, administrators, parents). As Selwyn (2011) noticed, the managerial core of the school and the governance structure of the school system have a major influence on the way digital media are used and, hence, how communication constitutes the school as an organization. Interestingly enough, this development is highly contingent, being influenced by the educational governance structure of the respective school system. Hence, we have to deal with two different cultures or social worlds within the school, which are mutually dependent but each constitutive of school in different ways: teaching and learning as well as administration and management.

Historically, schools have always been mediatized worlds. If we go back to the creation of the public school system in England, or the Prussian school system in Germany, media played an important role in justifying or arguing for their foundation as well as in the pedagogical and administrative subsystems within any individual school. If we think about books, blackboards and chalk on the one hand and 'pigeon holes' for teachers, log-books or print-outs on the other hand, we can identify various forms of mediatized communication besides the dominant face-to-face communication between teachers and their students. Using Krotz's categorization of mediatized communicative processes, we can observe similar patterns in the two identified school worlds, which constitute the 'media ensemble' (Morley, 2007, p. 200) of teachers and administrators (Table 17.1).

As a summary, we can identify different processes in which media play an important role within a school, following Schulz's extension of mediatization theory (Schulz, 2004, pp. 88–90): (1) Spatial and temporal

Table 17.1   Communication in mediatized school worlds

	Teaching and learning	Administration and management
Direct interpersonal communication	Negotiation of paper-based or digital homework, e-mail communication between teachers and students	Discussion and sharing of learning content, grades, etc. (paper-based or digital) among teachers, with administration and management, e-mail communication with parents
Mass communication	Content distribution, e.g., via textbooks, film presentation, digital learning resources	Teacher pigeon holes, bulletin boards, school websites, school information system
Interactive communication	Digital learning environments, game-based learning	School management information systems, performance feedback systems

extension of the scope of human communication by media technologies, for instance, by using software to support individual learning outside the regular school time; (2) substitution or transformation of existing social processes by new media, for example, the use of computer games for learning; (3) amalgamation and parallelization of media practice with other social action, for example, by using interactive whiteboards in traditional classroom settings; and (4) accommodation of social change by the sheer existence of media in society, for example, school-wide technology plans for curriculum integration. The four forms of communication are well suited to understanding the recent media change but do not acknowledge the potential of adding new forms of communication which have not been in place before. Especially in the school setting, we can identify this form as an addition, when information and communication technology (ICT) is used as a learning tool in a way that is distinct from any previous pedagogical process using ICT (e.g., using simulation software in science classes).

3. Educational governance and transcultural mediatization in schools

Especially in education, the dimension of culture (and its derived governance structure) has to be taken into account to understand the 'moulding forces of the media' (Hepp, 2012). Media can be regarded as spaces for judgements and reactions by teachers, unions and politicians. Especially the emergence of 'mainstream national media' in the UK has influenced the conversation about education (also Couldry, 2004). Couldry (2003) identifies two types of intersecting meta-capital: (a) the state as stipulator of educational policy and (b) the media as the arbiter of 'real facts'. While Couldry's perspective of media capital in education is mainly focused on mass media and the construction of pedagogic authority, our emphasis is on educational media supporting individual and group learning processes and organizational media for collaboration within schools and the specific role of the school in promoting media literacy.

Taking into account the current popular discussions in Germany (originally derived from the Anglo-American discussion on school effectiveness, school improvement and school-based management) on educational governance (e.g., Altrichter, Brüsemeister and Wissinger, 2007), we introduce a three-tier framework model that resembles the well-established distinction in sociology between macro, meso and micro levels (Figure 17.1).

On the macro level, the relation between media change and educational policy can be mapped. On the micro level, the focus of mediatized communication is on the teaching and learning processes in the classroom. The meso level attracts specific interest in communicative action in relation to the school as an organization. In the following sections, we provide examples of the three-level model and the interweaving processes using the UK

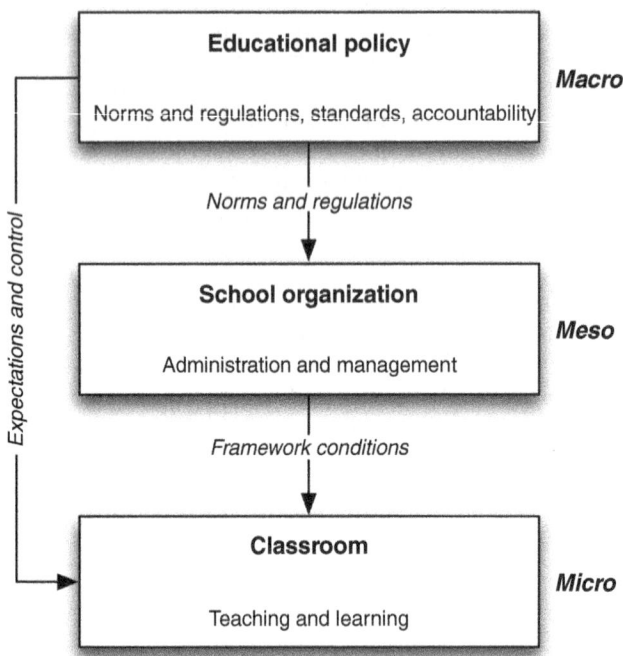

Figure 17.1 Three-level model of educational governance

and Germany as references for very different school systems: the UK with a governance structure of centralized decentralization, and Germany with decentralized centralization. As we regard the meso level as the intermediate layer that helps us to understand the ongoing interplay between the levels and emphasizing the process perspective, we reordered the typical micro–meso–macro structure.

Micro level: Media and the classroom

The current situation for teaching and learning with and about digital media is very different in the UK compared with Germany. There is an obvious difference between the use of media in the classroom (media education) and the support of critical and reflective thinking about media and their role in society (media literacy). While the first is embedded in the UK's National Curriculum and has been supported by large-scale equipment programmes since the 1990s (e.g., National Grid for Learning, DfEE, 1997), German teachers have no direct curriculum-based incentive to use ICT in their classrooms, and national and state-funded programmes are rather rare. Hence, educational technologies are less prominent in German schools (student:computer ratio of 10 to 1), while UK schools rank among the most equipped of all countries of the OECD (Organisation for Economic Co-operation and Development) (student:computer ratio of 4 to 1; OECD, 2011). Furthermore, educational media such as interactive whiteboards can be found in nearly every UK classroom, while German schools are struggling with budget limitations and ambivalent perspectives on the pedagogical value of ICT in the classroom. Regarding the concept of media literacy, Livingstone and Van Couvering (2008) try to 'emphasize the continuities between old and new media and information and communication technologies by extending the term "media literacy" or "literacy" in general to encompass a converged concept of media and information literacies'. If we follow their argument, then technological advances lead to an increasing range of media contents which are available on computers, and, hence, support and extend established ICT-literacy-related constructs rather than new technical and cognitive competencies. In this respect, the tradition in German classrooms is different from the UK: media literacy as a critical–reflective communicative practice has played an important role in Germany since the critique by Baacke (1973) and its extension within the media pedagogical discourse as *Medienbildung*, *Medienerziehung* and *Medienpaedagogik* (NB: only available in German, e.g., Baacke, 1997; Marotzki and Jörissen, 2010).

The micro level has been addressed extensively in educational research in relation to ICT and learning. Mainly focused on the measurable impact of educational technologies on student learning outcomes, the empirical evidence is rather weak (e.g., Cuban, 2001; Hattie, 2009). For the UK, there are plenty of studies to explain the cause-and-effect relation between the provision of ICT and the impact on education: more student-centred and constructivist, supporting higher-order learning and enhancing students' learning experiences and possibilities (e.g., Selwyn, 2011; Somekh, 2000; Yang, 2012).

In order to explain the specific situation in German schools, I will refer to our recent empirical study, which was conducted in 2010 among teachers in secondary schools in Germany's largest federal state, North Rhine-Westphalia (Breiter, Welling and Stolpmann, 2010). Based on a representative survey (1,500 teachers from 93 schools) and six case studies with qualitative interviews, the study aimed to understand the interdependence of the three levels of educational governance with regard to media literacy and the use of digital media for teaching and learning. Unlike other studies in Germany, we focused specifically on the role of the school as an organization and the accompanying framework conditions at the regional and policy levels.

To summarize the results, in order to reflect the process of mediatization in German secondary schools: more than half of the participating teachers use media at least occasionally (daily or once a week) in class. Teacher-centred classroom management using laptop, presentation software and projector is still the dominant practice. This reflects the slowly changing patterns within schools and it demonstrates a high level of inertia, regardless of the ongoing media innovations outside the school and the media ensembles of both students and teachers. The use of media for teaching and learning is further limited by the enduring relevance of materiality in the learning process, which is still significant even though the use of digital media has advantages over existing practices. This reflects the unbroken popularity of traditional media like books. The data show an intergenerational gap in digital media use, whereby teachers think 'good' media for students are media for learning; 'bad' media are media used in their leisure activities. The teachers' perception of students' use of media is often labelled with deficits. Further discrepancies are induced by the teachers' fundamental lack of understanding of many of the students' individual media practices outside school. With respect to media literacy, the beliefs of teachers are characterized by a strong focus on risks and dangers. In conclusion, we could find different dimensions of uncertainty and ambivalence. The ongoing, rapid evolution of digital media has an impact on everyday life in school, and numerous forms of digital media have 'forced' their way into school (e.g., Wikipedia, interactive whiteboards or tablet-PCs). In this context, teachers retreat to well-established and familiar patterns in an attempt to maintain orientation and the capability to act and communicate within mediatized worlds.

Macro level: School governance and educational policy

Transnational pressures on changing education policy enforced by international non-governmental organizations have been observed already by several scholars (e.g., Martens, Rusconi and Leuze, 2007). As Phillips (2011) pointed out, UK education policy has historically observed the German education system in order to learn, adopt or reject this 'role model'.

> There has been a consistent tendency over that long period [past hundred years, AB] to refer to the German example in education at one extreme to promote ideas for change and development ('do this and we shall be as successful as the Prussians') and at the other extreme to warn against innovation and reform ('do that you will end up as bad as the Prussians'), with various shades of attraction and repulsion in between.
>
> (Phillips, 2011, p. 1)

Phillips researched various sources, from travel documents of the 19th century by English students and professors, to studies by Her Majesty's Inspectors of Schools on the vocational school system in Germany in the 1980s, to the discussions after PISA on educational measurement and its resulting performance tables.

The process of mediatization affects the teaching profession and the school system in a twofold way. Communicative processes change while digital technologies become more and more available. Educational reform is part of social change, which is inextricably connected with media change. Modern education policy is globalized due to transnational institutions such as the OECD (e.g., PISA) or the International Association for the Evaluation of Educational Achievement (IEA) (e.g., The International Mathematics and Science Study (TIMSS) or Progress in International Reading Literacy Study (PIRLS)). Their influence on education policy has changed significantly during the last decade (Martens, Rusconi and Leuze, 2007). Nevertheless, the relation between UK and German education is of particular interest, as I argue that the 'direction of indirect influence' has been reversed from Germany to the UK. Besides transcultural invariables deeply embedded into the culture of a school system and the values and beliefs of the teaching profession, we can detect culture-specific adoptions of change, which can be observed first in the UK and are later invisibly transported to Germany. Furthermore, the process of mediatization is enforcing this phenomenon (e.g., Lingard and Rawolle, 2005).

As one outstanding example, the perspective on education in Germany changed tremendously from an input-oriented perspective to an output-orientation with metrics and indicators (Huber and Gördel, 2006). Media served as amplifiers, even more as digital media were available to distribute, interpret and reanalyze the data on student achievement. The huge gap between student achievements within Germany started an ongoing discussion about the quality of education, its measurability and the related policy decisions. Especially, the question of the best 'school structure' dominated the public discussion. Most federal states introduced central student achievement tests. Additionally, external evaluations and inspections were implemented and imposed on schools. Even more, the bad results from the PISA study in 2001 ('PISA shock') initiated a countrywide movement to collect data from students, teachers and schools. Besides the official efforts, which were often consolidated into 'education reports' on the state and federal levels and into policy documents by researchers, grass-roots activities were started using social networking sites. As external evaluations of teachers and/or schools, let alone rankings based on standardized tests, were hitherto unknown in Germany, the public availability of ratings of teacher performance by students and parents evoked a general legal and ethical discussion. Hence, the availability of digital media fell on a fruitful ground of social change.

Compared with Germany, some processes happened approximately ten years earlier in the UK. In 1988, the UK government launched the Education Reform Act (e.g., Flude and Hammer, 1990), aiming to radically change the governance structure of the school system, from the control of local administration to the school embedded in a central accountability mechanism (e.g., Pierson, 1998). Within this framework, the availability of school-based data on accountability was crucial, as all schools could be compared in league tables, displaying compliance with the then newly introduced state standards and observed by the inspectorate. Taking one step forward in the mediatization of school governance, all schools were requested to deliver data in real time and of a pre-defined quality, which could only be done by computer-based school information systems.

Directly related to ICT on the macro level, the new coalition government in the UK decided to close Becta, the central body responsible for the government's ICT initiatives in schools. Consequently, as Yang (2012, p. 107) states, 'the abolition of Becta indicates a shift from the top-down, government-led effort to integrate ICT into education to a bottom-up approach driven by local needs'. In Germany, there never was a central agency, and the federal states have different policies to support the provision of ICT in schools. The legal division between the state being responsible for general education provision, curriculum, teacher education and teacher employment, and the school district being responsible for school buildings, facility management and administration, is unique in the world. This shared responsibility and the limited autonomy of the school and its management lead to constant budget struggles about the cost for ICT infrastructure and educational media (for more details, see Breiter, 2001). Traditionally, the strong central control with standards and accountability in the UK, with the National Curriculum and the assessment regime, has a strong influence on how teachers are willing to use the potential of educational technologies. According to Yang (2012), the pedagogical standards defined in the curriculum assessment regime have a significant impact on teachers' pedagogical practice. For Germany, no corresponding evidence can be found. First, federal standards for the core subjects were introduced only in 2005 (KMK, 2005), and there is not much experience of their relevance; second, the new federal standards do not contain any link to ICT skills or media literacy; and, third, research shows that German teachers are rather reluctant to follow federal or state standards, as they have no direct impact on their everyday teaching. In contrast, in the UK, every Key Stage in the National Curriculum defines measurable goals for media literacy. Selwyn (2011) pointed towards another transcultural difference between the UK and Germany: the influence of interest groups and supra-national institutions that enforce the use of educational technologies. As part of his critical approach to the political economy of education, Selwyn (2011) uses several examples from interactive whiteboards to notebook initiatives to support his argument.

Meso level: Schools as mediatized organizational worlds

According to our research, the meso level of schools has been underestimated with regard to its role in the transformation process. Here, the perspective of mediatization has to be divided into two general streams: educational media and organizational media. Since the creation of the public school system, education has been inextricably linked with media. In educational research, the teacher him- or herself is often regarded as the most influential 'medium' in the learning process of students. Besides this very general understanding of media, the school is still governed around books, with deeply rooted values and orientations of teachers. This has not much changed over the decades with the advent of digital media like computers, learning management systems, interactive whiteboards or digital content. Apparently, we can observe significant transcultural differences in adoption and appropriation of ICT in German and UK schools (Kolo and Breiter, 2009). In our understanding, the organizational culture of schools has a crucial impact on these differences. We base our findings on the empirical research within the Priority Programme 'Mediatized Worlds' (see Footnote 1) on two in-depth case studies in schools, with a methodological mix of participant observations, qualitative interviews and quantitative analyses of log files from school information systems (Breiter, Welling and Schulz, 2011).

Following Weick (1995), organizations can be considered as networks of actions based on their own distinctive cultures and subcultures, which in turn are formative for their members. Thus, an organization involves processes of designing an order of action ('organizing'). He considers this process of organizing as the way in which people make sense through an ongoing communicative process of action, selection and interpretation. According to him, organizations are neither static nor stable entities, but communicative negotiation processes are continuously taking place when processing ambiguities or attributing meaning. This shows that organizations form their environment, and their members act within a self-constructed organizational reality. The attribution of meaning in organizations takes place in loosely coupled systems where the individual members have a large scope of decision-making. In his early work, Weick (1976) described schools and universities as prototypical organizations of this type. The process of attribution of meaning can be explained by the characteristic of 'enactment'. This is the process in which people in organizations (re)produce their environment by means of their communicative actions, thus making perceptible what they think: 'when the action of saying makes it possible for people to then see what they think' (Weick, 1995, p. 20). Hence, daily practices play an important role, and they become manifest in everyday life in various, partly ritualized ways, as can be exemplified in schools: teachers meet before the start of class to talk and to have breakfast together, members of the school board are regularly present in the breaks to be available, and joint festivities promote staff cohesion in an informal way. Moreover, everyday life at school offers many opportunities for spontaneous and intended encounter and communication, for instance, joint meals in the canteen, incidental encounters in the building or formal meetings.

Based on Weick's basic assumptions, approaches to the communicative constitution of organizations have been developed further. Putnam and

Nicotera (2010) assign communication a central role in the ontology of an organization. For this understanding, the interaction of the members is decisive: 'A pattern or array of types of interaction constitutes organizations insofar as they make organizations what they are, and insofar as basic features of the organization are implicated in the system of interaction' (McPhee and Zaug, 2009, p. 27). With this, McPhee and Zaug try a balancing act between the static understanding of an organization and a dynamic, constructive perspective, introducing four dimensions of the communicative constitution: membership negotiation, self-structuring, activity coordination and institutional positioning. In our empirical study in two large inner-city schools (see Footnote 1), we could identify the four dimensions as being constitutive for schools (see Table 17.2).

Furthermore, media appropriation influences the communicative processes, particularly between staff and management. The media ensembles of teachers for communicative action are shaped by six factors (Breiter, Welling and Schulz, 2011): (1) expected flow of communication, that is, how fast and secure is the transport of the message; (2) range of the usable media ensemble (from paper-based to digital); (3) time and effort for mediated communication from the perspective of rationalization; (4) quality of communication in respect to the risk of misunderstanding between direct interpersonal and mediated communication; (5) binding power of communication, that is, documentation of conversation with parents; and (6) lack of skills for using new forms of mediated communication accompanied with a high level of uncertainty among teachers.

As a hindering factor, our study could identify the role of the school's organizational culture in media integration. The results confirmed previous international research findings that the principal plays a central

Table 17.2 Four dimensions of schools as communicatively constituted organizations

Membership negotiation	Relationship between teachers and school, school-specific scripts, relevance of school culture for the negotiation process (e.g., identification, belonging, leadership)
Self-structuring	Communication between teachers, interactions guiding the school in a certain direction, creation of arenas for negotiation (e.g., staff meetings, working groups), with explicit and implicit rules
Activity coordination	Interactive joint construction of working processes by teachers, students and administrators, use of different instruments for coordination (e.g., curricula, asset management, class rosters or pigeon holes)
Institutional positioning	Development and creation of consistency of the school's external communication (e.g., school board, authorities, inspection and local community)

role in change processes in schools (e.g., Blumberg and Greenfield, 1986; Day, Harris, Hadfield, Tolley and Beresford, 2000; Green, 2010). Our study revealed that there is a statistically significant increase in media use by teachers if the principal (and school management) has a pronounced interest in digital media and if the school's leadership is open to innovation. A similar positive statistical effect can be seen with regard to the teachers' assessment of the available technology infrastructure. Furthermore, the principal can initiate and consolidate cooperative structures among staff, which results in positive stimuli for media integration. Wherever the pedagogical objectives and goals for media integration are discussed within the school and are defined in a technology plan (for a cross-country comparison, see Breiter (2001)), a positive correlation with the use of media is found. Schools and their leaders in Germany have relatively limited autonomy compared with UK schools. Head teachers are mainly teachers and only secondarily managers. The process of mediatization has – to a certain extent – undermined this separation. Digital media cannot be differentiated between infrastructure (district) and learning applications (state). Hence, the school is the place to link the two perspectives together. While school leadership has been an integral part of school research in the USA and the UK (Leithwood, 1994; Sergiovanni, 1996), it is relatively new in the German context, and only available in the German language (e.g., Wissinger, 2000). School-based management as the new governance model in the UK and the discussion about it in the USA are highlighting a new role of principals as 'transformational leadership' (Leithwood, 1994), being the 'agents of change' (Fullan, 2002).

In this context, mediatized communication becomes a central aspect of school development processes, with school leaders being the main gatekeepers. They appropriate their own media ensembles while being forced to report to and inform their governing bodies, parents and local community. The organizational change due to educational reforms that are connected to issues of accountability, rankings and competition is increasing the pressure on schools. Here, we find an overlap between the pedagogical and administrative realms of the school. Within the pedagogical realm, teachers are oscillating between school-level engagement and the interest group within the culture of their teaching subjects. Within the 'administrative subculture' (Selwyn, 2011, pp. 93–4), Selwyn points towards new public management and 'audit cultures of standardised content, assessment, official inspections and target-led performance' (p. 93). Looking at the UK development, it is obvious that administrative processes were the target for pushing digital technologies in schools. Digital technologies offer 'an ideal means to help school organizations to become more flexible, adaptable and entrepreneurial in the business dealings' (p. 19). In this transformation process, school leaders can be regarded as 'mediatization agents'. They establish and control power structures, have budget control, and organize access to information systems and the mediatized communicative processes between school management and staff, parents and the local community. This highlights the overlapping, cross-level processes which go beyond the traditional micro–meso–macro perspective.

4. Conclusion

Given this, the understanding of schools as mediatized worlds provides us with a theoretical frame to observe organizational change in line with media change in a specific social world. Furthermore, the communicative construction of the school as an organization clarifies the interdependence between the social, the media and school reform, framed by politics, by regional education authorities and by schools and their stakeholders. In the process of mediatization of education, as with other technological innovations, it has to be kept in mind that there is a constant struggle between social and technological determinism. Educators, especially, tend to believe that the next technological wave will solve pedagogical and organizational problems.

> To avoid the threat of 'technological determinism', it is tempting to defend adamantly 'social determinism', which in turn becomes so extreme [...] that even the most open-minded engineer becomes a fierce technical determinist bumping the table with virile exclamations about the 'weight of material constraints'. These gestures have no other effect but to trigger even moderate sociologists to insist even more vehemently on the importance of some 'discursive dimension.'
>
> (Latour, 2005, pp. 144–5)

Media are both technological and social and, as such, new technologies are discovered in a process of research and development and 'set the conditions for social change and progress' (Williams, 1990, p. 13). On the other hand, technologies are a 'by-product of a social process that is otherwise determined' (p. 13).

Educational research has a longstanding tradition of examining teaching and learning processes, but the organizational world of schools is less prominent. Furthermore, books have been the constitutive medium for schools over generations, embedded in a very stable socio-economic system. If we take the ongoing process of mediatization in all social worlds, this will play an important role for educational change, enforced by organizational reform. In schools as mediatized worlds all four processes of Schulz's analytical framework can be found. With the presented examples, we identified both unique and shared patterns of transformation across the countries as well as across the micro, meso and macro levels. The limits of traditional approaches of understanding media, communication and organizational change in schools became obvious. There is no static description of change and, hence, communicative processes need to be captured by wider process models across the three levels for understanding social–cultural phenomena, such as Elias' (1978) concept of 'figurations'. For Elias, figurations are 'networks of individuals' (p. 15) which constitute a larger social entity through reciprocal interaction – for example, by joining an organization such as a school or a classroom. The usefulness of this extension from the model of educational governance to a process model of educational change within mediatized worlds needs to be further developed.

Note

1. The research was funded by the Deutsche Forschungsgemeinschaft in the priority programme 1505 'Mediatized Worlds' (Funding number: BR 2273/10–1).

References

Altrichter, H., Brüsemeister, T. and Wissinger, J. (eds.) (2007) *Educational governance. Handlungskoordination und Steuerung im Bildungssystem* (Wiesbaden: VS Verlag).

Baacke, D. (1973) *Kommunikation und Kompetenz* (München: Juventus).

Baacke, D. (1997) *Medienpädagogik* (Tübingen: Niemeyer).

Blumberg, A. and Greenfield, W. (1986) *The effective principal. Perspectives on school leadership*, 2nd edition (Boston, MA: Allyn & Bacon).

Bourdieu, P. and Passeron, J.-C. (1977) *Reproduction in education, society and culture* (London: Sage).

Breiter, A. (2001) 'Digitale Medien im Schulsystem: Organisatorische Einbettung in Deutschland, den USA und Großbritannien'. In: *Zeitschrift für Erziehungswissenschaft*, 4(4), pp. 625–39.

Breiter, A., Welling, S. and Schulz, A. H. (2011) 'Mediatisierung schulischer Organisationskulturen'. In: Hepp, A. and Krotz, F. (eds.) *Mediatisierte Welten: Beschreibungsansätze und Forschungsfelder* (Wiesbaden: VS Verlag), pp. 96–117.

Breiter, A., Welling, S. and Stolpmann, B. E. (2010) *Medienkompetenz in Schulen* (Berlin: Vista).

Couldry, N. (2003) 'Media meta-capital: Extending the range of Bourdieu's field theory'. In: *Theory and Society*, 32(5–6), pp. 653–77.

Couldry, N. (2004) 'In the place of a common culture, what?' In: *Review of Education, Pedagogy and Cultural Studies*, 26(1), pp. 3–21.

Cuban, L. (2001). *Oversold and underused: Computers in classrooms* (Cambridge, MA: Harvard University Press).

Day, C., Harris, A., Hadfield, M., Tolley, H. and Beresford, J. (2000) *Leading schools in times of change* (Milton Keynes: Open University Press).

DfEE (1997) *Connecting the learning society: National grid for learning; the Government's Consultation Paper* (London: Department for Education and Employment, HMSO).

Elias, N. (1978) *The history of manners. The civilizing process* (New York: Pantheon).

Flude, M. and Hammer, M. (eds.) (1990) *The Education Reform Act 1988: Its origins and implications* (London: Falmer).

Fullan, M. G. (2002) 'The change leader'. In: *Educational Leadership*, 59(8), pp. 16–21.

Green, R. L. (2010) *The four dimensions of principal leadership. A framework for leading 21st-century schools* (Boston, MA: Allyn & Bacon).

Hattie, J. A. C. (2009) *Visible learning: A synthesis of over 800 meta-analyses relating to achievement* (London: Routledge).

Hepp, A. (2012) 'Mediatization and the "moulding forces" of the media'. In: *Communications*, 37(1), pp. 1–28.

Hepp, A. (2013) *Cultures of mediatization* (Cambridge: Polity Press).

Hjarvard, S. (2012) 'Doing the right thing: Media and communication studies in a mediatized world'. In: *Nordicom Review*, 33(1), pp. 27–34.

Huber, S. G. and Gördel, B. (2006) 'Quality assurance in the German school system'. In: *European Educational Research Journal*, 5(3), pp. 196–209.

KMK (2005) *Bildungsstandards der Kultusministerkonferenz* (Bonn: Sekretariat der Ständigen Konferenz der Kultusminister der Länder in der Bundesrepublik Deutschland).

Kolo, C. and Breiter, A. (2009) 'An integrative model for the dynamics of ICT-based innovations in education'. In: *Digital Culture & Education*, 1(2), pp. 89–103.

Kozma, R. H. (ed.) (2003) *Technology, innovation, and educational change. A global perspective* (Washington, DC: ISTE).

Krotz, F. (2007) 'The meta-process of "mediatization" as a conceptual frame'. In: *Global Media and Communication*, 3(3), pp. 256–60.

Krotz, F. (2009) 'Mediatization: A concept with which to grasp media and societal change'. In: Lundby, K. (ed.) *Mediatization: Concept, changes, consequences* (New York: Peter Lang), pp. 21–40.

Latour, B. (2005) *Reassembling the social – An introduction to actor-network-theory* (Oxford: Oxford University Press).

Leithwood, K. (1994) 'Leadership for school restructuring'. In: *Educational Administration Quarterly*, 30(4), pp. 498–518.

Lingard, B. and Rawolle, S. (2005) 'Mediatising educational policy: The journalistic field, science policy and cross field effects'. In: *Journal of Education Policy*, 10(3), pp. 361–80.

Livingstone, S. and van Couvering, E. (2008) 'Converging traditions of research on media and information literacies'. In: Corio, J., Knobel, M., Lankshear, C. and Leu, D. (eds.) *Handbook of research on new literacies* (New York: Lawrence Erlbaum Associates), pp. 103–32.

Lundby, K. (ed.) (2009) *Mediatization: Concept, changes, consequences* (New York: Peter Lang).

Marotzki, W. and Jörissen, B. (2010) 'Dimensionen strukturaler Medienbildung'. In Herzig, B., Meister, D., Moser, H. and Niesyto, H. (eds.) *Jahrbuch Medienpädagogik 8: Medienkompetenz und Web 2.0* (Wiesbaden: VS), pp. 19–39.

Martens, K., Rusconi, A. and Leuze, K. (eds.) (2007) *New arenas of education governance – The impact of international organizations and markets on educational policymaking* (Houndmills, Basingstoke: Palgrave Macmillan).

McPhee, R. D. and Zaug, P. (2009) 'The communicative constitution of organizations: A framework for explanation'. In: Putnam, L. L. and Nicotera, A. M. (eds.) *Building theories of organization. The constitutive role of communication* (New York: Routledge), pp. 21–47.

Moores, S. (2012) *Media, place and mobility* (London: Palgrave Macmillan).

Morley, D. (2007) *Media, modernity and technology: The geography of the new* (London: Routledge).

OECD (2011) *PISA 2009 results: Students on line. Digital technologies and performance.* Volume VI (Paris: Organisation for Economic Cooperation and Development).

Pelgrum, W. J. (2001) 'Obstacles to the integration of ICT in education: Results from a world-wide educational assessment'. In: *Computers & Education*, 37, pp. 163–78.

Phillips, D. (2011) *The German example. English interest in educational provision in Germany since 1800* (London: Continuum).

Pierson, C. (1998) 'The new governance of education: The conservatives and education 1988–1997'. In: *Oxford Review of Education*, 24(1), pp. 131–42.

Putnam, L. L. and Nicotera, A. M. (2010) 'Communicative constitution of organization is a question: Critical issues for addressing it'. In: *Management Communication Quarterly*, 24(1), pp. 158–65.

Schulz, W. (2004) 'Reconstructing mediatization as an analytical concept'. In: *European Journal of Communication*, 19, pp. 87–101.

Selwyn, N. (2011) *Schools and schooling in the digital age* (London: Routledge).

Sergiovanni, T. J. (1996) *Leadership for the schoolhouse* (San Francisco, CA: Jossey-Bass).

Shibutani, T. (1955) 'Reference groups as perspectives'. In: *American Journal of Sociology*, 60, pp. 562–9.

Somekh, B. (2000) 'New technology and learning: Policy and practice in the UK, 1980–2000'. In: *Education and Information Technologies*, 5(1), pp. 19–37.

Visscher, A. J., Wild, P., Smith, D. and Newton, L. (2003) 'Evaluation of the implementation, use and effects of a computerised management information system in English secondary schools'. In: *British Journal of Educational Technology*, 34(3), pp. 357–66.

Weick, K. E. (1976) 'Educational organizations as loosely coupled systems'. In: *Administrative Science Quarterly*, 21, pp. 1–19.

Weick, K. E. (1995) *Sensemaking in organizations* (Thousand Oaks, CA: Sage).

Williams, R. (1990) *Television, technology and cultural form* (London: Routledge).

Wissinger, J. (2000) 'Rolle und Aufgaben der Schulleitung bei der Qualitätssicherung und -entwicklung von Schulen'. In: *Zeitschrift für Pädagogik*, 46(6), pp. 851–65.

Yang, H. (2012) 'ICT in English schools: Transforming education?' In: *Technology, Pedagogy and Education*, 21(1), pp. 101–18.

Part VI
Conclusion

18
Mediatization: Concluding Thoughts and Challenges for the Future

Lynn Schofield Clark

1. Introduction

Mediatization is a theory. Or, perhaps more accurately, mediatization is a word that brings together scholars who are engaged in an international conversation about the role of communication technologies in relation to social and cultural change. The scholars who have contributed to this volume have been actively engaged in this conversation.

This concluding chapter, therefore, reviews some of the primary contributions these scholars have made to the conversation. It considers the themes that shape the boundaries of the discussion and explores the partners that various scholars bring with them as they consider its contours. The chapter also explores how various contributors draw upon differing approaches to reasoning as they study the role of media in social change, and highlight new questions that emerge in these contributions that drive forward the theories related to processes of mediatization.

The chapter also attempts to widen the frame of the discussions of mediatization theory by considering the bold claim that lies behind the impetus for the development of mediatization theories: that theories about change matter, and that scholars of mediatization can enable us to consider what is happening in our present-day lives so that we can make the best possible choices regarding our joint future. In this sense the theory has a largely underexplored pragmatic dimension, following Peirce's sense of the pragmatic as the productive crafting of sharper habits of thought that are particularly pertinent to our collective existential situation (Peirce, 1958; see also Hickman, 2007). As this chapter will argue, mediatization holds the potential not only to make a significant contribution to the study of media

---

This chapter incorporates insights from Andreas Hepp, Grace Chiou and Klaus Bruhn Jensen.

and social change, but to offer prescient insights and counsel for those shaping the media industries through policy and practice. Part of the challenge for mediatization theory moving forward, then, will involve identifying new intellectual partners as we consider our collective situation, and, thus, this concluding chapter reviews both where the theory has taken us so far and where we might go in the future. As this chapter will suggest, by utilizing a dialectical and narrative method of abductive reasoning developed in relation to critical/cultural studies, those of us engaged in the conversation of mediatization may be able to contribute to helping people to envision the choices we face as a global society and, even more so, what might happen if we choose one particular course of action (or inaction) instead of another.

The first section of this chapter reviews the differing approaches to reasoning that have guided the thinking in this volume. The second section is organized into three parts. First, we consider the status of medium theories as they garnered public attention in the 1960s, when they spoke of the then-new media as expressive of the zeitgeist of the moment. Next, we ponder the zeitgeist of the current era, considering the proliferation of data and of distributed networks that have arisen in the context of globalization and the scholars and commentators who are taking the lead in shaping public understanding of these issues. Finally, we turn to the work of media activists who have been striving to address themselves to the urgent concerns that have arisen in relation to the current zeitgeist. The chapter concludes by suggesting that, as both the loosely defined descendants of medium theory – those celebrated writers who embrace what I term a celebrated theory of mediatization – and a host of media activists are already working to shape the discourses and policies of digital media and its role in social change, they are self-evident partners for those within the mediatization conversation, as there are those among both scholars and activists who are convinced that media change does have consequences in the lives of the world's citizens. The chapter thus considers what it would mean to foster connections between media activists, celebrated writers and mediatization scholars, suggesting that this expanded conversation might help us to envision not only a better understanding of the internet now but also a synthetic way of considering the possibilities for what the evolving communication media could be, and could mean, for future generations.

We begin, then, with a review of where this volume has taken the conversation so far.

2. Mediatization and mediatized worlds

As Krotz has noted in this volume and in earlier writings, mediatization is a socially driven process that conditions all other processes (Krotz, 2007; 2009). Jansson and Andersson (2012) fittingly explain mediatization as the process through which 'the maintenance and development of lifeworlds and the relationships between them are increasingly dependent on, and moulded by, media technologies, representations, and institutions' (p. 175; see also Hepp, 2009; Livingstone, 2009). In earlier influential work, Schulz (2004) proposed four different aspects of mediatization: (1) media extend the natural limits of human communication capacities; (2) media provide a substitute for social activities and social institutions; (3) media amalgamate with various non-media activities in social life; and (4) actors and organizations of all sectors of society accommodate to media logic.

There are several themes that emerge within the preceding chapters that suggest a common framework for the mediatization conversation as it is occurring presently. First, each of these chapters underscores the variety of ways in which differing societal institutions come to interact with, shape and become shaped by the media. The contributors operate from the shared assumption that there is no singular 'media logic' that can be identified or applied in relation to every institution or practice, and thus they seek to clarify the theory's contours by elaborating on its discontinuities.

Second, as an outgrowth of this desire to complicate any tendency to view the process of mediatization reductively, the contributors recognize that all individuals participate in communicative action within the plurality of what Krotz and Hepp (2013) have termed 'mediatized life-worlds' (p. 146). In other words, people live in relation to a plurality of lifeworlds; we are each simultaneously encompassed in what Hecht and his colleagues (2004) have elsewhere termed personal, enacted, relational and communal identities (see also Jensen's (2010) discussion of interpersonal, mass and networked communication). Each of these spaces requires differing forms of communicative action, and, as communication media have been developed to address these communicative practices, their protocols and their use give shape to the lifeworlds we inhabit.

Third, those in mediatization are interested in sorting out how our human need for connection through interpersonal communication is and has been imbricated in the rise of autonomous industries that profit from our desire for these connections. In some ways, this approach draws upon Bruno Latour's actor–network theory, and views mediatization as 'the process by which collective uses of communication media extend the development of independent industries and their circulation of narratives, contribute to new forms of action and interaction in the social world, and give shape to how we think of humanity and our place in the world' (Clark, 2011; see also Hepp, 2013, pp. 49–50, 56–7).

The contributors in this volume also raise a host of new questions, and they get to these by embracing diverse strategies of *deductive, inductive* and *abductive reasoning* in order to bring to the surface new ways of conceptualizing mediatization as a social process. Few in this volume embrace a form of *deductive* reasoning and view mediatization as a hypothesis to be tested, although this is an approach that appears as students begin to understand the processes of reasoning. In this approach, scholars (and students) might identify differing aspects of social phenomena, create hypotheses about these, and, usually, find positive evidence in support of a general meta-theory of mediatization. It is worth noting that not many who are interested in mediatization have sought to *disprove* the theory, as it is accepted infer-entially among those who are currently writing about it; among them, mediatization seems to be the best explanation given the evidence.

Many in this volume embrace an *inductive* approach to the study of medi-atization, utilizing the concept as a panorama that opens new questions that require further research. Christensen, for example, explores the role of com-munication media in migration as an instance of mediatization; Knoblauch considers the visit of Benedict XVI to Germany as an example of the medi-atization of religion, in particular its role in a transformation to 'popular religion'; Breiter discusses the school as a 'mediatized world' across micro, meso and macro levels; Hepp, Berg and Roitsch research social media as one moment of the mediatization of community-building; and Thimm, Dang-Anh and Einspänner consider the emergence of Twitter in relation to politics and civil society as example of the mediatization of politics. Passoth, Sutter and Wehner investigate software-based data allocation as part of mediatiza-tion, whereas Storey and McDonald analyze changes in romance, and Röser and Peil consider changes in domestic lifeworlds of home. Each of these contributions offers examples of *inductive reasoning*, in that the contribu-tions aim to explore a new area related to mediatization, not so much to offer confirmation (or disconfirmation) of the general theory as, rather, to explore new questions that emerge if we presume that mediatization offers the best framework available for studying the process of how media play a role in social change.

Others in this volume similarly embrace an inductive approach, but are somewhat more sceptical of mediatization's distinctiveness as a framework and theory, opting to consider various cases (or aspects of cases) in rela-tion to existing social theories. Perhaps, these scholars argue, the cases under examination are explained adequately in relation to theories of cos-mopolitization, urbanization or modernization; at the very least, scholars must consider complementarities among these theories. Such inductive rea-soning leads scholars in this vein to consider what might be the unique contribution of mediatization theory to other bodies of social theory (and, in related work, how mediatization theory might differ from its close rela-tive, mediation theory; see Couldry, 2012 and in this volume; Livingstone, 2009). Some contributors to this volume, therefore, seek to identify com-monalities between the propositions of mediatization and the propositions of other social theories (Vickers, 2006). Couldry and Fornäs consider gen-erative ways in which the social theories of Bourdieu, Ricoeur and others offer complementary understandings of field theory and culturalization that might inform methods of studying mediatization. Hjarvard considers how Gibson's notion of affordances and Goffman's concept of territory provide ways of thinking about how new media structure and multiply our practices of interacting with one another. And Lundby wonders whether the rise of self-narratives in digital storytelling offers a nod to increased personalization and the desire for connection amidst felt distraction, thereby linking scholarly with therapeutic narratives of healing and wholeness.

Less common so far in the work formally recognized as mediatization is that involving abductive reasoning. *Abductive* reasoning may involve both deductive and inductive processes, but also involves a creative element that looks to unifying conceptions, according to Charles Sanders Peirce, who coined the term (1931; see also Burch, 2013). Abductive reasoning demands new terms to explain some phenomenon that previously escaped explanation. It is especially common in science, medicine and law, when a diagnosis is demanded yet explanations are only partial (Walton, 2005). In general, abduction has more to do with *coherence* than deduction, and, thus, abductive reasoning may involve not only rules of logic but also, significantly, visual and narrative thinking (Jensen, 1991; Thagard and Shelly, 1997). In many ways, the initial developments of both mediatization theory and medium theory were instances of abductive reasoning, attempts to explain something for which there was no singular cohering concept, although until this point scholars within mediatization theory have largely elided the more diagnostic and future-oriented aspects of abductive reasoning.

Some within mediatization theory and medium theory have embraced *analogical reasoning*, which is a form of reasoning with a relationship to both the inductive and the abductive. Analogical reasoning involves presenting an argument by drawing comparisons between a new concept and something already understood, thus identifying unifying concepts so as to point towards the future. This form of reasoning relies upon the fact that the human capacity for understanding is enhanced when new information is presented as part of a recognizable pattern. In this volume, Krotz clarifies the concept of 'media' within mediatization research. Based on this, he reviews the emergence of cultures of reading and the rise of perspective, advancing the idea that the IT concept of augmented reality might signal a similarly transformative shift. If we can understand the rise of perspective and the attendant changes in culture, art and cognition as a story of mediatization, the story of augmented reality may be a similarly provocative narrative that is suggestive of the role of media in contemporary change, he argues.

A second form of abductive reasoning is the *thought experiment* (Sorensen, 1992). Following Peirce, Thomas Kuhn used the phrase *thought experiments* to explain the creative aspect to abductive reasoning that can result in a coherent explanation:

> Thought experiments can disclose nature's failure to conform to a previously held set of expectations. In addition, they can suggest

particular ways in which both expectation and theory must henceforth be revised.

(Kuhn, 1962, pp. 241, 261)

Thought experiments have had a significant place within the development of quantum mechanics and relativity, as well as in many developments within philosophy.

In this volume, the chapter by Deuze incorporates elements of both the analogical and the thought experiment. Drawing a parallel between Husserl's concepts of living in and of the world and Habermas' concern with the colonization of the systemworld and lifeworld, Deuze introduces a concept of the multimediatization of the lifeworld to consider how we experience living in a world in which our understandings of reality, and perhaps reality itself, can be edited. He does this by borrowing from Sonesson an exploration of parallels between the ways we each experience life as 'open to invention' and also enclosed in an omnipresent network beyond our making or understanding, in much the same way as the characters in Casares' novel (and in the television programme *Lost*, which was based on that novel) experience themselves with agency even though their souls are, in a certain sense, trapped in a project beyond their making. Ultimately, however, Deuze sees the project of mediatization as an exercise in considering the relation of the self to others and to reality in media life, and, through the fictional stories he mentions, he argues that mediatization offers a way for us to consider the ethical and aesthetic challenges related to questioning what it means to take responsibility for ourselves on our own and in connection with others in our mediated society.

The thought experiment and analogical reasoning are particularly interesting in light of the history of the medium theory or media ecology tradition. Earlier theorists in the medium theory tradition, such as Neil Postman, embraced this analogical reasoning approach, with mixed results (Clark, 2009; Man Kong Lum, 2006). Others, such as Meyrowitz (1985), succeeded in modelling abductive reasoning to create an argument about how television removed barriers between generations and ushered in more egalitarian social relations. Meyrowitz (along with others in the medium theory tradition) has been criticized for embracing a form of technological determinism that downplays the factors beyond technology that contribute to social change. Whereas mediatization theorists generally recognize and seek to avoid the problem of technological determinism, it is important to note that both the analogical and the thought experiment of medium theory also make a contribution that can be recovered for mediatization theorists going forward: they rely upon narrative and visualization to develop not only coherence but also a *diagnosis*. In this sense, the approach of abductive reasoning that has been a part of the medium theory tradition goes beyond the deductive and inductive, opening to the imaginative in a way that strikes people as poetic, elegant, and possibly in the realm of the affective rather than merely the rational/logical. And these descriptive words first came to be associated with theories of the media in relation to the work of Marshall McLuhan.

3. What made Marshall McLuhan compelling?

The North American public intellectual tradition of the 1950s and early 1960s had elevated scholars like John Kenneth Galbraith, Oscar Handlin and Richard Hofstader to bestseller status. McLuhan, like these scholars and also like his contemporary Daniel Boorstin, experienced a cool reception among his academic peers, even as his ideas achieved influence in the public realm. In part, this was because McLuhan's writings had a distinctly *predictive and diagnostic* rather than a *deductive or rational* quality. Scholars in the social sciences and humanities are trained to be sceptical of prediction or diagnosis, and are instead interested in unmasking, demystifying and exposing the hidden arrangements of power, following Ricoeur (1970). To add to McLuhan's problems among scholars, many of his predictions have been proven wrong, as both his critics and his devotees have pointed out (Carr, 2011b; Strate, 2006).

But, then, how is it that McLuhan's ideas gained such purchase during the time period in which they were first expressed? In part, of course, McLuhan did present his thought experiments in the framework of a story of dramatic change that made sense to people at the time. He built upon the public interest in the role of media in social change with an intellectual career that coincided with the rise of television in North American society. In 1950, when only 9 per cent of US homes had televisions, McLuhan had been at the University of Toronto for just four years and was completing his first major work, *The Mechanical Bride*, which looked at the role of advertising in culture. By 1955, when 64.5 per cent of US homes had televisions, McLuhan's Communication and Culture seminars had attained Ford Foundation funding and had gained popular support among graduate students for their prescience in speaking about the changing media landscape (Library and Archives Canada, undated; TVB, 2012). And by 1960, when 92.6 per cent of US homes had televisions, McLuhan was on the verge of publishing what was to become his bestselling book, *Understanding Media: The Extension of Man* (1964), and its predecessor, *The Gutenberg Galaxy* (1962). McLuhan spoke of the revolutionary role of television and visual culture at a time when people were first experiencing the ways in which television was reshaping and disrupting the daily habits and routines of individuals, businesses and governance throughout society. This lent McLuhan's ideas a certain emotional resonance, to use Barthes' (1980) term, striking a chord with the listener, who knows that something is dramatically different and who longs for a narrative structure in which to make sense of that knowledge. McLuhan offered explanations for what this new television era heralded, and, while some of those explanations proved less accurate than others, the style in which he delivered what he called his 'probes' were well suited to the clipped and suggestive staccato of the soundbite era. In addition to the fact that television's diffusion and influence in every facet of society made explanations necessary, then, his appeal also rested in part in how his delivery conformed to the 'media logics' of television (Altheide and Snow, 1979).

Television adoption skyrocketed worldwide, along with both the advertising industry and the counter-culture (Frank, 1998; Lears, 1994). Just as societies around the globe simultaneously experienced a succession of anti-war, environmental, civil rights, indigenous rights and women's rights movements, television and 'mass' media made the consequences of these changes widely available around the world. Whereas few today would credit television alone for these societal revolutions, there is little doubt that witnessing in one's own living room the moving coverage of Vietnam and of civil rights protests constituted a new relationship between the narratives of news and the collective experiences of families (Gitlin, 1981). Few then dwelled on the constructed nature of what they saw, instead feeling themselves to be witnesses to the unfolding of world history in a manner not previously imagined.

McLuhan's metaphors of the global village and of hot and cool media articulated the zeitgeist of the moment, offering a way of understanding the new situation as well as hints of what it might portend for the future. Still, his was not the only voice discussing culture and technology. Harold Innis, Wyndham Lewis and Albert Lord, among others, contributed to a new framework for considering media in terms of its form rather than the content that it delivered, while in Britain the Centre for Contemporary Cultural Studies developed frameworks for considering the relationship between popular culture and subcultures. But this new North American framework that concentrated on foregrounding the medium was nowhere more popularly expressed than in McLuhan's *Understanding Media* and his dictum, 'the medium is the message'.

Interesting for us to ask, then, is this: what did the theories propagated by Marshall McLuhan and his contemporaries *accomplish*? I argue that the theories of 'the medium is the message' gained such widespread credence because people were simultaneously becoming aware of television's tendency to celebrate populism while also contributing to the rise of an elite class of celebrities across a broad range of social institutions. People were primed to consider the implications of television culture in comparison to the print culture of the past, and, thus, they were interested in developing comparative perspectives. But McLuhan's ideas went beyond the study of patterns in past and present relations of media and society. He also offered thought experiments, including a glimpse of the future in his concept of the 'global village'. He was not alone in giving voice to this vision of an interconnected world, but his theories articulated a perspective that, coupled with other voices of the time, enabled people to collectively raise a new set of politically engaged questions that, admittedly, were not even on the agenda for medium theorists. Such questions include the following. First, is everyone in the global village allowed to speak – and should they not be? Second, what would media for and by indigenous people look like? And, third, are there smaller groups that can be served by communication media that are not presently served? These are questions that emerged in media studies in the 1970s, 1980s, 1990s and beyond in relation to queer theory and gender studies, post-colonial theory and critical race theory, and theories of the subaltern. But the synthesis of these perspectives within media theory might not have been possible without the attention to the medium of television and its role in historical change first articulated in the circles of McLuhan and his followers. Even Raymond Williams felt compelled to address his thoughts to the popularized viewpoints of Marshall McLuhan in the 1970s (Lister, Dovey, Giddings, Grant and Kelly, 2009). This illustrates that, even though McLuhan's theories were viewed as problematic, they served as a catalyst for the development of thought that became a key strain within media theory to the present day. This is the kind of work that mediatization theorists can do today.

4. Speaking from the Zeitgeist

Today, as in Marshall McLuhan's day, the media environment is viewed alternately with suspicion and as a source of hope and promises. Like the thought experiments of its 1960s predecessor Marshall McLuhan, scholars and commentators who might be said to embrace a *celebrated theory of mediatization* (or a soft technological determinism) speak with the same recognizable voice of poetics and prophecy. We are living through an 'expansion in expressive capability', as Clay Shirky (2008) declares, celebrating the collaboration of amateurs and the increasing capacity for wisdom that is possible in venues such as Wikipedia. 'The future presented by the internet is the mass amateurization of publishing and a switch from "Why publish this?" to "Why not?",' he writes. Just as the simultaneous eruptions of social movements and technological change emerged in the 1960s, so, too, do societies across the globe wonder at purported linkages between the internet and the Arab Spring. Our longing for explanations is exemplified in popular and diagnostic texts, whether from Malcolm Gladwell or in video form such as in Michael Wesch's early YouTube video essay, 'The machine is us/using us'. Because of the way search algorithms learn from users, 'we will need to rethink copyright, authorship, identity, ethics, aesthetics, rhetorics, governance, privacy, commerce, love, family, ourselves', Wesch argues in an explanatory and prophetic essay viewed more than a million times within the first four months of 2007 alone.

There may be no single Marshall McLuhan figure who could emerge to offer a fragmented, hyperlinked, augmented and viral interpretation of our current engagement with technology. This may be because, in the years after the global financial meltdown of 2008–09 and awareness of the intractable problems of continuing tyrannical political leadership, the zeitgeist also speaks of a world overwhelmed with data and defined by not only perpetual contact but also surveillance (Katz and Aakhus, 2002). Jaron Lanier, 'father' of virtual reality technology and *Second Life* designer, was perhaps one of the earliest defectors from the triumphalist view of free information that populated Silicon Valley ideology for its early decades (Turner, 2006). In *You are not a gadget*, Lanier (2010) argued against conventional wisdom, stating that the internet is eroding our ability to interact with one another and is actually stifling our creativity. He extended the argument further in 2013 with *Who Owns the Future?*, a book that borrows from Homer to name Facebook, Google, Twitter and Amazon as 'siren servers', entities that draw us to them so as to obtain our personal information (he calls it 'theft') and then sell it for their gain. In his wonderfully titled book *To Save Everything, Click Here*, Morozov (2013) similarly adopts abductive reasoning in his identification of 'solutionism', an approach borrowed from engineering that, he argues, presumes that 'big data' can be mobilized to explain and predict human behaviour – a limited perspective, as he strongly argues.

Nicholas Carr (2011a) and Mark Bauerlein (2009) offer even more popularized narratives of how the internet is changing us: through distraction and shallow thought in Carr's analysis, and by making us 'dumber', in Bauerlein's. In a more sophisticated and poignant narrative, Sherry Turkle (2012) argues that our reliance upon communication technologies to mediate our personal connections makes us less capable of maintaining the deep relationships we all desire. Each of these treatises similarly employs narrative in an abductive approach to explore how it is that new media are playing a role as 'moulding forces' in relation to societal change.

Recent well-received entries that might be characterized as part of a celebrated theory of mediatization are exploring issues specifically related to internet protocols and search engines. Vaidhyanathan (2011) wonders whether the initial idealism inherent in Google's beginnings can truly foster the democratic and free relationship with information that its founders had originally envisioned. Turow (2012) exposes changes in the advertising industry that have led to non-transparent data collection processes that shape what we see and are able to consume online. And MacKinnon (2012) smartly highlights what she terms the 'corporate sovereigns of the internet', exploring how these entities make non-transparent decisions that affect our freedoms. Moving beyond analysis to diagnosis, MacKinnon asks how technology could and should be governed so as to support the rights and freedoms of people around the world. What is happening requires a response, as these and other authors in the celebrated theories of mediatization camp argue: institutions of society cannot keep pace as the power shifts from institutions to individuals, and in particular to individuals who are at the controls in relation to the internet's design (Mele, 2013). What is needed, as McChesney (2013) argues, are stronger institutional reactions to the internet. Lanier (2013) agrees. The internet's transparency has been one-way, he argues: these companies can benefit from our 'free' sharing of information, yet we receive no financial benefit in return, and we cannot even see what information is shared, with whom or to what ends. Lanier's diagnosis includes a proposal for what he terms a 'micro-finance' plan: we would each get a tiny compensation each time Google or Apple acquires information from us. This policy would enable us all to identify ourselves as economic actors who are contributing to the system from which companies like Google and Apple are benefitting, he says.

Following in the emergent tradition of celebrated mediatization theorists, this chapter argues that we in media studies, and specifically in mediatization, need a better way of not only mapping the present and of seeing how patterns might cause harm – a true mark of the critical tradition – but we also need a means of extending current trends outward so as to envision multiple possible future scenarios and the courses of action that these might require. For, while it is certainly the case that we cannot expect to predict the future with accuracy, this does not absolve us of moral responsibility regarding the future towards which our collective actions are moving us. Mediatization theories that are rooted in contemporary experiences and that direct attention towards the future would, thus, share common ground with what Bergman (2009) termed Charles Sanders Peirce's orientation to 'hope-driven inquiry embedded in experience, processes of interpretation, and communal practices' (p. 256). The goal of the reasoning behind mediatization theory, therefore, would be not to reach towards objective truth, but to move society towards socially sustainable habits of action, following Peirce's lead.

In this sense, mediatization, with its interest in positive change through analysis and diagnosis, might embrace what Collins (1998; 2000), following William James, terms 'visionary pragmatism', seeking not to reach a conclusive end but, rather, to see the scholarly enterprise as part of an ongoing journey struggling towards an ethical end (see also James, 2009, on the fact that this is a hallmark of US black feminist pragmatism in particular, and Couldry, 2012, writing on ethics in media studies). Collins (1998) proposes that contemporary social inquiry must address itself to these questions:

> First, does this social theory speak the truth to people about the reality of their lives? [...] Does this social theory equip people to resist oppression? Is this social theory functional as a tool for social change? [...] Does this critical social theory move people to struggle? For oppressed groups, this question concerns how effectively critical social theory provides

moral authority to struggles for self-definition and self-determination. (pp. 198–9)

These seem worthy questions to ask of a body of theory that seeks to address itself to understanding how change is occurring, and what role communication technologies play in relation to those changes.

5. Honouring Aaron Swartz

Finally, it is important to consider how it is that mediatization theorists can play a role in commenting on and participating in envisioning actual changes in our media systems. To do this, theorists will need to consider how to act as bridges between critical actors and the social movements that work beyond research institutions. Individuals and groups in the realms of practice and activism are much more directly involved in the processes of change, and, as they must address the ethical and political problems that arise on a regular basis, those in academia could – and should – work to support their efforts.

While envisioning possible futures and offering diagnoses is not a conventional part of the social scientist's or the humanist's scholarly toolkit, it is a much more common strategy among media activists, who must motivate others to see possibilities and dangers so as to elicit action. In 2013, as this volume was reaching its final stages, the world became familiar with the work of media activist Aaron Swartz because of his untimely death, and, thus, it is worth considering how work such as that of Swartz and others might intersect with the aims of mediatization theorists. Aaron worked tirelessly to raise awareness about SOPA, the Stop Online Piracy Act that proposed to give the US government the power to shut down access to particular websites. New York University Professor Clay Shirky's tribute was particularly relevant:

> The last time I saw Aaron, we were talking about [the organization Swartz founded called] Demand Progress, progressive politics, and ways of producing citizen-driven political change. What was so striking about Aaron is that he always wanted to solve the harder problem, not just to find some issue-specific workaround, but to understand how whatever system he was thinking about worked, and then to understand how to make it work better, however unusual such changes might be.
>
> (Shirky, 2013)

Maybe Swartz read medium theories, the predecessors to mediatization theory, or the celebrated theories of mediatization in his work, but, clearly, he was convinced that media change does relate in some way to the changes we see, or might see, in our lifeworlds. In a speech he gave describing the successful campaign to stop SOPA, Swartz put forth a narrative of what was going on and what would happen if we did not challenge this bill. But he also articulated a vision of what was possible if US citizens did succeed in stopping this bill, and it was a vision laden with metaphors and analogies: the internet as a global village, an equal set of opportunities, a level playing field. All of these are predicated on a vision of the internet and its possibilities and are related not only to what it was and is, but to what it could be.

What would it mean to build a bridge between media activism and mediatization theories? How could those of us in the mediatization conversation learn from activists and celebrated mediatization theorists so as to investigate avenues that could enrich the perspectives of activists, deepen their work, and help us all to better understand what is at stake in the changes that are happening right now in our media institutions that, in turn, are shaping and will continue to shape our media worlds?

Fields of study can and do undergo change. Should mediatization theorists take on the challenge of partnering with media activists as well as those embracing the abductive approach through analogous reasoning and thought experiments, we too will be a part of important changes in our field. The field of psychology offers an instructive model. Once dominated by studies of deviance, in recent years the field has begun to focus on what is now termed 'positive psychology' in the US, or what began controversially as the study of happiness and has evolved into studies of health indicators around the world (Csikszentmihályi, 2008; Fredrickson, 2000; Gardner, 2009; Seligman, 2002). More recently, sociology has begun to explore more diagnostic and abductive approaches as well, with some corners embracing a model of prosocial behaviour that looks, for instance, at the study of generosity and empathy as a means of questioning the individualism that is believed to fuel so much motivation in the global economic system (Decety and Ickes, 2011; Smith, 2012). What might mediatization theories look like if they were to consider what might have happened if the protests against US Senate-sponsored corporate control of internet censorship had failed and legislation had been permitted to pass in 2010? What if theories offered a positive vision for how democratic engagement could be achieved if certain regulations were enacted and put into practice?

6. Conclusion: Our challenge

'Creative abduction', as Umberto Eco argued, 'leads to and requires that the players/actors propose that which may be assumed to support the creative becoming' (Capozzi, 1997). In today's context of communication and cultural change, we as researchers are expected to think not only about what is, but about what we collectively might become. By engaging in an iterative process of figuring out what works in particular contexts, researchers in mediatization may be in a better position to tease out both the explanatory and the concrete use value of differing approaches, thus offering important contributions that bridge between research, social movements and societal institutions.

Digital, satellite and mobile media make it impossible to consider a future that is not deeply intertwined with the futures of all other beings on the planet. We are part of an interconnected network that is not as egalitarian as is sometimes assumed, but is not completely dystopian, either, as Galloway and Thacker (2007) have pointed out. We, therefore, need ways to think about this interconnection, and the ways in which communication technologies have both served and continue to serve as 'moulding forces' (Hepp, 2012, p. 1; 2013, p. 54). We need to consider how this interdependence came to be, what it looks like as it evolves and reshapes our societal institutions, and how its protocols shape and will continue to shape our collective future.

Scholars cannot be expected to do the work of activists, yet we can be partners with people who are working to envision what might happen if we as a society do or do not act in certain ways in response to the pressing challenges that face us and that do relate to the emergent characteristics of digital and mobile media. If we understand ourselves reflexively as being in relation to those who share the role of shaping interpretation and public discourse, we will be envisioning scholarship as a source for habits of thought and ethical action. We will want to affirm that there is no singular direction, and no singular diagnosis. But what we need may be more attempts at coherent descriptions and prescient diagnoses, and more willingness on the part of scholars in mediatization to offer some counsel on what could happen if we as a society collectively embrace this or that course of action in the future. In short, it may be that our task today in mediatization theory is akin to that of visionary pragmatism. In the words of Martin Luther King, Jr, it may be that we must 'hew out of a mountain of despair a stone of hope'.

References

Altheide, D. and Snow, R. P. (1979) *Media logic* (Beverly Hills, CA: Sage).

Barthes, R. (1980) *Camera lucida: Reflections on photography*, trans. R. Howard (New York: Hill and Wang).

Bauerlein, M. (2009) *The dumbest generation: How the digital age stupefies young Americans and jeopardizes our future (Or, don't trust anyone under 30)* (New York: Jeremy P. Tarcher/Penguin).

Bergman, M. (2009) 'Experience, purpose, and the value of vagueness: On C. S. Peirce's contribution to the philosophy of communication'. In: *Communication Theory*, 19, pp. 248–77.

Burch, R. (2013) 'Charles Sanders Peirce'. In: Zalta, E. N. (ed.) *The Stanford encyclopedia of philosophy* (spring 2013 edition). http://plato.stanford.edu/archives/spr2013/entries/peirce/, date accessed 11 March 2013.

Capozzi, R. (1997) *Reading Eco: An anthology* (Bloomington, IN: Indiana University Press).

Carr, N. (2011a) *The shallows: What the internet is doing to our brains* (New York: W.W. Norton & Company).

Carr, N. (2011b) 'McLuhan at 100'. In: *Rough type blog*, 18 July. http://www.roughtype. com/?p=1505.

Clark, L. S. (2009) 'Theories: Mediatization and media ecology'. In: Lundby, K. (ed.) *Mediatization* (New York: Peter Lang).

Clark, L. S. (2011) 'Considering religion and mediatization through a case study of J + K's big day (the JK wedding entrance dance): A response to Stig Hjarvard'. In: *Culture and Religion*, 12(2), pp. 167–84.

Collins, P. H. (1998) *Fighting words: Black women and the fight for social justice* (Minneapolis: University of Minnesota Press).

Collins, P. H. (2000) *Black feminist thought: Knowledge, consciousness, and the politics of empowerment*, 2nd edition (New York: Routledge).

Couldry, N. (2012) *Media, society, world: Social theory and digital media practice* (Cambridge, Oxford: Polity Press).

Csikszentmihályi, M. (2008 [1990]) *Flow: The psychology of optimal experience* (New York: Harper Perennial Modern Classics).

Decety, J. and Ickes, W. (2011) *The social neuroscience of empathy* (Cambridge, MA: MIT Press).

Frank, T. (1998) *The conquest of cool: Business culture, counterculture, and the rise of hip consumerism* (Chicago: University of Chicago Press).

Fredrickson, B. L. (2000) 'Cultivating positive emotions to optimize health and well-being'. In: *Prevention and Treatment*, 3.

Galloway, A. and Thacker, E. (2007) *The exploit: A theory of networks* (Minneapolis: University of Minnesota Press).

Gardner, H. (2009) *Five minds for the future* (Cambridge, MA: Harvard Business Review Press).

Gitlin, T. (1981) *The whole world is watching: Mass media in the making and unmaking of the new left* (Berkeley: University of California Press).

Hecht, M., Warren, J., Jung, E. and Krieger, J. L. (2004) 'A communication theory of identity'. In: Gundykunst, W. (ed.) *Theorizing about intercultural communication* (Thousand Oaks, CA: Sage).

Hepp, A. (2009) 'Differentiation: Mediatization and cultural change'. In: Lundby, K. (ed.) *Mediatization: Concept, changes, consequences* (New York: Peter Lang), pp. 135–54.

Hepp, A. (2012) 'Mediatization and the "molding force" of the media'. In: *Communications: The European Journal of Communication Research*, 37(1), pp. 1–28.

Hepp, A. (2013) *Cultures of mediatization* (Cambridge: Polity Press).

Hickman, L. (2007) *Pragmatism as post-postmodernism: Lessons from John Dewey* (Bronx: Fordham University Press).

James, V. D. (2009) 'Theorizing black feminist pragmatism: Forethoughts on practice and purpose of philosophy as envisioned by black feminists and John Dewey'. In: *Journal of Speculative Philosophy*, 23(2), pp. 92–104.

Jansson, A. and Andersson, M. (2012) 'Mediatization at the margins: Cosmopolitanism, network capital and spatial transformation in rural Sweden'. In: *Communications: The European Journal of Communication Research*, 37(2), pp. 173–94.

Jensen, K. B. (1991) *Handbook of qualitative methodology for mass communication research* (London: Routledge, Chapman & Hall).

Jensen, K. B. (2010) *Media convergence: The three degrees of network, mass, and interpersonal communication* (London: Routledge).

Katz, J. E. and Aakhus, M. A. (eds.) (2002) *Perpetual contact: Mobile communication, private talk, public performance* (Cambridge: Cambridge University Press).

Krotz, F. (2007) *Mediatisierung: Fallstudien zum Wandel von Kommunikation* (Wiesbaden: VS).

Krotz, F. (2009) 'Mediatization: A concept with which to grasp media and societal change'. In: Lundby, K. (ed.) *Mediatization: Concept, changes, consequences* (New York: Peter Lang), pp. 19–38.

Krotz, F. and Hepp, A. (2013) 'A concretization of mediatization: How mediatization works and why "mediatized worlds" are a helpful concept for empirical mediatization research'. In: *Empedocles. European Journal for the Philosophy of Communication*, 3(2), pp. 119–34.

Kuhn, T. (1962) *The structure of scientific revolutions* (Chicago, IL: University of Chicago Press).

Lanier, J. (2010) *You are not a gadget* (New York: Vintage).

Lanier, J. (2013) *Who owns the future?* (New York: Simon & Schuster).

Lears, J. (1994) *Fables of abundance: A cultural history of advertising in America* (New York: Basic Books).

Library and Archives Canada (undated) 'Old messengers, new media: The legacy of Innis and McLuhan'. http://www.collectionscanada.gc.ca/innis-mcluhan/index-e. html, date accessed 12 February 2013.

Lister, M., Dovey, J., Giddings, S., Grant, I. and Kelly, K. (2009) *New media: A critical introduction* (London: Routledge).

Livingstone, S. M. (2009) 'On the mediation of everything'. In: *Journal of Communication*, 59(1), pp. 1–18.

MacKinnon, R. (2012) *Consent of the networked: The worldwide struggle for internet freedom* (New York: Basic Books).

Man Kong Lum, C. (2006) *Perspectives on culture, technology and communication: The media ecology tradition* (Cresskill, NJ: Hampton Press).

McChesney, R. (2013) *Digital disconnect: How capitalism is turning the internet against democracy* (New York: The New Press).

McLuhan, M. (1962) *The Gutenberg galaxy: The making of typographic man* (Toronto: University of Toronto Press).

McLuhan, M. (1964) *Understanding media: The extensions of man* (New York: McGraw-Hill).

Mele, N. (2013) *The end of big: How the internet makes David the new Goliath* (New York: St Martin's Press).

Meyrowitz, J. (1985) *No sense of place: The impact of electronic media on social behavior* (New York: Oxford University Press).

Morozov, E. (2013) *To save everything, click here: Technology, solutionism, and the urge to fix problems that don't exist* (New York: PublicAffairs).

Peirce, C. S. (1931–58) *Collected papers of Charles Sanders Peirce*, vol. 5, edited by Hortshorne, C. and Weiss, P. (Cambridge: Harvard University Press).

Ricoeur, P. (1970) *Freud and philosophy: An essay on interpretation* (New Haven: Yale University Press).

Schulz, W. (2004) 'Reconstructing mediatization as an analytical concept'. In: *European Journal of Communication*, 19(1), pp. 87–101.

Seligman, M. E. P. (2002) *Authentic happiness* (New York: Free Press).

Shirky, C. (2008) *Here comes everybody: The power of organizing without organizations* (New York: Penguin Press).

Shirky, C. (2013) 'Tribute to Aaron Swartz'. In: *The Telegraph*, 13 January.

Smith, C. (2012) 'Grasping the big sociological picture shaping the moral lives of college students today'. In: *Journal of College and Character*, 13(3), online.

Sorensen, R. (1992) *Thought experiments* (New York: Oxford University Press).

Strate, L. (2006) *Echoes and reflections: On media ecology as a field of study* (Cresskill, NJ: Hampton Press).

Thagard, P. and Shelly, C. (1997) 'Abductive reasoning: Logical, visual thinking, coherence'. In: Dalla Chiara, M.-L., Doets, K., Mundici, D. and van Benthem, J. (eds.) *Logic and scientific methods* (Dordrecht: Kluwer), pp. 413–27.

Turkle, S. (2012) *Alone together: Why we expect more from technology and less from each other* (New York: Basic Books).

Turner, F. (2006) *From counterculture to cyberculture: Stewart Brand, the Whole Earth network, and the rise of digital utopianism* (Chicago, IL: University of Chicago Press).

Turow, J. (2012) *The daily you: How the advertising industry is defining your identity and your worth* (New Haven, CT: Yale University Press).

TV Basics (2012) *A report on the growth and scope of television*, June 2012 (Television Bureau of Advertising, New York). http://www.tvb.org/media/file/TV_Basics.pdf.

Vaidhyanathan, S. (2011) *The googlization of everything (and why we should worry)* (Berkeley, CA: University of California Press).

Vickers, J. (2006) 'The problem of induction'. In: Zalta, E. N. (ed.) *The Stanford encyclopedia of philosophy*. http://plato.stanford.edu/entries/induction-problem/, date accessed 16 April 2008.

Walton, D. (2005) *Abductive reasoning* (Tuscaloosa, AL: University of Alabama Press).

Wesch, M. (2007) 'The machine is us/ing us'. http://www.youtube.com/watch?feature=player_embedded&v=NLlGopyXT_g#!, date accessed 31 January 2007.

Author Index

Subject Index

Printed and bound by CPI Group (UK) Ltd, Croydon, CR0 4YY